The Nature of
Politics

"La Dame de Brassempouy," one of the earliest known representations of a human head, demonstrates the prehistoric origins of intentionality, art, and the quest for human self-awareness (see p. 252). Photograph courtesy Musée de l'Art Préhistorique de St. Germain-en-Laye.

ROGER D. MASTERS

The Nature of
Politics

YALE UNIVERSITY PRESS

New Haven & London

Published with assistance from
the Mary Cady Tew Memorial Fund

Set in Palatino type.

Printed in the United States of America.

Library of Congress Cataloging-in-Publication Data
Masters, Roger D.
The nature of politics / Roger D. Masters.
p.   cm.
Bibliography: p.
Includes index.
ISBN 0–300–04169–1 (cloth)
0–300–04980–3 (pbk.)
1. Political science. 2. Biology. 3. Biopolitics. I. Title.
JA80.M37 1989
306'.2—dc19   88–7652
                                                              CIP

The paper in this book meets the guidelines for permanence and
durability of the Committee on Production Guidelines for Book
Longevity of the Council on Library Resources.

10 9 8 7 6 5 4 3 2

To the memory of
LEO STRAUSS

CONTENTS

FIGURES AND TABLES

TABLES

PREFACE

Human nature has been at the foundation of thinking about politics since the ancient Greek philosophers developed the concept of "nature" as we know it in the West. As political philosophy is conventionally understood today, however, human nature is no longer the subject of scientific inquiry in the precise sense of formulating hypotheses and subjecting them to empirical tests. Instead, political theorists in the twentieth century have generally been content to analyze ideas about human nature and politics.

This separation of political theory from scientific research on human nature is doubtless related to what C. P. Snow called the divorce between the "Two Cultures." In our universities, the natural sciences are divided from the humanities and social sciences, with courses and teachers organized on the basis of the fields or disciplines they consider. As a result, despite excellent popularizations of the latest scientific findings, most academic studies of human behavior do not integrate an understanding of biology and evolution with the analysis of politics, economics, or sociology.

The situation is beginning to change as research based on biology spreads in all of the social sciences. As will be evident from the citations in this work, a number of scholars now link the study of humans with relevant research in other life sciences. To date, however, these endeavors have had relatively little effect on our understanding of human social behavior. In particular, contemporary biology has not had a major impact on political philosophy, which still seems to be a field concerned with the ideas of famous theorists instead of a scientific discipline with a long history.

There is a dual irony in this fact. First, the tradition of political philosophy arose and flourished in the hands of thinkers who did not make such rigid distinctions as those now practiced in our universities and our intellectual life. Plato's *Republic* presents an educational curriculum that includes the disciplines we call mathematics, physics, chemistry, and biology, as well as fields we consider to be philosophic and political in character; Aristotle wrote at least as widely on matters of biology and physics as on politics or ethics. In both the Lyceum and

the Academy, not to mention other ancient schools, the contemporary divisions between scholarly disciplines did not exist.

The second irony of the gap between the Two Cultures is the proliferation of scientific research that bears directly on political theory (for
example, see Wilson 1975, 1978; Barash 1977; von Cranach 1979;
Gruter and Bohannan 1983; Fetzer 1985; Ruse 1986; Alexander 1979,
1987). Evolutionary biology makes possible a deeper understanding
of human origins and the emergence of political institutions. Neurophysiology, neurochemistry, experimental psychology, ethology, and
ecology provide empirically based information about human nature.
In the last generation, the fossil record of human origins has been
greatly expanded and the mechanisms of inheritance (the structure
and function of DNA) understood for the first time; the science of
social behavior among animals has been enriched by direct observation in the field, by laboratory experiment, and by theoretical models
of natural selection.

These developments in the life sciences pose one of the central
intellectual paradoxes of the second half of the twentieth century. At a
time when the traditional concerns of philosophers are more amenable to scientific analysis than at any period since the inception of
Western political thought, scientific inquiry and political philosophy
have generally been divorced. Humans have, for the first time, the
capacity to engage in genetic engineering—and thus the power to
create new forms of human existence—yet the social sciences remain
largely untouched by research in the biological sciences.

There are exceptions, to be sure. There is an emerging subfield in
political science known as biopolitics (Thorson 1970; Somit 1976;
Wiegele 1979, 1982; White 1981; Schubert 1983b, 1985; Corning 1983;
Watts 1984; White and Losco 1986), but this academic approach is
limited so far to a small number of scholars. The study of human
nature and politics from the perspective of the life sciences has not yet
become an accepted approach in any of the social sciences. Still less
has it become a commonplace to subject political beliefs and public
policies to the scrutiny of the methods and findings of natural science.

It seems fair to assume that this state of affairs is not likely to
survive the continued advances in the natural sciences. Over the next
generation, barring nuclear war and the demise of advanced civilizations, research in the life sciences will doubtless expand our knowledge and our ability to manipulate biological phenomena. The political process must sooner or later be fundamentally affected by the
power to change not only the environment but also the behavior and
genetic composition of humans themselves (Kass 1971; Blank 1981). It
follows that the need for a better understanding of the relationships

between the scientific and philosophical approaches to human nature and politics will grow and persist.

This book addresses that need by viewing human politics from a perspective that is consistent with both the tradition of Western political philosophy and the findings of contemporary biology. Rejecting the view that social science will be totally absorbed by (or "reduced" to) biology, I presume that the behavior of our species—which Aristotle so accurately termed the "political animal" (*zoon politikon*)—is in many important respects unique in the natural world. But unlike those social scientists who have ignored biology or assumed that its use in studying humans is ideologically motivated, my analysis seeks to overcome the gulf between scientific research and human self-awareness.

This may appear an unlikely undertaking for a political theorist who studied under Leo Strauss at the University of Chicago. Of the political philosophers in this century, Strauss seemed the most critical of attempts to extend the scientific approach to the study of political things. For Strauss, perhaps more than for any of his contemporaries, the task of scholarship was to recover the art of philosophic reading in order to understand the greatest thinkers of the Western tradition. Both in his classes and in his writing, Strauss taught how to read the so-called Great Books and decried the substitution of scientific assumptions for the perspective of political philosophy (Strauss 1953, 1964). More recently, this challenge has been restated provocatively by Allan Bloom (1987).

Why should one of Strauss's former students dedicate to his memory a book that seeks to transcend the gap between the natural and the human sciences? Based on his reading of ancient political thought, Strauss himself was acutely aware of the importance of relating the study of human politics to the natural sciences. Indeed, for Strauss this was the issue of our times (Strauss 1953, 7–8). My book should therefore be seen as a continuation of his goal.

Without Strauss's teaching, it would have been difficult to recover the understanding of Western political philosophy needed to approach the perennial issue of human nature in a way consistent with contemporary natural science. I myself would not have seen either the gravity of the problem or a means of responding to it without the good fortune of having studied with him. Hence it is only proper that, in attempting to return to the wholeness of the enterprise of such thinkers as Rousseau, Hobbes, and Aristotle, my efforts be dedicated to the teacher who reminded his generation that this was the foremost task confronting our time.

I set forth in this work the foundations of a "naturalist" approach to the age-old theoretical questions of human nature (parts 1 and 2) and the state (parts 3 and 4). The first four chapters focus on human nature from the perspective of biological research, considering the status of human selfishness and altruism, of our participation in social groups, of human languages and cultures, and of politics itself. I then explore the origin of the centralized state by linking contemporary theories of natural selection to the study of social cooperation in political philosophy, game theory, and history. In the last two chapters, I summarize the implications of this evolutionary approach to human society, indicating why behaviorism and its theoretical concomitant, the fact-value dichotomy, will be replaced by a new naturalism capable of establishing standards of natural justice. Notes on technical points, an integral component of this part of the argument, are placed at the end in order not to distract the general reader. A companion volume, entitled *The Nature of Obligation,* will apply these general theoretical perspectives to issues that are conventionally treated in different disciplines within the social sciences.

My central thesis can be summarized in simple terms. Human behavior is as open to scientific study as the behavior of any other living being. But human societies are different from social groups among nonhuman primates or other animals. Although laws, customs, and governments are a response to situations similar to those leading many other animals to cooperate, human language makes it possible for our political and social institutions to take on a life of their own. Each human culture is a self-perpetuating system that becomes part of the environment facing the individual; rules that a child learns to obey have developed over time—and, if lasting, have been subject to influences transcending human choice and will. Since natural selection can have an impact on the origins and functioning of man-made institutions, the old academic controversy of nature versus nurture needs to be replaced by research on the complex interactions between cultural and biological factors.

The implications of this return to naturalism are summarized in the Epilogue, which shows how an evolutionary approach to human social behavior offers a reasonable basis for judging the rightness or justice of political institutions. Unlike the nihilism and relativism that have predominated in the West over the last century, an evolutionary approach provides objective criteria for preferring a constitutional regime in which citizens are subject to the law and play a legitimate role in political life. While evolutionary biology also explains the necessities that challenge civilization and its institutions, this naturalistic approach can help us to formulate more decent and humane standards of social life.

I am, of course, aware of the so-called naturalistic fallacy which has so often been condemned by logicians and methodologists. But when the doctor prescribes a treatment, we don't normally object that this practice bridges the logical distinction between the facts of diagnosis and the value of health. Biology, like medicine, has much to teach us about our species and the risks we confront by ignoring the natural basis and consequences of our habits of life.

This scientific perspective on human politics paradoxically leads toward a view of "natural justice." A return to views akin to those of Aristotle on the basis of contemporary research in the biological sciences will seem extremely puzzling. On the one hand, the textbooks tell us that Aristotle was apparently hostile to the concept of evolution; on the other, his political and biological theories were often used to support antiscientific orthodoxies. It is all the more difficult to keep an open mind toward the possibility of a return to naturalism because we have been told for so long that a scientific understanding of human nature needs to be entirely value-free. Despite these habits of thought, I can only hope some readers will consider my analysis of human nature, society, and politics with the seriousness the issue deserves.

The predicament in which we find ourselves at the end of the twentieth century is not trivial. Our species can obliterate itself with nuclear weapons, create genetic monsters, or destroy the physical environment through mindless pollution. Terrorists claim the intensity of their "commitment" is an adequate justification for their violence; barbarians within and without challenge the concept of civilization as an unsubstantiated preference; relativists scoff at the notion that there could be any reason whatever for standards of right and wrong.

A scientific understanding of human behavior should be presumed to be at least as difficult and demanding as nuclear physics, molecular genetics, or ecology. Unfortunately it often seems to be assumed that, because we are human, it will be easy for us to understand what humanity entails. Such an error is probably not unrelated to the events that have led our species to the brink of extinction. It is time to take seriously again the Socratic injunction, "Know thyself."

Acknowledgments

My deepest intellectual debt, as mentioned earlier, is to Leo Strauss, but there are other obligations I should note. My interest in contemporary ethology as a means of approaching philosophic issues arose in conversations with the late John Roddam (at that time working on *The Changing Mind,* a small but elegant book that deserved more attention than it received); he directed my attention to the popularization of ethology by the late Robert Ardrey (whose enthusiasm and willingness to admit error became useful to me as evidence of the possibility that biological research could be related to humanistic concerns). At professional meetings and in correspondence, a number of scholars have tried, often vainly, to extend my understanding of biological matters; since there is safety in numbers (and alphabetical ordering), I hope that responsibility for my errors will not be imputed to any of the following: Richard Alexander, Edward Berger, Ivan Chase, Irenaeus Eibl-Eibesfeldt, Carl Gans, Ben Ginsburg, Ken Korey, Paul MacLean, Michael McGuire, Thom Roos, Fred Strayer, Christian Vogel, Frans de Waal, Edward O. Wilson, and the many others whose works I have cited. Equally valuable has been the attempt of many social scientists to explain to me their disciplines: Paul Bohannan, Napoleon Chagnon, Mario von Cranach, William Durham, Paul Ekman, Don Elliott, William Foltz, Robin Fox, Siegfried Frey, Fred Greenstein, Margaret Gruter, Jack Hirshleifer, John Lanzetta, Gregory McHugo, Howard Margolis, Sidney Tarrow, and Lionel Tiger. Of incalculable importance has been discussion of philosophical matters with numerous friends: Allan Bloom, Hiram Caton, Joseph Cropsey, Terrence Marshall, Heinrich Meier, Thomas Pangle, Michael Platt, Arlene Saxonhouse—not to mention many other colleagues and students over the years. Last but not least, I have benefited from discussion and fellowship with political scientists for whom an understanding of the life sciences is as central as it has become for me: Larry Arnhart, Carol Barner-Barry, Fred Kort, Steven Peterson, Glendon Schubert, Jim Schubert, Albert Somit, John Wahlke, Meredith Watts, Elliott White, Tom Wiegele, Fred Willhoite, and other members of the Association for Politics and the Life Sciences. While I have surely forgotten to name others to whom I am indebted, it would be impossible to omit two friends and colleagues: Denis Sullivan, whose indispensable collaboration in the research described in chapter 2 makes it impossible to say where my ideas begin and his end, and Henry Ehrmann, whose willingness to listen to my observations on the world during our weekly walks was often more important than he will ever know.

Research support over the past twenty years has come from a number of institutions. A fellowship from the John Simon Guggenheim Foundation in 1967–68 provided the leisure to study contemporary biology for an uninterrupted year; the foundation's confidence that a political theorist could do such a thing was in many ways the critical prerequisite for the work that has followed. Experimental studies of the effects of facial displays in politics, conducted with Denis Sullivan and John Lanzetta, have been funded by the Harry Frank Guggenheim Foundation, the National Science Foundation, the Maison des Sciences de l'Homme (Paris), and Dartmouth College, which also supported my sabbatical leave during 1985–86. Preparation of the manuscript was aided by a grant from the Gruter Institute for Law and Behavioral Research. However impersonal some modern bureaucracies may be, these institutions have met my needs effectively and have earned my sincere gratitude.

Since this volume represents over twenty years of reflection and research, much of it has already appeared in provisional form; while intended from the outset as part of this study, the earlier articles have in each case been substantially revised. Permission to reprint segments from the following is gratefully acknowledged: "Of Marmots and Men: Animal Behavior and Human Altruism," in Lauren Wispé, ed., *Altruism, Sympathy, and Helping* (New York: Academic Press, 1978), pp. 59–77 (chapter 1); "Facial Displays and Political Leadership," *Journal of Social and Biological Structures* (1986), 9:315–46 (chapter 2); "Genes, Language, and Evolution," *Semiotica* (1970), 2:295–320 (chapter 3); "Politics as a Biological Phenomenon," *Social Science Information* (1975), 14:7–63 (chapter 4); "The Biological Nature of the State," *World Politics* (1983), 35:161–93, and "Why Bureaucracy?" in Elliott White and Joseph Losco, eds., *The Biology of Bureaucracy* (Lanham, Md.: University Press of America, 1986), pp. 149–91 (chapters 5 and 6); and "Ostracism, Voice, and Exit: The Biology of Social Participation," in Margaret Gruter and Roger D. Masters, eds., *Ostracism: A Social and Biological Phenomenon* (New York: Elsevier, 1986), pp. 231–47 (chapter 7). In each case, colleagues who edited these publications were of immense help, but none should be held accountable for the changes leading to the current volume.

The Nature of
Politics

PART I

Human Nature

The "nature of man" has been debated since the origins of Western political thought in ancient Greece. Although this issue reflects deeply rooted assumptions about social life, it is often treated in terms of images of human nature that are not based on empirical knowledge. To explore human nature from the perspective of the natural sciences, it is convenient to begin with the individual, though this is far more difficult than it might at first appear. Contemporary biology shows that the characteristics of an animal are not fixed and unaffected by its setting or life history. Nor can it be assumed that traits identified by the observer will be mutually exclusive. Humans—like other animals—are highly variable and likely to show contradictory traits. The first requisite for a rigorously scientific approach to human nature is therefore willingness to abandon the belief that answers are either/or: our behavior can be both innate and acquired; both selfish and cooperative; both similar to that of other species and uniquely human.

CHAPTER 1

Animal Behavior and Human Altruism

Selfishness and Altruism in Western Thought

Are human beings by nature cooperative and altruistic, or is human nature intrinsically egoistic and competitive? This fundamental question is as old as, or older than, the Western tradition of political theory. For the pre-Socratic philosophers, as for moderns like Hobbes, men are naturally oriented to individual gain; for these thinkers, cooperative behavior is merely a culturally acquired restraint on the desires of competitive individuals. In contrast, Plato and Aristotle as well as Hegel and Marx view human beings as naturally social, so that cooperation and altruism are at least as natural for our species as rivalry.

The question of human nature had therefore already been posed with clarity in ancient Greece. The pre-Socratics developed a frankly egoistic or hedonistic theory of human nature, in which cooperative or altruistic behaviors are necessary evils for calculating, selfish individuals.[1] Best known from the speeches of Thrasymachus in Plato's *Republic*, this hedonistic view treats human laws or customs as "restraints" on nature. As Antiphon the Sophist puts it in *On Truth* :

> Men draw life from the things that are advantageous to them: they incur death from the things that are disadvantageous to them. But the things which are established as advantageous in the view of the law are restraints on nature, whereas the things established by nature as advantageous are free. Therefore things that cause pain do not, on a right view, benefit nature more than things that cause pleasure; and therefore, again, things which cause suffering would not be more advantageous than things which cause happiness—for things which are really [truly or in truth] advantageous ought not to cause detriment, but gain. . . . Take the case of those who retaliate only after suffering injury,

3

and are never themselves the aggressors; or those who behave well to their parents, though their parents behave badly to them; or those, again, who allow others to prefer charges on oath, and bring no such charges themselves. Of the actions here mentioned one would find many to be inimical to nature. They involve more suffering when less is possible, less pleasure when more is possible and injury when freedom from injury is possible. (Antiphon *On Truth*, in Barker 1960, 96–97)[2]

In short, since humans naturally seek individual gain or pleasure, cooperation and altruism can be explained only as the result of social custom or convention—and thus are essentially learned.

Both Plato and Aristotle, following the tradition apparently inaugurated by Socrates, contest this position. For example, when Aristotle asserts that man is by nature a political animal, he directly challenges the Sophists' assertion that human society rests on contractual or conventional obligations among calculating individuals. Aristotle's view rests on a developmental or evolutionary account of social cooperation:

The household is the partnership constituted by nature for [the needs of] daily life; Charondas calls its members "peers of the mess," Epimenides of Crete "peers of the manger." The first partnership arising from [the union of] several households and for the sake of nondaily needs is the village. By nature the village seems to be above all an extension of the household. Its members some call "milk-peers;" they are "the children and the children's children." This is why cities were at first under kings, and nations are even now. For those who joined together were already under kings: every household was under the eldest as king, and so also were the extensions [of the household constituting the village] as a result of kinship. This is what Homer meant when he says that "each acts as law to his children and wives;" for [men] were scattered and used to dwell in this manner in ancient times. . . .

The partnership arising from [the union of] several villages that is complete is the city. It reaches a level of full self-sufficiency, so to speak; and while coming into being for the sake of living, it exists for the sake of living well. Every city, therefore, exists by nature, if such also are the first partnerships. For the city is their end, and nature is an end: what each thing is—for example, a human being, a horse, or a household—when its coming into being is complete is, we assert, the nature of that thing. . . . From these things it is evident, then, that the city belongs among the things that exist by nature, and that man is by nature a political animal. He who is without a city through nature rather than chance is either a mean sort or superior to man. (Aristotle *Politics* 1.2. 1252b–1253a)[3]

When some men rule others for their common benefit, Aristotle maintains, this situation is natural and in the interest of all; cooperation is natural, first within the family or extended kin group, and later by extension in the city. Not only is altruism or sharing virtuous, but such virtue is the full development of human nature, not merely a conventional restraint on individual pleasure or gain. For Aristotle, the Sophist understanding of human nature is inadequate.

Among moderns, the same issue separates individualistic hedonists like Hobbes and Locke from the continental tradition stemming from Hegel and Marx (Macpherson 1962; Strauss 1953; Masters 1977). As these examples suggest, the perennial question of altruism and selfishness has immense consequences for one's understanding of the origins and limits of political and social obligation. Opposing views tend to suggest different psychological theories as well as different ethical and legal ideals.

Theories of human nature are not merely normative preferences unrelated to scientific inquiry. The great thinkers of the past always took into consideration the science of their time, just as empirical science inevitably raises moral and philosophical questions. Hence it is of the greatest importance to assess the bearing of contemporary scientific evidence on this persistent problem of political philosophy and psychology.

Animal Behavior, Social Cooperation, and Human Nature

In the last generation, advances in the biological sciences have led to renewed debates concerning human nature. Scientific comparisons between humans and other species, though still criticized in some quarters, are possible—and even essential—provided they are drawn with adequate care and specificity (Lorenz 1974; von Cranach 1976; Rosenberg 1980; Kitcher 1985; Fetzer 1985). In particular, research in population genetics and ethology, often popularly described as "sociobiology" (Wilson 1975; Caplan 1978), seems directly relevant to the issue of human altruism and competitiveness (Alexander 1979, 1987; Stent 1979; White 1981; Gruter and Masters 1986; Ruse 1986).

Contemporary evolutionary theory should not be confused with the opinions of past generations. In the late nineteenth and the early twentieth centuries, Darwin's theory of evolution was interpreted to mean that natural selection favored the "survival of the fittest." Social Darwinists thus used a conception of natural competition to justify laissez-faire capitalism. Today's biologists have abandoned such a view of natural selection, not to mention its transformation into an ideological defense of free enterprise.

Since fitness is now defined as the capacity to transmit genes to succeeding generations, it is usually said that evolution merely favors those organisms producing more than the average number of offspring—and hence exhibiting an "advantage in differential reproduction" (Simpson 1967, 221–24). As a result, it is "simply the fit, rather than the 'fittest,' who survive" (Dobzhansky 1955, 112). In the last few years, this approach has been redefined as "inclusive fitness," since animals tend to maximize the proportion of their own genes transmitted to subsequent generations whether or not these genes are carried by their own offspring (Hamilton 1964; Trivers 1971; Wilson 1975; Barash 1977; Alexander 1979).

On the surface there is a striking similarity between the logic of hedonists like Antiphon the Sophist and that of evolutionary biologists (for example, Wilson 1975, 118–21, 341–44, 415–17). For Antiphon the Sophist, the proof that men are naturally selfish is that when individuals are unobserved, they violate the laws: "A man, therefore, who transgresses legal rules, is free from shame and punishment whenever he is unobserved by those that made the covenant, and is subject to shame and punishment only when he is observed" (Barker 1960, 95; cf. Plato *Republic* 2.359c-360d). Genetic theorists use exactly the same argument with reference to animal behavior when describing the selective advantage of "disguised cheating and sham cooperation" (Campbell 1972, 30).

Clearly the Sophist tradition, as well as its modern equivalent derived from Hobbes, provide an extremely insightful analysis of the theoretical issue posed by cooperation among individually competing organisms. But modern biology leads one to question whether this problem is appropriately viewed from the perspective of the individual organism (or phenotype); now biologists speak of genes, not individuals, as "selfish" (Dawkins 1976). Despite similarities in logic, the Sophist perspective is very different from one according to which an organism's "advantage" or "interest" is measured by the fate of its genes rather than by its immediate pleasures and pains. Some Sophists denied, for example, that it would be natural to sacrifice in favor of one's child (Gernet 1923, 182), let alone to prefer one's sister's offspring to one's own. In contrast, theories of inclusive fitness show how such apparent "self-sacrifice" can be the most effective way of increasing the proportion of an individual's genes in the next generation.

Granted the limitations of "pop sociobiology" (Kitcher 1985), it is thus a major error to confuse contemporary theories of inclusive fitness with the outmoded individualism of Social Darwinists. True, some population biologists have concluded that altruism is highly unlikely to be favored by natural selection; following this interpretation, it has been claimed that humans are naturally selfish, and that our social cooperation results from cultural or learned mechanisms (Campbell 1972, 1978). But others have argued that altruistic behavior can be favored by natural selection, at least under some conditions (Wilson 1975; Alexander 1979).

The concept of inclusive fitness thus does not by itself solve the question of whether humans are naturally selfish or altruistic (Barkow 1978; Schubert 1981; Alexander 1987). Theoretical arguments based on the presumed "selfish" competition between isolated genes have been challenged on the grounds that they ignore the importance of evolution at the level of the genome as a whole (Alexander and Sherman 1977). Indeed, research at the molecular level suggests that genetic sequences can overlap, so that the concept of the gene as a totally discrete unit may not always be consistent with the physical properties of DNA strings (Kolata 1977; Rosenblatt et al. 1988).

Although formalizations derived from abstract genetic theories or models in economics and game theory are extremely useful (Hamilton 1964; Maynard-Smith 1978; Axelrod 1983; Hirshleifer 1987), the debate concerning human nature can hardly be resolved without considering empirical data from ethology (Schubert 1981, 1983b). Arguments derived from population genetics often focus on a presumed gene for altruistic bravery (Wilson 1975; Campbell 1978), as if cooperative behaviors detrimental to individual survival would be transmitted genetically only if a distinct gene existed for them. It is essential to consider this assumption in the light of observed animal behavior.

One of the most obvious examples of what is commonly called altruistic self-sacrifice occurs when an individual fights and dies in defense of the group. This behavior is often taken as a test of human altruism, on the assumption that fighting within a group is a sign of individual competitiveness or selfishness, whereas fighting between groups is evidence of altruism. Territorial defense by individuals— presumably selfish or competitive—has therefore been contrasted with "real group conflicts," in which altruistic individuals cooperate to defend their group's territory against another group (Campbell 1972, 24).

Ethology shows, however, that *inter*group rivalry is not simply the opposite of *intra*group conflict, such as establishment and defense of individual territory or social dominance. Competition within the group is not merely selfish, nor is defense of the group a case of pure altruism. In many social vertebrates, and especially among primates, physical traits or behaviors can satisfy more than one function, depending on circumstances.

This multifunctionality of behavior deserves examination. Competition is often related to rivalry for dominance, whether in the form of status in a dominance hierarchy or as control over territory (Lorenz and Leyhausen 1973, 120–36). In many species, including primates, such dominance seems to be correlated with reproductive success (Hall and DeVore 1965, 72–77; Southwick, Beg, and Siddiqui 1965; Barash 1977; Alexander 1987, 24–30). In these cases, highly dominant males leave behind a disproportionate percentage of offspring in each generation. Hence a trait that gives its possessor an adaptive advantage in sexual encounters often has effects on other social behaviors as well.

It is usually assumed that dominance behaviors, including privileged access to receptive females and a tendency to serve as the focus of group "attention structure" (Chance 1967), are individually beneficial traits. Classical theories of population genetics account for the natural selection of the competitive behaviors usually associated with dominance. But in different settings these very traits can also produce defense against predators or other groups of the same species. For example, dominant baboon males move rapidly to counter any threat to the band as soon as they are alerted by the warning signals of peripheral juveniles (Bert et al. 1967; DeVore and Hall 1965; Kummer 1971; Goodall 1986a). Since such behaviors are conventionally described as "altruistic bravery," a traditional selective process may well account for an ambivalence between competition and social cooperation.

If the selection pressure in favor of traits associated with intragroup dominance is high enough, these traits will have a selective advantage even if some of their possessors die or do not reproduce because of increased vulnerability to predators or other groups of the same species. Natural selection could simultaneously favor both the adult males' traits of size, strength, or intragroup aggressiveness *and* bravery or risk-taking in defense of their group. Under many circumstances, the cost of these traits to those who are wounded or killed would be less than the average benefit they confer on those who are not. This is, in fact, what is meant by evolutionary fitness.

Natural selection can thus account for acts of what is conventionally called altruistic behavior among individuals who compete for reproductive success. Given the multifunctionality of bodily or behavioral traits in complex vertebrates like the primates, it is risky to limit theoretical discussions to a "gene for altruism" (especially since biologists define altruism technically in terms of an organism's genetic contribution to future generations). There is every reason to assume that among primate species with relatively elaborate patterns of socialization and group structure, both selfish and cooperative behaviors are favored to some extent by selection.

This ambivalence is especially clear in the social behavior of chimpanzees, the nonhuman primate most closely related to our own species. "We cannot hope to understand the role played by aggression in the ordering of chimpanzee society without consideration of the equally powerful forces of social attraction. It is the interplay of these two opposing forces, aggressive hostility and punishment on the one side and close and enduring friendly bonds on the other, which has led to the major social organization that we label a community" (Goodall 1986a). If such opposed behaviors and motivations are observed in chimpanzees under naturalistic conditions, similar factors may well be innate in *Homo sapiens*.

It could be objected that population genetics establishes strict limits to the altruism possible among primates like ourselves; because genetic competition restricts the innate social cooperation possible among vertebrates, only social insects with sterile worker and soldier castes could develop complex social systems comparable to a human civilization but based on instinctively programmed altruism. According to this argument, vertebrate sociality reaches its limit with packs of wolves and troops of chimpanzees, which include at best only several families (Campbell 1978).

As a description of human nature, this conclusion cannot be pushed too far. There is, of course, an important truth in the distinction between insect societies, based on innate behavior patterns that are genetically possible in species with haplo-diploid genetic inheritance, and human civilizations, whose foundation depends on learned cultural behavior. The argument, however, pretends to address the existence of cooperation and self-sacrifice as integral parts of the human behavioral repertoire, and as such tends to confuse the analysis of individuals with the evolution of social systems.

Among primates, it is probably unwise to attribute social structure to presumed instincts of individuals, on the assumption that relatively clever animals (like chimpanzees or wolves) have more complex societies than species with less noticeable learning abilities. If one measures sociality in terms of complexity, hamadryas baboons may well have a more intricate social structure than wolves or chimpanzees (cf. Kummer 1971 with Reynolds 1967, 1968 or Goodall 1986a); baboons and rhesus monkeys form lasting structured groups and exhibit such potentially altruistic behaviors as vigilance, dispute settlement, and defense against predators (Southwick, Beg, and Siddiqui 1965). In all of these species, two or three dominant males sometimes form coalitions and assist each other in maintaining their status (Altmann 1967; de Waal 1982, 1984). Indeed, even such an apparently pleasurable behavior as primate grooming is in part social and cooperative, controlling parasitic disease and maintaining the dominance structure (Sparks 1969). Ethologists who have studied the behavior of primates and of young human children are often struck by the similarities (Montagner 1978; Strayer 1981; Barner-Barry 1981; Gruter and Masters 1986).

One could, of course, dismiss these details as minor corrections. When arguing that "human complex social interdependence greatly exceeds that of wolves or chimpanzees," for instance, Campbell (1978) had in mind civilizations like "ancient China, the valleys of the Indus and the Ganges, and Aztecs, Mayas, and Incas." Such large-scale societies are crucial for those who argue that human altruism is sociocultural rather than genetic in origin. Since this view is shared by many social scientists, it is worth examining.

The claim that human nature is inherently selfish rather than co-operative cannot merely mean that empires and large-scale civilizations were produced by cultural evolution. Were that the case, there would be less to this argument than meets the eye. It is generally agreed that these forms of human culture were the result of cultural evolution. As an assertion about human nature, the statement that altruism is sociocultural implies that genetic competition places a narrow limit on natural cooperation in any human group—and the case of high civilizations is viewed as confirming evidence. If so, however, altruism must have been "socially induced" even in the smaller human societies that antedated the emergence of civilized empires and survived alongside them until the twentieth century.

For such an argument to concern human nature (rather than the circumstances that led to the formation of centralized states), it is necessary to equate "complexity" with "civilization" in a way that is doubly vulnerable to criticism. On the one hand, the cultural complexity of preliterate human hunter-gatherers now appears to be far greater than was assumed by those who dismissed such peoples as primitive; it will no longer do to characterize the peoples of preliterate human cultures as purely hedonistic or selfish individuals of limited intelligence and understanding of the natural world (Lévi-Strauss 1962). On the other hand, it is also probably a mistake to equate the size or stratification of an animal society with the social interdependence of its members. Quite the contrary, contemporary ethology points to a wide variety of social patterns as alternative strategies for survival, often in response to the ecological setting. Hence the structure of social behavior need not be considered solely, or even primarily, as a direct result of the altruism or competitiveness of individuals. Where, then, do observed variations in sociability come from?

Of Marmots and Men

Recent work on the social behavior of animals has begun to explain the difference between species whose members live in isolation or in colonies as a function of their typical environments. Rather than attributing the apparent complexity of social structures to abstractly defined instincts of individuals, biologists compare the ecological niche of different species—or of populations of a single species—in order to explain animal behavior. The results of this approach show the error of assuming that vertebrate social complexity is caused in a simplistic manner by individual traits.

For example, Barash (1974) has presented a general theory of the evolution of marmot societies. Marmots (the genus Marmota) are rodents, of which the most familiar is the woodchuck (figure 1.1). Different species of this genus have highly varied patterns of social organization.

> The woodchuck, *M. monax,* is best known east of the Mississippi, where it most commonly inhabits fields and forest ecotones at low elevations. . . . In this comparatively equitable environment, woodchucks are solitary and aggressive; the association between adult male and female is essentially limited to copulation, the only lasting social tie being the mother-young nexus, which itself terminates at weaning when the young disperse. (Barash 1974, 415)

Apart from aggressive encounters between adult males, *M. monax* thus seems to approximate Rousseau's famous description of the "state of nature" in which humans originally were solitary, "without war and without liaisons" (Rousseau *Second Discourse* part 1).

Although these woodchucks seem to illustrate the minimum of sociability in the natural world, not all marmots have this mode of life:

> By contrast, the Olympic marmot (*M. olympus*) is highly social, living in distinct, closely organized colonies usually composed of

Figure 1.1
The Woodchuck

From the *Encyclopedia Americana*, 29 (1984), 140. An excellent picture of the
woodchuck's behavior is found in Robert Frost's poetry ("A Drumlin Woodchuck,"
copyright 1936 by Robert Frost and renewed 1964 by Lesley Frost Ballantine.
Reprinted from THE POETRY OF ROBERT FROST, edited by Edward Connery Lathem, by
permission of Henry Holt and Company, Inc.):

One thing has a shelving bank,
Another a rotting plank,
To give it cozier skies
And make up for its lack of size.

My own strategic retreat
Is where two rocks almost meet,
And still more secure and snug,
A two-door burrow I dug.

With those in mind at my back
I can sit forth exposed to attack
As one who shrewdly pretends
That he and the world are friends.

All we who prefer to live
Have a little whistle we give,
And flash, at the least alarm
We dive down under the farm.

We allow some time for guile
And don't come out for a while
Either to eat or drink.
We take occasion to think.

And if after the hunt goes past
And the double-barreled blast
(Like war and pestilence
And the loss of common sense),

If I can with confidence say
That still for another day,
Or even another year,
I will be there for you, my dear,

It will be because, though small
As measured against the All,
I have been so instinctively thorough
About my crevice and burrow.

several adults (most commonly one male and two females), two-year-olds, yearlings, and the young of the year. This species is highly tolerant and playful, commonly feeding in social groups of three to six individuals. No territories or even distinct individual home ranges are maintained; all parts of the colony are equally available to all colony members. Dominance relationships are generally indistinct and nonpunitive. Olympic marmot social life is characterized by a high frequency of 'greeting behaviors' . . . apparently associated with individual recognition. (Ibid.)

As Barash's analysis makes clear, the difference between the individualistic woodchuck and the sociable Olympic marmot (figure 1.2) is strongly correlated with their environmental niches. *M. monax* benefits from "a relatively long vegetative growing season" and exploits its favorable environment by population dispersion. *M. olympus* inhabits "the alpine meadows in Olympic National Park, Washington . . . at or above timberline where they experience very short growing seasons of 40 to 70 days" (ibid.). Under these harsher conditions, a more elaborate colony structure has selective advantages.

It would make relatively little sense to attribute this difference in social organization to learning on the part of Olympic marmots, though undoubtedly some components of marmot behavior are learned. Moreover, it is not even clear that *M. olympus* is more social than *M. monax*. Rather, different social patterns are best understood as species-specific adaptations to varied ecological niches (Martin 1972, 429). The isolated individuals of *M. monax* represent an effective means by which the species has adapted to the environment of fields and low-level forests, just as the colonies of *M. olympus* are an adaptive response to the harsher conditions of the alpine meadows.

Barash provides further evidence for such an interpretation. Another species, the yellow-bellied marmot (*M. flaviventris*), not only inhabits environments intermediate to those of *M. monax* and *M. olympus*, but also exhibits social behaviors intermediate to these more extreme cases. Within this one species, variations in social structure can be correlated with ecological niche (Barash 1974, 419). Using the contemporary theory of natural selection, Barash thus shows how various marmot species and populations have evolved behaviors and social structures adapted to their environments. From this perspective, instead of deriving society from abstractly defined attributes of the individual, one can speak theoretically of the strategy of a gene pool or population (Ehrlich et al. 1975; Slobodkin 1964; Maynard-Smith 1978).

Three major points follow from Barash's work. First, at least one

Figure 1.2
The Olympic Marmot

(top) "A group of Olympic Marmots inhabiting an Alpine meadow. From the right, they consist of an adult male, two adult females and one juvenile. Groupings of this sort are common among this species, whereas they are not found among woodchucks inhabiting low elevation environments." Photograph by D. Barash. (bottom) "Olympic marmot alarm calling." Photograph by J. Spurr. Reprinted by permission of the publisher from David Barash, Sociobiology *and* Behavior, *pp. 58, 82. Copyright 1977 by Elsevier Science Publishing Co., Inc.*

behavioral trait of the Olympic marmot is unusual and difficult to explain on narrowly hedonistic or pleasure-seeking grounds. As an adaption to environmental severity, *M. olympus* females "produce litters in alternate years only." After careful examination, Barash concluded that "biennial breeding is thus apparently a genetically determined characteristic of this species, just like annual breeding in the woodchuck" (Barash 1974, 418). This form of birth control sharply contrasts with the generally prolific breeding of other rodents and might superficially be described as altruistic self-restraint.

Second, as Barash insists, Wynne-Edwards's (1962) theory of group selection is "unnecessary as an explanation of . . . the unique reproductive strategy exhibited by the Olympic marmot." All that need be assumed is that "traditional" natural selection operates "upon each individual" and produces "the reproductive performance likely to generate the maximum number of surviving offspring" (Barash 1974, 418). Although "kin selection" and "interdemic selection" may be more important than Barash suggests (Wilson 1975, 1978), verification of such theories is not indispensable for demonstrating the existence of genetically controlled cooperation or altruism among vertebrates.

Third, and perhaps most important of all, the isolated adults of the woodchuck *M. monax* do not represent the absence of social life (cf. Lorenz and Leyhausen 1973, 120). This is perhaps most difficult for us to understand, since it is tempting to conclude that Olympic marmots are social, whereas woodchucks are solitary or asocial. Such a Rousseauistic interpretation ignores the behavioral mechanisms required for the dispersal of the young, who are forced to leave their mothers in both species. The explanation, on closer inspection, is that different marmot species have evolved differing tolerances for a persisting bond between maturing young and adults.

Apparently aggressive interactions between members of a species must therefore be understood as fundamentally social behavior. Maturing infants in both woodchucks and Olympic marmots are rejected by their mothers after a certain stage of development. When young Olympic marmots were experimentally removed from their home colony and later reintroduced, they were received "in an unusually aggressive manner" similar to contacts between woodchucks (Barash 1974, 417). The degree of rejection would thus not seem to be a measure of "individualism," but rather an aspect of behavioral development and population structure characterizing a species in its ecological niche (Masters 1979a).

Similarly, primate mothers are often observed to reject their maturing infants at the stage when infant peer groups begin to form. Although the precise details vary in different species, one researcher concludes that, in general, "the more the mother rejects the infant, the more dependent does the infant become" (Kaufman 1974, 60). Even where increased maternal hostility to an infant does not prolong the mother-infant bond, one could hardly conclude that the behavior involved is antisocial. Among primates, "rejection increases the tendency to attachment . . . at the same time as it progressively denies the person of the mother as the object of attachment, thus leading to major attachments to other objects, an essential requirement of advanced societal living" (ibid. 59).

Individuals of the same primate species often exhibit different social patterns in different settings (for example, Jay 1965; Ripley 1967; Sugiyama 1967). Beyond the complexity and variety of the behavioral adaptations of marmots, monkeys, and humans, we thus see different solutions to the ubiquitous problem of the survival of species as breeding units. When observers identify some of these behaviors as cooperative and altruistic—or describe animals as competitive or selfish—they are thus classifying forms of interaction, not discovering a fundamental natural trait of individuals that necessarily causes species to form more or less complex groups (Gruter and Masters 1986).

Social behavior cannot be reduced to or entirely derived from individual traits without reference to the complex interplay of species and their environments. Campbell was correct when he suggested (1965b) that it is insufficient to derive social structures from a psychology of individual motivations. To be sure, it would also be inaccurate to deduce individual motivations from characteristics of groups or species. Contemporary biology stresses the importance of distinct levels of analysis and the danger of reductionism in relating one level to another (Anderson 1972; Jacob 1977; Masters 1973a). There is no easy answer to the study of complexity.

The Evolution of Human Altruism

The behavior of species as diverse as marmots and primates thus shows that altruistic or cooperative social behavior can be genetically transmitted in vertebrates without postulating group selection. Modern biology provides excellent reasons for reasserting the view that human competition and cooperation are both in part innate and in part learned (Eibl-Eibesfeldt 1971). Evidence of this ambivalence can be found not only in ethology, but also in research in such diverse fields as psychology and hominid evolution.

From a psychological perspective, observation suggests that all humans are likely to respond to some situations in a competitive way and to others in a cooperative manner. While a natural tendency to be altruistic or competitive can refer to situations—any human is more likely to cooperate with others facing the same life-threatening crisis— it is more often thought to concern differences between individuals. The question of human nature is usually taken to mean the latter: Do some (or all) humans tend to compete or to cooperate in most situations? Because "character" or "personality" can be defined as the way an individual responds to a new or ambiguous situation, this issue can be illuminated by psychological research.

Recent studies have shown that many personality traits, ranging from altruism and empathy to aggressiveness and criminality, are influenced by heredity as well as by the individual's environment (Hoffmann 1981; Wilson and Herrnstein 1986; Rushton, Littlefield, and Lumsden 1986; Cloninger 1986, 1987). Such analyses have often been attacked by behaviorists who stress individual conditioning (Kuo 1967) and by liberals or Marxists emphasizing the role of social environment (Halle 1965; Lewontin, Rose, and Kamin 1984); for these critics, it is ideological to claim that human character and ability could be innate to any significant extent. Despite methodological errors in earlier research on the heritability of personality traits (Kamin 1974; Dorfmann 1978; Gould 1981), the independent roles of heredity and environment are now increasingly evident for traits of both cooperative and competitive behavior.

The classic studies of what is popularly called the "nature and nurture" question have compared identical twins (whose genes are identical) with fraternal twins (who, like any pair of siblings, share one-half of their genes by descent). Although twins separated at birth and reared apart can also be contrasted with twin pairs raised together, studies using this method were properly criticized because the social environments of the separated twins are often similar, making it impossible to distinguish the effects of genes and social environment (Kamin 1974). Statistical comparisons using very large samples of identical and fraternal twins reared at home avoid this difficulty, since the family and sociocultural environment are the same for both members of each twin pair, whereas the two types of twins differ in genetic similarity (Eaves 1988). Additional research strategies extend the comparisons from twins to siblings, more distant family members, and the children of identical twins (Rose et al. 1979).

Repeated studies show that both aggressive and altruistic personality traits are highly heritable, but that individual experience is roughly equal in importance (Rushton, Littlefield, and Lumsden 1986; Holden 1987; Plomin and Daniels 1987; Eaves 1988). Particularly interesting are studies showing that infants have distinct patterns of social response that are manifest as early as two to four months (Izard, Hembree, and Huebner 1987; Izard 1988); extremely introverted or extroverted children at two years of age remain so later in childhood and exhibit distinct psychophysiological patterns as well as different social behaviors (Kagan, Reznick, and Snidman 1987, 1988). Contrary to much popular belief, the tendency to approach others cooperatively does not seem to be associated with family income, education, or social status to the same degree; those who claim that the socioeconomic environment accounts for virtually all human behavior tend to forget how much they differ from their own siblings. While environmental factors do indeed influence these behavioral traits, the most important experiences seem to concern individual life history rather than social class or culture.

While the precise genetic mechanisms involved in the inheritance of personality are open to question, the existence of individual differences in the probability of cooperative and competitive behavior is consistent with evolutionary principles (Cloninger 1986; Feierman 1987). There is every reason to believe that we have evolved from early hominids, like *Australopithecus africanus*, who lived in small groups characterized by a combination of cooperation and rivalry (Coppens et al. 1976, esp. 548; Humphrey 1976, 310–12; Thompson 1976; Isaac 1978). Nonverbal cues associated with both aggressive and cooperative behaviors are similar in nonhuman primates and humans (van Hooff 1969; Masters et al. 1986); differences in social behavior observed among chimpanzees (Goodall 1986a) or young children (Montagner 1978) are consistent with the view that the individual's personality results from a combination of innate and acquired factors.

Evolutionary anthropology thus agrees with psychology and human ethology: both genetic and cultural causal processes apparently contribute to both human cooperation and human competition. If so, it is plausible to assume that the balance between aggressiveness and sharing behavior could be a variable trait. From an evolutionary perspective, such diversity of response would be adaptive in a species with a complex behavioral repertoire facing changing social and physical environments.

This view of human nature puts a new light on Freud's treatment of social taboos as restraints on the pleasurable drives of individuals. Without endorsing Freud's poetic dichotomy of "eros" and "thanatos," something like this ambivalence does indeed seem to be natural. To be sure, some taboos are purely cultural in origin. But consider the taboo against incest, which—even if not absolutely universal—is probably the most widespread of these cultural prohibitions. There is good evidence that the avoidance of interbreeding with close kin has a biological element (Bischoff 1972). Inhibition of immediate individual pleasures can occur in other animals as well as in humans.

The argument of Freud's *Civilization and Its Discontents* is generally consistent with this ethological evidence. Broadly speaking, Freud argues that the most serious psychological conflicts confronting the human individual were produced by cultural evolution and its effects on the ambivalence of human nature—not by human nature itself. It has been said that "Freud was wrong in believing that length of *time* in evolutionary history is the problem" underlying the tension between competition and cooperation in humans (Campbell 1972, 32), but Freud may well have been correct after all. Assuming that both selfish pleasure (hedonism) and cooperation (altruism) are partly innate and partly learned in our species, could human evolution have altered the balance in a potentially dangerous way?

Prior to the neolithic revolution, hominids lived for at least several million years in small hunting and gathering groups (Morin 1973; Thompson 1976; Lovejoy 1981). If primate sociology and anthropology give us a clue, dominance and group defense probably became more advantageous (and hence the selective pressure in favor of them more marked) as population densities increased the frequencies of group interaction. Sometime in the three million years or more of hominid evolution prior to the emergence of civilization, humans developed languages. By the time of the oldest cave paintings, at least eighteen thousand to twenty thousand years ago, some forms of ritual and magic were in existence (Bataille 1980). Hence, since the Pleistocene, we can assume something like a culture as a complex symbolic system for social coordination.

As long as the size of human groups remained relatively small, the ambivalence between altruism and selfishness need not have been a more serious problem for our species than for baboons, chimpanzees, or rhesus monkeys. A high proportion of all males in the early human populations would exercise dominant behaviors if, as among many baboon, chimpanzee, and rhesus groups, two or three out of ten to fifteen males formed a dominant alliance coordinating group behavior. It would not be hard to explain genetic as well as cultural selection for traits that produced dominance within the band, an ability to lead the hunt, and "altruistic bravery" in defending the group (figure 1.3).

In this hypothesis, rapid evolution to very large populations over the past ten thousand years—made possible by agricultural food surpluses—has required an enlarged scope of cooperation and an equally enlarged arena of in-group competition or threat behavior. This extension of both human cooperation and human competition to broader objects was, of course, made possible only through cultural

Figure 1.3
Altruism and Leadership in Preliterate Human Societies

a. Indian Rock Drawing from New Mexico

b. Indian Rock Drawing from Michigan

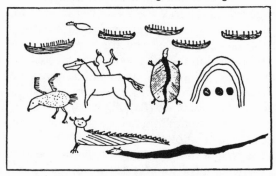

(a) A rock drawing found near a precipitous trail in New Mexico. It warns the "reader" that, while a mountain goat (with horns) may hope to pass safely, a rider on horseback is certain to fall. From Ellis 1984, 1–2. Because the picture represents the use of human intelligence to produce a durable "warning call," it is a visible image of human altruism in a preliterate culture. (b) "The five canoes at the top carry fifty-one men, represented by the vertical strokes. A chieftain called Kishkemunasee, 'Kingfisher,' leads the expedition. He is represented by the bird drawn above the first canoe. The three suns under three arches show that the journey lasted three days. The turtle symbolizes a happy landing, and the picture of a man on a horse shows that the warriors marched on quickly. The courageous spirit of the warriors is captured in the drawing of the eagle, while force and cunning are evoked in symbols of the panther and serpent." From Ellis 1984, 1–3. The image thus represents both leadership and altruistic behavior in intergroup conflict.

means. But this rapid sociocultural evolution we call history has put enormous strains on our species.

Time is indeed a major variable. Large-scale human civilizations have been superimposed on a species with a long history of cooperative competition in small bands. Even within contemporary societies, groups of ten to fifteen males have persisted as key units: boards of directors, cabinets or councils of ministers, sports teams, and so on (Tiger 1969). Success in agonistic or aggressive behavior within such a small cooperative group seems to correlate with reproductive success in many primates. The persistence of similar groups suggests that humans retain an analogous primate heritage even within large-scale social systems. What is different in civilization is the scope of the society with which individuals identify (Gruter and Masters 1986). And that difference is clearly cultural, necessitating very strong social "indoctrination," including on occasion a heavy dose of xenophobia, not to mention run-of-the-mill ethnocentrism (Campbell 1965b; Reynolds, Falger, and Vine 1987).

Cultural norms must therefore play a very strong role in reinforcing the appropriate behaviors in human societies. Depending on the cultural context, however, these norms may reinforce either competition (selfishness) or cooperation (altruism). All that we know of cultural variability, especially between Eastern and Western civilizations, would seem to confirm this connection between the evolution of more complex sociopolitical units and the extraordinary differences in behavior patterns from one population to another. But this means that wide cultural variability in our species is a sign of stress, insofar as our primate heritage has ill prepared the human animal to live in enormous, impersonal social systems (Tiger 1987). The transient character of political communities during recorded history underlines the instability of very large societies, in which the subtle mixtures of competition and cooperation—well adapted for small groups—are easily destroyed.

In this context, political philosophy can be understood as a response to the predicament facing human civilization. Precisely because the ambiguity of cooperation and competition is natural to humans, it is never completely clear how we should relate to each other. And because both selfishness and altruism have a natural root that has been transformed by cultural change, it is rare that political institutions are universally acceptable and stable. Hence, humans continually seek the "right" or "just" way of organizing their social life in the hopes of establishing standards for justifying, improving, or criticizing existing institutions.

As these reflections indicate, research in comparative animal behavior can ultimately contribute to the debates that have traditionally engaged philosophers (Masters 1975b, 1978a, 1978b; Somit 1976; White 1981). If so, the concept of natural justice—once at the center of political philosophy (Strauss 1953)—needs to be reconsidered in the light of contemporary ethology. Just as Aristotle rejected the relativism of the Sophists on the grounds that good or just behavior combines both conventional and natural elements, ethologists are coming to view varied cultural practices and norms in a naturalistic framework (Bischoff 1972; Eibl-Eibesfeldt 1971; Tiger and Fox 1971; Wickler 1972a; Stent 1979; Ruse 1986; Alexander 1987).

There is, of course, a risk in such speculations. The history of Social Darwinism should be ample warning that the attribution of "natural" status to definitions of justice can easily become ideological. Simplistic teleology is dangerous because it can be transformed into a defense of particularistic social opinions or national prejudices. Nonetheless, the refusal to consider the biological roots of human political and social life is also untenable; rejecting a natural component in human altruism can be as ideological as was Social Darwinism.

Many will be unconvinced by the foregoing argument. Comparisons of humans with other animals seem to ignore the most important feature of our species, namely, the large human brain, with its attendant capacity for learning, symbolic communication, and self-consciousness. But this generally accepted view ignores a crucial scientific problem. Where did our big brains come from?

At first glance, the increased cranial capacity of *Homo sapiens* would seem to be an unambiguously adaptive trait. Larger brain capacity appears to be associated with more complex learning, the ability to cope with "problems of interpersonal relationships" (Humphrey 1976), and hence better probabilities of survival and reproduction for the mutants that first carried this trait. Reflection indicates, however, that larger head size at birth also increases the danger to mother, infant, or both during childbirth (Montagu 1968).

The transition to the bipedal stature characterizing toolmaking hominids had consequences for females that are sometimes forgotten in abstract discussions of "the nature of man." The biomechanics of walking on two feet shifted the position of the pelvis, constraining the birth canal (figure 1.4); the prolonged labor associated with human childbirth is presumed to be a response to this problem (Johannson, personal communication). The fetus's head remains a principal stress in the birth process, even though neoteny (that is, delayed development during the early phases of ontogeny), associated with the prolonged helplessness of the human infant, permitted birth of a proportionally smaller fetus than would otherwise be the case (Hass 1970;

Figure 1.4
The Female Birth Canal and Upright Posture

a. Pelvic Structure in Australopithecines and Humans

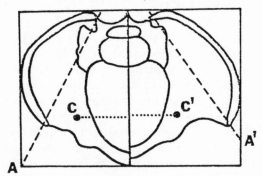

b. Birth Canal in Hominid Evolution

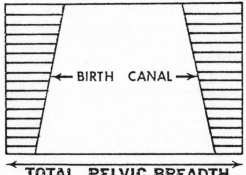

(a) Upper view of left half of the pelvis of modern man compared to right half of
Australopithecus *pelvis. "The total morphological pattern of the australopithecine
specimen yields a more advantageous position of the hip musculature than the
modern condition. The greater angulation of the iliac blades in australopithecines is
thus not indicative of an intermediate gate pattern but rather of a generally smaller
birth canal in the pelvis." From* C. Owen Lovejoy, "The Locomotor Skeleton of
Basal Pleistocene Hominids," *9th Congress, Union Internationale des Sciences
Prehistoriques et Protohistoriques, Colloque 6 (Paris: CNRS), 170.*
*(b) Enlargement of the human female's birth canal compared to that of
australopithecines (ibid., 171). Since pelvic structures were already adapted for
bipedal locomotion in autralopithecines, these changes in birth canal reflect a
distinct selective trend accommodating a larger fetal brain in recent hominid
evolution (compare figure 1.5).*

Gould 1977). It follows that the pressures of natural selection limiting brain size among primates could only have been increased by the transition to bipedal stature; for the pregnant woman, even today, the mutant fetus with an exceptionally large brain represents a survival risk to both mother and child.

The adaptive advantages of increased cranial capacity thus had correlative disadvantages. Moreover, it is not clear why this particular evolutionary trend occurred when it did in hominid evolution. The fossil record suggests that the earliest hominids maintained a brain size of approximately 800 cc for up to three million years after the initiation of toolmaking; within the last five hundred thousand years, brain size has increased considerably. Since this evolutionary trend is not correlated with other known developments in technology, life style, or bodily structure (figure 1.5), the emergence of the large human brain (averaging 1,400 cc) has never really been explained (Caspari 1968; Holloway 1968; Mettler 1962).

One possibility, rarely discussed, is that changes in hominid proto-culture occurred *before* the most recent increases in brain size and made them possible (cf. Isaac 1978). If our small-brained ancestors extended their cooperation to childbirth, at least to the extent of providing assistance to mothers in cases of difficulty, the increased mother-child mortality in case of a large-brained fetus would have been counterbalanced for the first time. If so, a pattern of social cooperation would have shifted the cost-benefit ratio, permitting the obvious advantages of the large brain for adults to come into play (Morin 1973). Without some such factor, it is hard to see how the increased size of the infant head would not have continued to be a selective disadvantage (Fisher 1987).

Observations of childbirth in free-ranging primates seem relatively rare, suggesting that it is not a social event for other primates (for example, van Lawick-Goodall 1969, 370). Chimpanzee females apparently give birth more easily than humans (DeVore, personal communication; Goodall 1986a and personal communication). When a female baboon was seen immediately after childbirth, "none of the other animals in the group actually approached her. On the contrary, on several occasions she tried to move close to some of them, and these sometimes moved away from her" (Hall and DeVore 1965, 85).

True, childbirth in some existing preliterate tribes is also not a social event. But the human mother can be instructed on delivery, and social assistance is available in case of complications. It would be necessary, of course, to spell out and examine in detail the hypothesis that new forms of social cooperation between the pregnant mother and other members of the group became feasible in the last five hun-

Figure 1.5
Growth in Hominid Cranial Capacity

a. The Evolutionary Path to *Homo sapiens*

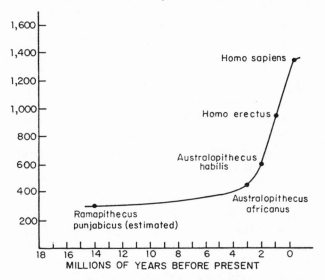

b. Structural Change in the Human Head

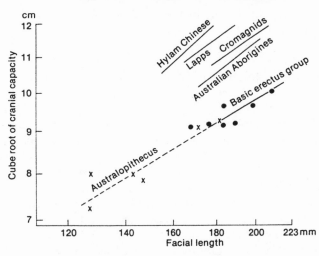

(a) Increase in brain size during human evolution. From Wilson 1975, 548; redrawn from Pilbeam. (b) Cube root of cranial capacity versus facial length for hominids. From Gould 1977, 398.

dred thousand years. Surely it is possible that positive feedback between increased social cooperation and the benefits of larger brains might account for the puzzling way in which the hominid brain increased to its present average size of 1,400 cc.

The hypothesis that the large hominid brain is the consequence of social cooperation, and particularly of educating or assisting women in order to reduce mortality in childbirth, has many interesting ramifications. It implies, for example, that the adaptive significance of the enlarged cortex might be primarily associated with the life cycle and activities of females, particularly with reference to the birth and care of infants (cf. Schubert 1983a, 1985). Whereas many accounts of the expansion of hominid evolution focus on male activities, such as hunting, group defense, or knowledge of the terrain, an explanation based on social cooperation emphasizes a factor that otherwise would have limited evolution toward larger brain size.

The development of social cooperation in human childbirth might therefore explain the relationship of brain size to complex social systems while avoiding a hidden difficulty in the usual account of hominid evolution. In the study of other species, biologists have often found that behavioral changes must have occurred before physiological ones; although bodily mutations sometimes influence behavior, modifications in animal behavior can create the selective advantage for subsequent mutations influencing body structure (Mayr 1958; see chap. 4, n. 3). It is often argued that humans cooperate in society because they have big brains. Perhaps the truth is that we have big brains because we cooperate in society.

From the "Nature of Man" to "Human Nature"

The hypothesis that increased brain size was made possible by cooperative behavior suggests an empirical answer to the perennial theoretical debates about human nature. If even the physiology of *Homo sapiens* is that of a social and cultural animal, it would become difficult to argue that human sociability is not a constituent element of our nature (cf. Portman 1961). Such an argument is, however, difficult if not impossible to prove: falsification of the hypothesis would require evidence of social behavior, which does not usually form fossilized traces capable of lasting for a half million years.[4] Nor can we perform experiments on the australopithecines or *Homo erectus* in order to determine the kinds of difficulties encountered during birth and the likely consequences of cooperation during the evolutionary transition to increased cranial capacity.

These difficulties perhaps help explain why political theorists have so often disagreed about the nature of our species. The fundamental propositions on which both philosophers and social scientists base their understanding of human behavior are, in many cases, just as difficult to confirm as the hypothesis just outlined. Consider, for example, the famous and ringing sentence at the outset of Rousseau's *Social Contract* : "L'homme est né libre, et partout il est dans les fers" (1.1). The ambiguities in this formulation make it hard to interpret or refute with empirical evidence; while Rousseau's phrase has immense rhetorical power—or, indeed, perhaps for that very reason—textual analysis confirms that it can hardly be used as a scientific hypothesis without further explanation.

The first difficulty in interpreting Rousseau's assertion is grammatical: the first verb has sometimes been assumed to be in the past tense ("Man was born free, and everywhere he is in chains"), sometimes in the present tense ("Man is born free, and everywhere he is in chains"). Since the French *"est né "* will support either reading, Rousseau's statement can be and has been taken to refer either to the origins of hominid evolution or to the artificial status of political communities in the present. In the first case, Rousseau means that certain social institutions did not exist at the outset of human history; in the second, he is arguing that they are unnatural here and now.

A second and related difficulty concerns the reference of the word *l'homme*: does Rousseau mean the entire human species or each individual human being? If Rousseau meant the latter, it is usually presumed that his usage does not imply a limitation to males, but even the gender of the reference is not clear (Keohane 1982). Does the word *fers* refer to political institutions like the centralized state, to formal slavery, or to any form of social and economic inequality? Is the word *libre* meant to include the absence of any obligation or duty to others, the freedom from formal legal requirements, or a degree of independence from all lasting social interactions (as in the "state of nature" of Rousseau's *Second Discourse*)?

Rousseau's famous phrase could refer to the evolutionary origins of the entire species, the current condition of civilized societies, or the status of obligations incumbent on individuals. It could focus on institutions or on individual behavior. Although the sentence could be interpreted as including a reference to his other writings, even the relationship to Rousseau's earlier work has given rise to critical confusion. It should hardly be surprising, therefore, that there is disagreement not only about the meaning of that one phrase, but that similar theoretical endeavors by other philosophers and social scientists give rise to controversy.

Perhaps the difficulty in defining the nature of our species is that we have sought answers too quickly. It has been suggested above, on the basis of evidence from animal behavior, that humans are by nature both cooperative and competitive, and that both of these behaviors are partly innate and partly learned. This seems to indicate that the most divergent theories are in part correct, which is hardly of much help. It is little wonder that the works of political philosophers are relegated to the history of ideas—and that social scientists spend little time seeking to define the nature of man.

As the example of Rousseau's famous line indicates, part of the difficulty lies in terminology. The word *man* is inherently ambiguous and should probably be abandoned in all serious discussion. Not only does it confuse the entire species (*man* as *mankind*) with the individual (*man* as *a man*), but it blurs the status of varied kinds of groups or societies and, of course, can minimize the difference between a man and a woman. Since all of these factors are potentially important variables in explaining an empirical observation like the enlarged human brain, the theoretical confusions introduced by speaking of "the nature of man" in the abstract should be avoided at all costs.

To shift the focus of theoretical discussion to a scientific ground, it is therefore necessary to move more slowly and cautiously. In seeking to provide a foundation for the social sciences as well as for political philosophy we should speak of human nature and then specify more accurately when the discussion refers to the species, to a society, or to the individual. In Plato's *Republic,* Socrates is twice compelled to take a longer path than he at first expected (2.357a–367e; 5.449e–451b). We would do well to emulate Socrates in this respect and take a longer route to the study of what it is to be a human being.

PART II

Social Behavior

Nature and culture are integrated in virtually everything that humans do. Despite our deeply rooted habit of thinking in terms of polar opposites (instinct versus learning; the innate versus the acquired; genes versus environment), research in the life sciences shows that humans are more complex beings than one might assume from popular opinions and beliefs.

Instead of starting from oversimplified dichotomies or reductionist concepts, it is therefore well to look carefully at the empirical phenomena of social behavior. Part 2 focuses on nonverbal and verbal means of communication to show how humans relate to each other in practice. While all members of our species share a common repertoire of behavior, each language and culture develops a distinct way of describing the world and the way humans ought to live in it. Rather than accentuating the reductionism feared by many ideological critics, a biological approach to human behavior explores the unique mechanisms underlying social change and therewith makes it possible to transform metaphors or images about human nature into rigorous questions for inquiry.

CHAPTER 2

Bonding, Aggression, and Flight

Human Nature and Social Behavior

The demonstration that human behavior is a compound of contradictory impulses has important theoretical consequences. Ethological studies of social life show us that human societies and governments cannot be adequately explained by supposedly invariant natural traits or instincts like altruism or selfishness. Political and social theories can hardly be credible if they rest on superficial definitions of human nature.

The interaction between individual characteristics and the social environment is of primary importance in understanding the obvious differences between human cultures. Even for other species, the environment is as much a determinant of social behavior as the "nature" of the animal. Does this mean that human nature is a *tabula rasa* contributing nothing but the ability to learn the rules or customs of each society?

According to evolutionary theory, animal behavior is as subject to natural selection as any other bodily trait (Roe and Simpson 1958). Ethologists have shown that the social life of other animals—and especially of nonhuman primates—is based upon species-specific behaviors that have evolved as adaptive responses (Lorenz [1931–63] 1970–71; Hinde 1982). Whereas the behaviorist psychologists of the early twentieth century spoke of undifferentiated "drives," Konrad Lorenz (often described as the father of modern ethology) spoke of each innate behavior as a distinct "action pattern" or "consummatory motor coordination" with its own instinctive "appetite"; as a result, Lorenz argued, animal behavior can be described in terms of a "parliament of instincts" in which conflicts between impulses are resolved (Lorenz [1961] 1966).

To analyze the political relevance of human nature, therefore, one must first ask whether there is an innate repertoire of human social behavior from which diverse social patterns emerge depending on ecology, cultural environment, and individual development. For other animals, such a repertoire provides the building blocks for behavioral variations between individuals or groups. Does our species have a behavioral repertoire or "biogrammar" akin to that of other animals (Tiger and Fox 1971), or has learning emancipated humans from the systems of behavior found in other species?

HUMAN NATURE IN PHILOSOPHY AND PSYCHOLOGY

This question about human nature was posed long ago in Plato's *Republic*. In that work, Socrates argues that the character of a human society is found in the behavior of its people rather than in material objects or physical surroundings (*Republic* 4.435e) and goes on to contrast three cultural patterns familiar in the ancient world:

> Isn't it quite necessary for us to agree that the very same forms and dispositions as are in the city are in each of us? . . . It would be ridiculous if someone should think that the spiritedness didn't come into the cities from those private men who are just the ones imputed with having this character, such as those in Thrace, Scythia, and pretty nearly the whole upper region; or the love of learning, which one could most impute to our region, or the love of money, which one could affirm is to be found not least among the Phoenicians and those in Egypt. (Plato *Republic* 4.435e–436a)

This remark implies that cultural differences are a response to such environmental variables as climate, geography, or economic system (cf. Aristotle *Politics* 7.7.1327b–1328a; Rousseau *Social Contract* 2.8–10). But if humans have a common nature, how do these differences arise? As Socrates points out, the environment cannot influence social customs unless it manifests itself in individual human behavior or personality.

Plato leads us to see that this question raises a serious difficulty for anyone seeking to understand human nature. Granted that cultural differences must be revealed in the behavior of individuals, *where* in the human organism do these observed differences reside? Some humans are characterized by bravery ("spiritedness"), some by intellectual occupation ("love of learning"), and some by desire for material wealth ("love of money"). Reflecting on this fact, the Platonic Socrates observes:

But this now is hard. Do we act in each of these ways as a result of the same part of ourselves, or are there three parts and with a different one we act in each of the different ways? Do we learn with one, become spirited with another of the parts within us, and desire the pleasures of nourishment and generation and all their kin with a third; or do we act with the soul as a whole in each of them once we are started? This will be hard to determine in a way worthy of the argument. (Plato *Republic* 4.436a)

For Socrates, the definition of human nature depends on the specificity of psychological principles or "drives": the hypothesis that human behavior is a function of "the entire soul"—akin to the Lockean view of a *tabula rasa* whose responses depend entirely on life experience—is contrasted with a differentiated repertoire of responses arising from distinct "things" or principles.

In ancient Greek thought, this issue had been raised by Sophists like Antiphon, for whom human behavior is the result of a single, ubiquitous pleasure-pain calculus (Barker 1960, 96–97). Modern empirical psychologists have long tended to follow a similar view, derived from the assumptions of Hobbes, Locke, and other "social contract" theorists (Masters 1977) and developed further by behaviorists in the tradition of Hull and Skinner (Peters and Taijfel 1972). In our day, the contrary view, according to which distinct psychological principles coexist and conflict, is often associated with Freud.

For simple hedonists like Antiphon or Hull, because one positive reinforcement can easily be substituted for another, human behavior is extraordinarily plastic and is shaped almost entirely by the environment and training. For those who insist on the heterogeneity of human nature, like Freud, competing desires are more difficult to eradicate, limiting the extent to which social restraints can mold or change the individual. The question raised by Socrates in the *Republic* obviously concerns an enduring difficulty in understanding human nature and social institutions.

If social behavior is the result of individual learning, one could speak of society as the result of a social contract between previously independent individuals, as did Hobbes, Locke, and Rousseau. Such theories are called into question, however, if humans naturally have a repertoire of behavior, including social bonding, that is not reducible to a single, homogeneous process like conditioned reinforcement. Posed in this way, philosophical debates concerning human nature can be fruitfully illuminated by research in ethology, neurophysiology, and social psychology.

To be called natural or biological, social responses would have to be rooted in the human brain, characteristic of normal growth and development, and universal or at least very widespread across different cultures. Even if human ethology reveals a species-specific repertoire of social behavior, moreover, there must be some way that these natural impulses or responses are combined with individual learning and cultural norms to produce the observed variations in human activity. Is there scientific research that explains this process?

Unlike disputes about abstract definitions of human nature, these questions can be addressed by observing how people act and react using methods derived from ethology and social psychology. We now know much about the structure and functions of the human brain and the way the nonverbal behavior of one individual influences others among nonhuman primates as well as humans. Since emotional responses and nonverbal displays are among the most universal elements of human behavior, they can be described, observed, and studied experimentally. Cross-cultural evidence can be related to similar types of behavior in nonhuman primates and used to explore the basic repertoire of human social interaction and its relationship to culturally learned behavior.

THE NATURE OF ANIMAL BEHAVIOR

Recent biological research shows that a simplistic nature-nurture dichotomy is no longer tenable (Simpson 1969; Gruter and Bohannan 1983; Kitcher 1985; Alexander 1986). Over the past generation, many careful studies of animal behavior in wild or semi-wild settings have revealed the complexity of social interactions and group structures once dismissed as instincts of little relevance to human cultural variation. Combined with continental ethological theories (under the influence of Lorenz, Tinbergen, and Hinde) and American experimental research, these findings have led to a rejection of the narrow stimulus-response model of behavior and its replacement by a more complex view (Masters 1976a; von Cranach et al. 1979).

One consequence of this trend has been the abandonment of the traditional notion of animal drives. What used to pass as the ubiquitous appetites or drives—hunger, sex, and the like—have been shown to be functional categories rather than psychological mechanisms or causes of behavior (von Cranach 1976). Each species satisfies these functions by activities that are combinations of particulate elements: orientation reflexes ("taxes"), innate or acquired motor coordinations, physiological states of readiness or "moods" (often reflected in "intention movements" or displays of a behavioral "tendency"), and "releasing mechanisms" triggered by the appearance of "key stimuli" (to mention only the best-known components of classical ethological theories).

Animal behavior typically consists of sequences of such components, some acquired or learned (either during "critical periods" of development or more flexibly throughout the life cycle) and others innate (Hinde and Stevenson 1971; Moyer 1969; Eibl-Eibesfeldt 1979; Hinde 1982). Which of these elements may be individually learned or modified by experience and which are more or less invariant depends on the species being studied. Whatever the case for a particular animal, virtually no mammal is entirely driven by instincts that are insensitive to development and individual experience; hence, as one biologist has remarked, the distinction between nature and nurture as competing causes is rather like asking whether the area of a rectangle is "caused" by its length rather than its width (Alexander 1986).

Although popularizations of ethology (for example, Ardrey 1963; Lorenz 1966) have led many to believe in ubiquitous instincts of aggression, territoriality, or altruism, these categories should be understood in functional terms—that is, as consequences of behavior, identified by the observer, that may (but need not always) be adaptive for a species in a particular setting. Animal behavior itself consists of concrete actions or motor coordinations, only some of which (like eating, copulating, sleeping, attacking, fleeing, or grooming) are "consummatory behaviors" directly satisfying physical needs; other actions include "displays" or "intention movements" reflecting the probability (a "mood" or "tendency") that an individual will engage in a consummatory behavior or serving as communicative signals ("releasers" or "rituals") in social groups (Lorenz 1967; Hass 1970; von Cranach et al. 1979; Hinde 1982).

An animal's behavior therefore reflects a combination of distinct elements, in which inherited and learned components are integrated in various ways (Lorenz [1931–63] 1970–71). Social interaction consists of the signals or cues that individuals use to adjust their behavior to each other as well as the contexts in which consummatory behaviors are exhibited. For example, the category of sexual behavior includes both the signals ("displays" or "intention movements") indicating a willingness to mate and the specific circumstances in which mating occurs. For animals who form pair-bonds for life, like gibbons, a single male and female will direct the behavioral displays only to each other; for other species, like chimpanzees, in which mating takes the form of temporary consortships, displays will be directed at different individuals from time to time.

Given the variety of consummatory behaviors, intention movements, and ritualizations within and between species, it seems at first difficult to generalize about animal behavior. The observer can, however, classify behavioral elements or social displays according to function, without reference to the innate or acquired causes of their development. Animals can approach, avoid, or remain in proximity ("bond") to each other: each of these relationships is a functional outcome of the interaction between individuals. While the consummatory behaviors of attack, flight, and copulation are the clearest manifestation of approach, avoidance, or social bonding, other consummatory behaviors or intention movements can have the same effect: eating, for example, is a solitary behavior for some animals and a social event for other species (Blurton-Jones 1987).

The categories of approach, avoidance, and social bonding thus provide a general way of classifying animal behavior without prejudging the role of innate or acquired traits (cf. Herbst 1975). In a survey of the behaviors that precede mating among vertebrates, for example, Morris (1956) was able to show that the observed displays ("courtship rituals") combine intention movements of attack or threat, flight or avoidance, and bonding in varied ways. Displays associated with these three types of social response seem quite general in animal social life, if only because easily recognized (or "ritualized") signals of attack, flight, and bonding are likely to be adaptive for animals living in social groups.

Plato's question concerning human nature can be restated in terms of the descriptive categories of attack, flight, and bonding. If humans exhibit a natural repertoire of behavior organized in terms of different "things" or principles ("parts of the soul"), these three categories of behavior would have distinct properties, whereas if humans engaged in all three kinds of behavior on the basis of a single process of conditioning ("with the entire soul"), each kind of response would depend solely on the experience of the individual. The single pleasure-pain calculus predicated by thinkers like Antiphon or Hobbes implies that social bonding occurs only for individuals who thereby increase the frequency of pleasure; in this view, humans have somehow emancipated themselves from the differentiated drives or instincts found in other animals. If Plato's Socrates is correct, on the other hand, behaviors associated with social bonding cannot be entirely derived from individual experience or expectations of generalized pleasure; in this tradition, social behavior is as natural for humans as for other social animals.

RHETORIC, NONVERBAL BEHAVIOR, AND LEADERSHIP

To convert the age-old debates about human nature into a scientific problem, it is necessary to specify the kind of behavior to be observed and studied. Traditionally, philosophers discussed this issue in terms of the "passions" or feelings. But if these emotions and impulses are to be called natural, they must be studied in a form that permits one to distinguish between passions that are cultural and those that are innate. Otherwise, as Rousseau stressed in his critique of Hobbes, socially induced desires could be compounded with natural ones (Rousseau *Second Discourse*, pt. 1).

If humans have a repertoire of social responses like other animals, it should be evident in our nonverbal behavior. Among the nonverbal displays of primates, facial gestures are particularly important in social interactions (van Hooff 1969; Chance 1976; de Waal 1982; Hinde 1982). For example, the human smile seems to be an innate motor coordination, since it is exhibited under similar circumstances by virtually all normal infants (including blind children who cannot have learned to smile by watching others); while seeing others may facilitate the appearance of this response, the smile is as characteristic of normal human development as any innate or species-specific trait in another mammal (Hass 1970).

Humans exhibit facial displays similar to those of monkeys and apes (figure 2.1), and these muscular movements are an exceptionally strong stimulus with comparable expressive and social properties in all known human populations (Ekman and Oster 1979; Plutchik 1980). Facial gestures thus have a dual function, since they both express emotions (inner states or feelings of the individual) and serve as social signals for others in the group (Lanzetta et al. 1985; Masters et al. 1986).

Facial displays and other nonverbal behaviors are especially important as cues of dominance and subordination in nonhuman primate bands, where leaders are constantly being observed by subordinates. It should hardly be surprising, therefore, that similar phenomena exist in the relationship between human leaders and followers, whether in groups of children (Montagner 1978; Barner-Barry 1981) or in adult life (Masters 1976a, 1981a; Eibl-Eibesfeldt 1979; Schubert 1985). Facial displays thus provide a concrete and observable starting point for exploring human social behavior, especially since such phenomena allow us to analyze what humans actually do—in contrast to the indices or correlates of behavior usually studied in conventional social science (Wahlke 1979; Schubert 1981).

Although nonverbal behavior is now studied with scientific tech-

Figure 2.1
The Evolution of the Human Smile

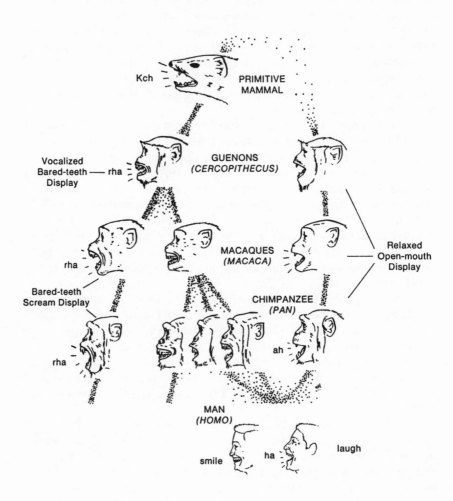

Comparison of human expressions of smiling and laughter with the bared-teeth displays of lower primates and primitive mammals. From Wilson 1975, 228, redrawn from van Hooff.

niques, it is a traditional focus for the thinkers interested in human nature and social interaction (Hundert 1987/1988). Rhetoric was once the principal science for the study and training of political leaders. In ancient Greece, the discovery that persuasive techniques could be analyzed and taught—generally credited to the Sophists—seems to have been a critical step in the emergence of the first schools of political science (Wheelwright 1966; Barker 1960). Restated by Plato, notably in the speeches of Thrasymachus in the *Republic* and the title figure of the *Gorgias*, this approach to rhetoric began with a focus on matters of verbal presentation and organization. By the time of Aristotle, however, the communication of emotion by nonverbal as well as verbal means had become a major element in the science of rhetoric (Arnhart 1981, esp. chap. 6).

The importance of nonverbal communication in traditional studies of rhetoric is evident if one consults older manuals for popular use. For example, William Scott's *Lessons in Elocution; or a Selection of Pieces in Prose and Verse for the Improvement of Youth in Reading and Speaking*, published in 1820, begins with lessons on "Elements of Gesture" taken from Walker's *Speaker* :

> There is the language of emotions and passions as well as of ideas. To express the latter is the peculiar province of words; to express the former, nature teaches us to make use of tones, looks and gestures. When anger, fear, joy, grief, love, or any other active passion arises in our minds, we naturally discover it by the particular manner in which we utter our words; by the features of the countenance, and by other well known signs. And even when we speak without any of the more violent emotions, some kind of feeling usually accompanies our words, and this, whatever it be, hath its proper external expression. Expression indeed hath been so little studied in public speaking, that we seem almost to have forgotten the language of nature, and are ready to consider every attempt to recover it, as the labored and effected effort of art. But nature is always the same; and every judicious imitation of it will always be pleasing. Nor can any one deserve the appellation of a good speaker, much less of a complete orator, till to distinct articulation, a good command of voice, and just emphasis, he is able to add the various expressions of emotion and passion. (Scott 1820, 54–55)

To teach public speaking, therefore, the first lessons concerned a "system of gesture, suited to the wants and capacities of school boys" (ibid. 9).

In addition to general devices for holding the body in an appropriate manner, students were taught the facial gestures associated with human emotions. "Every part of the human frame contributes to express the passions and emotions of the mind, and to shew in general its present state. . . . Especially the face, being furnished with a variety of muscles, does more in expressing the passions of the mind than the whole human frame besides" (ibid. 28–29). Since rhetorical skill requires appropriate use of nonverbal cues of the face as well as the body, the specific facial displays associated with each emotion were an important subject of study.

Although it is widely assumed that "nature teaches us" to use expressive behavior (as Scott's rhetorical manual put it), individuals perform similar behaviors in distinct ways that have a major impact on observers; as a result, today as in the past, those seeking power often take lessons in the hope of being more successful when appearing in public. Nor is this variability merely a local phenomenon: as the traveler soon learns, nonverbal behavior varies somewhat in different cultures and contexts. Facial displays do not seem to be a rigidly fixed or invariant characteristic as they combine innate and learned features.

The importance of such nonverbal behavior is evident in historical anecdotes about famous statesmen. In recent times, for example, it has been said that facial displays were critical in the success of leaders as diverse as Hitler (Shirer 1941, 454), Churchill (Gilbert 1981, vol. 6, 228), Mao (Terrill 1980, 159), and Eisenhower (Greenstein 1982). The emergence of television has, of course, made this process more salient.[1] Any complete understanding of the way individuals compete and gain power must consider the symbolic gestures of emotion and dominance that originated in hominid evolution but have been subtly influenced by human cultural practices.

The relationship between natural and cultural elements in human social behavior can therefore be explored by studying the effects of leaders' facial displays. Experimental methods make it possible to compare the emotions and attitudes elicited by similar nonverbal gestures in different countries (Masters and Mouchon 1986; Masters and Sullivan 1986). As a result, the scientific analysis of facial displays and rhetoric can be used to test the assumption, derived from the philosophic tradition of Hobbes and Locke, that human social behavior is plastic and culturally determined in all important respects.

Facial Displays and Social Behavior

Scientific research has now discovered more precisely how facial gestures serve as cues of emotion and of leadership. Studies in ethology, neurology, social psychology, education, and political science clarify the role of nonverbal displays in eliciting submissive, cooperative, or hostile attitudes in the observer. Whereas traditional manuals of rhetoric were based on intuitive "systems of gesture" like that cited above, we now know much about the evolutionary origins of facial displays, about the neurological structures that process these stimuli, and about the way that cognition and emotion interact when human adults respond to images of a political leader.

Analysis of nonverbal behavior is, however, paradoxically difficult (Frey et al. 1983). As one linguist put it, "we react to gestures as to a secret and complex code, written nowhere and known by no one, but understood by all" (Sapir 1970; cited by Coulomb-Gully 1986, 44). Rigorous study of facial displays is complicated not only by their subtle variability, but because they can both express an individual's emotional state and impress the observer by triggering an emotional or behavioral response.

Under the pressure of natural selection, expressive cues easily perceived by others were most likely to evolve as means of coordinating social behavior (Darwin [1872] 1965). Facial displays thus can have a communicative function quite independent of their role in expressing emotions. Although a smile is universally decoded as an expression of positive emotion (Ekman and Oster 1979), this display may coordinate the behaviors of sender and receiver even if the expressor is not happy—and, indeed, smiling may be more often used as a social signal than as an expression of happiness (Kraut and Johnston 1979).

The social role of the smile is evident from psychological experiments showing that it is harder to condition an aversive stimulus to a happy face than to a face expressing fear (Orr and Lanzetta 1980) or anger (Ohman and Dimberg 1978). Presumably, a happy face is a poor stimulus for arousing fear because humans are predisposed to associate this display with pleasurable outcomes. For some ethologists, the smiling component of a happy face is an innate signal that evolved as a reassuring cue, particularly for the young infant (Morris 1967, 120–25).

When primates interact, their status can typically be inferred from their display behavior. Changes in dominance are foreshadowed by slight but significant modifications in facial and bodily gestures (de Waal 1982; Goodall 1983; McGuire and Raleigh 1986). Since the effect of these behaviors on observers is critical in the process of hierarchy formation (Chase 1980b, 1982), cues of dominance and submission play a role both for the interacting individuals and for the group as a whole.

Among humans, facial expressions are an equally important factor in social relationships. From birth, human neonates recognize and imitate these nonverbal displays (Meltzoff and Moore 1977). Since mother-infant interaction is based in part on subtle facial cues (Papousek and Papousek 1979), it is perhaps not surprising that human females decode the facial displays of infants with greater accuracy than males (Babchuck et al. 1985).[2] Conversely, infants differ in their responses to similar displays of their mother, revealing personality traits that persist in later development (Izard, Hembree, and Heubner 1987; Izard 1988).

As the child matures, nonverbal behavior and especially facial displays play a critical role in the development of interaction with peers. Among preschool children, such cues produce distinctions between leaders and followers between the ages of three and five (Montagner 1978; Strayer 1981; Barner-Barry 1981). The effects of facial cues at this age have been demonstrated experimentally: when two children enter a room in which a single toy has been placed, the ultimate possessor can be predicted from their initial facial displays (Zivin 1977). In extreme cases, stable personality traits can be associated with such differences in nonverbal behavior (Kagan, Reznick, and Snidman 1987, 1988).

Specific structures in the brain control the process of perceiving and responding to the facial gestures of others; if these sites are damaged, normal social interaction is interrupted for nonhuman primates as well as humans. Monkeys subjected to experimental lesions of the temporal poles or amygdaloid nuclei (figure 2.2a-c) and released in free-ranging groups are unable to bond to others and tend to be ostracized (Kling 1986). In a human patient, damage to these sites in the brain was associated with difficulties in social interaction and an inability to decode emotion from the facial displays of others (Kling 1987). There even appear to be single neurons in the temporal cortex that are specialized to respond to the face of a conspecific (Gross 1983; Rodman and Gross 1987; Posner et al. 1988).

The ability to name another's face is controlled by different structures in the human brain than those involved in the recognition of well-known faces (figure 2.2c). Damage to the sites associating names and faces constitutes a distinct deficit (prosopagnosia), in which emotional response to the face is present but naming known faces is inhibited (Tranel and Damasio 1985). The human central nervous system is thus highly structured to perceive, decode, and respond to facial displays; unlike the *tabula rasa* theories of Hobbes, Locke, and some early behaviorists, contemporary neurology shows that the capacity for social behavior is preprogrammed in the human brain (Changeux 1983; Shepherd 1983; Gilinsky 1984).[3]

At the physiological level as well, expressive displays play an important role in primate social behavior. Among vervet monkeys, the leader has higher levels of whole blood serotonin than subordinates; in the course of naturally occurring status changes, serotonin levels drop in the formerly dominant individual and rise in his successor. This physiological mechanism seems to be controlled by the sight of submissive display behavior. The leader's serotonin level falls, just as if he had lost status, when he is either isolated from the group or prevented from seeing submissive displays by a one-way mirror (McGuire and Raleigh 1986; Raleigh and McGuire 1986). Experimental evidence suggests that similar hormonal processes are present in human children (Montagner 1978) and adults (Madson 1985a, 1985b).

For humans, the importance of decoding and responding to facial displays can be illustrated in other ways. Autistic children cannot interpret the emotions in the facial displays they see, perhaps because they focus attention on the lower portions of the face and do not attend to the eyes (Denckla 1986a). In teaching learning-disabled children, it has been found that complementarity in the facial display behavior of tutor and student is predictive of success, whereas matching of tutor and pupil on other personality variables was not correlated with effective results (Sapir 1985).

Because nonverbal behavior has so many effects, the study of facial displays is a particularly useful way to explore the complexity of human social and emotional behavior. An emotional experience affects the muscles associated with facial expression, even though the results need not be visible (Fridlund and Izard 1983; Cacioppo and Petty 1979; Vaughan and Lanzetta 1980; Englis, Vaughan, and Lanzetta 1982). When experimental subjects are asked to imagine they are happy, the cheek muscle (zygomat) producing a smile is activated; the muscle that lowers the eyebrows (corrugator) is most likely to be active when a subject is asked to imagine being angry, though this muscle is activated to some extent whenever attention is being focused (Schwartz et al. 1976). These effects explain why the face so often reflects the individual's inner state or feeling (or, to use a traditional formula, why the face is a mirror of the soul).

An individual's facial gestures are not simply reactive, however, since they can play an active role in changing inner states or feelings. In one experiment, actors were instructed to manipulate facial muscles one at a time without knowing the emotional display that was being generated: the result was a physiological reaction similar to that of the emotion being posed (Ekman, Levenson, and Friesen 1983). Sometimes called "facial feedback," this reaction suggests that a ritualized gesture performed because the occasion seems to demand it—

Figure 2.2
Localized Structures in the Human Brain
for Processing Nonverbal Cues

a. Cross-Section of Cerebral Cortex

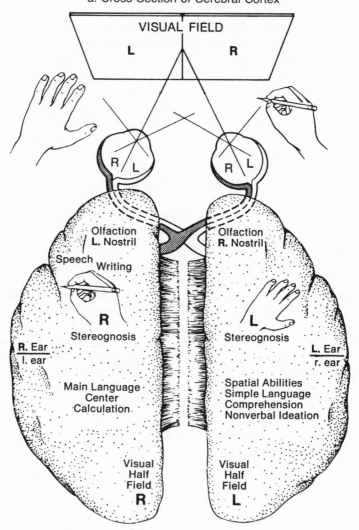

(a) Lateralization of nonverbal and linguistic functions in the human brain, using schematic representation to show "the relative specialization of the two hemispheres and their relations to sensory inputs and motor outputs. Cutting of the corpus callosum is shown in the midline." From Shepherd 1983, 584.

b. The Amygdala and the Limbic System

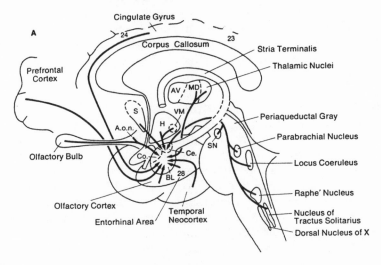

c. Structures for Seeing and Naming

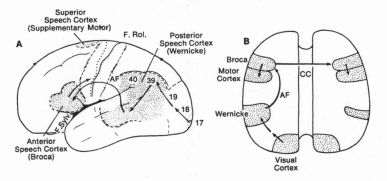

(b) Vertical section showing "parts of the brain with . . . inputs to the amygdala. Abbreviations: A.o.n., anterior olfactory nucleus; AV, anteroventral thalamic nucleus; BL, basolateral amygdaloid nucleus; Ce., central amygdaloid nucleus; Co., cortical amygdaloid nucleus; H, hypothalmus; MD, dorsomedial thalmic nucleus; RF, reticular formation; S, septum; SN, substantia nigra; VM, ventromedial hypothalamic nucleus." From Shepherd 1983, 539 (fig. 29.9a). Outputs from the amygdala follow distinct pathways (ibid., fig. 29.9b). These structures form essential components of the "limbic system" associated with emotional response and memory, distinguishing the mammalian brain from that of reptiles (MacLean 1983). (c) Structures associated with "seeing and naming" (588, fig. 31.15). From Neurobiology *by Gordon M. Shepherd. Copyright © 1983 by Oxford University Press, Inc. Reprinted by permission.*

such as the smile associated with a greeting display—can influence the actor's own feelings (Laird 1974). Hence the motor coordinations that produce facial displays are linked in complex ways with both physiological substrates of feeling and the thoughts or verbal expressions associated with our inner states (Fridlund, Schwartz, and Fowler 1984; Leventhal 1984).

Facial displays are also powerful stimuli that influence observers in predictable ways. When mothers look at their infants, they tend to imitate the facial display they observe (von Cranach et al. 1979); adults who watch pictures of facial displays of other humans—or even of chimpanzees—can be observed engaging in the same mimicry. Whether this is due to a sharing of emotion or a neurological link between the perception and expression of facial displays (Gilinsky 1984), the face is not a neutral or "unconditioned" stimulus, but rather one whose effects have been "prepared" by human evolution (Lanzetta and Orr 1980, 1981; Orr and Lanzetta 1980).

Since the capacity to decode and respond to facial displays is functionally necessary for normal social behavior, it should not be surprising that the facial displays of political leaders can influence observers' emotions and attitudes. These effects of nonverbal behavior can be demonstrated experimentally by showing viewers videotapes of known leaders exhibiting expressive displays that have been selected according to criteria from ethology and social psychology. Cross-cultural studies confirm that different kinds of facial displays by leaders are accurately decoded even when viewers have strong prior attitudes that bias judgments to some degree (Masters et al. 1986; Masters and Sullivan 1986; Sullivan and Masters 1988; Masters and Mouchon 1986). Although these facial displays elicit distinct emotions, the viewers' emotional responses and judgments depend on their prior attitudes as well as on what they have just seen.

Findings in many disciplines thus demonstrate that facial displays derived from hominid evolution play an important role in social interaction. Although based in human biology, this system of communication is not rigidly invariant or narrowly determined by genetic factors. The social environment also plays a decisive role in causing the behavior we observe. For example, damage to the sites in the brain that process facial cues (notably lesions of the temporal poles or amygdaloid nuclei) produce different symptoms in caged and in free-ranging monkeys (Kling 1986).

Although facial displays clearly have universal aspects (Ekman and Oster 1979; Eibl-Eibesfeldt 1979), members of different societies exhibit somewhat different expressive behavior, especially in public settings (Birdwhistell 1970). These cultural expectations can change responses to similar facial displays (Masters and Sullivan 1986). Even within a single society, the prior attitude of the viewer, the individual performance style of the actor, and the context can all have independent effects on the emotional reactions and judgments elicited by a given type of display. Since individual learning and cognition as well as social tradition are integrated with innate patterns of emotional response and nonverbal display, this system of communication is particularly suitable as the focus for studying the interaction of nature and nurture in human social behavior.

The Human Repertoire of Facial Displays

Facial displays, like other nonverbal cues, blend different muscular movements into graded signals on a number of dimensions (Sebeok 1968; Altmann 1967; Kendon 1981). Technically called "analogical signals" (see chap. 3), nonverbal displays both vary continuously in their intensity and blend different elements or components: "All displays including facial expressions are usually the resultant of more than one behavioral impulse in conflict. Attack and retreat, affinity and sexuality, care-giving and exploration all interact to produce the graded facial, vocal, and postural signals that determine appropriate social interactions" (Plutchik 1980, 284–85). In addition, variability in response to facial display behavior can be due to other nonverbal or verbal cues, to the social context or setting, and to the prior experience or status of the interacting individuals. As a consequence, it has been hard to define gestures that have predictable emotional effects; "seemingly identical body movements supply the activity for quite different cue classes" (Birdwhistell 1970, 166). While this phenomenon is found in animal communication generally (Gray 1963; Smith 1969), it is particularly relevant to the study of human facial displays.

Ethologists approach this problem by analyzing the way highly stereotyped, or ritualized, displays form a system of communicative signals. Developing one of Darwin's insights, for example, Leyhausen has shown that displays of anger and fear in cats can be arrayed in terms of a two-dimensional chart (figure 2.3): as the intensity of each emotion or motivation increases, the displays become more marked—with every conceivable blend of the two emotions producing a recognizable pattern (Lorenz and Leyhausen 1973).

Social psychologists studying human emotional behavior have found much the same kind of system. While some researchers stress stereotyped patterns that are unambiguous cues of emotion (Ekman 1979), others suggest that these displays are arrayed in dimensions or

Figure 2.3
Cats' Displays of Readiness for Defense or Attack

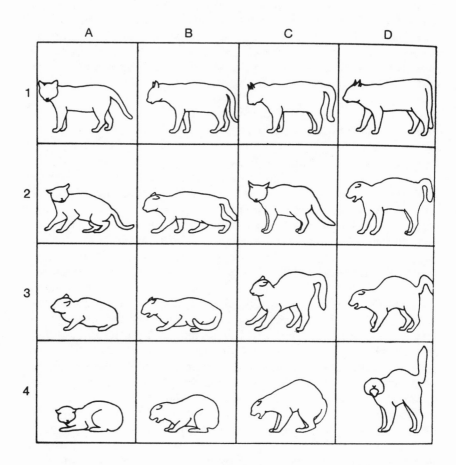

"Expression of readiness for defense or attack in the cat. 1 A–D horizontal: from 'neutral' to maximally aggressive; A1–4 vertical: from 'neutral' to maximally defensive. The other squares show corresponding superimpositions. No posture has been interpolated, all are drawn from photographs or film. Under suitable conditions every stage may be experimentally elicited in the same animal." Reprinted by permission from Lorenz and Leyhausen 1973, 302; and Paul Leyhausen, Katzen—eine Verhaltenskunde *(Berlin and Hamburg: Paul Parey Scientific Publishers, 1982).*

"clusters" (Osgood 1966). The convergence between primate ethology and social psychology helps to explain how individual or cultural variability arises on the basis of an underlying human behavioral repertoire resembling that of the nonhuman primates (Chevalier-Skolnikoff 1973; Plutchik 1980; Masters 1976a; Ekman, Friesen, and Ellsworth 1972).

As a first step in identifying our repertoire of social behavior, the classifications of human emotion and primate nonverbal display by four eminent scholars—Osgood, Plutchik, van Hooff, and Fridja—are compared in terms of emotional words that human subjects distinguish reliably (table 2.1).[4] Although differences in classification are evident (Plutchik and Fridja each speak of eight distinct dimensions or categories, whereas Osgood presents a four-dimensional model of human emotions and van Hooff describes five basic "systems" or clusters of primate displays), there is considerable overlap in the classification and description of primate behavior and human emotion.

At least three functional categories of social displays and emotions—anger, threat, or aggression; fear, evasiveness, or flight; and happiness, affiliation, or social reassurance—are distinguished in all of these classifications (see also Morris 1956; Hirschman 1974; Masters 1976b). While other kinds of emotion and behavior, such as sadness or generalized arousal, are often highly important, these three categories of nonverbal behavior obviously play a central role in the social behavior of humans as well as of nonhuman primates.

Because a facial display can be a social cue even when not expressing an emotion, terms are needed to describe the ensemble of expressed emotions, social signals, and observer's responses that may be implicated in various ways by nonverbal behavior. While many psychologists speak of the broad difference between positive and negative emotions (for example, Ekman 1979), Chance (1976) has used the term "hedonic" (pleasurable) and contrasted this dimension with "agonic" (competitive) behaviors associated with either threat or fear.

The facial displays corresponding to these dimensions can be described in terms of the precise muscular movements they involve. Displays called "happiness/reassurance," "anger/threat," and "fear/ evasion" are clearly distinguished in van Hooff's classification of the gestures of nonhuman primates (1969) as well as in the analysis of human facial expressions of emotion by Ekman and his colleagues (Ekman, Friesen, and Ellsworth 1972; Ekman and Oster 1979; Ekman 1979). The cues involved in these three types of behavior can be objectively defined (table 2.2) and are readily evident even from still photographs.

Table 2.1
Dimensions of Nonverbal Behavior in Social Psychology and Ethology

Trait Attribution[1]	Osgood (1966) Cluster[2]	van Hooff (1973) System[2]	van Hooff (1973) Cluster[2]	Fridja (1973) Cluster[2]	Plutchik (1980) Subjective[2]	Plutchik (1980) Behavior[2]	Plutchik (1980) Function[2]	Plutchik (1980) Trait[2]
Strong Determined Self-Confident	Determination	Show (VI)[3]			Controlled (f)		Activation	
Angry Threatening Aggressive	Anger-rage (Cluster F)	Aggressive (III)	Aggressive & Bluff	Distant (b)[3]	Anger	Attacking	Destruction	Aggressive
Comforting Helpful Reassuring	Pity-sorrow (B)	Comfort	Affinity	Positive (c)[3]	Acceptance	Affiliating	Incorporation	Trustful
Evasive Insincere Untruthful	Suspicion-distrust (L)	Avoidance (IV)[3]		Distant (b)[3]				
Joyful Happy Amused	Quiet-pleasure (H)	Play	Play	Positive (c)[3]	Joy	Cooperating	Reproduction	Gregarious
Interested Eager Curious	Expectancy (J)			Control (f)[3]	Expectancy	Exploring	Exploration	Controlled
Confused Puzzled Bewildered	Surprise (C)	Excitement	Excitement	Surprise (e)	Surprise	Stopping	Orientation	Dyscontrolled
Fearful Anxious Worried	Anxiety-fear (A & E)	Submissive (IV)[3]	Submissive	Negative (a & d)	Fear	Escaping	Protection	Timid
Disgusted Disdainful Scornful	Disgust (G)			Rejection (g)	Disgust	Repulsing	Rejection	Distrustful
Sad Downcast Gloomy	Despair (D)			Negative (a)[3]	Sadness	Cry for help	Reintegration	Depression

[1]Triads of related descriptive terms used in experimental studies of description and emotional response to expressive displays (Lanzetta et al. 1985; Masters et al. 1986).

[2]Categories used in author's classification (category label is in parentheses after name for trait in author's system). Plutchik (1980) categorizes "subjective" state or emotion felt by individual, "behavior" or visible display, "function" or social consequence, and "trait" or attribute of individual displaying behavior.

[3]Part of category only.

Table 2.2
Criteria for Classifying Facial Displays

	Anger/threat	Fear/evasion	Happiness/ reassurance
Eyelids:	opened wide	upper raised/ lower tight- ened	opened wide, or normal, or slightly closed
Eyebrows:	lowered	lowered and furrowed	raised
Eye orientation:	staring	averted	focused, then cut off
Mouth corners:	forward or low- ered	retracted, nor- mal	retracted and/ or raised
Teeth showing:	lower	variable or none	upper or both
Head motion:			
Lateral	none	side-to-side	side-to-side
Vertical	none	up-down	up-down
Head Orienta- tion:			
To body	forward from trunk	turned from ver- tical	normal to trunk
angle to verti- cal	down	down	up

Source: Masters et al. 1986, table 2.

While there are other important facial expressions (including sad-ness, disgust, boredom, and so on), the three categories in table 2.2 provide a basis for analyzing many typical cues in human nonverbal behavior. Not only are displays of happiness/reassurance, anger/ threat, and fear/evasion widely recognized as having the same mean-ing in different human cultures (Ekman and Oster 1979), but their social significance in face-to-face groups has been observed among both children and adults.

Among children to the age of about two years, agonic displays determine dominance status, whereas after that time the dominant child often shows superiority through hedonic gestures (Strayer and Trudel 1984). In play groups of three to five year-old children, the most aggressive child is normally not the most dominant member of the group; the leader is more likely to be self-assured and to use hedonic displays as a means of reassuring others (Strayer 1981; Barner-Barry 1981). Indeed, it is not unusual for highly aggressive displays to be characteristic of a marginal member of the group, whose behavior seems to reflect frustration and low status rather than dominance (Montagner 1978). Similar patterns have been observed in many human cultures, suggesting that social status is often communicated by these facial displays and other nonverbal behaviors (Eibl-Eibesfeldt 1979; Hinde 1982).

For human adults, the effects of nonverbal behavior seem to depend in part on the way displays of happiness/reassurance, anger/threat, or fear/evasion are expressed, and in part on the appropriateness of the behavior to the setting in which it occurs. As in other species, the establishment and maintenance of dominance depends not only on dyadic interaction, but also on the observation of competitive contests by third parties (Chase 1980b, 1982; McGuire and Raleigh 1986; Raleigh and McGuire 1986); among chimpanzees, for example, the types of social signal just described are carefully observed by all members of the group and provide a reliable indication of changes in status (de Waal 1982; Goodall 1986a). Whatever the cultural differences in the display rules governing human facial gestures, therefore, it is reasonable to expect that this mode of communication plays an important role in social organization and control.

Due to the impact of television, the contemporary citizen can see images of political leaders on a daily basis. The ease with which this viewing situation can be approximated under laboratory conditions makes it possible to explore systematically the emotions and judgments produced by leaders exhibiting different types of facial displays. Because the observer's response to nonverbal behavior influences social status among primates generally, experimental studies using videotapes of known and meaningful leaders are a plausible approach to the ethology of human social interaction. Although such experiments are to some extent artificial, particularly because they differ from face-to-face situations where all participants are physically present, the television viewer is in a situation not entirely unlike the bystander watching two other members of the group.

Since these experiments have been described in detail elsewhere (for a review, see Lanzetta et al. 1985), a brief description of the method should suffice. Short videotape segments of political leaders, recorded during routine television news coverage, were selected according to the criteria summarized in table 2.2 (for still images taken from these displays, see figure 2.4). After pretests confirmed that these segments were perceived as displays of happiness/reassurance, anger/threat, or fear/evasion, they were presented to groups of fifteen to thirty adults or college students with image only, sound only, or sound plus image (and, in one experiment, with filtered sound plus image or with a written transcript only). Studies in the United States have focused on President Reagan (Sullivan et al. 1984; McHugo et al. 1985; Masters et al. 1986), the eight Democratic candidates for the presidency in 1984 (Sullivan and Masters 1988), and actors posing as congressional candidates (Plate 1984). Experiments in France used excerpts of Socialist Prime Minister Laurent Fabius, Gaullist Prime Minister Jacques Chirac, and right-wing Front Nationale leader Jean-Marie Le Pen (Masters and Mouchon 1986; Masters and Sullivan 1986; Masters and Muzet [unpublished]).

After completing a questionnaire on prior political opinions, attitudes toward the media, and socioeconomic background, viewers were shown excerpts and asked to describe each leader's behavior on nine scales (ranging from 0 to 6), each of which was defined by a triad of terms (strong–determined–self-confident, angry-threatening-aggressive, comforting-helpful-reassuring, and so on); self-reports of emotional response were recorded on similar scales. In the French experiments, verbal labels for scales were translated from English to French, verified with local scholars, then translated back from French to English; any terms giving rise to ambiguities were dropped.

Experimental groups of American and French viewers discriminate accurately between leaders' displays of happiness/reassurance, anger/threat, and fear/evasion. When average scores for perceived happiness, anger, and fear are compared, the scale congruent with each kind of display is consistently rated higher than scales corresponding to the other types of display. This is so both for Americans watching President Reagan (figure 2.5a) and for French viewers seeing displays of Reagan or comparable excerpts of three French leaders (figure 2.5b).

Social signals of happiness/reassurance, anger/threat, and fear/evasion are communicated by means other than facial gestures. Even when subjects silently read the text of the messages used in the videotapes, heard the message without the picture, or saw the excerpts with the sound filtered (so that nonverbal cues were not accompanied by a meaningful message), their descriptions were similar (Masters et al. 1986). Though the level of emotional intensity attributed to Reagan after a silent reading of his text was lower than that described in the

Figure 2.4
*Facial Displays of Happiness / Reassurance, Anger / Threat,
and Fear / Evasion*

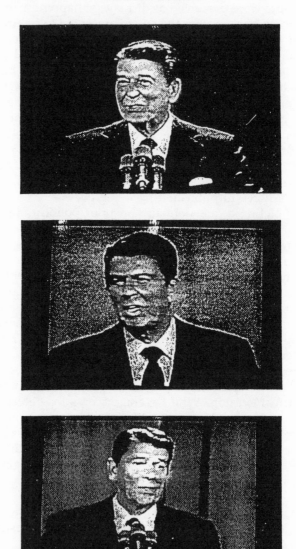

*Photographs of televised images of leaders' displays used in experimental studies,
from Masters et al. 1985, figure 1.*

other experimental conditions, these similarities confirm the stability of responses to nonverbal behavior found by ethologists and social psychologists. At least in the case of a homogeneous excerpt, the emotional characteristics attributed to the verbal message seem to parallel those elicited by the facial display.[5]

These results do not depend on recognition of the leader's face. In another experiment, one group of viewers was shown videotapes of all eight Democratic candidates for the 1984 presidential nomination, as well as of President Reagan, in January 1984—before the first caucuses or primaries, at a time when some of the politicians involved were unknown to most of the subjects and the majority of Americans; a second group of viewers saw exactly the same videotapes in October 1984, three weeks prior to the election (when most of the candidates were well known to almost everyone). Discrimination between kinds of displays was not influenced by prior attitude or recognition of the candidates. To be sure, each of the nine candidates was perceived somewhat differently, and between January and October, more happiness and strength was attributed to the displays of two leaders whose status had improved, Reagan and Jackson. But whether it was seen with sound plus image or with the image alone, in no case was there any confusion between a display defined objectively as neutral and one characterized as happy/reassuring (Masters et al. 1985; Sullivan and Masters 1988).

Because nonverbal cues vary on a multiplicity of dimensions, single verbal scales may not capture the entire response to an emotional display (Plutchik 1980). When responses on all nine descriptive scales were factor analyzed, however, the same underlying factors are implicated in verbal descriptions of President Reagan by American viewers and of Prime Ministers Fabius and Chirac by the French (Masters and Sullivan 1986). These factors appear to be relatively consistent for excerpts seen without sound, heard without the image, and seen with filtered sound that obscures the verbal message, and even for reading the text (Masters et al. 1986).

Each type of display also has characteristic effects on viewers' emotions, which can be measured experimentally by monitoring physiological reactions (either in the autonomic nervous system or in the facial muscles associated with emotional displays), as well as by asking for verbal self-reports (Cacioppo and Petty 1979; McHugo et al. 1985). When videotapes are presented with both sound and image, the three expressive displays produce different psychophysiological responses (figure 2.6). All excerpts activate the corrugator muscles to some degree, reflecting the lowering of the eyebrows associated with focusing visual attention, but this reaction is strongest in reactions to displays of anger/threat. In contrast, the zygomatic muscles associated with smil-

Figure 2.5
Average Descriptive Scores on Scales
Congruent with Videotape Excerpts of
Happiness / Reassurance, Anger / Threat, and Fear / Evasion

a. United States

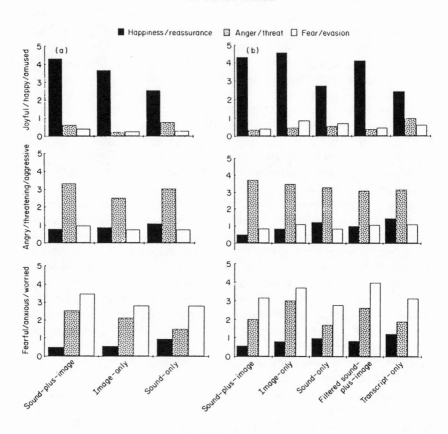

Mean intensity ratings on descriptive scales (0–6) for excerpts of leaders in France and the U.S. (a) Adult ratings of President Reagan in three media conditions, American experiment #1 (N = 65). (b) College student ratings of President Reagan in five media conditions, American experiment #2 (N = 145), from Masters et al. 1986.

b. France

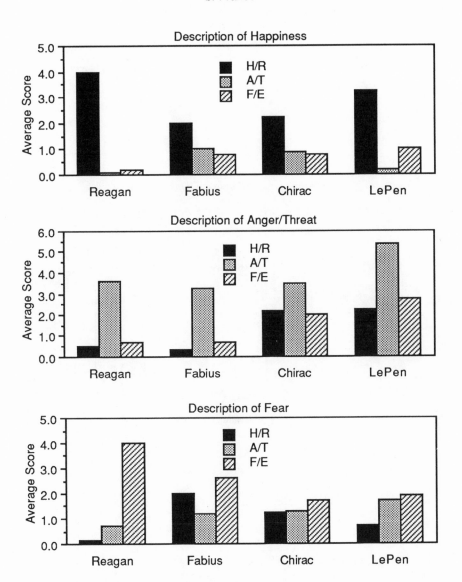

(c) *French students' ratings of President Reagan, in sound-plus-image condition, Université de Paris-I pre-test (N = 16); French students' ratings of Fabius, Chirac, and Le Pen in sound-plus-image, image-only, and sound-only conditions combined, experiment at Université de Paris-X (N = 65), from Masters and Sullivan 1986.*

Figure 2.6
Physiological Responses to Facial Displays of a Leader

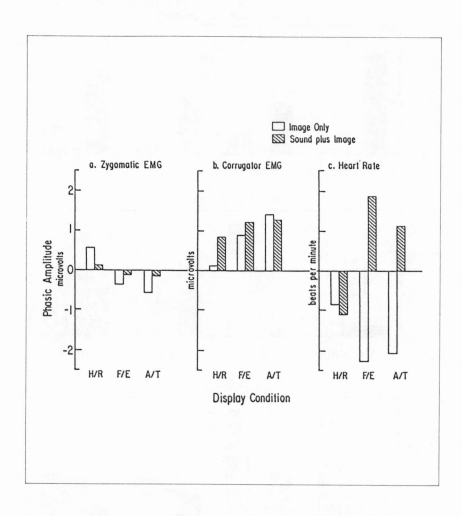

Brow (corrugator) and cheek (zygomatic) muscular reactions and heart rate as changes from pre-exposure baseline when watching displays of President Reagan exhibiting happiness / reassurance, anger / threat, and fear / evasion. American experiment #3, from Lanzetta et al., "Emotional and Cognitive Responses to Televised Images of Political Leaders," in Sidney Kraus and Richard Perloff, eds., Mass Media and Political Thought, *p. 98. Copyright 1985 by Sage Publications. Reprinted by permission of Sage Publications, Inc.*

ing are activated in response to seeing happy/reassuring excerpts, but relaxed when seeing displays of either anger/threat or fear/evasion.

When the same facial displays are seen without the sound, the immediate psychophysiological reactions are similar but greatly amplified (figure 2.6). Although seeing the displays also influences heart rate and skin conductance, the effects on facial muscles associated with emotional response are especially good evidence that the three kinds of facial displays are indeed distinct elements of a behavioral repertoire.

Human emotional responses are, of course, more than mere physiological reactions: the feelings that matter in politics are subjective states that can be verbalized and shared with others. In the experiments discussed above, verbal reports of emotional reactions were also recorded after subjects saw each videotape excerpt. As in other experimental studies of emotion (Vaughan and Lanzetta 1980; Englis, Vaughan, and Lanzetta 1982), the viewer was asked whether he or she felt "afraid, angry, disgusted, uneasy or confused, happy or joyful, hopeful or comforted, sympathetic or inspired," with the responses being registered as scores ranging from 0 to 6. Since these verbal reports are consistent with psychophysiological measures when both are recorded for the same experiment (McHugo et al. 1985), the 0–6 self-reporting scales were used to measure emotional responses to videotapes of leaders in both France and the United States.

Such experiments show that nonverbal displays of political leaders elicit similar emotions in different cultures. Factor analysis of the scale scores for self-reported emotion shows a striking congruence between French and American viewers (figure 2.7). In both countries, the emotions reported during experiments reflect two virtually identical factors, one positive (self-reports of joy, comfort, support, and interest) and the other negative (anger, disgust, fear, and confusion). These two factors, which parallel the hedonic and agonic modes of primate social behavior identified by Chance (1976), have also been found to underlie public opinion surveys of emotional responses to American leaders (Abelson et al. 1982; Lau and Erber 1985; Marcus in press).[6] Humans have inherited a repertoire of social signals and emotions that continue to play an important role in interactions between leaders and followers.

Emotion and Judgment in Politics

The study of nonverbal behavior reminds us that humans are not always as rational as we might want to believe. Facial displays associ-

Figure 2.7
Positive and Negative Emotions after Seeing Leaders

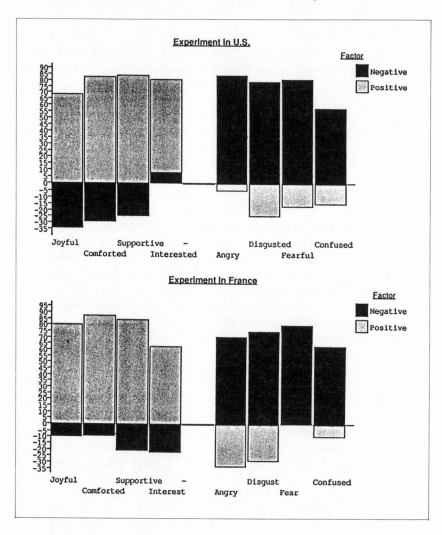

*Each bar represents factor loading on a scale for self-reported emotion; black bar =
"Negative" Emotional Factor; dotted bar = "Positive" Emotional Factor. U.S.
data: Experiment #2 (N = 145)—happy/reassuring, anger/threat, and fear/
evasion displays of President Reagan, all media conditions combined. French data:
Nanterre experiment (N = 65)—happy/reassuring, anger/threat, and fear/evasion
displays of Prime Ministers Fabius and Chirac, all media conditions combined.
From Masters and Sullivan 1986, figure 3.*

ated with the expression of emotion as well as with social dominance seem to convey similar information when exhibited by political leaders or by children (not to mention chimpanzees). One can recognize this fact, however, without implying that there are no differences between adults and either children or chimpanzees: philosophers as diverse as Aristotle (*Rhetoric*) and Rousseau (*First Discourse*) insisted on the vital role played by emotion in human thought and reasoning while distinguishing between humans and other animals. To understand the effects of facial displays in human politics, it is essential to consider the role of verbal or cognitive judgments in responses to nonverbal cues of emotion or status.

While the image of the face communicates important information, humans normally integrate these cues with verbal messages—and this process may either weaken the effect of the nonverbal display or modify its direction. At the psychophysiological level, the activation of facial muscles associated with emotional behavior is stronger and more differentiated when the image is seen alone than when it is seen with sound. In other experiments as well, the combination of a verbal and a visual channel of information can modify the impact of facial displays on the emotions and judgments of the viewer (Sullivan et al. 1984; McHugo et al. 1985; Lanzetta et al. 1985). The effects of watching leaders thus depend to some extent on distinct processes of emotion and judgment elicited by verbal and nonverbal channels of communication.[7]

FACIAL DISPLAYS AND POLITICAL ATTITUDES

Under some circumstances, a leader's nonverbal behavior can have important effects on political attitudes as well as emotional responses. In the study using displays of all the presidential candidates in the 1984 election, viewing short excerpts had significant effects on attitudes toward the leaders. While candidates differed greatly in the evocative effects of their happiness/reassurance displays, the same excerpts of Reagan became more effective in October (when his reelection seemed assured), whereas the displays of Mondale and other rivals had either similar or weaker effects as the election approached (Sullivan and Masters 1988).

Further evidence that a leader's nonverbal displays can influence the political attitudes of some viewers came from experiments using news stories with different images of President Reagan in the background. In these studies, videotapes were excerpted from television news and edited so that some of the stories could be presented to different groups with silent images of either happiness/reassurance, anger/threat, or neutral displays accompanying the news commentary (Sullivan et al. 1984). Because the message and the context were the same for all subjects, it was possible to measure the influence of variations in the facial displays on viewers' emotional and cognitive responses.

Among the results of this experiment, two are particularly relevant here. First, there was a difference between the way males and females integrated their emotional and cognitive responses: whereas male viewers were more accurate in recalling the kind of image in the background of the news stories, these silent displays elicited more distinct emotional reactions for female viewers than for males. Not everyone need react the same way to a nonverbal display. Whether related to differences in the behavioral strategies of chimpanzee males and females (de Waal 1984), to greater cerebral lateralization of human males (Masland 1983), to different patterns of integrating emotion and cognition in response to a moral dilemma (Gilligan 1983), or simply to differences in the attitudes of males and females to President Reagan, gender is a potentially important factor in human social and political life (Tiger 1969; Schubert 1983a, 1985; Plate 1984; Watts 1984).

A second major finding in this experiment was that male viewers with neutral attitudes toward President Reagan were highly influenced by his facial displays, whereas silent images in the background of news stories did not produce a significant change in the attitudes of females. Male and female viewers who either liked or disliked the president did not modify their prior opinions merely because they saw a set of news stories with more images showing happiness/reassurance, anger/threat, or neither in the background. Hence the only significant effects of a display dissociated from the verbal message were on male viewers who were neutral at the outset (Sullivan et al. 1984).

Both the influence of nonverbal behavior and the importance of judgment and political opinion are illustrated by these results. When we lack other information or are indifferent, facial displays are most likely to have an independent effect on our emotional responses and attitudes; otherwise, our judgments and even our emotions are a product of what we think as well as of what we see. In much the same way, viewers with weaker or less developed political opinions are those most likely to be swayed by television instant analysis and news commentary on an event they have just seen (Newton et al. 1988).

FACIAL DISPLAYS AS A CAUSE OF VIEWER RESPONSES

Even if viewers' attitudes change after seeing a leader, it does not follow that the emotions communicated by the face were the cause of these differences. Seeing an image could merely trigger preexisting attitudes. To discover whether attitude changes are correlated with the positive emotion transmitted by a leader's nonverbal displays, one can analyze postexperimental attitudes using multiple regression techniques (which measure the relative effects of different factors on a particular response).[8] In this way, it is possible to compare the impact of viewers' emotional responses and their perceptions of a display with the effects of their prior opinions (whether about the leader, about political parties, or about issues).

This analysis reveals three points worth emphasizing. First, viewers' attitudes are influenced independently by emotional responses to nonverbal displays and by prior attitudes. Second, these emotional responses are influenced by the perceived intensity and homogeneity of the leader's display behavior. Finally, but of great practical importance, different leaders vary in their performance of similar displays, and these differences seem to be associated with their political success or failure.

In the study of American presidential candidates in 1984, viewers' emotional responses had a significant effect in modifying postexperiment attitudes to most of the rivals. For all leaders except Mondale, it was the positive emotional response to a happy/reassuring excerpt, and not the response to a neutral one, that was significantly associated with favorable changes in attitude. By way of contrast, such cognitive attitudes as party identification, agreement with the leader's position on issues, or judgments of the candidate's leadership ability were less likely to have an independent effect on viewers' post-test attitudes. These results were also found for responses to excerpts seen without the sound, indicating that emotions stimulated by the nonverbal display are indeed an independent cause of attitude change (Sullivan and Masters 1988).

The effects of nonverbal behavior thus depend, in part, on the way different individuals perform similar social behaviors. Of particular significance is the effect of nonverbal displays that are perceived as blends of distinct emotions (Izard 1972; Ekman and Friesen 1982). A simple measure of this phenomenon is the ratio of descriptions of hedonic cues (happiness and reassurance) to agonic ones (anger and fear) in image-only presentations of happy/reassuring displays.[9]

For the happy/reassurance displays seen in image-only condition in the 1984 American presidential study, the correlation between the sample's average descriptive blend ratio of a candidate and the positive emotion elicited by that display is .82. The happy/reassuring excerpt of Walter Mondale, which was perceived as more blended (average hedonic/agonic ratio = 2.3) than comparable excerpts of Reagan (ratio = 3.7), Hart (ratio = 4.6), McGovern (ratio = 4.0), or Glenn (ratio = 3.6), elicited significantly lower self-reports of happy emotion than did a similar excerpt of other candidates. This effect is also evident in responses to different displays by a single leader: the correlation between average perceived blend-ratio and average positive emotional responses to happiness/reassurance, anger/threat, and fear/ evasion displays of President Reagan was .85 for supporters and .75 for critics.

Similar results were found in experiments in France in February 1986, one month before legislative elections. Viewers were shown videotapes of then Socialist Prime Minister Laurent Fabius and his main rival, the Gaullist Jacques Chirac. Of the two, Fabius was less effective in eliciting positive emotion and agreement from his supporters than was Chirac, the eventual winner of the March 1986 legislative election (Masters and Muzet). Multiple regression analysis confirms that Fabius' happy/reassurance excerpt was relatively ineffective in activating partisans (Masters and Sullivan 1986).

Experiments therefore show that viewers' emotional responses to a leader can be associated with changes in attitudes after seeing them. In both France and the United States, a leader whose facial displays were perceived as more blended than those of his rivals failed to transmit positive emotion to his potential supporters. As among other primates (van Hooff 1969), human leaders exhibiting cues of fear and insecurity are unlikely to be effective as leaders. While there are indeed cultural differences between the role of anger/threat cues in France and the United States (Masters and Sullivan 1986), emotional responses to nonverbal cues provide a natural foundation for judgments of leaders.

SOCIAL CONTEXTS AND RESPONSE

The social context in which displays are seen modifies viewer responses both within a single society and from one country to another. The psychophysiological responses of viewers with different attitudes toward President Reagan were not significantly different when he was the only stimulus figure, whereas presentation of Reagan and Hart in the same viewing session produced significant effects of prior attitude on psychophysiological arousal (Lanzetta et al. 1985; McHugo and Lanzetta 1986). Seeing rivals also produced interactions between prior attitude and type of display on verbal descriptions of leaders in both France and the United States (Masters et al. 1986; Masters and Sullivan 1986), even though prior attitudes had not influenced such descriptive ratings in experiments using a single stimulus figure. In one French study, excerpts that produced "consensual" responses by viewers of the right and the left when originally shown on television became polarized when presented just before an election (Masters and Muzet [unpublished]). As ethologists have shown (Lorenz [1931–1963] 1970–71), the sight of a conspecific is not a fixed stimulus whose effects are independent of the situation.

The status of the participants can also influence responses to nonverbal displays of human leaders, as it does among other primates. In the study using videotapes of all American presidential candidates in 1984, significantly stronger emotions of happiness were elicited by identical excerpts of Reagan, Hart, and Jackson three weeks before the election than in January; descriptions and emotional responses to excerpts of other candidates were not significantly different in the two samples (Masters et al. 1985). When the same displays of Reagan and Hart were shown in February 1988, viewers—and especially women—had significantly more negative feelings toward Hart (Carlotti 1988). Changes in a leader's status thus modify the evocative power of the same stimuli.

Despite cross-cultural similarities between France and the United States, an interesting difference was noted between the two countries. The relative strength of emotional responses to displays of happiness/reassurance and anger/threat seems to differ in the United States and France. While viewers decode and respond emotionally to these gestures in similar ways, happiness/reassurance is more likely to elicit positive or hedonic ("warm") emotions in the United States, whereas French viewers respond at least as positively, if not more so, to displays of anger/threat.

American viewers report significantly more joy or happiness when seeing a leader like Reagan exhibit displays of happiness/reassurance than in response to an anger/threat display (Lanzetta et al. 1985; McHugo and Lanzetta 1986). In contrast, similar groups of French viewers do not differ significantly in emotional responses to happiness/reassurance and anger/threat excerpts of powerful leaders like Fabius and Chirac; if anything, anger/threat actually elicited more positive emotion from supporters than did happiness/reassurance. While subjects in both countries respond negatively to displays of fear/evasion, therefore, French viewers seem to expect more authoritative or aggressive behavior from those who hold high public office, whereas Americans are less likely to report positive emotions after seeing a leader exhibit anger/threat (Masters and Sullivan 1986).

These results could be viewed as confirming the conventional description of French culture as somewhat more hierarchical or status-conscious than that of the United States. Experimental research thus shows how a phylogenetically derived system of social communication can be "recruited" or "ritualized" in different ways by human societies (Lorenz 1967; Sebeok 1968; Lumsden and Wilson 1981) and reveals the complex interactions between nonverbal cues derived from the primate social repertoire, cognitive attitudes of individuals, and social or political contexts. The question of Plato's Socrates can thus be answered using the experimental methods of modern science: Emotional responses located in distinct structures in the human brain play an independent role in human social and political behavior.

The Human Behavioral Repertoire and the Triune Brain

Despite Rousseau's explicit suggestion that philosophers use experiments to study human nature (Rousseau *Second Discourse*, Preface), such methods have not generally been used to resolve the psychological question posed in Plato's *Republic*. Socrates asks whether three human experiences—to "learn," to "feel anger," and to "desire the pleasures of nourishment and generation and their kin" —are all properties of "the entire soul" or whether they involve distinct "things" or elements of human nature (Plato *Republic* 4.436a). In the ensuing dialogue, Plato presents us with an answer based on observing the behavior of young children (441a) and animals (441b) as well as adults (439e–441a). Contemporary experimental evidence in neurology, ethology, and psychology confirms the Platonic insistence on the heterogeneity of our nature.

Observation of both animals and humans shows that there is a natural difference between the behaviors associated with pleasures and those that occur when we feel anger or other competitive emotions. Facial displays of hedonic or pleasurable emotion are associated with gestures that signal a readiness for non-hostile social interaction and affiliation; agonic or competitive displays, whether of anger and threat or of fear and submission, are different from these hedonic behaviors in different human cultures as well as in nonhuman primate species. These three kinds of display elicit distinct reactions in the human observer both at the physiological and the verbal or conscious levels: viewers who see another person exhibiting gestures of happiness/reassurance, anger/threat, or fear/evasion respond in different ways, although cultural tradition can modify the relative level of response to each type of display.

The third human attribute discussed by Plato's Socrates—our capacity to learn—is distinct from both hedonic and agonic emotions or social signals. Our learning takes the form of verbal information that is distinctively human (whereas the nonverbal displays of the human face are similar to those of other primates), and the opinions that a person has learned can modify the effect of nonverbal cues of happiness/reassurance, anger/threat, or fear/evasion. The experiments described above suggest that the observer responds to the sight of another with a physiological reaction largely determined by that person's status and display behavior. When viewers are asked to describe their emotions verbally, however, their self-reports depend to a greater degree on their political opinions. Conscious or verbal expression of emotion cannot be entirely predicted on the basis of the nonverbal stimuli, even in the case of facial displays that produce reflexive physiological responses.

There is much additional evidence in favor of a natural distinction between the three attributes of human experience discussed by Socrates in the *Republic*. The difference between purely "selfish" behaviors solely related to the individual's self-preservation, and those responses that reflect emotion and social bonding, has been traced to the evolutionary divergence of the mammals from reptiles. Only among mammals is the mother capable of recognizing an infant's distress call as a social signal eliciting nurturant behavior (MacLean 1983). This evolutionary difference gave rise to distinct structures in the brain—most notably the limbic system, in which the emotional experience of mammals and primates is primarily localized.

Research on the structure of the brain indicates that primate brains have a more complex structure than those of other mammals. In describing the central nervous system of primates, and especially of humans, MacLean has therefore spoken of the "triune brain": in addition to the brain stem (which arose with reptiles and is characterized by autonomic responses directly associated with individual survival) and the limbic system (with which mammalian species acquired emotion and social bonding), the radically enlarged cerebral cortex of primates reaches its apogee in humans (MacLean 1983; Sagan 1977). Hence the different kinds of behavior observed in the experiments described above can be traced, at least in part, to distinct structures in the human brain.

MacLean's concept of the triune brain provides empirical support for the tripartite psychology presented in Book 4 of Plato's *Republic* (436a–441c). It is not hard to associate the brain stem (which MacLean calls the "R-complex" to symbolize its reptilian origins) with the "part of the soul" or psychological principle that Socrates calls "appetite"—that is, the individual's "pleasures of nourishment and generation and their kin." What the Platonic Socrates calls *thymos*, or "spiritedness"—the psychological principle associated with anger, guilt, and human emotion—seems to be primarily associated with the limbic system and other structures derived from the specifically mammalian brain. And reason or speech (*logos*)—the primary basis of human learning—is located principally in the cerebral cortex, whose expansion during hominid evolution has been so dramatically documented over the last generation of research on prehistoric fossils.

Like Freudian psychology (which obviously reflects a similar psychological structure, albeit with the more poetic terminology of id, superego, and ego), Platonic psychology is thus consistent with differentiations in the structure of the human brain as well as with observed patterns of human behavior. Contemporary scientific research thus contradicts the attempt to derive all human social behavior from an undifferentiated and individualistic pleasure-pain calculus of "the entire soul." Human nature has not been totally emancipated from its evolutionary origins.

Competitiveness among human beings—or, for that matter, among other animals—cannot therefore be used to proclaim that all society is "unnatural" or "artificial" (Portmann 1961). Because facial displays communicate information independently of the emotions they express, this nonverbal system of social signals contradicts the philosophical tradition in which the individual is viewed as an isolated being. Nor can it be argued that human learning reflects a simple process of conditioning, in which social stimuli take on meaning and produce effects solely on the basis of the individual's prior experiences. Although such conditioned learning is of course important in other primates as well as in humans, the different effects of a smile and a threatening frown are as much species-specific traits as any element of human physiology and behavior.

As a description of the mechanisms underlying human social behavior, the *tabula rasa* psychology of Hobbes and Locke—as well as its prolongation in the psychological tradition that treated the human brain as an undifferentiated "black box" whose responses were entirely due to individual learning and experience—must be abandoned. Although human nature is complex, it can be understood by using scientific methodologies. This does not mean, however, that the concept of a pleasure-pain calculus that gave rise to the psychological tradition of Antiphon the Sophist, Hobbes, Locke, and modern behaviorists like Skinner was merely foolish: such theorists transposed onto the nature of the individual processes that function at the level of the evolution of species. Nonetheless, it is no longer adequate to assume that society is entirely the result of human volition or agreement, or that the plasticity of our social behavior is due to an absence of human nature (as was also claimed by existentialists). We have an innate behavioral repertoire that can be used to qualify human beings as social animals.

CHAPTER 3

Society, Language, and Cultural Change

Individual Behavior, Social Structure, and Human History

An age-old theoretical question is answered by evidence that the repertoire of human expressive and social behavior is based in biology: both competition and cooperation are indeed natural for our species. As the only basis of a naturalistic understanding of politics, however, the discovery that nonverbal displays function as a universal system of social communication proves either too much or too little. If facial gestures like those of other primates explain human social behavior, why did some civilizations evolve beyond the scale of the small groups characteristic of most primates? On the other hand, if the variety of human societies can be explained only by invoking speech and cultural tradition, of what relevance are minute variations of facial muscles? An adequate theory of politics must explain the difference between "stateless societies" (organized on the basis of informal face-to-face social relations) and states (with much larger populations as well as formal governments)—and a constant is usually insufficient to explain variation.

In the last chapter I considered how brief expressive acts influence observers, whereas cultural and political systems are ongoing structures of social interaction. Any stable society presupposes a pattern of organizing the human behavioral repertoire; cultures rest on rules that govern, among other things, circumstances in which the expression of happiness, anger, or fear is appropriate or taboo. While human societies also invent new forms of symbolic activity, even these cultural phenomena have meaning only in the context of a coherent system of behavior.

The analysis of social communities as whole units raises a further philosophical (and theological) issue concerning human nature. Why and how do human cultures change from time to time and place to place? For what reasons did human civilization as we know it come into being? The description of social systems cannot be a static matter, for states rise and fall, and customs or laws change. Many political ideologies and religious teachings seek to persuade believers that the existing and accepted way of life is the only conceivable way; while understandable enough, such explanations dissolve under the scientific evidence of human variability and change.

The problem of cultural diversity was at the root of the discovery of nature by the ancient Greek philosophers. Prior to the emergence of that theoretical concept, myth and religious ritual had provided an account of both the origins of the universe and the proper rules governing human behavior. For instance, an epic like the *Enuma elish*, which played a central part in the spring festivals of Mesopotamian civilization, also served as a legitimization of political power, an account of the organization of the heavens, and a religious prescription for obligations to the gods (Pritchard 1958). What we now call science and religion could be fused only as long as comparisons between societies were not legitimate (cf. Plato *Republic* 1.327a); when Greek thinkers following Thales began to explore "natural science," it was in part due to their awareness of the relativity of human cultural practices as contrasted to the constancy of other natural things (Masters 1977).

In the Christian tradition, cultural variation and change have been interpreted predominantly in terms of the biblical account of human origins. For over two thousand years, it has been widely believed that human life should be understood as the product of God's creation and man's original sin. Individual human behavior could therefore be explained by the story of Adam and Eve, and history could be traced to human sin and God's will. Natural science challenges the conventional belief in this account as a literal description, though the Bible can be—and for many, still is—taken as a symbolic and ultimately true interpretation of human existence.

At least among scientists, the account of the special creation of man in *Genesis* is no longer taken literally; Darwin's basic conception of organic evolution can be considered as accepted, albeit with some important modifications (Dobzhansky 1955, chap. 6; Simpson 1967, chap. 16; Mayr 1963, chap. 1). All forms of life can therefore be viewed as the product of a trial-and-error process (Rensch 1966, 62–63; Dobzhansky 1955, 130, 133; Lorenz 1967, 16; Campbell 1965a; Dawkins 1987) or a "stochastic game" that populations of organisms play against the rest of nature (Slobodkin 1964).

Although the human body does not seem to have been exempt from evolutionary processes, it is often argued that human beings are radically different from other forms of life because culture is transmitted by learning rather than genetic inheritance. As one leading botanist has written: "Our minds and our social organization contribute far more to human nature than our bodies. . . . Our minds, our foresight, and our social structure, although they are the products of evolution, are nevertheless completely real and new. They set us apart from animals just as truly as if they had been specially created" (Stebbins 1967, 50–51). According to this view, which is widely shared by social scientists (for example, Geertz 1965), evolutionary principles explain the origins of *Homo sapiens* but are of minimal relevance to the structure and development of human societies and cultures.

This conventional interpretation presumes that only humans create behavioral patterns and technologies that adapt to or control the environment; ultimately, it is assumed that there is a radical distinction between human learning and animal instincts. Such a simplistic dichotomy between nature and nurture has, however, been destroyed by modern biology (Dobzhansky 1962; Bonner 1980). Not only has something akin to cultural variation been observed in species as diverse as bees (Sebeok 1967a), langurs (Jay 1965; Ripley 1967; Sugiyama 1967), and Japanese monkeys (Kawamura 1963; Tsumori 1967), but a genetic component has been suggested in such apparently learned human characteristics as language capability (Lenneberg 1964; Masland 1983), anxiety neurosis and other personality traits (Ferris 1969; Cloninger 1987), and even gender-based role differentiation (Tiger 1969; Watts 1984).

The common belief that man freely controls his own evolution (for example, Halle 1965) is contradicted by increasing evidence of the unintended consequences of cultural practices on the human gene pool (Muller 1960; Garn 1967; Alland 1967)[1] as well as on the environment (Ophuls 1977). More to the point, since organic evolution can fruitfully be understood as a process of problem-solving, sociocultural systems seem subject to mechanisms analogous to those governing biological phenomena (cf. Gerard 1960; Slobodkin 1964; or Lumsden and Wilson 1981, with Gould 1963). As Lorenz boldly put it ([1961] 1966, 260), "historians will have to face the fact that natural selection determined the evolution of cultures in the same manner as it did that of species." While human learning makes possible relatively sophisticated mechanisms of adaptation, is cultural evolution subject to principles like those governing survival and change in other species?

Some evolutionary biologists and social scientists have begun to reconsider the striking analogies between organic and sociocultural evolution (Steward 1955; Tax 1960; Sahlins and Service 1960; Campbell 1960, 1965a; Alland 1967; Fox 1967; Tiger 1969; Wilson 1975; Dawkins 1976; Chagnon and Irons 1979; Cavalli-Sforza and Feldman 1981; Gruter and Bohannan 1983; Lopreato 1984). These analogies cannot be dismissed as mere metaphors or equated with the scientism of nineteenth-century Social Darwinism, for modern evolutionary theory explains how common biological needs can be met by parallel but different bodily features or behavior patterns (Simpson 1967; Rensch 1966). For the biologist, such "analogies" or parallelisms must be distinguished from "homologies," which reflect the presence of a single mechanism in phylogenetically related species (von Cranach 1976).

For example, binocular vision is homologous in most primates, whereas the different kinds of eyes or wings of insects, birds, and bats are analogous or parallel developments in different evolutionary lines (Dobzhansky 1955, 228–34). There is nothing metaphorical or scientistic about these analogies between species; they simply reflect the nondirected or opportunistic process by which natural selection can satisfy a given function, like sight or flying, in different albeit parallel ways. And without identifying the function that is satisfied by a given organic structure or form of behavior, biologists have found it impossible to analyze the mechanisms underlying evolution (Pittendrigh 1958).

From the evolutionary perspective, the cultural variability of *Homo sapiens* is a means of adapting to environmental change and exploiting new ways of life or "ecological niches" (Dobzhansky 1962, 20); "culture is a biological adaptation with a nongenetic mode of inheritance depending on symbolic content rather than on fusion of the gametes" (Spuhler 1959, 12). The transmission of cultural behavior through human learning is thus an evolutionary mechanism that is parallel or analogous—in the precise biological sense of these terms—to the transmission of adaptive traits by inheritance (Cavalli-Sforza and Feldman 1981).

Just as learning is a means by which an organism gains information about its environment, so genetic endowment can be understood as a means of conveying information to succeeding members of a species (Lorenz 1967, chap. 3; Marais 1969, chap. 3). As Gerard points out, "the problem of fixing experience is universal; the mechanisms involved are highly particular" (1960, 225). Since the evolution of parallel but distinct solutions to common problems or biological functions follows the pattern of a nondirected trial-and-error process in all other organisms, it is hard to see why human cultures should be unique in this respect.

Everything we know of the origin of human cultures indicates that they were an unplanned response to the problem of survival and adaptation (Washburn and Avis 1958; Washburn and Howell 1960). "Culture is the means whereby man adapts himself to his natural and social environments and to his pre-existent cultural milieu. The history of this adaptation is the story of cultural evolution. Like biological evolution, the processes of the evolution of culture are selective ones" (Willey 1960, 111). Although early proponents of an evolutionary anthropology erroneously described a unilineal historical sequence, composed of stages that were everywhere identical, such patterns are relatively rare in organic evolution; far more common, and more revealing, are the mechanisms and processes of adaptation that lead to analogies in the evolution of different lines of descent (Simpson 1967).

Old World monkeys (*Cercopithecidae*) and New World monkeys (*Ceboideae*) are now known to have evolved separately from different prosimians, yet both lines independently developed a parallel range of species, including some that move by brachiation and some with longer or prehensile versus shorter tails, to exploit similar environmental conditions (Washburn and Hamburg 1965). The same phenomenon of independent but parallel adaptations to similar ecological conditions has been described among human cultures as "multilinear evolution" (Steward 1955; Braidwood 1960; Willey 1960).

If human social systems are natural adaptations somehow akin to the varied social structures found among primates, we need a means of describing overall patterns of social interaction. What is the link between the observed nonverbal or verbal behavior of individuals and the society or culture as a whole? Most social scientists have filled this gap with concepts of social structure (class, roles, kinship groups, and so on) or historical events (economic development, social mobility, revolution). Such concepts remain ad hoc constructs without a scientific foundation, however, unless they can be derived from the evolved social capabilities of *Homo sapiens*. To understand human social structures and historical change, the behavioral repertoire humans share with primates needs to be linked to the cultural or political systems of behavior that seemingly take on a life of their own.

Society as a Communicative System

Every social system consists of patterns of individual behavior out of which lasting social structures are formed. Humans, like other animals, engage in many actions in addition to the displays of happiness/ reassurance, anger/threat, and fear/evasion described as components of the human social repertoire in chapter 2. We eat, sleep, and copulate as well as avoid, threaten, or bond with others; emotions of sorrow and excitement cannot be entirely reduced to feelings of happiness, anger, or fear (Plutchik 1980). A social system, whether among humans or other animals, defines the circumstances in which all such consummatory behaviors and displays occur or are inhibited. Consider the social structures associated with mating in varied animal species: a pair-bond (as in gibbons) and a temporary consortship (as in chimpanzees) differ in the probabilities that the appropriate display and copulatory behaviors will occur between a given male and female.

For other animals as well as for humans, social relationships can be considered as rules or expectations governing the time, place, and social partners toward whom different elements of the behavioral repertoire of the species are possible. To place the study of human social systems on a biological foundation, it is first necessary to explain how animals, who cannot enunciate these rules in speech, know when to behave in different ways (Hearne 1987). Ethologists have discovered that primates learn a considerable portion of their behavior, and that even a single species will form different social structures in varied environmental circumstances (DeVore 1965; Morris 1969; Barash 1977; Dunbar 1988). Whether innate or acquired, the cues regulating social interaction permit adaptation and change. If understood correctly, this ethological approach can be used to describe human societies as well as groups of primates.

How can displays like those discussed in chapter 2 function as social signals? Ethologists speak of intention movements when describing animal behaviors akin to human facial expressions. A threat, for example, signals the potentiality of a physical attack if the target animal does not flee or exhibit behaviors that cut off the interaction (Lorenz [1961] 1966; Hass 1970). In the absence of inhibition or other interruption, gestures of the anger/threat category seem to initiate a sequence that leads to the consummatory behaviors of violent aggression. In a similar way, it seems only too evident that displays of fear and evasiveness are intention movements related to flight and avoidance, whereas displays of happiness or reassurance ought to signal pleasurable social interaction. It would be a serious mistake, however, to assume that the inner state ("mood"), the visible gesture or display, and the functional consequence form a unitary system.

In fact, the functional or social consequence of an animal display is often quite different from the intention movement from which it originated. Not all threat displays have the result of communicating aggressive intent or hostility. One of Konrad Lorenz's most important findings was that a threat display could become a stimulus facilitating social bonding and thus reassuring the observer (Lorenz [1961] 1966;

[1931–63] 1970–71; Lorenz and Leyhausen 1973); experiments with humans have found precisely the same thing (Sullivan et al. 1984; Lanzetta et al. 1985). Similarly, fear/evasion displays can evolve into cues that signify a submissive relationship to a more dominant member of the group. In the evolution of mammalian social behavior, intention movements originally associated with flight or avoidance have thus been ritualized into social signals permitting ongoing interaction between dominant and subordinate members of a group.

By ritualization, Lorenz and other ethologists mean that stereotyped motor coordinations of one animal have become a "key stimulus" or social signal for others, reliably triggering a particular response. When this happens, observation of the ritualized display is said to be a "releasing mechanism." In nontechnical terms, a display comes to have predictable meaning for other animals of a species. This process occurs in animal social behavior because natural selection can operate on a behavior or display as well as on any other bodily trait.

Among humans, for example, the sight of an infant's smile functions as a "key releaser," stimulating the observer to a particular physiological or emotional response. From an evolutionary perspective, this was probably adaptive insofar as it increased the parental care received by helpless infants (Babchuk, Hames, and Thomason 1985). Whether an infant actually smiles because of an inner feeling of happiness or distress from intestinal gas (Hass 1970) would be irrelevant to the selection of the smile as ritualized cue, as long as the resulting provision of care tends to increase the reproductive success of human adults. In this instance, the provision of care and parent-child bonding are functional consequences of the smile as a social signal (whatever the neurological, somatic, or developmental factors that produce smiling behavior in infants).

Lorenz's finding that threat displays could strengthen the bonds between animals describes a social outcome that evolved in some species but not in others. Among most reptiles, threat displays have not developed this ritualized status as social cues. It is therefore dangerous to extrapolate findings concerning the social behavior of any one species to other animals (for example, Ardrey 1963), as if ethology described constant relationships between specific kinds of display behavior and functional consequences. Although functional categories derived from cross-species comparisons can be used to describe human behavior, the exact consequences of each type of social interaction must be studied with care (von Cranach 1976; von Cranach et al. 1979).

There should be no confusion about the status of flight or avoidance, attack or threat, and bonding between individuals, the basic categories discussed in chapter 2. "Aggressive behavior" is a verbal label used by the human observer to describe a constellation of actions that are physiologically and socially divergent in any one species (Moyer 1969) as well as in different species. Early in his career, Lorenz discovered that, among many kinds of birds, a "conspecific" was not a single thing; from a bird's perspective, the releasers functioning as a cue to indicate the presence of another bird of the same species are quite diverse, depending on the social context in which two individuals find themselves (Lorenz [1931–63] 1970–71). In the social life of any animal, such signals or releasers do not occur in isolation from each other, but rather form a communicative system.

The cues of flight, agonistic challenge, and bonding form distinctive configurations in different kinds of animals, or even in groups of the same species. A social structure depends on which individuals flee, attack, or bond to each other; such patterns can be described, at least in principle, as rules stating, for example, that primate mothers do not normally attack their own infants; maturing juveniles of one or both sexes normally migrate away from their natal group; males are attracted to estrous females (DeVore 1965; Lancaster 1986). To see the utility of this way of approaching social structure, it will be useful to describe some of the varied patterns found in nonhuman social systems.

In chapter 1, the behavior of woodchucks and Olympic marmots was contrasted. It would be inaccurate to describe one of these species as aggressive and the other as cooperative. Rather, we can now say that woodchucks tend to avoid each other (except for mating), with dispersion being maintained by aggressive displays; in contrast, small groups of Olympic marmots bond and frequently direct greeting behaviors to each other, while exhibiting aggressive threats toward other conspecifics. Once such social structures are described as patterns of avoidance, aggression, and bonding, it is possible to explain differences within and between species as adaptations to the environment (Barash 1974, 1977).

This way of conceptualizing social structures is at the opposite extreme from the so-called genetic reductionism criticized by those hostile to biological approaches to human behavior (Lewontin, Rose, and Kamin 1984). While flight or submission, threat or attack, and reassurance or bonding are indeed found in other species, they are functional categories of analysis defined primarily in terms of observed communicative signals. Some birds signal the intention to mate with a courtship ritual; humans often communicate this intention with words or culturally prescribed actions. In either case, the same question can be posed:

do the informational cues—whether learned, innate, or some combination of the two—give rise to lasting bonds between the mating pair? Although the pair-bond is not a physical thing like a wing or a leg, the difference between such a relationship and a passing consortship or sexual encounter is as real as any other biological phenomenon.

The utility of describing social systems in terms of the signals that regulate individual and group behavior is not limited to the ritualized displays of animals (Hearne 1987). Since nonverbal displays are cues, or signs, providing information about the likely responses of others, categories used to analyze them can also describe human verbal or cultural symbols that perform the same function. In animal behavior, flight or submission, anger or threat, and reassurance or bonding are organized into patterns that produce social structures like the mother-infant bond, the male-female mating pair, or the dominance structure of adult males—the social relationships that constitute what the ethologist or social scientist would call a society (Fox 1975). Presumably the same approach should help us to understand how social relationships arise from human verbal or cultural symbols that communicate one individual's intention to avoid conflict, to attack, or to bond to another.

A society, whether of humans or of other animals, can therefore be understood as a system of communicative behavior (Whorf 1956; Hall 1969; Birdwhistell 1970; Bonner 1980; Mehler 1986). There is nothing radically new about this approach. Both linguistics and molecular biology have taught the necessity of approaching complex, evolving systems from the perspective of information on the assumption that observed phenomena result from the operation of a basic program. In both linguistics and molecular biology, these programs presuppose a "grammar," or set of rules, for combining the constituent elements. Much the same could be said concerning Lévi-Strauss's structural analysis of myth and social structure, which has had such a wide effect in cultural anthropology (for example, Lévi-Strauss 1958; [1944] 1967; [1955] 1974).

The study of society as a system of communication can explain how varied customs and practices arise from the natural repertoire of human social behavior. Unlike some structural-functional models in sociology, such a structural account of a society need not be static. Because informational cues about how others are likely to respond will be more or less accurate and useful in different environments, social signals can be subject to the pressures of natural selection, cultural preference, or human choice. When this happens, social structures can change and adapt to new needs and circumstances. In short, by viewing a society in terms of the behavioral cues that give members information about each other, evolutionary analysis can be extended to human cultures as well as to the social behavior of other species.

Language, Culture, and Evolution

THE FUNCTION OF LANGUAGE

Once social structures are viewed as a pattern of communication, it is possible to tranform the parallels between human history and organic evolution from a metaphor to a scientific hypothesis. Because social animals need information about each other's likely responses, the behavioral cues that serve as social signals fulfill an adaptive function. According to neo-Darwinian theory, traits that have a significant influence on an individual's reproductive success are usually subject to natural selection, and reliable information about the behavior of others is as important to humans as to any other animal. To study whether the process of change in human societies is in some sense analogous to the evolution of species, it is necessary to specify how socially relevant information is communicated, not only from one individual to another, but from one time and place to another.

Whatever the importance of nonverbal gestures and facial displays, there can be no question that speech is the primary mode of transmitting human culture. One needs only to visit a country where neither the spoken language nor the writing is understood, as is the case for the average American traveling in mainland China today, to appreciate the limits of nonverbal communication. Even considering every possible use of hand and body gestures as well as facial displays, such cues convey only a small proportion of the information needed to predict the behavior of others and carry out one's own intentions.

Human speech and language can also communicate over broader ranges of time and space than the face-to-face interactions in which nonverbal gestures are effective. Among animals, behavioral displays or ritualizations are often transmitted from generation to generation as innate behaviors or as imitative gestures, whereas human cultures involve complex recipes and rules, not to mention laws, that often require some form of verbal explanation. As a result, human rules can be communicated to people who are not physically present in the same place, making possible the extension of social customs and laws to much larger populations than other mammalian social groups. To consider whether human social changes can be compared to evolutionary processes, therefore, our focus has to shift to the specifically human system of communication by means of spoken and written language.

THE ANALOGY BETWEEN GENES AND LANGUAGE

Like all living things, human sociocultural systems must provide for both repetition of responses that permit relatively stable functioning, and development of new capacities to respond adaptively or evolve (Campbell 1965a).

> At each stage and at each level, the system or subsystem presents to the environment a structure which has at least some aspects of a template, and so can lead to the production of more of itself; and at least some aspects of a program or set of operational rules, so that the kinds of responses it will make to certain situations are roughly indicated . . . Repetition or cyclic production of the same entities is, of course, necessary to biological existence, but it is not sufficient for biological change. Gene duplication without gene mutants (which then continue the duplication mode) would allow no evolution at the molecular level and only limited reassortment above this. Cell division without (irreversible) differentiation would blot out ontogeny and, by obstructing phenotypic expression, also sharply constrict evolution. Stereotyped behavior and fixed views do not favor cultural development; the new idea, a sort of social mutant . . . is needed. (Gerard 1960, 257–58, 260)

From this perspective, sociocultural systems provide a mechanism for transmitting learned responses from one generation to another with sufficient repetition so that relevant experience is not lost, and with sufficient flexibility so that relevant innovations can be adopted.

This does not mean, of course, that sociocultural systems are always perfectly adapted, either in terms of their internal functioning or their relationship with the broader environment (Beals and Siegel 1966). But the same could readily be said of biological species, which do not always function perfectly or evolve in the direction of better adaptation; like species, human cultures can pass through phases of gradual or rapid change, adaptive radiation, decline, or ultimate extinction. Successful adaptation presumes a balance between repetition and innovation, and this balance will necessarily depend upon the precise relationship between the environment and a living population, be it an animal species or a human culture.

Stated at this level of generality, an analogy between biological and cultural processes may seem relatively unobjectionable but also trite; to go further, it is necessary to specify the medium through which repetition and innovation are transmitted from generation to generation in human societies. That human beings are distinguished from other known species by the use of verbal language has been emphasized by theorists since the Greeks (Aristotle *Politics* 1.2.1253a); unlike animal communication, human language permits the formation of symbols that can be repeated, modified, and even created without reference to immediate sensory stimulation (Sebeok 1965, 1967a, 1968; Critchley 1960; Gray 1963; Bastian 1965; Altmann 1967). One is thus led to wonder whether there may be analogies between verbal symbols—as well as the cultural symbols derived from them—and the mechanisms of repetition and innovation in organic evolution.

Several writers have suggested such parallels (Spuhler 1959). "If genes and mutation were the great inventions for speeding change at the molecular level, and gamete formation and fusion at the cellular level, so were the nervous system and the engram at the individual level, and language and other information flow—and the cerebral mechanisms that mediate this—at the social level" (Gerard 1960, 264). Dawkins (1976) introduced the concept of the "meme" as a cultural equivalent of the gene; more recently, Lumsden and Wilson (1981) spoke of "culturgens" as biological units of analysis. Whatever the intuitive appeal of such comparisons, it is necessary to describe objectively what is meant by a symbol, meme, or culturgen and to show that the presumed similarities rest on objectively defined parallels in structure and function.

Although evolutionary biologists can legitimately speak of different species as having an analogous trait, such a comparison presupposes a precise definition of the functions being served and the traits that serve them (Masters [1973a] 1976). For example, the comparisons between expressive displays in humans and primates reveal some analogies, but only because we can define functional categories of nonverbal behavior and describe objectively the facial gestures that serve these functions.

Analogies between genes and the verbal symbols of a human language are promising because, at the outset, we have no difficulty understanding that both systems function as sources of information in transmitting recipes or rules of behavior that control social organization. As one leading student of insect societies noted:

> Most social behavior of insects is genetically determined, while most social behavior of man is culturally determined through symbolic communication. . . . Although this great difference in the basic mechanisms of social evolution lies at the root of the uniqueness of man as contrasted to the social insects, symbols have many functional attributes of genes. Variation, isolation, and selection are operative factors in the evolution of both genetic and symbolic systems. (Emerson 1958, 331)

Some of these parallels between genetic material and human speech are striking (Gerard, Kluckhohn, and Rapoport 1956; Sebeok 1967a; Jacob et al. 1968; Jakobson 1970). But in order to show that the analogy is neither forced nor fanciful, the structural features and functional attributes shared by genes and verbal languages must be described in detail.

One characteristic of human languages that sets them apart from most if not all animal languages has been called "duality of patterning" (Hockett 1958, 1959): human speech is composed of meaningless units (phonemes) that are combined into symbols that convey meaning (morphemes). The genetic code (figure 3.1), based on a "genetic alphabet" of four nucleotides, has this same duality of patterning (Beadle 1963; Beadle and Beadle 1966; Ayala 1978; Stebbins and Ayala 1985). Moreover, like words in a human language, genes are transmitted not in isolation but in sequences whose structure (chromosomes) could be compared to the structure of utterances or sentences. Since the meaning of a word, like the phenotypical expression of a gene, depends in part on the context in which it appears, Hockett should have spoken of threefold patterning.

The linguist Roman Jakobson, who originally insisted that "linguistics belongs to the social sciences and not to natural history" (cited by Sebeok 1967a, 83), came to emphasize the importance of this structural similarity between human languages and genetic material:

All the detailed and specified genetic information is contained in molecular coded messages, namely in their linear sequences of "code words" or "codons." Each word comprises three coding subunits termed "nucleotide bases" or "letters" of the code "alphabet." This alphabet consists of four differing letters "used to spell out the genetic message." The "dictionary" of the genetic code encompasses 64 distinct words which, in regard to their components are defined as "triplets," for each of them forms a sequence of three letters. Sixty-one of these triplets carry an individual meaning, while three are apparently used merely to signal the end of a genetic message . . . The subunits of the genetic code are to be compared directly with phonemes. We may state that among all the information-carrying systems, the genetic code and the verbal code are the only ones based upon the use of discrete components which, by themselves, are devoid of inherent meaning but serve to constitute the minimal senseful units,

Figure 3.1
The Genetic Code

FIRST RNA NUCLEOTIDE BASE	SECOND RNA NUCLEOTIDE BASE				THIRD RNA NUCLEOTIDE BASE
	U	C	A	G	
URACIL (U)	PHENYLALANINE	SERINE	TYROSINE	CYSTEINE	U
	PHENYLALANINE	SERINE	TYROSINE	CYSTEINE	C
	LEUCINE	SERINE	STOP	STOP	A
	LEUCINE	SERINE	STOP	TRYPTOPHAN	G
CYTOSINE (C)	LEUCINE	PROLINE	HISTIDINE	ARGININE	U
	LEUCINE	PROLINE	HISTIDINE	ARGININE	C
	LEUCINE	PROLINE	GLUTAMINE	ARGININE	A
	LEUCINE	PROLINE	GLUTAMINE	ARGININE	G
ADENINE (A)	ISOLEUCINE	THREONINE	ASPARAGINE	SERINE	U
	ISOLEUCINE	THREONINE	ASPARAGINE	SERINE	C
	ISOLEUCINE	THREONINE	LYSINE	ARGININE	A
	START / METHIONINE	THREONINE	LYSINE	ARGININE	G
GUANINE (G)	VALINE	ALANINE	ASPARTIC ACID	GLYCINE	U
	VALINE	ALANINE	ASPARTIC ACID	GLYCINE	C
	VALINE	ALANINE	GLUTAMIC ACID	GLYCINE	A
	VALINE	ALANINE	GLUTAMIC ACID	GLYCINE	G

Legend:
NEUTRAL
AROMATIC
BASIC
ACIDIC
SULFUR-CONTAINING

The "Dictionary of the Genetic Code" is tabulated here in the language of messenger RNA. The code is universal: all organisms, from the lowliest bacterium to man, use the same set of RNA codons to specify the same 20 amino acids. In addition, AUG serves as a 'start' codon to signal the beginning of the messenger-RNA transcript, and UAA, UAG and UGA serve as 'stop' codons. The code is highly redundant in that several codons specify the same amino acid. Nevertheless, certain point mutations (single substitutions of one nucleotide-base pair for another in the DNA molecule) may change a codon so that it specifies a different amino acid. Point mutations have been grouped together. . . Point mutations that result in the substitution of one amino acid for another of the same group ("conservative" mutations) usually lead to subtle changes in the structure and function of a protein. In contrast, point mutations that result in the substitution of one amino acid for another of a different group may lead to drastic changes in the protein. Because of the clustering of amino acids of similar type, most point mutations lead to conservative substitutions and hence to minor changes in proteins." From Francisco Ayala, "The Mechanisms of Evolution," Scientific American, copyright © 1978 by Scientific American, Inc. All rights reserved.

i.e. entities endowed with their own, intrinsic meaning in a given code . . .

The similarity in the structure of these informational systems goes, however, much farther. All the interrelations of phonemes are decomposable into several binary oppositions of the further indissociable distinctive features. In an analogous way, two binary oppositions underlie the four "letters" of the nucleic code: thymine (T), cytosine (C), guanine (G), and adenine (A). A size relation (termed "transversion" by Freese and Crick) opposes the two pyrimidines T and C to the larger purines, G and A. On the other hand, the two pyrimidines (T vs. C) and, equally, the two purines (G vs. A), stand to each other in a relation of "reflexive congruence" or "transition" according to Freese's and Crick's nomenclature: namely, they present two contrary orders of the donor and acceptor. Thus T:G = C:A and T:C = G:A. Only the twice opposed bases prove to be compatible in the two complementary strands of the DNA molecule: T with A and C with G. (Jakobson 1970)

Hence one could say that both genes and linguistic symbols have the same structural attributes: discrete, meaningless components (phonemes or nucleotides), structured into "binary opposition" by means of "distinctive features," are combined into meaningful units that form longer, functional "strings" or messages.

These structural parallels need not mean that there are functional or evolutionary analogies between genetic and linguistic systems for coding information. The existence of discrete or "digital" units that function only in combinations, which in turn form longer sequences, could be attributed to generalized principles of hierarchical organization: something akin to triadic patterning is found at the atomic and molecular levels (atomic particles, atoms, and molecules; atoms, molecules, and compounds). Nonetheless, the appearance of such a structure as a means of coding and transmitting information is not inevitable, as can be seen by comparing alphabetic and hieroglyphic or ideographic systems of writing (figure 3.2). Alphabetic writing shares triadic patterning (letters, words, and sentences), whereas hieroglyphic or ideographic writing is typically dyadic (symbol and sequence of symbols).[2]

The functional and evolutionary differences between these two kinds of writing are good evidence of the unique properties of triadic coding systems. Whether hieroglyphic or morphemic writing systems all stemmed from the Sumerians or were also invented independently by the Chinese and the Maya of Yucatan, it is generally argued that

Figure 3.2
Hieroglyphic and Alphabetic Writing

Forms of writing, from the top: Mayan glyphs, Egyptian hieroglyphs, Phoenician alphabet, and Roman. From Masters 1971, 829.

alphabetic or phonemic writing was only invented once, by the Phoenicians (Hockett 1958, chap. 62; Landar 1966, chap. 4; Langacker 1968, 65–66).[3] After its invention, however, the alphabetic system showed an extraordinary capacity of adaptation and diffusion, spreading far more rapidly and widely than any of the known hieroglyphic or pictographic systems. Moreover, it has been claimed that modern technology developed in Graeco-Judaeo-Christian civilization because the metaphysical prerequisites for Western science are most fully present in cultures using an alphabet (Derrida 1967).

Although our system of writing is not the only one possible, an alphabet has advantages as a means of coding the information contained in human speech. Since such writing is phonetic, it permits more or less the same flexibility as speech itself. This differential advantage of alphabetic writing over hieroglyphs or pictograms is that of a triadic informational coding structure as compared to a dyadic one; significantly enough, human speech has the same advantage by comparison with animal gestures and sounds (Sebeok 1962; Bastian 1965). It seems likely that the triadic patterning characteristic of the genetic code, human speech, or alphabetic writing permits more effective communicative functioning and faster evolutionary adaptation than systems with merely two levels of variable coding units.

Biologists have frequently used the analogy between genetic material and alphabetic writing—a system that itself imitates phonetic speech—in order to explain the structure of the genetic code.

An analogy may be useful to visualize how the molecules of DNA can function to transmit heredity. Innumerable words, sentences, and messages can all be represented by different combinations of the 26 letters of the alphabet, as they can also be conveyed by the two "letters" of the Morse Code— a dot and a dash. The genetic alphabet consists of only four letters—the four nucleotide bases. . . . Four letters are nevertheless capable of specifying the differences between countless genes. The number of possible permutations of four letters in a word consisting of n letters is 4n. . . . We now think of genes as sections of the molecular chains of DNA, which contain genetic messages coded in particular sequences of nucleotide bases. As Pontecorvo put it: "The analogy of the genetic material with a written message is a useful commonplace. The important change is that we now think of the message as being in handwritten English rather than in Chinese. The words are no longer units of structure, of function, and of copying, like the ideographic Chinese characters, but only

units of function emerging from characteristic groupings of lin-
early arranged letters." (Dobzhansky 1962, 37, 39)

But does this analogy between alphabetic writing and the genetic
code represent a parallelism in the precise, biological sense, or is it
merely a heuristic metaphor?

THE DIFFERENCE BETWEEN HUMAN SPEECH
AND ANIMAL DISPLAYS

Since Altmann (1967) has criticized Hockett's conception of duality of
patterning, it is necessary to indicate why this criticism is not relevant
to the notion of triadic patterning attributed to both genetic material
and human languages. In technical terms, any informational coding
system can be analyzed in terms of the linguistic properties of "arbitrary" versus "iconic" representation and "digital" versus "analogical" coding. As Altmann defines these concepts, "a message is iconic
to the extent that the properties of the denotata [things signified] can
be mapped onto properties of the corresponding messages"; non-
iconic representation is "arbitrary." Messages are "digital" when they
"are primarily quantitized, all-or-none signals, discrete rather than
continuous," whereas "analogical" information codes contain "communicative, continuous variations" that convey meaning by more-or-
less (Altmann 1967, 339–40).

These technical distinctions help us to understand the difference
between animal communication and human speech. The communicative language of bee dances is, in technical terms, analogical since the
angle of the bee's waggle can vary continuously, and iconic since this
angle represents the angle of the source of honey relative to the sun
(Sebeok 1967a; Sebeok 1968). The gestures and vocalizations of most
vertebrates are usually arbitrary, whether their communicative signals are digital, as in the all-or-none difference between certain complex bird songs, or analogical, as in the continuous range of facial
grimaces and sounds of many primates (Marler 1965; van Hooff 1969)
or the bodily postures of mammals more generally (see figures 2.1 and
2.4). By contrast, human speech rests on a digital code, since the
difference between one phoneme and another is normally an all-or-
none matter (Sebeok 1967b), and apart from onomatopoetic forms,
the relation of phoneme to denotation is usually arbitrary (for exceptions, see Brown 1958, 111–39; Lévi-Strauss 1958, 103–8).

These categories are relevant to human speech because what
Hockett calls duality of patterning (Hockett 1958, 1959) presupposes a
duality of digital coding units. While Altmann is correct in pointing

out that all communicative systems rest on potentially meaningless units, such as muscular contractions, that are combined into communicative signs (Altmann 1967, 347–49), Hockett's conception presupposes that the meaningless units of human speech are digital: for example, a phoneme is intended and perceived as either an *a* or an *o*, not as a sound on an unbroken continuum (1958, chap. 1). Since a continuous variation of sound frequencies is produced by the human vocal apparatus (Bastian 1965), our verbal languages reflect the emergence of a distinct level of meaningless, digital components (phonemes) between the continuously variable physical substrates and the signs themselves.

Although languages use different sets of phonemic contrasts, the capacity to distinguish between phonemes is now known to be innate. At birth, the human infant can discriminate the acoustic properties of the phonemic contrasts used in all known languages. By the eighth month, however, the child begins to lose the capacity to differentiate speech sounds not used in the languages of the social environment. After puberty, the reorganization of the central nervous system makes it extremely difficult to acquire the ability to match pronunciation and hearing of such foreign speech sounds, as is obvious to anyone who has tried to learn to speak a new language as an adult (Galaburda 1986; Mehler 1986). The human brain has evolved an innate capacity for language in which the distinct processes involved in understanding speech, talking, reading, and writing are localized in precise neurological circuits (figure 3.3).

Whereas animals inherit the capacity to decode meaningful cues of sound and gesture, humans have thus a natural capacity to understand and speak any language (Lenneberg 1964). Like genetic material and biological systems generally, the system functions by producing a multitude of variants, some of which are selected as adaptive or useful in specific environments. In this case, the central nervous system of the infant inherits the ability to discriminate any phonemic contrasts, but the neurological pathways corresponding to those speech sounds not encountered in childhood are subjected to negative selection as the brain develops. Similar phenomena seem to exist for elements of intonation and phrasing that form abstract elements of language at the level of utterances (Mehler 1986).

These characteristics of human speech indicate the importance of what has been called triadic patterning. Sentences or sequences of words or morphemes, the third or most complex level of speech, provide analogical communication since we can talk about more or less anything. This level rests on two distinct tiers or levels of information coding, however: phonemes (which are strictly digital) and mor-

Figure 3.3
Localization of Speech Functions in the Left Hemisphere

a. Essential Components of the Speech Mechanism

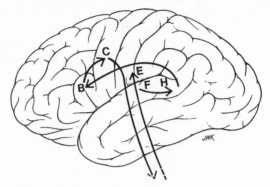

b. Mechanisms Required for Speech Comprehension and Speech
Formulation

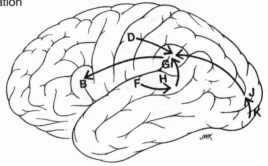

(a) *"Sounds are 'heard' in the auditory receptive area of the left temporal lobe F,
and analysed in the adjacent areas of the temporal lobe H. Motor patterns for the
production of speech are established in Broca's area of the frontal lobe B, which
controls the motor outflow to the speech mechanisms C. Proprioceptive feedback
from the muscles and movements of the speech organs returns to the sensory areas
of the post-central region E. The sounds of the person's speech provide further
feedback. These sensorimotor activities become closely associated in a coordinated
pattern of neural activity." From Masland 1983, 43. (b) "The essential area is in
the region of the supramarginal gyrus G. Within this area are established the
linkages between the neural patterns of the spoken word and the various sensory
experience derived through vision (K–J) and feeling (D). An association between
area G and Broca's area B is required for the initiation of speech." From Masland
1983, 44. Reprinted by permission from Pavlidis and Miles, eds.,* Dyslexia
Research and Its Applications to Education. *Copyright © 1983 by John Wiley.*

c. Mechanisms Required for Written Language

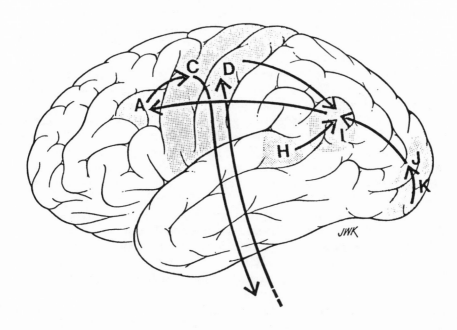

(c) "The visual patterns of the written symbols are perceived in the primary visual area K and analysed in the adjacent visual association area J. In area I, they become associated with the sound of the word or letter analysed in the auditory association area H. Note also that this centre for written language is just posterior to the angular gyrus, which is the area for spoken language (see figure 3.3b). As is also the case with spoken language there is a direct outflow to the frontal lobe A which controls the movements of writing through the motor area C. Again, there is feedback to the sensory area D from the muscles and joints involved in writing. Thus within these closely integrated structures there develop the multisensory motor patterns of neural activity that underlie writing." From Masland 1983, 51. Reprinted by permission from Pavlidis and Miles, eds., Dyslexia Research and Its Applications to Education. *Copyright © 1983 by John Wiley.*

phemes (which are primarily digital insofar as the difference between morphemes or words is all-or-none, but also analogical insofar as human languages permit the addition of inflectional affixes such as plurals, tenses in verbs, intonations, and so on). Technically speaking, plurals, verb endings, and the like are distinct digital morphemes, but since they never stand in isolation, the varying combinations of roots and affixes could be treated as partially analogical (Hockett 1958, 242–44). Since actual human speech is therefore both digital and analogical (Sebeok 1962), these technical features seem less important than triadic patterning as the basis of our languages.

Alphabetic writing preserves the triadic structure of speech, since letters are digital codes, words principally digital but secondarily analogical, and printed pages analogical. In contrast, nonalphabetic writing does not rest on a level of digital representations that by themselves fail to carry meaning. Whereas letters are iconic representations of phonemes, with few exceptions pictograms, hieroglyphs, or ideograms are arbitrary representations of spoken morphemes or words (though, of course, such symbols are often iconic representations of the thing denoted).

Detailed comparisons of different kinds of writing thus suggest that imitation may not be the central feature of communicative systems.[4] The dimension of arbitrary versus iconic representation seems less important for coding capacity than the difference between a system of signs, whether composed in analog or digital fashion, and a system of triadic patterning in which all functional units of coding are themselves combinations and permutations of digital but nonfunctional components. The latter can be either arbitrary (phonemes in speech) or iconic (letters in alphabetic writing). In the genetic code, the nucleotides would seem to be partly arbitrary coding units (insofar as each of the four nucleotide bases is used in the triplet code for different amino acids, apparently without reference to the proteins ultimately produced) and partly iconic coding units (since the cell's production of proteins depends on the fit between DNA and RNA molecules).

The capacity of informational coding systems with triadic patterning to adapt more rapidly than simpler structures arises from the economy of means. The incremental difficulty of adding to the stock of coded items is reduced considerably if an entirely new symbol or combination of existing discrete symbols is not needed. Since the primary, nonfunctional units of a triadic system can be either iconic or arbitrary, human speech is capable of approximating the efficiency of a genetic coding system in which the basic nonfunctional units are partly iconic. The analogy between genes and language is more than a vague metaphor.

TRANSFORMATIONAL GRAMMAR AND GENETIC MECHANISMS

Structural similarities between human language, alphabetic writing, and genetic material, however fascinating in themselves, are of limited theoretical significance unless the analogy leads to deeper insights. Triadic patterning is a purely formal characteristic, and recent advances in both linguistics and genetics have been achieved only by exploring dynamic processes within such complex structures. Hence it is necessary to consider the possibility of functional comparisons between genetic and linguistic systems.

After referring to the biologists' analogy between alphabetic writing and DNA, Jakobson lists further parallels between the structure of human speech and molecular genetics:

> The transition from lexical to syntactical units of different grades [in human languages] is paralleled by the ascent from codons to 'cistrons' and 'operons,' and the latter two ranks of genetic sequences are equated by biologists with ascending syntactic constructions, and the constraints on the distribution of codons within such constructions have been called 'the syntax of the DNA chain.' In the genetic message the 'words' are not separated from each other, whereas specific signals indicate the start and end of the operon and the limits between the cistrons within the operon, and are metaphorically described as 'punctuation marks' or 'commas.' They actually correspond to the delimitative devices used in the phonological division of the utterance into sentences. . . . (Jakobson 1970)

Hence the formal structural analogy between speech and the genetic code points to similarities between syntactical or grammatical rules of language and the functioning of DNA and RNA chains.

In the 1960s, biologists studying the mechanisms by which DNA and RNA regulate cellular functioning found that the strings of nucleotides in the chromosomes act as templates for the production of proteins (figure 3.4). The DNA in the cell nucleus can therefore be viewed as the source of a continuous series of coded messages, transmitted by complementary strings of messenger RNA that pass into the cell protoplasm and operating throughout the life of each organic cell (Beadle and Beadle 1966, chap. 20; Bonner and Mills 1964; Steitz 1988).

> The concept currently accepted is that genes act by determining the amino acid sequence of proteins, or rather, as the hemoglobin evidence shows us, polypeptide chains. . . . The genetic locus is thought of as the unit that specifies the amino acid sequence of

Figure 3.4
The Central Dogma of Molecular Biology

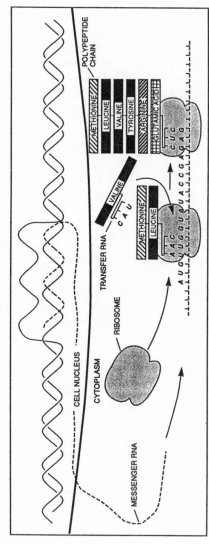

The "central dogma" of molecular genetics states that genetic information flows from DNA to RNA to protein. Genes are relatively short segments of the long DNA molecules in cells. The DNA molecule comprises a linear code made up of four types of nucleotide base: adenine (A), cytosine (C), guanine (G), and thymine (T). The code is expressed in two steps: first the sequence of nucleotide bases in one strand of the DNA double helix is transcribed onto a single complementary strand of messenger RNA (which has the same bases as DNA, except that thymine is replaced by the closely related uracil, or U). The messenger RNA is then translated into protein by means of complementary transfer-RNA molecules, which add amino acids one by one to the growing chain as the ribosome moves along the messenger-RNA strand. Each of the 20 amino acids found in proteins is specified by a 'codon' made up of three sequential RNA bases." From Francisco Ayala, "The Mechanisms of Evolution," Scientific American, copyright © 1978 by Scientific American, Inc. All rights reserved. While more recent research shows added complexity, including processes contrary to the "central dogma" as well as more detailed mechanisms in RNA transcription (Stebbins and Ayala 1985; Steitz 1988), the general picture outlined here seems to reflect the principles of molecular genetics.

one polypeptide. The cistron, or functional unit, . . . can be considered synonymous; i.e., it has the same physical limits as the
locus. Sites (or codons) are the subunits of the locus, each encoding the information for one amino acid. (McKusick 1964, 64)

Since each cell of a complex organism normally contains the same
complement of chromosomes in its nucleus, cell differentiation and
cell growth result from the capacity of a given genetic complex to
produce different messages at different times in different cells.

The functional units of the genetic code must therefore have a syntax and a grammar determining which genetic loci will be placed into
operation in a given cell at a given moment. Whereas each gene was
formerly viewed as an isolated unit, contemporary molecular biology
emphasizes the complexity of each gene locus and the varying regula-
tive functions of different parts of the DNA string (McClintock 1967;
Ayala 1978; Rosenblatt et al. 1988). According to one view, "a sizable
portion of the functional genes in differentiated cell types may be
regulatory genes" rather than "structural" genes that code an individual protein sequence (Britten and Davidson 1969).

Possible analogies between molecular biology and linguistics are
nothing short of astonishing. Within the last generation, the notion of
transformational or phrase-structure grammar has revolutionized linguistics (Bach 1964; Chomsky 1965; Foldor and Katz 1964). According
to this approach, speech can be viewed as the formation of "well-
formed" strings of symbols according to largely unconscious or pre-
conscious grammatical rules. The child's acquisition of language is thus
a process of learning transformational rules and not merely imitating
adult vocabulary or speech patterns (Brown and Bellugi 1964; Ervin
1964; Fraser, Bellugi and Brown 1968; McNeill 1968; Mehler 1986).

To understand the sense in which molecular biology could be described as a transformational grammar like that found in human languages, an example may be useful. A well-studied mutation in *Homo
sapiens* produces the so-called sickle-cell hemoglobin, which in homozygous individuals produces sickle-cell anemia (see note 1, above).
Like all proteins, the hemoglobin in human blood is composed of long
sequences of amino acids. More specifically,

the normal hemoglobin molecule is a tetramer, that is, is made up
of four poly-peptide chains: two identical alpha chains and two
identical beta chains . . . . The defect in sickle hemoglobin is limited to one peptide of the β-polypeptide chain . . . . When the
amino acid sequence of the aberrant peptide was compared with
that of the normal peptide that is replaced, the following was
found.

Hb A [normal]   valine-histidine-leucine-threonine-
                  proline-*glutamic acid*-glutamic acid-lysine

Hb S [sickle-cell] valine-histidine-leucine-threonine-
                    proline-*valine*-glutamic acid-lysine
                                        (McKusick 1964, 63)

A difference of one peptide on the chain thus transforms the normal hemoglobin into a mutant form (figure 3.5); while still a "well-formed string" in the sense that it is a stable molecule that functions as hemoglobin, the mutant has different properties from normal hemoglobin depending on the precise substitution that has occurred.

The mutation that produces sickle-cell hemoglobin can be traced to a transformation in one nucleotide of the DNA and RNA codes.

> The RNA code word for glutamic acid is UAG. The mutation responsible for Hb S and Hb C [another mutant hemoglobin, formed by substituting lysine for glutamic acid at the point where sickle-cell hemoglobin substitutes valine for glutamic acid] is a change in a single base, because the code word for valine is UUG and that for lysine is UAA. (U = uridine; A = adenine; G = guanine. In the DNA code thymine replaces uridine.) In the above code words, e.g., UAG, the order of the letters as given is not necessarily the correct one.[5] (Ibid. 64)

In short, the transformational grammar of the genetic code permits the substitution of either valine or lysine for glutamic acid at a particular locus of the β-polypeptide chain of the hemoglobin molecule. The transformation that produces this message is the substitution of a single base in the DNA or RNA sequence, since UAG (glutamic acid) can be transformed into either UUG (valine) or UAA (lysine) by changing a single nucleotide (or letter of the genetic alphabet). In just the same way, of course, a single phonemic substitution can produce different well-formed strings in English, such as "It is the *n*ame," "It is the *g*ame," or "It is the *s*ame."

Transformational grammar usually deals with linguistic patterns much more complex than the above example. Molecular biologists have not reached a full understanding of the syntax of the genetic material in the cell nucleus, though they are working rapidly in this direction (Bonner and Mills 1964; Britten and Davidson 1969; Handler 1970; Steitz 1988). The analogies between transformational grammar and genetic mechanisms might therefore promise to produce suggestive concepts and hypotheses in both linguistics and biology. For example, Jakobson cites a case in which biologists have profitably utilized linguistic terminology:

The strict "colinearity" of the time sequence in the encoding and decoding operations characterizes both the verbal language and the basic phenomenon of molecular genetics, the translation of the nucleic message into the "peptidic language." Here again we come across a quite natural penetration of a linguistic concept and term into the research of biologists who, by collating the original messages with their peptidic translation, detect the "synonymous codons." One of the communicative functions of verbal synonyms is the avoidance of partial homonymy (e.g., utterances substituting *adjust* for *adapt* to prevent the easy confusion of the latter word with its partial homonym *adopt*), and biologists question whether a similar subtle reason could not underlie the choice between synonymous codons. (Jakobson 1970)

Such borrowing of linguistic experience in the biologist's description of genetics should also, however, warn us of the dangers of simply equating these two informational systems. As Alfred Hershey put it after a careful analysis of different forms of DNA:

I conclude that DNA language is not human language and that information theory of the message variety is not serviceable for both. Consider a message A through Z in which sentence Z is a paraphrase of A. Then for the purposes of human communication, we have $A-Z = A-YA = A-Y$, and Z serves only to minimize errors of transmission. In the language of DNA chemistry, $A-Y$ and $A-YA$ are not equivalent, and open sequences of the type $A-Y$ may well be meaningless. Furthermore we can write $A-YA = N-YA-N$ for DNA language, a rule implying a degree of independence in the meaning of individual sentences not common in human messages. This second difference is only one of degree and DNA sentences must surely remain intact in the long run. . . . In short, DNA language is a chemical language obeying special topological rules, rules that are enforced by the special kind of twofold redundancy usually found in its messages.[6] (Hershey 1968, 563)

The difference between the acoustical channel used by human speech and the chemical channels conveying genetic messages should not be underestimated, for the properties of the communicative channel necessarily influence the structure and function of a coding system (Sebeok 1962, 1965).

One means of isolating the underlying similarities between the genetic code and speech, without erroneously overstating their identity, is to specify the broad class of systems to which both human and

Figure 3.5
Hemoglobin Molecules

a. Form of Hemoglobin Molecules

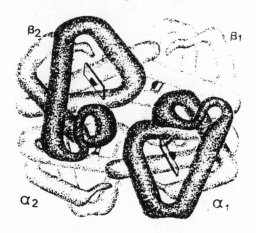

b. Amino Acid Sequence of Hemoglobins

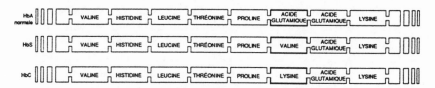

Illustration of the structure and mechanisms of hemoglobin from the French scientific journal La Recherche, *from Masters 1971, 832. (Note that there is no difference between the process described in this figure, as translated from the French, and that in figures 3.1 and 3.4). (a) "Like all proteins, hemoglobin from human blood is composed of long sequences of amino acids. More exactly,. hemoglobin is formed by four chains of polypeptides, two identical chains called 'alpha' and two chains called 'beta.' " (b) "The replacement of one amino acid, glutamic acid, by another in a section of the Beta chain produces two well-known mutations, HbS and HbC. HbS is famous because it is very widely spread in primitive tribes, where it has been observed that this hemoglobin mutation causes a characteristic anemia, 'sickle cell anemia.' That mutation is lethal if it is inherited from both parents (homozygote); if it is inherited from only one parent (heterozygote), the mutation confers a natural immunity against malaria."*

c. Genetic Code and Production of Hemoglobins

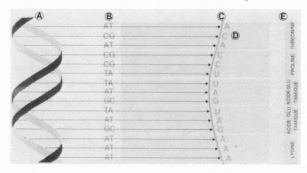

d. Shape of Red Blood Cells

(c) "The mutations producing the abnormal HbS and HbC hemoglobins come from the transformation of a single base (or 'letter') of the DNA helix (step A). A single chain of the helix is 'read' during the decoding (step B). (Here, by convention, the chain on the right). The sequence formed by the succession of bases or 'letters' on this chain is transcribed into a sequence of messenger RNA (step C) formed by the complementary bases, so that messenger RNA reproduces the 'message' of the other chain excepting for thymine T, which is replaced by uridine U. Messenger RNA is the 'mold' on which the synthesis of proteins is formed. Each triple of letters or 'codon' (step D) contains the information corresponding to an amino acid. A mechanism putting in action transfer RNA, ribosomes, and enzymes 'reads' the message contained in the messenger RNA and, facing each codon, attaches the amino acid corresponding to its predecessor. The chain of the protein (step E) is thus manufactured to the end of the sequence, which ends with a 'punctuation mark.' This protein has specific properties that depend narrowly on the composition of its chain. A single amino acid replaced by another can bring about the formation of an inactive protein or one having completely different properties. The codon that 'means' glutamic acid is uridine-adenine-guanine UAG. The substitution of the base uridine in place of adenine gives the codon UUG, which stands for valine. It is in fact this amino acid that replaces glutamic acid in hemoglobin HbS. In the same way, if adenine replaces guanine in UAG, this codon becomes UAA. This new codon codes for another amino acid, lysine, whose presence in the chain produces a new kind of hemoglobin, hemoglobin HbC." (d) "Left, the red blood cells of a man suffering from 'sickle-cell anemia' have a characteristic form, in the shape of a crescent or sickle, due to the presence of the abnormal hemoglobin, HbS. Right, normal red blood cells."

DNA languages belong. Transformational or phrase-structure grammar can be formulated in terms of set theory, relating such grammars
to the general mathematical theory of automata. Such mathematical
formulations provide a symbolic description of different means of
producing strings of coded units, the so-called abstract families of
languages, whose properties are defined without reference to the
concrete channel of communication used (Spanier 1969).

For example, generative grammars and the languages they produce
can be classified as "context sensitive" (if the generation of new symbols in a string is constrained by the symbolic context) or "context
free." Both the genetic code and human languages are in this sense
context-sensitive languages, whereas certain formalized languages
used by automata (or computers) are context free. Moreover, many
species of animals could be described as having a context-free language insofar as their communicative signals represent a general class
of events and gain a specific meaning only from the physical environment in which the signal is produced (Smith 1969). As a result, of
course, animal communication is more severely restricted to messages
triggered by stimulation from the nonlinguistic environment, be it the
organism's physiological state or external phenomena (Gray 1963). In
contrast, the meaning of each symbol in the genetic code or human
speech depends to a greater extent on the grammatical context of the
language itself, so that messages can be initiated with a greater degree
of independence from environmental stimulation.[7]

In less technical language, the difference between nonverbal communication (like human facial displays) and human speech lies in the
degree of independence of each signal from the environmental or physiological cues that trigger it. In nonverbal communication, whether
among humans or other animals, each cue seems to communicate information without reference to other cues in the coding system, so that the
grammar of cues is relatively simple; in order to interpret the signal, the
context that matters is primarily the environment or state of the organism emitting the display (rather than the other displays that precede or
follow each act).

In verbal communication, in contrast, each cue seems to encode
information only in combination with other cues in the system, so
that the grammatical rules are extremely complex. To interpret each
sound in a spoken utterance, the context that matters is primarily
(though not exclusively) the other sounds and words in the verbal
message rather than the environment or physiological state of the
speaker. While this contrast cannot be pushed too far, insofar as
previously seen displays can influence the significance of a nonverbal
cue just as the social or physical environment can transform the mean-

ing of a verbal remark, the distinctive characteristics of human language are surely linked to its relative independence from physical or environmental causes beyond the control of the speaker.

Human communication is extraordinarily complex because spoken messages are accompanied by nonverbal cues, not only of the face and body, but also of the voice. It is nonetheless possible to define objectively those features of verbal language that are distinct from the nonverbal communicative systems we share with other animals. These attributes of linguistic symbols help us to account for their principal characteristic: humans can think and talk about virtually anything, at almost any time. The independence or "openness" of human speech has often been noted as the reason cultural practices can become independent of genetic causation. What has not been so widely realized is that these very features also indicate why linguistic symbols might be compared to genetic material as a parallel system for encoding and transmitting information conducive to survival and reproductive success. The technical structural and grammatical properties of languages as compared to genes therefore suggest mechanisms by which human cultural change could approximate processes of organic evolution without being simply identical to it.

Symbolic Communication and Social Structure

Human cultures and political systems have been elaborated on the basis of a natural behavioral repertoire that evolved to regulate social interactions in small groups. We can now see how language and the resulting capacity to form symbolic representations in the absence of the thing represented made this transformation possible. A verbal utterance can directly fulfill the function of a nonverbal signal of bonding, threat, or flight ("I love you," "Pull over and show me your license!", "I surrender"), or a culturally defined object can be ritualized as a symbol that plays a similar role (a dozen roses, a policeman's uniform and badge, a white flag). Just as animal social structures are built up from combinations of elementary relationships (Chase 1980b), each based on a characteristic pattern of social signals, so human cultures develop as the combination of multiple structural relationships—with the critical difference that the verbal and nonverbal symbols of a human culture are no longer as tightly constrained by physical or social contexts as is animal social communication.

Three features of human culture become more intelligible when one thinks of social life in this way. First, quite obviously, is the plasticity and variability of human social systems. Since humans invent symbols to represent other symbols as well as natural things, cultures can ritualize socially important cues in myriad ways. Humans have the capacity to transform a natural object into a cultural message (a dozen roses as a sign of love), to invent and make objects that symbolize status or role (uniforms and badges), and of course to use speech instead of or to reinforce nonverbal behavior ("I surrender"). Because these multiple elements gain meaning from the context of other linguistic or cultural symbols whose variety is potentially infinite, as well as from a physical and social environment that is naturally finite, representations and transformations of the natural repertoire of social behavior have an almost unlimited complexity and variety.

A second feature of importance is the redundancy of cultural information. Different words can symbolize the same object ("a dozen roses" and "bunch of flowers"); different symbols can represent the same thing (the policeman's uniform and badge); a social function can be fulfilled by both verbal and nonverbal cues ("I surrender" and showing a white flag). Just as genetic information and verbal utterances are "buffered," or protected, against error by redundancy, the multiplicity of cultural cues for a social relationship make confusion less likely. As was shown in chapter 2, this redundancy extends to the facial display repertoire humans share with other primates and its use as a cultural cue; hence television viewers who lack other opinions about a political leader may form an attitude on the basis of a nonverbal display (even if it is merely in the background of a television newscast). Without redundancy, it would be difficult to understand how the openness and infinite variety of language and symbolic behavior could be organized into a coherent communicative system.

The third and in some ways most important property of cultural symbols is that they change. As Campbell (1960, 1965a) has shown, the characteristics of random variation and selective retention apply to any system of information in which elements vary independently, and can be selectively retained (or discarded) depending on the utility or adaptiveness of the variants. Because there are so many symbols and cues in a culture, variability can be subject to selection without either precluding change or producing catastrophe at every innovative event. Hence the same characteristics of language and symbolic representation that account for the diversity of human cultures and social systems also lie at the heart of cultural change and human history.

Human social structures are elaborated from cultural cues that either reflect the natural repertoire of social behavior directly or fulfill its functions symbolically. The categories of bonding, attack, and flight found in animal social behavior can take infinitely varied forms when shaped by human language and culture. An animal ritual or a human facial display can bond mother and child, a male and a female mating pair, juvenile males at the margin of a troop, or a pair of dominant males competing with a rival (to mention only some obvious possibilities). Building on this natural repertoire, a communicative system not constrained by physically visible cues radically increases the variety and complexity of the social structures available to human beings.

SOCIAL FACILITATION, BONDING, AND HUMAN SOCIAL STRUCTURES

To understand how verbal symbols can constitute social patterns, it is convenient to begin with cues that facilitate social bonding. In studies of human facial expressions, the greeting display was shown to be a universal gesture closely related to primate displays of social facilitation. In humans, however, this greeting can be, and typically is, reinforced by a verbal message such as "Hello," "Nice day," or "Good morning, sir." Such spoken greetings are the most elementary example of the way cultural communication elaborates the natural repertoire of social behavior, since these verbal messages represent or echo the basic primate response, signaling the absence of aggressive intent or inviting the partner to social interaction.

Greetings often play a more complex role. A greeting that is expressed in human speech immediately identifies the speaker's linguistic style and therewith can be a cue of group membership. This function of speech clearly has played its greatest role in identifying outsiders, whose accent or choice of words betrays their foreign origins; the biblical example of the password *shibboleth*, used by the Hebrews because the Philistine enemy could not pronounce the *sh* phoneme, illustrates the use of verbal symbols of greeting as the way of demarking friend and foe, group member and outsider. It need hardly be added that nonverbal cues (like the soldier's salute), styles of dress, and modes of body movement can also be recruited as cultural symbols of greeting, establishing distinct forms of social relationship.

Symbolic behavior can, moreover, generate bonds between humans in very different ways. The exchange of objects, fundamental to complex economic life, can establish a temporary reciprocity between humans even without the presence of a greeting display. Among some primitive tribes, barter between groups takes a ritualized form in which the goods being offered by one group are placed next to an encampment without face-to-face contact; the resident group then inspects the offer and sets out a counteroffer if interested; finally, the group initiating the exchange either consummates the bargain or takes back its own goods and leaves. Such a mode of establishing reciprocity is, of course, extremely crude and limited: it can be imagined only in social systems where competing groups lack means of cultural communication, like a greeting display, that allow more subtle verbal (or nonverbal) bargaining.

Economic exchanges as a form of temporary bonding are greatly facilitated by human speech. Contracts are an especially good illustration of this principle because of the role language plays in their negotiation, though displays such as the smile and the handshake at their successful conclusion (not to mention other uses of expressive behavior in the negotiating process) should not be ignored. Language makes possible an agreement to cooperate over a greatly expanded domain of activities and gives the first individual to perform the agreement a notion of the likely response (without being constrained to exchange only those things that could be placed side by side, as in the primitive trade described above). Other cultural symbols, however, can come to play a similar role in exchange—most notably, money.

As Aristotle noted (*Ethics* 5.5.1133a–1133b), money is a transformation of primitive barter and other such reciprocal agreements in trading behavior. Whereas the direct exchange of goods and services presumes that each side can agree on the equivalence of unequal things, money becomes a more universal symbol of this reciprocity; very different things, with quite diverse "use values," can then be exchanged whenever goods and services have comparable monetary (or exchange) value. One need not share Marx's view of this process in *Capital* to agree that the transformation of use values (which limit exchange to barter) into monetary exchange values created a new arena for social interaction in the form of the market economy.

The capacity of human speech to symbolize diverse objects and relationships, which change over time, is indispensable for the emergence of a market based on money. The English word *trade*, which can refer to an agreement to barter between two parties, has also come to mean a line of business (*trade* in the traditional sense of the economic activity that an individual has adopted), the kind of market in which one is participating (wholesale or retail trade), or the activity of exchanging symbols of the worth of other business firms (as in trading on the stock or commodity markets). As these instances suggest, cultural cues can take multiple forms not only because a single cue can have different meanings, but because new symbols (like money) can transform existing cues (a barter agreement), thereby opening up vast possibilities of cooperative and competitive activity in the market economy.

Agreements and contracts can be seen as providing social facilitation or bonds between individuals (typically, but not always, in competition with third parties). In economic exchanges, these agreements are usually for quite limited purposes. Primitive barter, for example, is an agreement limited to the physical exchange of goods present at the time; the limited liability contract to form a business firm typically engages the partners only with regard to a portion of their economic assets and personal lives. Even the money economy as a whole is normally limited to certain kinds of exchanges: in modern societies, for example, it is usually considered illegal to sell other human beings (slavery), sexual activity (prostitution), or the killing of another (the organized-crime "contract").

As these limitations on the market economy indicate, the cultural bonds established among humans can be viewed as rules for social interaction. When young children play, they typically engage in games with rules, either following cultural prescriptions or inventing as they go. Society itself, as social contract theorists since the Sophists have argued, can be viewed as an agreement to engage in social interaction according to mutually acceptable rules. The verbal and symbolic acts that facilitate social interaction and create social bonds can become explicit rules or norms of behavior. Laws make explicit, as a verbal injunction, the kind of social communication present in all animal societies.

The use of cultural symbols of reciprocity and exchange illustrates how the limited scale of primate social groups has been transcended by human societies. Animals often form bonds based on reciprocity between known individuals (Trivers 1981); as a result, the number of individuals in mammalian social groups is typically quite limited. In economic activity, humans can engage in reciprocal exchanges with a virtually unlimited number of others; with the invention of money, goods and services can be exchanged with others who are completely unknown (Aristotle *Politics* 1.9.1256b–1.11.1259a). Laws can also establish formal rules of behavior governing groups of varied size, permitting a social system to expand beyond the limits of the face-to-face group.

Since speech permits humans to name their own actions as well as external objects, each of these levels of social bonding can give rise to specific verbal labels. Naming behavior is thus central to the human social process (Hearne 1987). In many cultures, naming rituals for the newborn child symbolize the infant's integration into the society. Kinship relationships can be named (mother, mother's brother or uncle, identical twins) and, as cultural anthropologists have shown, in most societies these names specify a complex pattern of rights and obligations (Lévi-Strauss 1958, 1962). The bonds of the family or clan are thus represented not only by face-to-face recognition and nonverbal behavior, by habit and social interaction, and by a web of kinship terminology: the bond itself often receives the symbolic name of the kinship group or "jural community" (Bohannan 1963). As kinship is combined with, and ultimately transcended by, economic cooperation in the market economy, naming of the place of residence (town, city, or country) becomes increasingly important, not only as a mode of self-identification, but as a criterion of citizenship and access to legal or political rights

The importance of naming behavior in symbolizing social bonds extends to the modern nation-state, not to mention political parties, religious communities, clubs, and all sorts of lesser social organizations. Multiple ways of symbolizing a social bond provide additional means of eliciting emotional support and loyalty for the group. Among primitive clans, for example, the existence of totemic animals provides a symbolic identity that seems to reinforce the sense of community (a phenomenon that recurs in the symbolic naming of school or professional athletic teams, which so often provide a common focus for otherwise anonymous modern social communities). In all these ways—and more that can readily be imagined—human language and cultural symbols expand both the complexity and the scale of human social institutions compared to those of other primates (Reynolds, Falger, and Vine 1987).

THREAT, DOMINANCE, AND POLITICAL POWER

Human language and cultural symbols transform and elaborate other elements of the natural repertoire of human social behavior besides bonding. Examples of symbolic facilitation of social interaction have been given at a number of levels; the verbal statement or symbol can simply represent the nonverbal act of greeting, it can designate or establish a dyadic relationship or bond, it can facilitate exchange or temporary reciprocity between trading partners, and it can denominate a group or arena in which social interaction and loyalties are present. The same range of possibilities exists for the cultural transformations and ritualizations of the displays of anger, threat, and aggressiveness found in all social animals.

Displays of threat are often symbolically transformed into signs of relationships of dominance and subordination. Individual acts of threat reflecting the power of one individual over another can be represented by a verbal utterance (as illustrated by the policeman's command to a driver, "Pull over and show me your license"). Cultural artifacts (the policeman's pistol as well as his uniform) often symbolize the status or role of individuals who are expected to be dominant over others. Entire social groups as well as individuals can symbolize their location in the social dominance pattern and, in so doing, communicate their power in symbolic ways that are tantamount to a threat (the ritual displays of all-male groups twirling noisemakers and dancing in many traditional societies, or the ceremonial parades in which large military units symbolize the dominance of a political elite in our own day).

Just as speech can be used to negotiate reciprocal exchanges and thereby to facilitate egalitarian social interaction, language can be used to request changes to the benefit of one party in an exchange between unequals. When these requests take the form of orders from superiors in a formal organization, they are often visibly associated with threatening nonverbal displays (although they are perhaps more effective when presented along with the appearance of submissive or bonding behavior). Whether accompanied by a smile or a frown, the orders of military officers and corporate officials often function as symbolic threats. A subordinate's verbal request to improve the quality or quantity of the exchange can also be a symbolic threat, however, because it challenges the dominance of those in power; for this reason, what Hirschman (1974) called "voice" is a human manifestation of the animal social signals of threat and agonistic challenge (Masters 1976b).

The fact that cultural cues communicating threat can be expressed in verbal terms, without direct acts of a physical nature, may mask the persistent role of aggressive behavior in human social life. A cursory reading of most political discourse nonetheless confirms the ubiquity of symbolic terms that replace overt hostility with verbal challenge. While such words as *condemn, attack, charge, challenge, deny,* or *fight* are obvious in this regard, humans are ingenious in devising symbolic means of threatening others (ranging from the erection of statues by leaders to the wearing of armbands by protesters).

Although some cultural cues of threat and aggression are legitimate, others may not be consistent with accepted rules or laws governing social interaction. Illegitimate attack behavior is often what we call crime. Theft, rape, and murder can be defined as illegitimate or aggressive exchanges in which force must be used because the target would otherwise be unwilling to accept the desired transaction. Not surprisingly, criminal eruptions of violence in highly industrialized societies are usually attributed to deviant or marginal individuals, presumably because legitimate authorities should not need to resort to naked violence as a means of expressing their privileged access to goods and services. Even if politics and crime both involve coercion, the different perception of legitimate uses of threat is revealed by the general outrage when contemporary American leaders combine criminal and legal uses of their power.

Finally, cultural behavior can constitute symbolic (or real) threat at the level of entire social groups. In feuding societies and other cultures without formal governments, bands representing the kin group, clan, or village often enforce standards of behavior, acting in their own interest when threatening deviants and especially punishing members of other groups (Barkun 1963; Masters 1964; Gruter and Masters 1986). Within the state, the punishment of crime functions not only as an attack on the person of the criminal but also as a threat to potential violators of the laws. In international relations, the threat or actuality of war, with its consequent effect of unifying the in-group, also provides occasions for symbolic or actual violent behavior between communities.

In all these manifestations, the possible forms of agonistic behavior found in other primates are magnified enormously by the web of cultural communication. In particular, the broadened arenas of social interaction, facilitated by language and symbolic ritual, permit countless variations of displays of anger and threat. Much the same can be said, of course, of the third main category of our natural repertoire—flight, evasion, and the related displays of submission.

FLIGHT, SUBMISSION, AND SOCIAL COOPERATION

It would be tedious to catalog the varied ways in which language and culture permit humans to transform and elaborate the category of flight, evasion, and social submission. Obviously, verbal and nonverbal rituals analogous to animal displays of fear, evasion, and flight are widespread in human society: submissiveness toward those in authority can take the form of physical acts (bowing), verbal deference (saying "sir" or "ma'am"), or obeying orders and laws (paying taxes). Since displays of dominance and power do not automatically elicit such responses, social stability requires some means of expressing submissive behaviors as well as bonding or loyalty.

Perhaps less noticeable, but equally important, is the role of exit from a situation or group as a component of ongoing social interaction. Among nonhuman primates, out-migration from the natal band by either males or females plays a central role in social structure (Wrangham 1979; Lancaster 1986); similarly, departure is essential for the normal functioning of many human social structures. In most cultures, the maturing child is forced to leave the household on becoming an adult; only in this way is the family as an institution reproduced from generation to generation.

Exit also occurs, in a symbolic way, in economic exchange. Indeed, as Hirschman has argued, exit is the primary mechanism of the classical model of the competitive market, in which dissatisfaction is communicated only when "some customers stop buying the firm's products or some members leave the organization" (Hirschman 1974, 4). As in many primitive societies where dissatisfaction with attempts to exercise dominance leads to group fission rather than conflict (Lévi-Strauss [1955] 1974), the option of leaving a social group may confer a feeling of freedom and openness not found when bonds of loyalty preclude departure.

However, exit can be involuntary rather than voluntary. Within complex organizations, an employee can be fired before he has a chance to quit; governments can formally compel unwanted individuals to go into exile. In face-to-face societies, less formal social pressures can ostracize a supposed deviant by cutting off social interactions that might otherwise take place (Gruter and Masters 1986). Such actions involving compulsory exit for a targeted individual or group clearly represent powerful threats directed to other subordinates who might challenge those who are dominant.

Finally, exit behaviors can be characteristic of entire groups. From Moses' flight into Egypt to the exodus from Nazi domination in Europe during the 1930s, groups, whether formally constituted or informally gathered, have often fled social situations that were perceived as intolerable. Such population movements, along with migrations, military defeat, and the eradication of entire populations by conquerors, have played a central role in human history. What is often forgotten is that symbolic images of cultural purity and loyalty—superficially similar to those used in establishing and maintaining social bonds—have been associated with the most horrible examples of genocide and destruction. Even though most human civilizations have been formed by the merger of quite distinct ethnic or social groups, the claim of racial purity as a means of preserving a threatened society has, on more than one occasion, given rise to events like the Holocaust. Sometimes, the enforced exit of individuals and groups from civilizations is a total physical annihilation rather than a symbolic flight or submission.

The development of linguistic and cultural modes of organizing social behavior is thus not the unmixed blessing sometimes implied in academic studies of human evolution (Halle 1965). Here, however, the purpose is not to praise or blame the effects of human speech and culture, but merely to understand how they have made possible the evolution of such diverse social systems in our species. If we consider a human society as a communicative system, built on the natural repertoire of social behavior we share with other primates but transformed by our capacity to create linguistic symbols, the ancient question of where human civilizations come from can be converted into a scientific problem.

Culture as an Evolutionary Phenomenon

It seems likely that human culture is an extraordinarily effective adaptive mechanism because human verbal languages have the capacity to code and transmit information that is of the same order as that of the genes and is not attained by animal languages. Alternative explanations of human adaptability, such as those stressing the primary role of technology, can readily be related to the acquisition of speech: Although the use of tools has been observed in a number of other species (Hall 1967) and our australopithecine ancestors made and used tools (Washburn and Howell 1960), only insofar as the resulting way of life gave rise to speech was it possible for the hominids to achieve the spectacular rate of technological change and cultural variation witnessed during the last forty thousand years (Bounak 1958). The apparent diffusion of toolmaking techniques in Paleolithic hominid populations (Oakley 1959) is hard to explain without some form of verbal communication. While precise reconstruction of the evolutionary relationship between toolmaking and verbal symbols is probably impossible, technological change itself reflects the superimposition of diffusion on evolutionary patterns like those of organic life (Bordes 1960; Braidwood 1960).

The evolution of human languages themselves also reveals many of the patterns found in organic evolution, such as "adaptive radiation," progressive change, and extinction (Hockett 1958, chaps. 42–62; Critchley 1960, 289–91; Gerard, Kluckhohn, and Rapoport 1956). The main difference between genetic and linguistic systems is that the latter have a much greater capacity for hybridization: hence it is continuously possible for different linguistic communities to exchange information, something that is relatively rare in the gene pools of organic species (Mayr 1963, chap. 6; Kroeber 1952, chap. 9; Hockett 1958, chaps. 47–49).

This capacity of borrowing the experience coded in one language or culture and adapting it in another language and culture lies at the root of the phenomenon of diffusion, which was long used to attack the application of an evolutionary approach in anthropology (Steward 1955, chap. 5). Yet from the standpoint of a biological analogy between genetic and linguistic systems, the capacity for hybridization or borrowing among human languages explains a relatively obvious but crucial characteristic of human evolution: unlike most other phylogenies that have expanded throughout the planet and adopted widely differing ways of life, the hominid line has produced a single species with divergent cultures (rather than splitting into distinct species and genera).

For example, baboons (genus *Papio*) and macaques (genus *Macaca*) are closely related monkeys that have diverged due to geographic isolation, with baboons inhabiting Africa and macaques Asia; within these genera, different species have evolved in different environments (Washburn and Hamburg 1965). In contrast, human races are only imperfectly related to cultural or linguistic communities and, at least since the disappearance of Neanderthal man, one can view *Homo sapiens* as a single species with a common gene pool (Dobzhansky 1962, chap. 10; Korn and Thompson 1967, pt. 6; Brace and Montagu 1965).

It need hardly be added that the capacity to borrow experience or concepts from other populations reinforces strongly the adaptability of *Homo sapiens*. Since this permits human populations to exploit new modes of livelihood or technology without becoming distinct species, selective pressures favored the emergence of *Homo sapiens* as a primate whose survival depends on the acquisition of culture (Geertz 1965). Language would seem to be the decisive mechanism in this substitution of cultural divergence for genetic divergence. Whereas animal species are distinct to the extent that a population's gene pool is isolated (Mayr 1963), human languages, as any translator knows, are merely relatively closed systems of information coding, so that although truly identical equivalents are often nonexistent, rough approximations can usually be found or created given sufficient effort (Brown 1958, chap. 7).

A human sociocultural system based on a shared language is thus the functional analog for the species in organic evolution (Gerard, Kluckhohn, and Rapoport 1956, 9–10). Just as any biological species can be analyzed in terms of its gene pool and the relative frequency of various alleles or gene combinations within it, so any culture could be described in terms of a "symbol pool"—that is, the variety and statistical distribution of verbal or cultural symbols shared by a human population (Cavalli-Sforza and Feldman 1981; Lumsden and Wilson 1981). Like genes, which are templates or programs for converting energy and matter into organic cells and behavior, symbols are templates or programs for converting energy and matter into cultural artifacts and behavior.

Just as every organism (phenotype) results from the interaction of a unique genotype, or set of "norms of reaction," and its environment or life history (Dobzhansky 1955), each human individual is a personality resulting from the interaction of culturally inherited norms of reaction with a unique environment, life history, and natural potentialities. Since verbal messages become ways of structuring the world, different ways of talking and thinking can generate profound social controversy. It should therefore not be surprising that linguistic conflicts have had such political importance in non-Western societies during the postcolonial epoch (Fishman, Ferguson, and Das Gupta 1968) as well as in such multicultural industrial states as Belgium and Canada.

In suggesting that cultures are analogous to species, and human languages to genetic coding, it is not presumed that cultures are simply equivalent to languages; such reductionism would be absurd, as is evident from any attempt to equate an observed organism with its chromosomal complement. Granted that the relationship between language and culture is complex (Landar 1966), the primacy of symbolism in human behavior is evident (Duncan 1968; Thass-Thienemann 1968); as Edward T. Hall puts it, "culture is communication" (1959, chap. 5). The analogies proposed here confirm the role of symbolic language as a constituent element of human behavior. Institutions, whether national states, political parties, or kinship groups, can be said to exist as cultural realities only insofar as symbols exist that denote them.[8]

Since genes and chromosomes are observable organic compounds, whereas symbols or ideas are invisible, it will be objected that the analogy between verbal symbols and genes is essentially mystical. We would do well to remember that genes were originally defined by Mendel as factors whose existence could only be deduced from the effects they produce; even a generation ago, it could be said that "no one has ever seen a gene, but then neither has anyone actually seen a neutron or the nucleus of a hydrogen atom" (Brace and Montagu 1965, 37). Only recently have genes begun to be understood biochemically, and this knowledge is still insufficient to explain most observed organic structures (Simpson 1967, 279–80; Ayala 1978; Stebbins and Ayala 1985). One could say much the same of recent strides toward an understanding of the structure of language, and the limited but expanding knowledge of the relationship between linguistic structure and human behavior (Lévi-Strauss 1958, esp. chaps. 2–5; Lacan 1966; Derrida 1967).

Of particular relevance is the discovery of processes in genetic evolution that do not seem to be directly related to adaptation. Some species, for example, "can have thousands of copies of some genes as well as long stretches of DNA that do not code for proteins and are not considered to be genes at all" (Stebbins and Ayala 1985, 75). While some of these repetitive stretches of DNA may ultimately have functional significance as the basis of "new" genes, their emergence suggests that the processes of molecular genetics occasionally make their own dynamic contributions to evolution (Nur et al. 1988). Just as philosophers have long debated whether ideas have an independent effect on human history (and have usually been told by historians that this is not highly likely), geneticists have sometimes claimed that DNA exhibits an independent "molecular drive" in producing "seemingly meaningless repetitions"—only to be told by ecologists and evolutionary theorists that "traditional concepts of evolution suffice to explain the proliferation of such segments" (Stebbins and Ayala 1985, 75). In both cases, adaptation to the environment is doubtless the dominant pattern; in both cases, the exceptions that prove the rule may include some of the most important events in the development of radically new forms of life and society.

While further development of the many parallels between genetic and linguistic systems is not possible here, an example of the utility of this approach for the understanding of historical change may be appropriate. The principles of transformation operating within a system of coded symbols (be it a gene pool, a protein string, a language, or a cultural myth) make it possible to reconstruct evolutionary sequences from divergent structures even when direct historical data are unobtainable. In one of the first studies of this sort, analysis of amino acid sequences in the protein cytochrome c of twenty-one extant species made possible a reconstruction of the likely mutational transformations that could have produced these variants (Dayhoff 1969); as a result, research of this sort can use contemporary data to hypothesize an evolutionary tree, indicating both nodes of divergence and time scale. In much the same way, knowledge of the principles of mythical transformation permitted Lévi-Strauss to clarify questions of cultural evolution from nonhistorical structural data (1968, 185–224).

The structural and functional similarities between genes and languages therefore help to explain the immense variety and rapid rate of change observed in human culture since the Paleolithic epoch. That symbolic representation made social change possible, however, does not mean that language was the principal cause of the social structures and customs developed in various human populations. Genes themselves are the medium, not the only driving force, of organic evolution; the analogy between genes and verbal symbols suggests that cultural evolution, like the evolution of animal species, generally reflects a trial-and-error adaptation to changes in the ecological and social environments in which individuals live.

As a result, this approach need not imply ethnocentrism or evaluative bias in the study of human social systems. Nature is no more favorable to one species than to another; no one culture can claim to be the correct form of human existence, without reference to time and place. By treating human cultural variation as an evolutionary phenomenon, it should therefore be possible to address traditional philosophic questions such as the origins of the state in a way consistent with contemporary scientific research.

Political institutions, like the varied social structures of animal societies, presumably arose because they had become adaptive in some populations. Although such an adaptation could have occurred only because humans have been social beings for millennia, the state cannot be deduced directly from a definition of human nature. Governments and bureaucracies could emerge only when circumstances made a political system controlling large populations of nonkin consistent with the needs of humans formerly living in less centralized communities. Similarly, the conditions under which states disintegrate have to be transformed into an empirical question about the environmental conditions under which decentralized, fluctuating political authorities are adaptive for human populations.

A theory of sociocultural behavior and change that emphasizes the role of language as a functional and evolutionary analog of genetic material can avoid many pitfalls that have confronted earlier attempts to relate biological theories to human behavior. Such an approach fully reflects the uniqueness of *Homo sapiens*; no other animal is known to have a fully developed capacity for verbal language. At the same time, this perspective is compatible with the biological sciences, making it possible to consider whether natural factors shaping the behavior of other species also influence human political and social life. One can therefore avoid the twin dangers of assuming either that humans are merely animals or that we are in no way an animal species. On this basis, neo-Darwinian models of organic evolution can be used in the study of social and political systems without thereby invoking either genetic determinism or ideological justification for the status quo.

The resulting theory of human behavior could well claim to be synthetic in the same sense that modern biology is said to rest on a "synthetic" theory of evolution (Stebbins and Ayala 1985). In recent years, various forms of structural and functional analysis have become prominent in sociology, anthropology, and political science (Levy 1952; Lévi-Strauss 1958; Easton 1953, 1965a, 1965b; Kaplan 1957; Piaget 1970); such theoretical approaches have been opposed both from a more traditional standpoint, which emphasizes historical development and the uniqueness of each event, and from a behaviorist viewpoint, which stresses the need for experimental or quantitative analysis. All of these approaches have validity if utilized appropriately, but since the social sciences have lacked a common frame of reference, the proliferation of models and theories has often given the impression of chaos.

In biology, the concepts of structure or "being," function or "behaving," and evolution or "becoming" have been integrated thanks to the modern, synthetic theory. A similar intellectual coherence follows from the view that language provides a mechanism that is structurally and functionally similar to inheritance yet a product of social learning. If human speech is an evolutionary analog or parallel to genetic material, the concepts of structure, function, and evolution—and the correlative approaches of systemic, behavioral, and historical analysis—can be integrated in social science as they have been in the life sciences. Such an approach shows politics to be a distinctly human phenomenon that is nonetheless consistent with the principles of evolutionary biology.

PART III

Politics and the State

A consideration of the human implications of evolutionary biology can provide the basis for an empirical social science that is consistent with the tradition of philosophical discourse. Lest it be thought that this is absurd, it is important to understand more precisely why the very existence of a bureaucratically organized central government is a scientific problem. Because contemporary social scientists and philosophers have taken the state for granted, they have not found it necessary to pose fundamental questions about the nature of human social behavior. Once these conventional assumptions are questioned, it will be possible to integrate political philosophy, rational choice theories in the social sciences (ranging from economics to game theory), and evolutionary biology into a single approach to the nature of complex social behavior.

CHAPTER 4

Politics as a
Biological Phenomenon

Homo Sapiens in the Evolutionary Process

Approaching human nature as a phenomenon to be explained by the evolutionary process permits us to address central problems in political philosophy. Answers to several traditional questions have already been suggested: in debates whether human nature is fundamentally cooperative or competitive, whether humans are innately rational or fundamentally emotional, and whether culture is totally new or a product of the same evolutionary forces found in our genes, both sides have been partially correct. A similar understanding of human nature has been elaborated in what can be called the dialectical tradition of Western philosophy. Plato (as distinct from the Platonic Socrates) and Aristotle among the ancients, as well as Hegel and Marx in modern thought, all shared the view that simple dichotomies could not encompass human social life; all four thinkers stress the ambivalences of competition and cooperation, reason and emotion, and nature and human experience (Masters 1977, 1978a). In approaching humans in a complex way, however, this dialectical tradition has been characterized by yet another fundamental issue: Which has primacy, the causation of material factors or the principles of the form or "Idea"?

For Plato, all visible things are the product of a formative principle: the Idea or Form of the thing is prior to what we see, which is a mere representation or image of the Forms. For Aristotle, this teaching was apparently too divorced from the material world around us; Aristotle stressed the material and efficient causal processes seemingly given secondary importance by Plato, and taught that they were combined with formal and final causes akin to Platonic Ideas. Among the moderns, Hegel gives primacy to what he calls the Idea or Spirit: "pure thought" or, in more contemporary terms, the informational programs that generate the phenomena we see. Marx rebelled at this feature of Hegelian thought; while asserting that Hegel alone had understood the dialectics of change, Marx insisted that this dialectic had to give a primary role to the material, visible causes of human social life.

At first, one might wonder how a scientific approach could contribute anything to such a philosophic controversy. The naive assumption that science is purely materialist no longer goes unquestioned, however, even in physics (Heisenberg 1968; Capra 1975; Hawking 1988). In biology, the analysis of genes as templates for the production of complex molecular structures gives rise to a profound challenge to simple materialism: is the strand of DNA to be understood primarily as a material "thing" or as a carrier of information—"programs" directing cells to develop and function in a way consistent with an abstract "form" or strategy? Because human language is an evolutionary analog of the genes, the way a living organism is related to its genetic material is particularly germane to the traditional debates between materialists and idealists.

In addition, evolutionary biology can contribute to a better understanding of what is perhaps the most fundamental issue in the history of Western political thought: the so-called debate between the ancients and the moderns. For many students of political philosophy, the difference between the predominant thinkers of antiquity and those since the Renaissance is the most important question facing human thought (Strauss 1953); since at least Swift and Rousseau, this has been a major topic in political philosophy. According to the ancients, there does not seem to be a direction or "progress" in human history. Rather, for philosophers like Plato and Aristotle, as for historians like Thucydides, states rise and fall without testifying to a linear pattern of development. In contrast, modern thinkers as diverse as Hobbes, Locke, Hegel, and Marx seem to think that human reason and industry make possible a transformation of the natural world and a progressive change or development of the human condition (Masters 1977).

Evolutionary biology provides us with a rather different view of change. On the one hand, evolution helps explain how complexity can emerge and sequences of development seem to become irreversible when the transformations of simpler forms make it impossible to return to the earlier ecological system. The appearance of life itself represented just such a transformation of the physical system of the planet, as indeed did the emergence of *Homo sapiens* (Dobzhansky 1955, 1962). On the other hand, evolution is no longer viewed as a progress toward better forms or adaptations: as a trial-and-error process, genetic mutation and natural selection produce change without a single line of direction that could be attributed to a conscious intention or plan (Simpson 1967; Monod 1970; Pieron 1956; Gould 1977; Dawkins 1987).

Basic issues in history, political philosophy, and social science can therefore be clarified by considering in detail the relationship between living forms and the environment. What does it mean to describe evolution as the random mutation or variation of genetic material, subject to natural selection as well as processes like genetic drift? Almost obscured by the discoveries of geneticists in the last generation, the so-called new synthesis of twentieth-century biology has explored processes that can account for the existence of myriad forms of life, their transformation into new species or genera, and their ultimate extinction (Dobzhansky 1955, chap. 6; Mayr 1963, chap. 1; Simpson 1967, chap. 16; Rensch 1966). More recent debates, occasioned by the concept of "punctuated equilibria" (Gould and Eldredge 1977) concern the rates of change implied by this Darwinian approach, but do not challenge the basic perspective of evolutionary biology (Stebbins and Ayala 1985). Similarly, the concept of inclusive fitness developed by Hamilton (1964), which provides one of the bases of the controversial theory popularly known as sociobiology (Wilson 1975; Dawkins 1976; Barash 1977; Kitcher 1985), merely elaborates the neo-Darwinian understanding of natural selection.

Recent debates in the life sciences can hardly be understood and related to human social behavior without a solid grounding in the theoretical perspective shared by all evolutionary biologists. To bring together the implications of ethology and genetics it is therefore now essential to set forth the fundamentals of Darwinian biology in a more comprehensive fashion.

The Neo-Darwinian "Synthesis"

Theodosius Dobzhansky's prize-winning *Mankind Evolving* (1962) probably reflects the approach of contemporary biological theory as well as any other single statement. Written more than twenty-five years ago, his work represents the principles on which the last generation of biological research has been based. Precisely because Dobzhansky's description of neo-Darwinian theory and its relevance to humans antedates such controversial concepts as inclusive fitness and punctuated equilibria, it provides a perspective on more recent theoretical or ideological controversies (cf. Masters 1982a, 1984). Hence it is useful to begin from Dobzhansky's work, citing other comparable statements of the same period (Rensch 1966; Mayr 1963; Roe and Simpson 1958, chap. 1; Simpson 1967; Stebbins 1966) to confirm its representative character.

GENES, ENVIRONMENT, AND DEVELOPMENT

Dobzhansky began his analysis of the place of humans in the natural world by rejecting the radical distinction between human nature and culture:

> The thesis to be set forth in the present book is that man has both a nature and a 'history.' Human evolution has two components, the biological or organic, and the cultural or super-organic. These components are neither mutually exclusive nor independent, but interrelated and interdependent. Human evolution cannot be understood as a purely biological process, nor can it be adequately described as the history of culture. It is the interaction of biology and culture. (Dobzhansky 1962, 18)

Whereas twentieth-century social scientists have traditionally dismissed biological factors as little more than the unvarying drives underlying learned behavior, Dobzhansky insists on the interaction or feedback between cultural and biological processes.

Dobzhansky traced the erroneous opinions of non-biologists to a failure to understand the life sciences:

> Why do so many people insist that biological and cultural evolution are absolutely independent? I suggest that this is due in large part to a widespread misunderstanding of the nature of heredity . . . biological heredity, which is the basis of biological evolution, does not transmit cultural, or for that matter physical, traits ready-made; what it does is determine the response of the developing organism to the environment in which the development takes place. (Dobzhansky 1962, 21)

Although it is often assumed that the genes cause the bodily structure of any organism, biologists have abandoned a simple, one-to-one relationship between physical traits and genetics. Even on the level of plant life, the development of living beings is now understood as the result of an interaction between genetic and environmental factors.

The observed characteristics of an individual, the phenotype, are distinguished from the sum of the genes (or genotype) inherited by each organism. As Dobzhansky put it in an earlier work:

The question whether the genotype or the environment is more important in the formation of the phenotype or the personality is evidently meaningless (although frequently and acrimoniously discussed). The phenotype is the outcome of a process of organic development. There is no organic development without an organism, and no organism without a genotype. Equally, every organism exists in an environment and at the expense of an environment . . . any organism is the product of its genotype and of its life experience or biography. (Dobzhansky 1955, 74)

Or, in the words of George Gaylord Simpson, another eminent student of evolution:

The characteristics of any individual organism within a population are determined by the interaction of its heredity with its environment, in the broadest sense, as the organism develops and, to a less extent, thereafter as long as it lives. . . . Different genes have different effects, . . . but the whole chromosomal complement acts and interacts, and it is that complement as a complex unit that is the main determinant of heredity. It may be considered as setting a reaction range, sometimes rigidly narrow and sometimes very broad, within which the characteristics of the developing organism must lie. (Simpson 1958, 14)

Whether one prefers Dobzhansky's "norm of reaction" or Simpson's "reaction range," this interpretation calls into question the common opinion that acquired modifications or variations are simply caused by the environment or learning (nurture) as distinct from inheritance (nature).

To clarify the multiple causation that produces the phenotype, it is often convenient to distinguish between the genotype's reaction range at each stage of development and the genotypically determined pattern of growth (ontogeny) during the life cycle. While we often think of mutations as altering single traits, like the color of peas studied by Mendel, genetic variation also controls the rate of development of each phase in an organism's life history. As Gould (1977) has shown, such changes in ontogeny are doubtless more important in evolution than was at first realized.

The simplest level of analysis, at each developmental stage of an organism, concerns the reaction range of observed traits, like the height of a plant or the color of its flowers, under varying environmental conditions. Beyond certain extremes, the organism will die; within the range of viability, some environmental conditions will inhibit full development or successful reproduction (Lorenz [1950] 1971, 126). A plant will die if given too much or too little water; within the range of survival, its height will vary, depending on exactly how much water it gets. In contrast, flower color is often relatively invariant as long as the surrounding conditions permit the flower to form, but even such a trait can be conceived as having a reaction range that determines the environmental limits within which it will appear.

Although organisms often have traits that reveal a considerable degree of "phenotypical flexibility" (Mayr 1963, 146–48), much experimental work is needed to determine the reaction range for a structural or behavioral trait. As an example, figure 4.1 is the experimentally determined range of antennal reactions of the male codling moth, *Laspeyresia pomonella*, to various concentrations of a chemical compound that acts as a sex attractant (Roelofs et al. 1971).

Where the plasticity of an organism is extreme, the reaction range need not be linear and unimodal, as in figure 4.1. For example, the leaves of the plant called the water crowfoot (*Ranunculus aquatilis*) have a markedly different shape when submerged in water and when above the water level (Stebbins 1966, 19); if a reaction range were to be drawn for the leaf shape of the water crowfoot, it would have the form of a step function. In many animal species, both bodily structures and behaviors demonstrate such phenotypical plasticity, as is evident from seasonal variations in protective coloring and sexual behavior.

Since some environmental conditions can modify even relatively stable phenotypical traits, it is theoretically useful to treat the reaction range as an n-dimensional space whose shape represents the curves, like those in figure 4.1, for every relevant environmental factor. Although it is "a practical impossibility" to determine the precise limits of the total reaction range for any organism (Dobzhansky 1955, 75), the genotypical reaction ranges of some traits have been established for different human populations (Schreider 1972).

In addition to establishing the shape of the reaction range for each organic trait in all environments, the genotype establishes the developmental sequence of ontogeny. While one could view time as merely one dimension of the n-dimensional reaction range, developmental patterns are particularly important (Gould 1977). Many organisms exhibit critical periods during which failure to develop a given structure or behavior, due to the absence of appropriate environmental conditions, is irreversible.

The general pattern of interaction between genotype and environment during the life cycle has been pictured as a three-dimensional curve (Bloom 1964); for a given trait, a range of phenotypes is possible

Figure 4.1
Experimental Reaction Range: Male Codling Moth Antennal Responses to
Concentrations of Sexual Attractant Pheramone
(trans-8, trans-10-dodecadlen-1 o1)

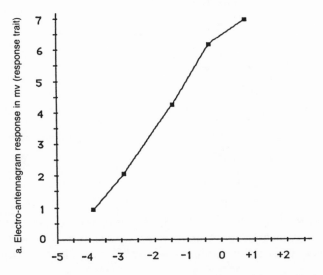

b. Concentration of attractant [Log_{10} Mg] (environmental condition)

From "Sex Attractant of the Codling Moth: Characterization with
Electroantennagram Technique," Wendell Roelofs et al., Science, *vol. 174, pp.*
197–99, 15 October 1971.

at each successive age, depending on the organism's environment and prior development (figure 4.2). As should be obvious, the variation at any age represents a synchronic reaction range, as in figure 4.1.

Where there are irreversible changes in ontogeny, the developmental reaction range can be viewed as a set of pathways, diverging at the critical periods of growth (figure 4.3). The development of social behavior in many primates, as well as such human traits as the acquisition of speech, follow this type of developmental process. For instance, rhesus monkeys raised in isolation, and thereby deprived of the environmental stimulation of conspecifics, exhibit many behavioral abnormalities (Harlow and Harlow 1963; Harlow 1971). Similarly, human children reared through adolescence in an environment without language and speech, as in the cases of "wild children"

Figure 4.2
Typical Developmental Reaction Range

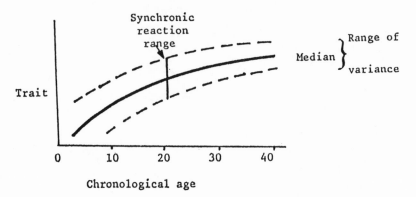

Chronological age

From Benjamin Bloom, Stability and Change in Human Characteristics,
copyright © 1964 by John Wiley. Reprinted by permission.

reared by animals (Rousseau *Second Discourse,* note c), are probably
incapable of acquiring full linguistic capabilities, and even nutritional
deficiencies in infant diet can have lasting effects on intelligence (Dubos 1968, 77–95).

Not all developmental pathways are narrowly constrained or irreversible (Dunn 1979). While the rhesus monkeys reared in isolation by
the Harlows exhibited serious deficits in mating and child-rearing,
many of these abnormalities do not occur when infants isolated from
their mothers are allowed to interact with peers (Hinde 1982). Learning deficits in humans are likewise subject to surprising remediation if
suitable intervention occurs in time: even children with diseases causing severe retardation can vary significantly in linguistic performance
(figure 4.3). For normal humans, therefore, it should not be surprising
that intelligence is a highly complex trait with bewildering interactions between inheritance and individual experience (Gardner 1983);
even where there is some evidence of possible inherited differences in
learning abilities, as in some forms of dyslexia, it has proven extraordinarily difficult to discover the limits of the reaction range or its precise
genetic basis.[1]

Exposure to an appropriate environment is a necessary but not
sufficient condition for the expression of a trait. The genotype establishes not only the environments within which the phenotype will be
viable, but also the degree to which an environmental variable will
influence future growth. Since the organism's structure and behavior
are a product of the interaction between genotype and environment

Figure 4.3

Relationship between Speech Development and IQ in the Mentally Retarded

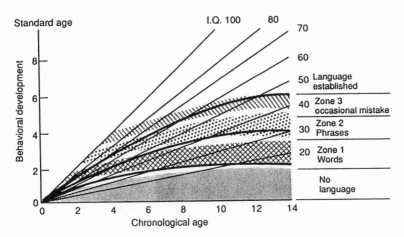

"Curved lines show empirically determined 'decay rates' of IQ in the mentally retarded. The shading indicates language development. An individual whose IQ at a given age falls into the dark area at the bottom has no language. One falling into the lighter areas is in one of three stages of language development, and will develop further until the early teens, with progress depending upon both IQ and age. Individuals in the white area above are in full command of language. After age 12–13, speech development usually 'freezes.' " From Lenneberg 1964, 79. Data based on a follow-up study of 61 mongoloids and 23 children with other types of retarding disease.

throughout life, the distinction between heredity and experience as distinct causes must be reexamined with care.[2] This does not mean that the effects of genotype and environment are indistinguishable:

> The contribution of the genetic and environmental variables may be quite different for different characteristics: to which blood group a person belongs is decided, as far as is known, entirely by the genotype and not at all by the environment; which language a person speaks is decided entirely by environment and not at all by genotype, except that some low-grade mental defectives may be unable to learn any language and the defect may be genetic. (Dobzhansky 1962, 44–45)

In studying variations within a population or species, the genetic and environmental variables can be distinguished, but the task is difficult because the development of each individual represents an interaction of genotype and environment throughout life history.

VARIABILITY IN HOMO SAPIENS

The genotype of *Homo sapiens* provides for a wide range of behavior in two senses: not only do individuals differ considerably, but standards of behavior (expected norms as well as observable statistical probabilities) vary greatly from one culture to another. Whereas the behavioral reaction range of bees or wasps seems to be narrowly determined, humans are capable of learning an extraordinary variety of actions. Here, however, we must beware of anthropocentrism. Because we are often unaware of the actual or potential range of variation in other animals, it is tempting to assert that the differences between one human being and another are far greater than differences within any other species (for example, Halle 1965, 129–31; Simpson 1967, 284).

Just as Dobzhansky has emphasized the physical variations in seemingly identical flies within the species *Drosophila pseudoobscura* or *Drosophila melanogaster* (1955 and other writings), marked behavioral differences in wasps and other insects have been noted by careful observers (Deleurance 1956; Portmann 1961). Since each genotype in a sexually reproducing species is unique, at least in theory (Dobzhansky 1962, 29–30; Mayr 1958, 352), it should be no surprise that Schaller (1965) found, after sufficient observation, that gorillas are individually distinguishable in both physique and behavior. Similarly detailed observation of chimpanzees (Goodall 1986a; de Waal 1982), baboons (DeVore and Washburn 1967; DeVore and Hall 1965; Hall and DeVore, 1965; Crook 1967; Bert et al. 1967; Kummer 1971), and langur monkeys (Ripley 1967; Sugiyama 1967; Jay 1963, 1965) shows that both individuals and groups of a species often exhibit variable behavior, especially in different natural settings.

These observations suggest that the plasticity of human behavior, both within and between societies, must be assessed cautiously. While the genotypical reaction range of *Homo sapiens* seems incomparably broader than that of other species, the precise difference is probably one of degree. Although the acquisition of verbal language distinguishes humans from other primates (Critchley 1960; Hockett 1959), individual learning and social custom do not make natural impulsions irrelevant in human behavior. On the other hand, learned or acquired behavioral components produce variation in other species, and the homeostatic response of virtually any animal can be described as a trial-and-error process (Pieron 1956; Gerard 1960).

POPULATION GENETICS AND THE EVOLUTION OF SPECIES

The adaptation of organisms to their environment is not solely a characteristic of individual phenotypes; species as a whole evolve through time. Although the distinction between individuals and populations is often ignored in discussing the relationship between nature and human culture (for example, Hockett 1958, 369), the evolution of populations is governed by different mechanisms from those by which individuals adapt over the life cycle.

Natural selection is no longer considered in terms of individual survival, but rather as the transmission of those genes whose reaction range makes survival and reproduction more probable. This process occurs in populations over generations, as mutations and genetic recombinations produce genotypes that leave relatively more offspring and only this sense (Muller 1960) are fitter than prior genotypes. Not only is it "simply the fit, rather that the 'fittest,' who survive" (Dobzhansky 1955, 112), but the decisive criterion of fitness is the ability to leave viable offspring or "advantage in differential reproduction" (Simpson 1967, 221–24). Defined in this way, reproductive success is measured by the transmission of genes whether they are carried by the organism itself or by close kin, not by the number of living offspring (Hamilton 1964; Wilson 1975; Alexander 1979).

Modifications of a phenotype, whether bodily changes or behavioral acquisitions due to learning, cannot be passed on to succeeding generations except insofar as they result from or enter heritable reaction ranges.[3] Since mutations occur constantly and sexual reproduction recombines the genes of both parents in each generation, species normally consist of a variety of genotypes, some of which will be more or less adapted or adaptable than others. The evolutionary process is analyzed by population geneticists in terms of the relative frequency of variants of given genes ("alleles") or combinations of genes ("polygenes") throughout a population. "The genes in populations of interbreeding organisms may be described as gene pools. The frequency of genes in a gene pool is determined by mutation pressure, selection, breeding structure, and other factors" (Caspari 1958, 122). While the phenotype of sexually reproducing species reflects the interaction between a unique genotype and its environment, the range of such genotypes thus depends on the statistical frequency of different alleles and combinations of genes in the population's gene pool.

This distinction must be stressed. For species as a whole, evolution operates through processes that can only be studied statistically and would not necessarily differ if each genotype determined an invariant phenotype regardless of environmental variation (as was more or less assumed by Mendel). There are thus two quite different levels on which inherited and environmental influences interact, and from the point of view of population genetics, the capacity of individuals to adapt, survive, and reproduce represents only one of the variables influencing evolution, namely, selection pressure. Other factors, such as genetic drift, mutation rates, population size, isolation, and hybridization are equally important in producing the various patterns of evolution observed in the fossil record or inferred from living forms (Rensch 1966; Mayr 1963; Stebbins 1967).

Under the influence of natural selection and these other factors, a population of organisms continuously replicates the genetic information contained in the species' gene pool. Insofar as the ultimate constraints on evolution arise from properties of the gene pool—and not, as at first might appear, from the characteristics of phenotypes (Moorhead and Kaplan 1967)—it is necessary to reverse our commonsense notion of observable phenomena. To understand the profound reversal of assumptions that this implies, one must reflect carefully on a remark attributed to Samuel Butler and now taken seriously by biologists (Pittendrigh 1958): "The chicken is the egg's way of making another egg." Slobodkin's formulation of evolution as a stochastic game (1964) or Dawkins's concept of the "selfish gene" (1976) are merely sophisticated treatments of the approach suggested by Butler's phrase.

Needless to say, most humans consider the visible phenotype, and not a theoretical construct like the gene pool, to be the stuff of life. Although we find it hard to treat other animals as transitory expressions of self-replicating genetic information, it is even more difficult (and, one is tempted to add, more unnatural) to view ourselves in this way. Yet from the perspective of the cosmos, biology teaches us that the primary reality may not be the physical or existential realm of which we are conscious, but rather the gene pool that we inherit and transmit to our descendants.

To be sure, natural selection normally acts upon the visible phenotype and not directly on the genome. Even here, however, life is often more complex than traditional theories assumed: as modern biologists have explored molecular genetics, phenomena have been discovered that seem explicable only on the basis of the structural properties of DNA. In some instances, it seems as though sequences of nucleotide bases have replicated themselves autonomously, as though there were a molecular drive underlying evolution (Stebbins and Ayala 1985). In at least one case, a chromosome has been found which "enhances its transmission by eliminating the rest of the genome" (Nur et al. 1988). While it is clear that all living phenomena cannot be reduced to molecular events alone (Simpson 1969), from the evolutionary perspective the organism serves as a vehicle for carrying genes (Dawkins 1976, 1982).

Regardless of one's response to such speculations, *Homo sapiens* continues to evolve genetically. In addition to factors influencing other species, the frequency of varied human genotypes can also be affected by cultural behavior. Modern medicine, for instance, has drastically reduced certain pressures of natural selection in many societies. Because the human gene pool is subject to the same evolutionary processes as other species (Dobzhansky 1962; Muller 1960; Sorenson 1971), discussion of the relationship between nature and culture must clearly distinguish genetic influences on individual human behavior from evolutionary processes affecting the species as a whole (Lorenz 1967; Blank 1981). While the first of these problems is illuminated by ethological comparisons between humans and other animals, the second cannot be studied without considering human history and comparing patterns of cultural change with the evolution of other species and genera.

Discussion of the perfectibility of human beings (to use a concept developed in Rousseau's *Second Discourse*) refers to the broad reaction ranges of hominid genotypes, permitting human individuals and societies to adapt to a wide variety of ecological niches. This capacity to learn and modify behavior is itself a biological adaptation, one that has been conspicuously successful as our species has increased in numbers and range over the last fifty thousand years. While human speech has decisive selective advantages for *Homo sapiens*, the capacity to learn a verbal language is itself genetically transmitted (Lenneberg 1964).

It may seem trite to remind ourselves that the variability of human behavior is itself the consequence of natural selection and that we can survive only within the limits of genetically determined reaction ranges. But humility is not the least of the potential benefits of a sound understanding of biology. Human societies could not escape the limits of evolutionary principles even if they were to adopt total eugenic control of their populations. Although such a step will probably be technically feasible within the next generation (Muller 1968; Taylor 1968; Fuller 1974), it would not supersede neo-Darwinian theory: eugenic practices would have to conform to the statistical principles of population genetics and would merely represent an alternative to random mutation and sexual recombination as reproductive processes. Given the unforeseeable consequences of genetic engineering and eugenic control, nature provides us with no assurance that conscious manipulation of the gene pool would guarantee the survival of the species (Kass 1971; Gaylin 1972; Rifkin 1983).

Human Behavior as a Biological Phenomenon

IMPLICATIONS OF BIOLOGY FOR THE SOCIAL SCIENCES

The neo-Darwinian or synthetic theory of evolution contradicts a sharp dichotomy between nature and culture. Although the actions of humans influence their physical surroundings, their phenotypes, and their species' gene pool, the physical and biological characteristics of *Homo sapiens* interact with the natural and social environment throughout individual development and social history. Simplistic assertions, such as "Man makes himself" or "Man's innate compulsions are genetic and ineradicable," do not reflect an understanding of human behavior when viewed as a biological phenomenon.

Five implications of this perspective should be emphasized. First, each aspect of human life must be analyzed without a priori assumptions concerning the cultural or natural status of the processes and functions involved. Phenomena that vary from one human population to another are not thereby totally cultural, as is evident from cross-cultural differences in the age of puberty (Johnston, Malina, and Galbraith 1971). Many natural characteristics of normal human beings presuppose individual learning and social tradition: such elemental actions as copulation, defecation, and eating are simultaneously biological and cultural.

Second, it is imperative to distinguish carefully between individuals, groups, and the entire species (Masters 1973a, 1973b). The causes and functional consequences of individual behavior cannot be simply generalized to populations, nor can phenomena discovered in groups or populations be simply equated with the species *Homo sapiens* as a whole. Much sloppy thought and writing—particularly of the type using the collective noun *man* to gloss over unwarranted generalizations—must be reconsidered with care. From a biological point of view, our species should be viewed as a gene pool reproducing itself through time as populations of phenotypes adapt to various environments.

This suggests a third implication of great importance. In the evolutionary process, the phenotype serves primarily as the carrier of the genes, not vice versa. If "the chicken is the egg's way of making another egg," our tendency to attribute primacy to the material and sensual universe of human experience, the realm of the human phenotype, may be an illusion. The greatest significance of many events may be their selective impact on our gene pool rather than their perceived consequences for individuals or societies (Alexander 1979; Chagnon and Irons 1979; Blank 1981). While the effects of modern medicine are obvious in this regard, a wide range of cultural and individual practices have important implications for the species' evolution.

A fourth conclusion follows: We must constantly beware of an all too human tendency to overestimate the importance of our own conscious intentions, plans, and rationalizations. One is almost tempted to propose, as a general rule, that the latent functions of human behavior are always more important than the manifest or intended consequences (Merton 1949; Levy 1952). Without going this far, it should be clear that the expression of purpose or motivation does not constitute a comprehensive explanation of human phenomena, since from a biological perspective one must explain the existence of human intentions as well as the selective consequences of the means of fulfilling them.

Fifth, and finally, biology reminds us of the crucial importance of time. Both the individual life cycle and the evolution of species represent sequences of events that are usually irreversible. Neither cell differentiation in ontogeny nor species differentiation in phylogeny can be entirely reduced to "the physical principles of repeatability, predictability, and parity of prediction and explanation" (Simpson 1969, 9–10). Biology, like the social sciences, thus deals with problems of historical development as well as collective processes that cannot be reduced to the sum of their individual components.

These five conclusions suggest the desirability of using the biological sciences, rather than physics or the philosophy of science, as a paradigm for the social sciences (Thorson 1970; Masters 1970; Schubert 1981). Unlike classical physics, the biological sciences deal with open systems of great complexity, in which time plays an essential role at the level of both individuals and populations. Whatever its status in physics (Gal-Or 1972; Hawking 1988), the traditional understanding of the second law of thermodynamics does not adequately explain life. Living systems can decrease entropy through time by evolving a more complex organization of matter and energy (Corning 1984), and on this crucial point, social systems are comparable to biological ones, not to the phenomena studied by classical physics (compare, however, Bohr 1958, 13–22 and Epilogue, note 2).

Both biological and social sciences study populations that reproduce themselves through a process capable of evolutionary change. In terms of physical systems, human life, like that of any other species, represents negative entropy or information—that is, a nonrandom distribution of matter and energy (Morin 1973). The individual's genotype and the species' gene pool cannot be fully understood in terms of their chemical composition, for it is the sequence and structural conformation of the nucleotide bases on the DNA chain, not the simple percentage of each nucleotide base in the cell nucleus, that encodes the information specifying the amino-acid sequences manufactured by each living cell.

In biology, as in the social sciences, complex structures cannot be explained solely in terms of the combinations and permutations of the simpler elements of which they are composed (Anderson 1972). At each higher level of complexity, new structures emerge that are best understood as a nonrandom organization of information, and structural properties at a higher level of complexity cannot be simply reduced to a manifestation of their components (Gleick 1987). This characteristic, which has been particularly notable not only in modern genetics (Stent 1969) but also in the analysis of the physiology of perception (Ohloff 1971; Stent 1972; Gilinsky 1984; Rodman and Gross 1987), has also been examined in human cultures by what is generally known as the structuralist school (Lévi-Strauss 1962 and other writings; Derrida 1967; Piaget 1970).

Although the convergence of structural analysis in the biological and social sciences cannot be examined further here, suffice it to say that any general theory of human life as a biological phenomenon seems to rest on the properties of complex systems that are capable of encoding, transmitting, and processing information (Pattee 1973). The model presented in the following pages can thus claim to overcome the obsolete dichotomy between nature and culture without thereby running the risk of a naive reductionism. The resulting theoretical approach makes possible not only a more coherent relationship between the social and natural sciences, but a better understanding of human politics as well.

GENES, CULTURE, AND LEARNING

Since each phenotype must fall within the reaction range of its genotype, the gene pool of a species can fruitfully be conceptualized as a system of information storage, processing, and transmission. Cultural roles or norms establish, in an analogous fashion, the reaction range within which individual personalities fall, depending on the specific experience of each human being; culture or tradition, like genetic inheritance, is a means of storing, processing, and transmitting information concerning adaptive responses to varied contingencies (Willey 1960, 111; Spuhler 1959, 12). Finally, the learning and memory of the individual establish a probable range of reaction to future environmental conditions and stimuli, both natural and cultural.

It is obvious that the informational systems of the human gene pool, a human culture, and a human individual do not exist in a vacuum; rather, each is an analytically separable component of a concrete physical system: the species *Homo sapiens* on the planet Earth, a human population adapted to a particular environment and ecological niche, and a human phenotype with its unique life history. Even more important, these three levels of information, each corresponding to a different level of physical system, form a nested series: each human population is part of the species, just as each individual is part of a population. Similarly, the three information-coding systems form a nested set: cultural norms must lie within the potentialities of the human gene pool, just as individual learning must lie within the potentialities of the individual's culture and genotype. Yet neither cultural norms nor individual learning can be simply reduced to the information coded in the human chromosomes, for both a verbal language and the central nervous system can function within limits as autonomous, open information systems.

To clarify the relationship between these three levels and types of information systems, a biological model of human behavior is set forth as a flow chart in figure 4.4. In this diagram, the species as a whole, an interacting population or society, and an individual each are represented by a pair of related systems: a physical or material system in its environment, and an information-coding, -processing, and -transmission system present in the physical system. Each of the less inclusive physical systems must lie within the reaction ranges determined by the higher level, although feedback mechanisms produce evolutionary changes at all levels of both physical and informational systems. To represent these differences, solid lines represent direct causation, dotted lines represent feedback, and the boxes represent analytically separable systems that evolve through time.

While the human individual's phenotype is a direct expression of genotypical potentiality in the environments encountered through ontogeny, it is also an expression of the cultural and social reality in which each human being lives. For example, the untreated color and texture of human hair is a phenotypical trait, reflecting the interaction of genotype and environment; hair style is a cultural phenomenon (and one that has had political significance in some societies). Since human cultures and societies encode, process, and transmit information through a communicative system that is neither entirely in the gene pool nor entirely in any one individual's brain and central nervous system, each of the three levels functions as an open system with a degree of autonomy.

A hierarchical approach like that in figure 4.4 serves as the basis for a pragmatic distinction between the social and biological sciences, since social evolution is, within limits, not reducible to physiological

Figure 4.4
Human Behavior as a Biological Phenomenon

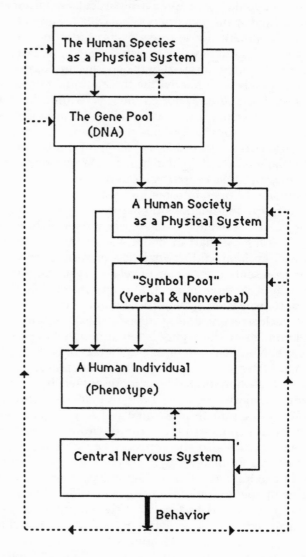

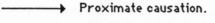

*From Masters 1975, figure 4. For distinction between proximate and ultimate
causes, see Barash 1977.*

causes. At the same time, the model avoids the common misconception that the existence of social or individual adaptation and learning supersedes biological processes and functions within the human phenotype. Above all, the schema reminds us that our species is an evolving system that cannot be entirely reduced to its constituent populations and individuals.

Human behavior is the product of an integration, within the brain and central nervous system of each individual, of phylogenetically selected information transmitted by the genes, historically selected information transmitted by language and cultural symbols, and individually learned information acquired during the life cycle. "Each person's constitution is therefore made up of the evolutionary past incorporated in the various forms of mental and biological memory" (Dubos 1968, 100). Individuals and societies can and do evolve new patterns of behavior, just as every species including our own evolves new physical and behavioral traits, but these changes (represented by the feedback arrows in figure 4.4) must be encoded in a relevant information system in order to become irreversible.

Since modifications in any of the physical systems must be coded in an information system if they are to influence future behavior, there are two general requisites for lasting change. First, the new structure or behavior must be accessible to the previously existing physical system; just as no single genetic mutation could give rise to wings on the human body, so a primitive human tribe could not invent the airplane. Second, once the modification or variation occurs (whether by accident or design), it must be encoded in the information-processing system, where its transmission to future generations either by cultural or genetic means will depend on the operation of selective mechanisms (Campbell 1960, 1965a).

The second criterion for adaptive change is particularly relevant to politics. Leonardo da Vinci's concept of human flight with artificial wings was not effectively realized until long after the Italian Renaissance; political ideals or inventions are often subjected to a negative selection pressure if they conflict too sharply with the opinions of the time. In the United States, the "Townsend Plan" and Huey Long's "Share-the-Wealth" program, viewed as "crackpot" in the 1930s (Morison 1965, 973–75), became respectable political proposals a generation later when rebaptized "Guaranteed Annual Income" (Stoffaes 1973).

As this example reminds us, the various systems sketched in figure 4.4 do not change at a constant, harmonious rate. Individuals may learn to solve problems before their society is ready to adopt their solution, as in the case of Leonardo da Vinci. Conversely, individuals may lag behind social change, refusing to abandon ideals or judgments that arose in earlier epochs. Contradictions between the expectations and behaviors of different individuals or groups are, as observers of *Homo sapiens* have long recognized, frequent in almost every human society. For this reason, if no other, politics is a characteristic feature of human life.

HOMO SAPIENS AS THE POLITICAL ANIMAL

The model presented above gives full weight to both the similarities and the differences between humans and other animal species. In particular, it focuses attention on the unparalleled extent to which *Homo sapiens* fulfills biological functions through cultural traditions and individual learning, and relates this specifically human adaptation to the development of verbal speech made possible by the complex human brain. As Edward T. Hall puts it, "people from different cultures not only speak different languages but, what is more important, inhabit different sensory worlds" (Hall 1969, 24).

To express the extent to which *Homo sapiens* is a species that cannot survive without culture and individual learning, some have spoken of "man as a cultural animal" (Geertz 1965; Montagu 1968). Others have used the phrase "the imperial animal" (Tiger and Fox 1971) or the "human animal" (Hass 1970) to express the duality of our species' nature. Perhaps, however, it is more fitting to use Aristotle's concept, "the political animal."

The model in figure 4.4 emphasizes the information-coding systems that enable populations and individuals to survive and reproduce. At the level of the individual phenotype, every cell carries in its nucleus the same complement of chromosomes, which provide a set of programs or rules governing both cell functioning and cell differentiation or growth: Cells produce different proteins when a portion of the chromosomal message is disinhibited or activated under given intra- or extra-cellular conditions, so that RNA templates produce the appropriate amino-acid sequence and assemble the resulting components into a specific protein molecule (Beadle and Beadle 1966; Stent 1969; Steitz 1988).

Individual behavior also represents an information-processing system. The brain responds to sensory stimulation in a highly structured manner that could be described as a physiological code since sense receptors and neuronal networks respond to preprogrammed features of the environment (Stent 1972). The sense of smell, for example, depends on the geometric shape of molecules in contact with the sensory apparatus and not merely on their chemical composition (Ohloff 1971). Because networks of brain cells are specialized in processing abstracted properties of a cue, sensory stimulation is communicated to the cortex through specialized neurological structures; ultimately, activation of a given neuronal sequence or pattern is coded as a specific message for the central nervous system (Moyer 1969; Changeux 1983; Gilinsky 1984; Rodman and Gross 1987).

In much the same way, cultures can be viewed as information systems based on a series of interrelated codes. To be sure, human cultures and societies elaborate complex systems of material artifacts— tools that manipulate the environment, symbolic objects, and works of art—that are "artificial organs" not transmitted through the gene pool (Hass 1970). But artifacts become extinct if humans cannot communicate the mode of producing, using, or understanding them; hence, without speech, variability is limited to those actions that can be visibly imitated, such as techniques of using preexisting objects or moving through the environment. While some species use tools, humans make them in unequalled variety, in all probability because only humans can communicate verbal instructions to program the production of tools (K. R. L. Hall 1967; Oakley 1959; Bounak 1958; Leakey 1981).

Like genetic material, speech is an information-coding system that allows previously successful modes of adaptation to be preserved. The analogy of computer programming is useful: While the physical hardware of a computer makes possible a range of programs, actual use of the computer depends on prior mastery of the relevant computer language, or rather of that part of the computer language needed for the task at hand. Once developed and stored in the computer, a program permits users to solve a problem without having to rewrite the original sequence of instructions. At the same time, continued computer use can lead to further evolution of the basic program as modifications solve new needs and problems.

The analogy between a human society and a cybernetic system has been developed in detail by Deutsch (1963). His presentation has a revealing shortcoming, since Deutsch fails to stress the analogies between man-made cybernetic information nets, such as the computer, and the information systems occurring in nature, like the gene pool or a human language (cf. Corning 1984). As a result, Deutsch limits the possible analogies between human society and biological systems to the individual organism (Deutsch 1963, 30–34, 77–78), despite increasing awareness that it is always a population that is the basic unit of evolution (Mayr 1963).[4] Nonetheless, Deutsch's model suggests the advantage of relating political systems to the process by which information is transmitted and communicated within human groups.

Just as there is a hierarchy of programs in a computer, so the information that governs human behavior has a structure. For example, the computer program establishing the procedure for user validation has a temporal and logical priority over user-initiated programs, since access to the computer presupposes satisfactory user validation. In much the same way, among the informational programs or rules that establish the probable range of individual human behaviors, some determine access to resources and relative status in cases of competing claims. These rules, whether in the form of written law or cultural practices and traditions, constitute what is often called the "regime" (Easton 1965b, chap. 12) or "political system."[5]

Because the genetic reaction range of *Homo sapiens* is so broad that humans must rely on culturally transmitted and individually learned information to survive and reproduce, the probability of contradictions between individuals or groups is exceptionally high. Moreover, the larger a human population and the more rapid its rate of social change, the greater the variation in the experiences or environments that condition individual learning, and in the information communicated to different members. Humans therefore often develop patterns of behavior that are not entirely congruent with the cultural and political norms of the society as a whole, or of other individuals and groups with whom they interact.

The diversity of individual responses to the same environmental circumstances is natural to a much greater degree than is suspected from the perspective of behaviorist psychologists for whom the organism is a passive "black box" responding to stimuli according to universal laws of behavior (Skinner 1965). The presumption that given circumstances elicit identical responses in different individuals is contradicted by studies of the precise localization of information processing in the human brain. Although each hemisphere of the brain normally provides different functions (verbal and linear processing in the left, nonverbal and holistic processing in the right) that are integrated in speaking, reading or writing (see figure 2.2a), individuals differ in their pattern of hemispheric specialization and in their strategies of processing and integrating the same sensory information (Masland 1983; Gilinsky 1984; Geschwind and Galaburda 1987; Kosslyn 1988). Because there are many different types of intelligence (Gardner 1983), humans vary greatly in their perceptions and thoughts as well as in their judgments or values.

Since the three pairs of systems in figure 4.4 are virtually never in complete equilibrium, a society's regime or political system has the function of determining the priority of potentially conflicting messages and rules of action. Because this function can be satisfied without the existence of a state—a social institution specialized in the establishment and enforcement of the "rules of the game"— politics is present in all human populations. Political systems can be identified even in primitive tribes without rulers or in contemporary international relations between states claiming to be sovereign (Masters 1964). Whether or not enforced by a central government, law functions as a program whose primary function is to channel the behavior of the individuals and groups comprising a society. Though laws also establish procedures for resolving conflicts, use of these mechanisms is, in a technical sense, a secondary function that reflects ambiguity or conflict in the interpretation of social rules by different individuals (Barkun 1963).

A Biological Definition of Politics

A distinctive characteristic of *Homo sapiens*, related to the evolutionary emergence of the large brain, language, and cultural diversification, is the sheer complexity of the factors contributing to human behavior. Morin (1973) has spoken of "hypercomplexity," arguing that the wide range of human adaptability necessarily implies an equally high risk of irrationality, insanity, and conflict; he speaks of our species as the "crisis animal" and suggests that its appropriate scientific designation should be "*Homo sapiens/demens*."

Such an understanding of human nature provides added rationale for the Aristotelian concept of the *zoon politikon*, the political animal. From a biological perspective, conflicts between the behavioral programs encoded in genes, in language, or in individual learning must be regulated, though not necessarily resolved, if the species is to survive. Just as a computer can be rendered inoperable by certain contradictory programs, an organism can be seriously disturbed, if not destroyed, when genetic and learned behavioral programs are in radical contradiction. This occurs, for example, when primates deprived of normal maternal care and social experience fail to learn behaviors congruent with innate propensities, leading to severe abnormalities similar to human psychoses and, in extreme cases, inability to copulate or rear young (Harlow and Harlow 1963; Harlow 1971).

Given the complex information which must be integrated by the human central nervous system, it should hardly be surprising that discontinuities between genetic, cultural, and individually learned behavioral programs constantly produce deviance and social conflict. The biological function of politics thus arises from the insufficiency of other modes of regulating social interaction. Laws, whether customary or written, do not suffice in all situations; as common experience has long indicated, they are all too easily broken. The political process, by which laws are changed, enforced, and challenged, would seem to be an inevitable counterpart of the "hypercomplexity" represented in figure 4.4.

In the common usage of the term, politics is a form of rivalry to determine which humans are permitted to transmit "authoritative" messages or commands to the rest of the society (Easton 1965a, 1965b). In this sense, high status and political office are in themselves symbolic messages; just as dominance in animal societies is communicated by gestures or personal recognition, humans represent social and political status by verbal and nonverbal symbols that organize social interactions (Maclay and Knipe 1972).

In a secondary sense, however, politics is also rivalry concerning the content of authoritative messages in a human population (Edelman 1964). While this is obvious when political conflict concerns the substance of laws or customs, behavior can be said to have a political element even when it is not openly directed to legal or institutional change. For example, novels or popular songs can convey crucial political messages, particularly in regimes where other channels of communication are closed to significant sectors of the population (Holland 1968; Green and Walzer 1969).

One can therefore define politics more precisely as behavior that simultaneously partakes of the attributes of bonding, dominance, and submission (which the human primate shares with many other mammals) and those of legal or customary regulation of social life (characteristic of human groups endowed with language). Politics is not merely what ethologists have called agonic or agonistic behavior (Altmann 1967): competitive rivalry for dominance exists in sports, on school playgrounds, and in business without thereby deserving the name politics. Nor is all behavior governed by legal norms automatically political: as cultural anthropology teaches us, legal or customary rules govern childhood, marriage, and the entire range of human social life.

Political behavior, properly so called, comprises actions in which the rivalry for and perpetuation of social dominance and loyalty impinges on the legal or customary rules governing a group. As such, political science has a peculiar status, for it lies at the intersection of ethology and anthropology—or, more broadly, at the point where the social and natural sciences meet. Indeed, this definition of politics may help explain why political theorists, at least before the middle of the nineteenth century, were almost always concerned with the definition of human nature and the relationship between nature and society.

While the biological approach suggested here is generally compatible with much recent work in political science, it permits the inclusion of dimensions that are frequently ignored. There is no reason to limit the analysis of biological variables in politics to the remark that human nature is "essentially uniform" or that "biological traits" are part of the "environment" of the political system (Deutsch 1963, 12, 29; Easton 1965a, 72). On each of the three levels of analysis distinguished above (the species, societies, and the individual), a biological definition of politics points to phenomena that have not traditionally been studied by political scientists.

For example, our species has not been "liberated" from natural constraints merely because of the tremendous extension of human technology (Meadows et al. 1972), and the possibility of "Limits to Growth" poses specifically political problems (Ophuls 1973, 1977; Sprout and Sprout 1971). Can one find, in biological evolution, criteria that would permit a better understanding of these new issues, if not guidelines for policy (Caldwell 1964; Corning 1971b)? In the study of modern societies, much has been said of the decline in power of legislatures and the rising influence of individual leaders. To what extent is this development—and the related increase in the phenomenon of charismatic leadership—linked to rapid social and cultural change? Can charisma be more fully understood in the context of ethological studies of dominance and submission (Hummel 1973; Larsen 1973; Sullivan and Masters 1988)? Do increased population densities, which produce behavioral disturbances in other species, rigidify dominance hierarchies and increase the frequency of pathological or aggressive behaviors (Bouthoul 1970; Galle, Gove, and McPherson 1972)?

Although the political behavior of individuals, whether leaders or followers, has traditionally been interpreted in terms of attitudes and interests, recent events often seem irrational according to these criteria. Biological research shows the role of physiological variables in dominance behavior (Corning and Corning 1972; McGuire and Raleigh 1986; Madson 1985a, 1985b). Are there natural factors that help to explain the different political behaviors of males and females (Tiger 1969; Dearden 1974; Watts 1984; Schubert 1985)? Are the physiological correlates of drug use relevant to political departicipation among the poor or powerless (Stauffer 1971)?

Even if the above questions were irrelevant to political analysis, they concern issues on which policymakers will necessarily make decisions of biological as well as political importance. What are the political implications of biomedical technologies that could drastically modify the human gene pool (Taylor 1968; Blank 1981; Rifkin 1983)? Proposals for

Zero Population Growth, genetic or drug screening, and mapping of the human genome have manifold political consequences (Attah 1973; Hemphill 1973). Should psychosurgical or psychopharmacological technologies be used as an alternative to the penal system, regulating deviant behavior without formal legal processes (Somit 1968; Corover 1973)? Should leaders be treated with drugs in order to limit their aggressive behaviors, thereby diminishing the risk of global warfare (Clark 1971)?

These issues, and many others like them, cannot be understood without reference to the biological sciences. Although it has been traditional to distinguish nature and culture, the resulting dichotomy between the natural and social sciences is contradicted not only by scientific findings, but by the dilemmas facing contemporary governments. Lest political science continue its isolation from the rapid developments in contemporary biology, it is important to treat political behavior as a biological phenomenon on both causal and functional levels.

In suggesting a biological definition of politics, human behavior is not thereby reduced to animal instinct or evolutionary necessity. Each of the three levels of systems distinguished in figure 4.4 is open; naive reductionism, whether in the form of "pop sociobiology" (Kitcher 1985) or "behaviorism" (Skinner 1965), is as outmoded as nineteenth-century Social Darwinism or eighteenth-century materialism. Complex living systems can be better understood as a reflection of structures encoding information and evolving in ways that are not always determinate and predictable (Anderson 1972; Gal-Or 1972; Morin 1973; Gleick 1987). Traditional philosophic debates about the nature of man have been inconclusive because the term *man* confuses heterogeneous levels of analysis and not, as is sometimes claimed, because our species lacks a nature.

Evolutionary Biology and Political Theory

In addition to improving our understanding of practical matters, the perspective of the life sciences can clarify many issues in the tradition of political thought. Three specific questions have already been mentioned. First, the debate between materialists and idealists. Second, the so-called quarrel of the ancients and the moderns; and finally, the relationship between human nature and politics. On each of these topics, evolutionary biology leads to a reformulation and clarification of questions that have long seemed insoluble.

MATERIALISM AND IDEALISM

The relationship between phenotype and genotype, which serves as one of the foundations of the neo-Darwinian theory of evolution, suggests a way of reconsidering the traditional debates between materialists and idealists. No species can survive unless its phenotypic representatives are sufficiently viable, in the environments where they live, to produce offspring; natural selection operates on the visible organism, not directly on the gene pool. Because the physical requisites of life are essential factors in organic evolution, biology at first appears to favor materialism, particularly as an alternative to the traditional theological account of creation. But this appearance is deceptive.

For those who no longer explain life as an act of God's creative will and divine plan, the relationship between genotype and phenotype shows the need for a more complex view than simple materialism. In individual life history, genes functioning as a set of instructions have a priority over the physical structures they produce; at the level of species, the gene pool represents phylogenetically evolved structures and adaptations to the environment that are transmitted from one generation to another. The development and life of the phenotype is directed by genetic information, which serves as a code or plan for the formation of organisms that fit the species' nature.

Biologists who reject the traditional concept of teleology associated with divine creation nonetheless admit a category of events that can be understood only in terms of what Aristotle called "formal" and "final" causes," although to avoid misunderstanding some speak of "teleonomic" processes rather than teleological ones (Pittendrigh 1958; Mayr 1974; Masters 1978a). Others use the term "ultimate causation" to describe the long-term effects of natural selection, as distinct from the "proximate causation" operating on the individual phenotype (Barash 1977, 37–39).

There does not seem to be a way to reduce biology to a single set of material causes, on the model of the seventeenth-century physics used by Hobbes and Locke. Nor can it be said that the physical and social environment necessarily causes species to have a particular characteristic, as Engels and some materialists in the Marxist tradition concluded: While adaptation to the environment is one of the factors in evolution, other characteristics of population genetics are due to genetic drift, sampling, and genomic structure—attributes of the informational system for transmitting genetic information, rather than of the material environment per se. Treating the gene pool as a constituent element of living forms is hardly mysticism, but it limits the scope of the mechanistic causation emphasized by traditional materialists.

Evolutionary biology points to the irreducible importance of processes at different systemic levels, much along the lines of Aristotle's conceptualization of four types of causality. Efficient causes are those actually producing or triggering the motions of living things; they include the sources of energy in the physical environment as well as stimuli impinging on each organism. Material causation is broader, since it includes those attributes of an organism that are necessary requisites of behavior as well as physical constraints that influence species over time and space (even without immediate physical effects on an individual). The central nervous system of each species, for example, is a material cause determining which environmental events can be perceived as stimuli; the ecological setting functions as a material cause of natural selection, favoring some genotypes over others. While both efficient and material causation concern the phenotypical or visible systems in nature, there is surely a meaningful difference between the causes whose presence or absence triggers or drives a specific event, and material factors that are necessary conditions without being an efficient cause of the phenomenon observed.

Other causal processes operate on the level of the genetic material and its mode of influencing the phenotype. Formal causation could be identified with the way an organism's basic shape and behavior are preprogrammed in the genome. A dog does not look like a cat or an elephant. In ontogeny, genes provide instructions for cellular differentiation and growth until the organism corresponds to the fundamental shape or Form (sometimes called "bauplan") of the species. Activity can also have a form. In the behavior of individuals, the characteristics of displays or environmental cues that function as releasing mechanisms are often inherited or at least influenced by the species' evolutionary past (Lorenz [1931–63] 1970–71). At this level, causation can be called formal because it concerns the genetic information controlling the material processes of growth, development, and behavior.

Final causation, perhaps the most difficult of the Aristotelian categories, represents the tendency of living forms to seek behavioral and functional responses consistent with the species' strategy of adaptation. Whereas formal causes concern the information coded in the genome, final causes concern the reasons we discover to explain why such information evolved. At the most general level, of course, the final cause is always the same, namely, relative advantage in the transmission of genes from generation to generation; for this reason, critics have often attacked discussions of biological adaptation as "just so stories," incapable of empirical verification (Lewontin, Rose, and

Kamin 1984). In extreme cases, the concept of final cause can be misused absurdly to imply that whatever exists is the product of evolution and natural selection, as in the classic "the nose evolved to hold up eyeglasses." Because there is a very real risk of converting the principle of natural selection into a justification for the status quo, analysis of final causation—which is to say, of adaptation to the environment—requires special care. To be convincing, such explanations need to show that the phenotypic traits claimed as adaptations actually have the presumed effects on reproductive success. This task is difficult. Not only should adaptive forms enhance the organism's contribution to the gene pool, but, given time for selection to operate, they should not occur in ecological settings where the presumed functional benefits would not arise (Barash 1977; Kitcher 1985).

Lest this formulation seem too abstract, consider its relevance to a human behavior such as greeting an old friend. Humans exhibit a natural (in the sense of species-typical) set of displays and gestures whenever two old friends see each other after an absence; in addition, each culture has verbal and nonverbal symbols of its own that are customary in this situation. The efficient cause of these displays is the circumstance of a meeting between acquaintances or friends after an absence. The material causes are more complex, since they include the features of the central nervous system that make possible individual facial recognition as well as those implicated in the production of the nonverbal and verbal greeting behavior. Other elements of the central nervous system are, however, equally important material causes of greeting behavior: if the motor cortex associated with the movement of facial muscles has been damaged, for example, some of the nonverbal displays associated with greeting will not be produced normally.

In contrast to these efficient and material causes of greeting behavior are the formal and final causes associated with the informational systems making communication possible. The form of a nonverbal greeting display, like the form of a verbal utterance of greeting, can be specified in abstract terms. The smile, defined as a pattern of the mouth, is a signal with communicative properties; similarly, the cultural forms used in greeting are defined at the level of the social system, determining which behavioral response is appropriate ("Bonjour, Monsieur" is more likely to be an appropriate greeting in France than in the United States—but can also occur if I meet a French acquaintance in New York).

The final causes of greeting displays are concerned with the adaptive functions that presumably explain their evolution. In many reptilian species, the behavioral repertoire does not include such social displays; clearly a greeting response will not be distinguished from other behaviors if an animal never encounters situations in which its survival will be enhanced by cooperative interaction with other members of its own species (MacLean 1983). Like formal causes, final causes are not directly visible, but they are essential in order to provide a complete evolutionary explanation of phenotypic traits and especially of social behavior (Roe and Simpson 1958; Lorenz 1967).

The phenomena traditionally stressed by materialist philosophers have been either efficient or material causes; idealists have tended to argue that formal or final causes have priority. It would seem that neither is correct to dismiss the other completely. Materialists and idealists were focusing on distinct but equally real problems. Neither the simplistic materialism that denies the independent role of ideas in human history nor the naive idealism that rejects material causation as a matter of principle is scientifically adequate. Among political philosophers, Aristotle exemplifies a theorist whose dialectical understanding encompasses both material and nonmaterial causal processes: his position thus seems more fully consistent with evolutionary biology than either that of Hegelians for whom the priority of the Idea is total, or of Marxists who take a mechanistic view of materialism.

THE QUARREL OF THE ANCIENTS AND THE MODERNS

Because the quarrel of the ancients and the moderns can be understood as a theoretical disagreement about the nature and direction of human history, it can be illuminated by evolutionary biology. There are, of course, other differences between ancient and modern philosophy. As Rousseau argues in his *First Discourse*, for example, the moderns replace the classic notion of "civic virtue" with a concern for "money and business" or utility; Hobbes, one of the foremost exponents of the modern view, denies there is a *"finus ultimus*, utmost aim, or *summum bonum*, highest good, such as is spoken of in the books of the ancient philosophers" (Hobbes *Leviathan* 1.11).

The theoretical controversy between the ancients and the moderns also concerns the relevance of a study of nature to political and social standards of right and wrong. Beginning with Machiavelli, and more fully developed in the tradition from Hobbes and Locke to Bentham, Mill, and contemporary social science, one strand of modernity has openly replaced the notion of virtue with a descriptive science of human behavior devoted to utility. In this view, nature at most establishes the individual's rights or claims, but not duties or obligations. Another strand of modern thought, represented most notably by Hegel and Marx, stressed the process of history; for these thinkers, standards of right and wrong are produced by culture and history rather than by individual choice and agreement. In neither case do the characteristic modern thinkers judge political life in terms of standards of excellence or virtue derived from human nature. Even the exceptional case of Rousseau seems to reinforce this difference between the ancients and moderns: though seeking to challenge his contemporaries in the name of ancient virtue (*First Discourse*), Rousseau derives natural standards of human behavior from the rights of the individual in a prepolitical state of nature (*Second Discourse*) and distinguishes sharply between humanly created political right and this natural condition (*Social Contract*).

The changed attitude toward standards of virtue that characterizes modern thought was intimately related to the belief that humans could conquer natural necessity and radically improve the human condition. This change can be associated with Machiavelli, who insists not only that he is opening a "new route" in philosophy (*Discourses on Titus Livy* 1, Introduction), but also that this novel teaching will help humans to control "fortune" or necessity (*The Prince*, chap. 25). As a result, the modern perspective shifts from virtue to utility as the means of achieving material political progress (Strauss 1953). If science makes possible a transformation of the human condition, clearly the useful is prior to the natural.

The issue dividing the ancients and moderns can therefore be restated in terms of the divergent concepts of human history that have predominated in the two epochs (Masters 1977). For the ancient philosophers, humans could at best observe and understand nature: scientific or philosophic knowledge was not expected to conquer natural necessity, overcome the political conflict between the rich and the poor, or produce a regime capable of lasting indefinitely (Plato *Republic* 8.546a; Aristotle *Politics* 7.9.1329a; 7.10.1329b; 7.13.1332a; Thucydides *History of the Peloponnesian War* 1.1–23). Following Machiavelli and especially Bacon, who was the first to speak explicitly of science "conquering nature" for "the relief of man's estate," the moderns imagined a scientific knowledge of nature capable of controlling necessity and emancipating political life from prior limitations. This view of historical progress is evident in Hobbes's claim that his theory made possible a commonwealth capable, at least in principle, of becoming "eternal" (*Leviathan* 1.11–16), as well as in Marx's assertion that humans could, and in time would, complete the "conquest" of nature and open an era of unparalleled "freedom" (*Economic and Philosophic Manuscripts of 1844* ; *German Ideology*).

Evolutionary biology speaks directly to the extent to which humans, through scientific knowledge of nature, can hope to achieve progress. The so-called modern project is hardly an absurd concept: modern genetics, as well as physics, chemistry, and the other natural sciences, has indeed achieved control over vast ranges of necessity by means of a more exact understanding of nature. At the same time, neo-Darwinian theory teaches that there is no inherent direction to natural change, and that all living species are subject to extinction just as individual organisms are subject to death. Each side in the quarrel of the ancients and the moderns touched upon a very profound element of truth, which may help explain the difficulty of resolving the debate.

As with many philosophical controversies, the issue seems insoluble until it is realized that each position deals with different phenomena. The pagan philosophers of ancient Greece did not live in communities that believed in the beneficent creation of the world as the willful action of an omnipotent monotheistic God; hence they could accept natural change without challenging religious dogma. According to Socrates in Plato's *Republic*, for example, the Muses themselves tell us that "for everything that has come into being there is decay" (*Republic* 8.546a). Even when Aristotle emphasizes the relatively unchanging character of nature as contrasted to the variability of human convention, he points out that natural things are subject to change (*Nicomachean Ethics* 5.7). Today one would have to agree: the solar system and all heavenly bodies, as well as all living things on earth, are characterized by change throughout a life cycle of birth, maturity, decay, and death. If the sun will one day burn itself out, not to mention the possibility that the entire universe may ultimately reach a state of perfect entropy, it is hard to understand what is meant by a definitive or "eternal" conquest of nature by means of human science (Hawking 1988).

The ancient view of the limits of progress could be said to focus on the overall pattern of evolutionary processes, and therewith on the question of human emancipation from the ultimate constraint of death that confronts all visible beings. Contemporary evolutionary theory concurs with the ancient view that there is no inherent directionality in the evolution or change in nature; human knowledge cannot conquer all natural necessities. Although human science may, to use Hobbes's analogy, make possible the creation of "artificial" forms of life (be they machines, animal chimeras, or human social systems) that can rival God's creation of animals for historical success (*Leviathan*, Author's Introduction), neither human artifacts nor other living beings can overcome all natural sources of change and decay.

The most famous exponents of the modern view do not respond effectively to this view of evolution: even those optimists who think of transcending the natural resource limitations of the earth through the colonization of space have to confront the ultimate death of stars like the sun, as well as the possibility of a collapse of the entire cosmos. Current models of the origin of the universe seem to approximate the cosmology of ancients like Empedocles more than that of moderns like Newton or Descartes; while only a few of the ancients, like Lucretius, seem to have understood something like biological evolution, the pagan philosophers' understanding of human history is remarkably consistent with modern evolutionary thought (Masters 1978a, 1983c).

The moderns could, however, be dealing with a different and much more limited phenomenon. Thinkers from Machiavelli, Bacon, and Hobbes to Hegel, Marx, and Engels, whatever their many differences, agree that human science can transform the day-to-day living conditions of the mass of mankind. For these moderns, this transformation would alter political and social life. It is hard to consider the effects of technology without agreeing to some degree. The impact of natural selection must have been substantially reduced to make possible the extraordinary growth in the total human population that has occurred over the last three centuries. Science and technology have probably modified daily life to a greater extent since 1900 than in the preceding two or three millennia: changes in science and technology have eradicated most epidemic diseases, expanded food supplies in both quantity and reliability, and produced human microenvironments that insulate human activity from temperature and weather.

At this level, the modern judgment has clearly been confirmed. Although the ancients were correct in thinking that the entire historical or evolutionary process could not be overcome eternally, they were wrong to assume that science and technology are incapable of controlling natural necessities in a way that can transform human society and politics over the short run. The optimism of modern political philosophers can therefore explain the immense political triumph of Western civilization in the nineteenth and twentieth centuries without being interpreted as an expectation of a total perfection of human existence; when moderns like Marx speak as if history will lead to the definitive establishment of unlimited plenty and happiness, one can suspect Victorian overoptimism rather than serious philosophic contemplation of human nature.

As this reflection suggests, reconsideration of traditional philosophic debates in the light of contemporary evolutionary biology can be very fruitful. Past philosophers were at a vast disadvantage when compared to our generation: On the one hand, we dispose of a theoretical understanding of the mechanisms of evolution that is more precise and complete than at any prior epoch; on the other, the data used to verify and deepen this theory—including fossil evidence, radioactive dating, and even comparison of the genetics and biochemistry of different species—are superior to those available even fifty years ago. Precisely for this reason, the theory of the evolutionary process and the findings concerning the emergence of the hominids have a central role in deepening our understanding of the human condition.

HUMAN NATURE AND THE STATE

Although the demonstration that human nature is intrinsically political appears to resolve the theoretical dispute about natural sociability, this issue points to the new insights made possible by the study of evolution. Many political philosophers have held that nature "dissociates" men (Hobbes *Leviathan* 1.13) or "little prepared their sociability" (Rousseau *Second Discourse*, Pt. 1). For such theorists, whose views can be traced to the Sophists in ancient Greece, political society is the result of an agreement or social contract among naturally selfish individuals for whom the gains of cooperation in a state are greater than the costs of continued competition in the "state of nature."

In this philosophical tradition, the state is unnatural because individual humans are naturally competitive or asocial. Paradoxically, contemporary research shows that although the premises of the social contract tradition in political theory are inadequate, its conclusion is sound. The existence of centralized states and governments is indeed a biological puzzle, even though empirical evidence from the study of human evolution, ethology, and cultural anthropology confirms the social and political nature of our species.

The premises of social contract theories can no longer be sustained. No living primate species studied by ethologists is totally asocial; as Köhler said, "it is hardly an exaggeration to say that a chimpanzee kept in solitude is not a real chimpanzee at all" (1959, 251). Although fossils of early hominids include little evidence of behavior as such, there are many indications of social life; by the Paleolithic epoch, our ancestors engaged in burial rituals, art, and complex toolmaking techniques—all of which imply some degree of social cooperation (chap. 1, note 4). As far as specialists are concerned, there is no question that *Homo sapiens* has always been a social animal; debate centers, rather, on the kind of group that was characteristic at various periods of hominid evolution (Portman 1961; Reynolds 1966; Fox 1967; Spuhler 1959; DeVore and Washburn 1967; Washburn and Howell 1960; Morin 1973; Thompson 1976; Isaac 1978; G. Schubert 1986).

This is not to say that the theories of Hobbes, Rousseau, and other social contract theorists were absurd; the issue they posed was very real, although it can now be stated more accurately in terms of human evolution instead of human nature. Hobbes was quite right to point to self-interest and competition as decisive problems undermining co-operation within the centralized state, just as Rousseau had good reason to challenge the presumption that inherited wealth, social class, and political institutions were part of the natural condition of mankind. Civil societies with governments and bureaucracies are nei-ther ubiquitous nor easily explained from the perspective of evolution-ary theory. Humans survived and flourished for millennia in face-to-face social groups or tribes that did not need the institution of a state; anthropological research has shown that politics exists in "stateless societies" and other primitive political systems without centralized bureaucracies (Fortes and Evans-Pritchard 1940; Lévi-Strauss [1944] 1967; Masters 1964; Harris 1977; Gruter and Masters 1986). The natu-ral status of the state is therefore not established by asserting that humans are naturally social and political.

In the tradition of thinkers like Aristotle, Aquinas, and Marx, for whom humans are naturally social, history or evolution led to the formation of political systems with organized governments. Even from this perspective, however, a definition of human nature is not adequate to explain the emergence of civilized societies and govern-ments. Since natural selection seems to prevent large-scale coopera-tive organizations like the centralized state among other mammals, the specific pattern of historical or evolutionary change leading to large-scale social systems remains a biological problem. In Book 1 of the *Politics*, Aristotle contents himself with a description of the rise of the city-state, or *polis*, without fully explaining how different human social systems came into being or why the state arose where it did. Marx argues that the division of labor gave rise to property, social class distinctions, and ultimately political authority; he does not give an account of the difference between humans and other animals that goes beyond the assertion that humans produce "freely" whereas other animals are limited by instinct or necessity (*Economic and Philo-sophic Manuscripts of 1844*; *German Ideology*).

Social contract theory, while misplaced as a description of human nature at the individual or group level, thus points to a problem not resolved by those thinkers for whom humans are naturally sociable: the origin of the state must be shown to have adaptive benefits for competing individuals who did not need to cooperate with strangers or support governments in order to survive and reproduce. Psycho-logical hedonists like Antiphon the Sophist and Hobbes therefore seem to have transposed to the individual a cost-benefit calculus like that reflecting the selective pressures against indiscriminate altruism in other species (Dawkins 1976; Campbell 1972).

For most traditional political theorists, explanations of political institutions are based on definitions of human nature that do not consider the evolutionary process in a way that is entirely consistent with contemporary biological theory. In accounting for social behavior, as for any phenotypical trait, the environment is as much a factor as the genotype (or nature) of an organism. Whatever one might say about this principle in general, it surely must be relevant to the emergence of the centralized state, since hominids have lived for so much of their evolutionary history in face-to-face groups of such a different scale and character.

From a biological perspective, the traditional concern of political theorists should be rephrased. Instead of seeking to deduce the existence of the state from human nature, we need to discover the environmental circumstances that could have led human political behavior to take a form so radically different from other mammalian social structures. More specifically, we need to find out why the natural selection against extending social cooperation to large impersonal groups was overcome. Why do people obey governments whose decisions often benefit genetic competitors, individuals or groups who are neither related to the law-abiding citizen nor guaranteed to reciprocate? In short, the problem facing political theory is not the origin of politics and society; rather, it is the foundation of civilization and the centralized state.

CHAPTER 5

The Nature of
the State

Is the State an "Unnatural" Phenomenon?

Modern governments and bureaucracies are, as Weber taught, typically related to states based on "rational-legal" norms of legitimacy (Weber 1956, 196–244). Such institutions are found in societies with comparatively large populations: in contrast to the hunter-gatherer band of fifty to one hundred members that characterized hominids for millennia, the complex societies associated with bureaucratically organized states require the cooperation of tens of thousands, or millions, of human beings. Such social cooperation, moreover, has costs for the participants: bureaucracies (as some politicians love to emphasize) absorb considerable financial resources, which citizens would often prefer to use for more immediate private consumption.

From the perspective of evolutionary biology, bureaucracies and the societies within which they emerge are surprisingly difficult to explain. Social cooperation in very large groups of animals seems to violate the basic premises of the neo-Darwinian theory of natural selection. The evolutionary process concerns behaviors as well as bodily structures (Roe and Simpson 1958), and if natural selection primarily tends to favor the reproductive success of individuals, cooperation or self-sacrifice that benefits unrelated strangers (particularly if they are not likely to return the favor) should be less adaptive than selfish or nepotistic behavior benefiting close kin and reciprocating conspecifics.

Serious consideration of this view led some biologists to wonder how altruism—or, to speak more precisely, helping behavior that can be exploited by nonkin ("sociality")—could ever occur in nature. While the problem was particularly relevant to the study of ants, bees, and other social insects, even many mammals exhibit more extensive social cooperation than might be predicted from a rigorous interpretation of natural selection at the level of the individual phenotype. But in no species is this problem as evident as in *Homo sapiens*. Beyond the traditional ethical concern for standards of virtue and vice, how does Darwinian theory explain the existence of large-scale state systems imposing legal obligations and using taxation to support bureaucratic institutions? Can the same explanations account for the growth of bureaucracy in the private sector (big business, big labor) as well as in government? Finally, do the common tensions we encounter in bureaucratic situations as well as the historical evidence of the periodic collapse of bureaucratically organized states and empires take on new light from an evolutionary perspective?

Over the past twenty years, similar issues have been posed almost simultaneously in conventional political science and in evolutionary biology. Following Anthony Downs's popularization of the well-known puzzles of welfare economics (1957), the question of collective goods became a commonplace in political science; symbolized by such models in game theory as the Prisoner's Dilemma and the Tragedy of the Commons, rational choice theory seemingly leads to the conclusion that cooperation in large-scale communities is always vulnerable to exploitation by "free riders," who benefit from the collective goods without supporting them. Unlike the more descriptive approach characterizing sociological research, formal cost-benefit models of human social cooperation thus rediscovered the traditional problem of the origin of the state, and, indeed, formulated it in a manner that was virtually identical to the social contract theory of the pre-Socratics in ancient Greece (Barry 1970; Olson 1982; Masters 1983a).

Biologists have focused on the same issue at the level of evolutionary theory, particularly since Hamilton (1964) introduced the concept of inclusive fitness to explain the existence of helping behaviors in animals. Insofar as natural selection is an optimizing mechanism that balances individual costs and benefits, it soon became evident that models derived from game theory could illuminate the behavioral strategies observed in different species (Wilson 1975; Maynard-Smith 1978). While the explanation of insect societies provided an important confirmation of the predictions of inclusive fitness theory, equally impressive empirical findings have shown the relevance of this approach to mammalian social behavior (Alexander 1974; Barash 1977) and more specifically to humans (Alexander 1977, 1979, 1981; Lumsden and Wilson 1981; Stent 1979; Chagnon and Irons 1979; van den Berghe 1979; Chase 1980a; White 1981; Axelrod and Hamilton 1981; Gruter and Bohannan 1983; Masters 1983a).

Cooperation generally entails some cost to the individual. To understand animal social behavior, biologists therefore have to discover

how individuals gain from cooperation and to show that these benefits exceed the costs. For example, under conditions of abundant and
continuously available resources, animals not subject to predation
tend to be asocial. In such situations, there is virtually no benefit from
cooperation that overbalances its costs in energy or time (Barash 1977;
Kummer 1979). Hence, in species like the lepilemur or the orangutan,
one finds asocial behavior that resembles Rousseau's state of nature to
a remarkable degree (cf. Rousseau *Second Discourse*, Pt. 1 and note j,
with Galdikas-Brindamour 1975; Masters 1978b).

According to the prevailing interpretation of inclusive fitness theory,
natural selection operates primarily, though not necessarily solely, at
the level of the individual (Williams 1966). If two organisms interact,
whether or not they cooperate can usually be predicted by a cost-
benefit calculus of the alternatives. This calculus need not be conscious;
indeed, it provides an explanation of the natural selection (sometimes
called the ultimate causation) of animal behavior in an extraordinary
number of species (Barash 1977, esp. 37–39). As in rational actor models
in economic theory, particularly when applied to questions of collective goods or public choice, all that need be assumed is that behavior
will vary as if it were a strategy chosen on the basis of cost-benefit
optimization (Maynard-Smith 1978; Hirshleifer 1978; Chase 1980a,
Margolis 1981).

In his well-known article introducing the concept of inclusive fitness, William Hamilton (1964) proposes four general "types of behavior" defined in such cost-benefit terms. When organisms interact, the
actor can derive either a net benefit or a net loss from his behavior,
and "neighbors"—that is, other organisms involved in the social
interaction—can likewise derive either a net benefit or a net loss. The
resulting fourfold table, rewritten to stress behavioral consequences
rather than subjective intention (Stent 1977; Masters 1979a),[1] has general relevance as a means of linking evolutionary biology to the study
of human institutions (figure 5.1).

This approach analyzes social behavior in terms of each individual's benefits and costs, on the assumption that observable outcomes
establish the net utility of the act. In economic theory, such cost-
benefit analysis is usually measured in monetary or materialistic
(economic) terms. Evolutionary biology substitutes long-range reproductive success—that is, the proportion of an individual's genes
transmitted to future generations of the species (Wilson 1975). Inclusive fitness thus differs from the traditional notion of survival of the
fittest in two important respects. First, natural selection favors the
ability of individuals to transmit their genes to posterity (rather than
their fitness in terms of health, power, beauty, or other physical

Figure 5.1
Hamilton's Four Types of Behavior

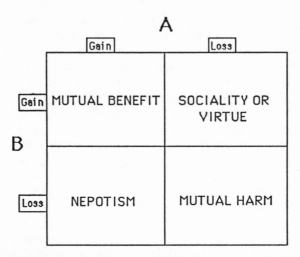

Modified from Hamilton 1964. Similar classification presented by Wilson 1975 and Barash 1977. Note that outcomes of Sociality (Virtue) and Nepotism (Selfishness) are labeled from the perspective of A; the same cells, from B's perspective, have the opposite character.

traits). Second, an organism's reproductive success can sometimes be furthered by assisting others instead of by mating (Barash 1977, 91–93; Alexander 1979).

Social biologists call the lower left cell of figure 5.1 *nepotism*, or kin selection, because the actor's positive payoff—a larger share of genes, in comparison to others, in future generations—necessarily involves favoring close kin as compared to more distant relatives or unrelated individuals.[2] In contrast, the upper left cell—*mutual benefit* (often called mutualism or reciprocity)—refers to situations in which two presumably unrelated individuals both gain from an action; among animals, such an exchange of benefits often rests on a mechanism of recognition or reciprocity that discriminates against noncooperative "free riders" (Trivers 1971).[3] *Mutual harm*, the lower right cell of figure 5.1, can occur when organisms gain more from denying themselves the use of a beneficial resource than from running the risk that it be preempted by rivals (Pierotti 1980; Wilson 1975, 119); when such interactions predominate, a species will tend to be *asocial* .

Since *nepotism*, *mutual benefit*, and *mutual harm* all refer to self-interested or "egoistic" behavior, all can be readily explained, depending on circumstances, as results of natural selection (Alexander 1974; Dawkins 1976). Situations in which an animal incurs a relative loss while potential competitors gain (the upper right cell in figure 5.1) seem harder to derive from evolutionary theory. Such group benefits or "giving" behaviors are instances of social cooperation between nonkin without personal reciprocity; anything that benefits the actor's kin is at least equally helpful to reproductive rivals and their offspring.

The cells in figure 5.1 can also be described as four categories of social partners: *kin* (others benefiting from nepotistic behavior), *allies* (others sharing mutual benefits), *nonkin* (others benefiting by sociality or the mere fact of group membership), and *enemies* (others excluded from the group that is sharing benefits, even at the risk of mutual harm). Whether a human action falls into one or another of these four cells—and hence, whether an individual responds to another as kin, as ally, as nonkin group member, or as enemy—depends on environmental conditions. At any time, moreover, humans may find a benefit in forgoing all social interaction, retreating into asocial isolation (a fifth possible consequence of Hamilton's categories). According to the circumstances, the same behavior, be it eating or defense against a predator, can thus be asocial or can generate shared benefits for kin, for allies, or for all group members.

As long as neo-Darwinian theory measured benefits (or fitness) in purely individual terms, it was hard to see how any social cooperation beyond the level of *mutual benefit* could occur. Helping behavior seemed unnatural, since an organism that loses net reproductive success to a conspecific should be at an adaptive disadvantage; hence even if a behavior that helps others should arise (whether from an individually learned response or from some genetic mutant), it should be deleterious and disappear. Discussion of this problem has been confused, however, by the use of the term "altruism" to designate helping behaviors: self-sacrificial intention is not the critical question, since the relevant evolutionary analysis concerns behavioral outcomes rather than motivation (Stent 1977; Masters 1981b). Properly framed, therefore, the issue concerns *sociality* or the very existence of social communities dependent on cooperation beyond the level of *mutual benefit* (Alexander 1977, 1979). Why do individuals refrain from selfish exploitation of others whenever they can gain by so doing? To use the old-fashioned term, what is the basis of virtue?

Hamilton's major theoretical contribution was to show that biologists had previously analyzed this phenomenon from too narrow a perspective. In addition to the genome of the individual, the costs and benefits of any behavior accrue to genes identical by descent carried in the phenotypes of kin. Hamilton pointed out that the concept of reproductive success had to be expanded to include the benefits of an animal's behavior for related organisms, since the effect of an action on the fitness of close kin—discounted by their coefficient of relatedness—would be as subject to natural selection as effects on the actor's individual fitness (Hamilton 1964). As a consequence, the measure of reproductive success is now described as inclusive fitness, that is, reproductive success or fitness *including* both an individual and that individual's close kin.

The approach to animal social behavior that resulted from Hamilton's work has been shown to be of immense explanatory value. In the present context, however, the concept of inclusive fitness does not substantially resolve the paradox of the state as a form of human social organization. Inclusive fitness theory can clearly explain why the haplo-diploid reproductive system permits the evolution of insect societies, or the circumstances in which mammals will direct helping behavior to close kin (Alexander 1974; Wilson 1975; Barash 1977). The theory can also explain many otherwise puzzling aspects of human behavior in the kin-based preliterate societies without centralized governments that have been studied over the years by anthropologists (Chagnon and Irons 1979; van den Berghe 1979; Masters 1984). But the centralized state as an institution requires social cooperation among nonkin in very large communities, which are as much of a puzzle from the perspective of inclusive fitness theory as from individual models of natural selection.

Inclusive fitness can explain why two unrelated individuals (or their close kin) might engage in helping behavior whenever they find themselves in ongoing relationships subject to future role reversals. Baptized "reciprocal altruism" by Trivers (1971) and formalized as the so-called tit-for-tat strategy in a repeated Prisoner's Dilemma (Axelrod and Hamilton 1981; Axelrod 1983), such models of mutually beneficial cooperation can easily be extended beyond a two-person situation. By considering the role of observers who identify those who cooperate or cheat and share this information, for example, Alexander (1987) shows that "indirect reciprocity" will function in much this way in small groups. The logic of cost-benefit calculations of inclusive fitness can thus explain cooperation and helping behavior among self-interested individuals in face-to-face societies. Using this approach, evolutionary theorists can account for the existence of small bands comprised primarily of extended kin, and even for the formation of larger tribal populations organized as clans or segmentary lineage systems in which there is a subtle mixture of cooperation and competition among kin-based groups (Fortes and Evans-Pritchard 1940; Masters 1964; Fox 1975). Inclusive fitness theory can thus help us to understand the likely pattern of hominid social organization over the four or five million years prior to the development of agriculture, as well as many of the particularities of the kin-based tribal societies encountered in the Western colonial expansion over the last four centuries (Korn and Thompson 1967; Chagnon and Irons 1979; Ortner 1983). In all of these settings, cooperation does not extend beyond the domain of kinship and face-to-face reciprocity and hence does not produce integrated societies whose size and power structure is difficult to explain by neo-Darwinian theory.

In analyzing very large-scale human communities, however, inclusive fitness theory leads to exactly the same conclusions as the older views of individual selfishness or reproductive success. The centralized state cannot exist without taxation, military service, and other actions of the subjects, who must contribute to collective goods that benefit members of the community indiscriminately; some of these social obligations, most notably in warfare, will inevitably fall in the category defined as helping or *sociality*. All such actions benefit other members of the society at a cost to the individual and his kin. The origin of bureaucratic institutions seems especially contrary to neo-Darwinian theory, for government officials often gain disproportionately when large states and empires extract the resources needed for their emergence and survival (Eisenstadt 1963). On theoretical grounds, humans, like other mammals, should not be expected to form cooperative societies with populations numbered in the hundreds of thousands or millions (Campbell 1972, 1975).

To resolve this problem, some biologists have invoked natural selection at the level of the group or species as a whole. Earlier theorists tried to account for social cooperation as a means by which animals contributed to the survival of their species, or at least to the survival of their own population (Wynne-Edwards 1963). Known as "group selection," this hypothesis confronted the theoretical objection that natural selection would normally undermine such behavior; any gene leading an organism to sacrifice short-term individual reproductive success for the benefit of the group as a whole would be at a disadvantage in comparison to genes carried by more "selfish" members of its species (Williams 1966). More sophisticated models of group selection have indicated possible exceptions to this general rule, but they are based on quite restrictive assumptions (such as small population sizes, sharply diverse ecological pressures, and high rates of natural selection). While these forces might explain social cooperation within relatively small groups (E. O. Wilson 1975; D. S. Wilson 1979), they do not seem adequate to explain the emergence of communities of thousands or millions of humans ruled by the institution known as the state.

The bureaucratic state—or, indeed, any society more extensive than the bands and villages characteristic of preliterate hunter-gatherers, pastoralists, or agriculturalists—thus remains an evolutionary puzzle (Masters 1983a). Since the time of Sophists in ancient Greece, political philosophers have been perplexed by the same issue and have posed it in a very similar manner. From the speech of Glaucon in Plato's *Republic* (2.357b–362c) to Hobbes's *Leviathan*, Locke's *Second Treatise of Government*, and Rousseau's *Social Contract*, the origin of the state had been explained on the assumption that individuals must gain more from entering large communities than they lose by forgoing opportunities to compete with nonkin. Hence the issue cannot be dismissed as an artifact of a politically biased commitment to genetic determinism, as some Marxist critics of sociobiology have charged (Caplan 1978); on the contrary, all social and political theory—from economics, rational choice or collective goods theory, and game theory to traditional political philosophy—must answer the same problem if it is to account for the existence and perpetuation of states and bureaucracies (Rosenberg 1980; White 1981; Masters 1982a, 1983a, 1983b).

Inclusive Fitness Theory and Human Social Institutions

As this exposition makes clear, contemporary neo-Darwinian theory requires a fundamental shift in our understanding of social behavior. Whereas political philosophers and social scientists usually treat the question of *sociability*—whether humans are naturally selfish or cooperative—as an attribute of human nature, biology now teaches us that the existence and structure of social groups varies, even within a single species, as a consequence of the interaction between animals and their environment. A species that is asocial in one setting may be social in others (Beckoff and Wells 1980; Wrangham 1980). From a scientific perspective, therefore, it is misleading to conceptualize social behavior as a constant natural trait (such as two eyes, one nose, and one mouth in the human face).

The conventional wisdom according to which biology can explain the existence of human society, but not the differences between human cultures, is thus inadequate: the emergence of large-scale human societies and formal legal systems must be treated as a scientific problem (Wilson 1975; Alexander 1977; Campbell 1972). The usual answers to this problem violate the premises of evolutionary theory because they assume that the state is beneficial to the group, results from chance, or is an act of human creation (for example, St. Thomas

Aquinas *Summa Theologica* 1–2, questions 90–97; Machiavelli *Discourses on Titus Livy* 1.2, 1.9). None of these conventional explanations is tenable without a careful consideration of the selective pressures against institutions like the state in other animals and during most of hominid evolution.

Since contemporary theories of natural selection stress the priority of individual reproductive success (E. O. Wilson 1975; Trivers 1981), one can never presume that a behavior has been selected because it redounds to the benefit of the population or species. But it is equally erroneous to assume that, as a matter of principle, natural selection never generates behavior of this sort (D. S. Wilson 1979; Masters 1981b). Indeed, much recent theoretical work suggests a dialectical relationship between individual inclusive fitness and group interest (Alexander and Borgia 1978; Layzer 1978; Wade 1980), particularly in a complex social species like *Homo sapiens* (Hoffman 1981; Margolis 1982).

Many species have specialized in one or two of the five kinds of behavior described as *asociality, nepotism, mutual benefit, sociality,* and *mutual harm.* But if environments change or are uncertain, a diverse and more plastic repertoire will be selected (Real 1980). Humans, thanks to larger brains and complex linguistic systems, seem to have exploited a broader range of social alternatives than most other animals. Moreover, the emergence of *mutual benefit* or *sociality,* not to mention occasions of *mutual harm,* in no way abolishes the adaptiveness of *nepotism* or, in appropriate conditions, *asociality.* In conventional terms, humans combine "selfishness" and "self-interested" cooperation with "altruism" and "spite" to an often bewildering degree (Stent 1979).

Social biology thus gives us a more precise understanding of the difference between human social behavior and that of other gregarious animals. Inclusive fitness theory leads to a prediction that the likely costs and benefits of alternative behaviors will vary depending on ecological circumstances and the individual's social role, prior experience, age, or sex. Humans, especially because of their intelligence, are capable of exploiting many if not all of the possible alternatives in a single day or even a single hour. Moreover, *sociality* or virtue among nonkin creates a situation in which cheating—that is, pretending to cooperate while actually engaging in *nepotism* ("selfish" behavior)— has greater payoffs than reciprocity, provided, of course, that it goes undetected (Plato *Republic* 2.359b–360d; Trivers 1981, 9–39; Willhoite 1981).

Humans manipulate this repertoire of social possibilities by means of a dual transformation of the cost-benefit calculus observed in animal behavior. At the individual level, the assessment of the interpersonal situation (the categories in figure 5.1) is transformed—usually in a conscious way, but sometimes through repression or self-deception—into a subjective motive. These psychological responses are further molded into sociocultural institutions, which, while superficially associated with a corresponding psychological motive, actually use diverse assessments of the world (Masters 1983a, table 1). Since each biological situation can generate any of the five motivational responses and each of the individual motives can produce behaviors at any of the five institutional levels, a reductionist science of human behavior is highly improbable if not impossible (Schubert 1981; Stent 1979; Anderson 1982).

Language, of course, is what enables humans to engage in this dual transformation of natural potentialities. In other species, although intention can be inferred from observed behavior (Lorenz [1931–63] 1970–71; Hearne 1987), subjective events cannot be perceived directly and so cannot serve as objective social signals or symbols. In contrast, human language permits this duality, since words can be used either in silent thought or in audible speech. Probably grounded in the unusual structure of phonemic utterances described above as triadic patterning, speech can thus establish cultural rules and social institutions based on shared meaning (Crook 1981). To put it more simply, language enables humans to establish cultures to a degree apparently impossible in other animals (Aristotle *Politics* 1.2.1253a; Hobbes *Leviathan* 1.4).

This property of speech makes it possible to link evolutionary theory with the conventional social sciences. Human institutions, in their bewildering variety and complexity, are constituted by the attributes defining who is included, who is excluded, and how participants are expected to behave. When social institutions are described, however, different levels of analysis such as the family, the business firm or market economy, and the state or community are distinguished. Mediated by psychological assessments and motives, these familiar institutions correspond in a rough way to categories of animal social interaction, but have been transformed as the result of human language.

Among humans, situations that other animals usually, though not always (Griffin 1976; Bonner 1980), "live" in an unreflective manner have become distinct and often contradictory phenomena of individual consciousness and cultural rules. This means that animal instinct and human learning are different ways of responding to similar problems created by environmental conditions and individual needs (cf. Aristotle *Politics* 8.17.1337a). Hence the concepts of inclusive fitness theory are relevant to complex human institutions like the state, even though human social behavior often has different proximate causes than that of other species.

Cost-Benefit Theories of Cooperation

As Brian Barry (1970) has argued, there are two broad traditions in the social sciences: economic models, in which aggregate phenomena are analyzed as if individuals rationally calculated the costs and benefits of alternatives, and sociological approaches, which treat entire systems as having properties that cannot be deduced from individual choices (cf. Mills 1959). A similar duality of methods can be discerned in the biological sciences (Williams 1966; Alexander and Borgia 1978; Masters 1982a). Since both inclusive fitness theory in biology and economic or rational actor models in the social sciences are based on a cost-benefit analysis, it has been argued that they can be integrated into a single approach (Hirshleifer 1977, 1987; Chase 1980a; Margolis 1982). This prospect is particularly relevant to research concerning the state, because rational actor theories of public choice or collective goods, akin to those in economics, have increasingly been adopted by political scientists (Downs 1957; Olson 1965, 1982; Hirschman 1974; Sullivan, Nakamura, and Winters 1980).

To indicate how inclusive fitness theory is related to social science, it is convenient to begin with game theory, which has been used by many social biologists to explain the costs and benefits of alternative behavioral strategies (Trivers 1971; Maynard-Smith 1978; McEachron and Baer 1982). In particular, the well-known Prisoner's Dilemma is a fruitful way of examining the problem of cooperation. This class of games has been widely used in the social sciences (Kaplan 1957; Axelrod 1980a, 1980b, 1981), and has also been applied in explanations of animal social life (Axelrod and Hamilton 1981; Axelrod 1983; Boyd 1988). For the sake of exposition, consider the following example of the Prisoner's Dilemma.

> Two men, A and B, have collaborated in stealing $20, which they split fifty-fifty. They have been caught and placed in separate jail cells with no possibility of communicating with each other. The jailer tells them that if both remain silent, evidence for a full prosecution is lacking and they will be released with a fine of $1 each (leaving both A and B with a net gain of $9 each). If one of the two talks, but the other does not, the prisoner who talks ("defector") will go scot free (net gain: $10), while the silent pris-

oner ("sucker") will be forced to return his share of the stolen
money and be fined $10 or given a comparable jail sentence (net
cost: -$10). If both talk, both forfeit the money and are fined $9 or
given a proportional term in jail (net cost: -$9 each). For A and B
jointly, this last result is the worst possible outcome, since all the
stolen money is forfeited and both are punished (fine or term in
jail). Yet it is this worst outcome for the two collectively that is
chosen if A and B decide their actions "rationally" on the basis of
a cost-benefit calculation. This follows because each individual
must try to gain the most (or lose the least) regardless of the
other's action in circumstances prohibiting communication. A
gains more (or loses less) by talking than by silence if B is silent *or*
if B talks; B, deciding separately, makes the same calculation.

The game matrix for this Prisoner's Dilemma is set forth in figure
5.2. This game has at least three essential conditions. First, the payoffs must be transitive (in the example, $+10 > +9 > -9 > -10$).
Second, each actor independently chooses a strategy that will maximize his gains (or minimize his losses). Third, communication or
behavioral coercion between the actors is not allowed. Under these
circumstances, as game theorists are fond of pointing out, it is rational
for both A and B to choose the outcome in which both lose, since for
each individual the strategy of talking (defecting) has a higher payoff
than silence (cooperating).

On a moment's reflection, figure 5.2 will be seen to contain the
same basic categories as figure 5.1 (derived from inclusive fitness
theory). The difference is that the Prisoner's Dilemma specifies a set
of environmental constraints and then seeks to predict the strategy
that will be chosen, whereas Hamilton's more general model defines
the basic options in any set of environmental conditions. Hence, the
Prisoner's Dilemma can be taken as a special case of the general
theory, albeit one that is particularly useful in explaining many coun-
terintuitive situations.

One major consequence of this similarity deserves emphasis. The
labels in these figures concern the four outcomes as defined from the
perspective of A. In the Prisoner's Dilemma, what is *nepotism* ("selfishness") from the perspective of A will be *sociality* or virtue ("altruism")
from B's point of view. One man's meat is another man's poison. Is it
any wonder that humans often suspect the motivations of others and
proclaim the innocence of their own intentions (even if, or rather
especially if, these intentions are consistent with their long-range self-
interest)? As Trivers (1971, 1981) has shown, humans seem to special-
ize in deceit to cheat on their partners, in moralistic aggression against

Figure 5.2
Prisoner's Dilemma: Nonkin

A's Strategy

	Silent	Talk
Silent	A= +9 B= +9 MUTUAL BENEFIT	A= +10 B= -10 NEPOTISM*
Talk	A= -10 B= +10 SOCIALITY OR VIRTUE*	A= -9 B= -9 MUTUAL HARM

B's Strategy

*Game matrix for a typical Prisoner's Dilemma. Assumptions: Two-person game in which communication or behavioral coercion between A and B is impossible and payoffs are transitive and commensurable (cheating > cooperating > joint punishment > virtue or being a "sucker"—or, to use conventionally adopted symbols, T > R > P > S). It is also necessary that "the positive effect of cooperation on the fitness of the recipient must exceed its negative effects on the fitness of the donor. This condition implies that R > (T+S)/2 > P (Boyd 1988, 214). In this example, T (cheating) = +10; R (cooperating) = +9; P (punishment) = -9; S (virtue) = -10. *Nepotism (private self-interest—here "cheating" by talking when other is silent) and sociality (virtue—here being silent while the other talks) are defined in terms of A's payoffs.*

those who cheat, and in deceitful imitation of compliance and morality to avoid punishment.

Even if the Prisoner's Dilemma is useful in analyzing such problems of social cooperation, what is gained by extending this model to evolutionary theory? To illustrate the unexpected consequences of linking game theory with inclusive fitness theory, consider a Prisoner's Dilemma in which the two prisoners are full siblings or father and son. If the coefficient of relatedness between A and B is 1/2, A's payoff for each cell of the matrix must be rewritten to include one-half of B's payoff (which also accrues to A), and vice versa. When we recalculate the game matrix in this way (figure 5.3), the strategy of cooperating

Figure 5.3
Prisoner's Dilemma: Kin

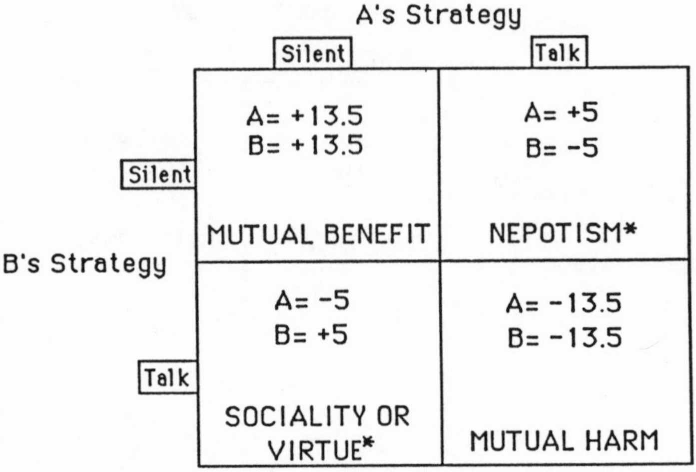

A's Strategy

	Silent	Talk
Silent	A= +13.5 B= +13.5 MUTUAL BENEFIT	A= +5 B= -5 NEPOTISM*
Talk	A= -5 B= +5 SOCIALITY OR VIRTUE*	A= -13.5 B= -13.5 MUTUAL HARM

B's Strategy

Game matrix for Prisoner's Dilemma with same assumptions as in figure 5.2, except that participants are kin (either full siblings or parent-offspring) with a coefficient of relatedness of r = .5). *Hence in each cell, A adds .5 of B's payoff in figure 5.2 to his own payoff, and B does the same for A's payoffs. *As in figure 5.2, nepotism (private self-interest) and sociality (virtue) are defined in terms of A's payoff.*

now dominates that of defecting for each prisoner, regardless of the response of the other. Rather than resulting in mutual harm, the same payoffs lead to cooperation and mutual benefit. It should be little wonder that organized crime is often structured in "families" based on pseudokinship, if not real kin relations, or that states often use symbols of kinship (fatherland, motherland, fraternity) to legitimate obedience (Reynolds, Falger, and Vine 1987).

The value of the payoffs in this example influences the outcome in a particularly interesting way. If the cost of a selfish strategy (defecting from the cooperative agreement by talking) is reduced without changing the other formal properties of the game, even kin will not cooperate. To see this, consider kin whose coefficient of relatedness is 1/2 (as in the last example) confronting a Prisoner's Dilemma in which the payoffs are the same except that the punishment if both talk is reduced from −9 to −3. As the game matrix of figure 5.4 indicates, cooperation is no longer the rational cost-benefit strategy even for

Figure 5.4
Prisoner's Dilemma: Kin (Reduced Punishment)

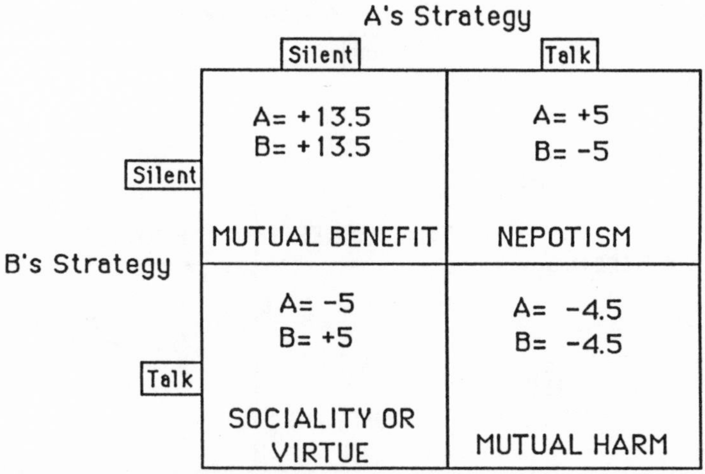

A's Strategy

	Silent	Talk
Silent	A= +13.5 B= +13.5 MUTUAL BENEFIT	A= +5 B= -5 NEPOTISM
Talk	A= -5 B= +5 SOCIALITY OR VIRTUE	A= -4.5 B= -4.5 MUTUAL HARM

B's Strategy

Prisoner's Dilemma with same assumptions as in figure 5.3, except that cost of punishment has been reduced; payoffs now: T = +10 > R = +9 > P = −3 > S = −10.

close kin; although virtue is the best policy if the other cooperates, it provides a worse outcome if the kinsman defects.[4] As parents often notice, children who cooperate when there is a significant outside threat—or when the punishment for fighting is high enough—often squabble over trivia (Trivers 1981).

When kin are confronted with a competitive situation like the Prisoner's Dilemma of figure 5.4, an alternative to more severe punishment of the guilty lies in greatly increasing the rewards of cooperation. If, for example, one promises a greater reward for mutual silence, and if the payoff for selfishness is not very much greater than that of mutual benefit, then a competitive game can also be converted into a cooperative one. For instance, the Prisoner's Dilemma of figure 5.4 becomes a cooperative game if the payoff for mutually beneficial silence is increased without enlarging the incremental benefit of defection over virtue (figure 5.5). Religions, by promising greater rewards for virtue in the afterlife, are an obvious example of social circumstances that can have this effect. In preliterate societies without a centralized government, for instance, competition between lineages or clans often put individuals in situations akin to a Prisoner's Di-

Figure 5.5
Prisoner's Dilemma: Kin (Increased Reward)

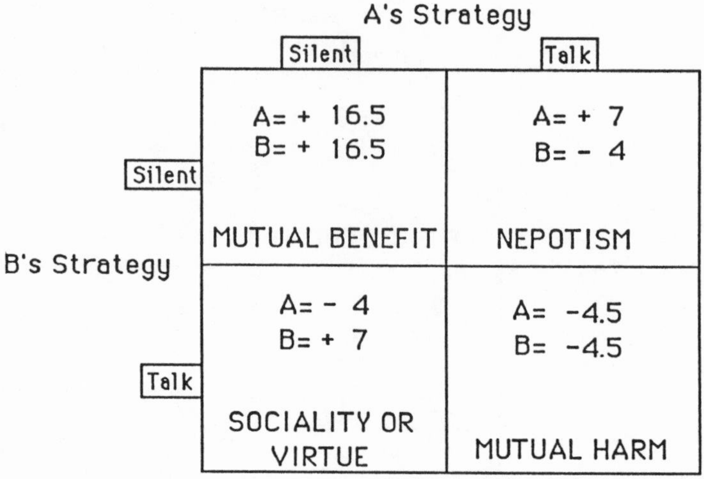

A's Strategy

	Silent	Talk
Silent	A= + 16.5 B= + 16.5 MUTUAL BENEFIT	A= + 7 B= − 4 NEPOTISM
Talk	A= − 4 B= + 7 SOCIALITY OR VIRTUE	A= −4.5 B= −4.5 MUTUAL HARM

B's Strategy

Prisoner's Dilemma with same assumptions as in figure 5.4, except that rewards have been increased; payoffs now: $T = +12 > R = +11 > P = -3 > S = -10$.

lemma; such clans or lineages are typically united by common ancestor worship and other rituals promising benefits for those supporting the kin group.

As these examples suggest, the cost-benefit calculus of inclusive fitness theory leads to the prediction that social cooperation is most likely either when the partners can gain mutual and reciprocal benefits, or when they are kin confronting an environment that either punishes selfishness severely or greatly rewards cooperation, or both. Unlike conventional theories of social cooperation, it will be noted that both the environmental circumstances and the kinship of the players can make a difference. In the structure of payoffs in figure 5.4, for instance, a relatively large punishment for the so-called sucker, or virtuous prisoner, actually contributes to the outcome of mutual harm instead of preventing it, because when both guilty parties are caught, their joint punishment is relatively small. Social behavior is influenced by both genes and environment.

Generalizing from this example, one can see the reasons that a rigorous punishment for deviant behavior need not be an effective deterrent if its administration is haphazard and unlikely, as well as the reasons for the extremely violent reactions to defection in social systems organized on the basis of self-help. In stateless societies where law is enforced by kin groups (Fortes and Evans-Pritchard 1940; Barkun 1963; Gruter and Masters 1986), as in organized crime, the feud or its equivalent can be effective as a means of enforcing cooperation within the "family."

Other natural factors that could inhibit or facilitate self-sacrifice or virtue can be illustrated by analyzing the Prisoner's Dilemma. For example, when confronted with multiple plays of a Prisoner's Dilemma like that in figure 5.2, the most reliable way to avoid mutual harm is called a tit-for-tat strategy, in which one responds with the same behavior that the other player or organism used in the previous round (Axelrod and Hamilton 1981). The virtuous response in a series of encounters between nonkin cannot otherwise be simply established as the best policy, because such a strategy is vulnerable to cheating by a free rider who thereby gets the benefits of the virtue of others without paying the costs.

From the perspective of game theory, therefore, social cooperation between nonkin usually occurs only in cases of mutual benefit such as those marked by relations of reciprocity (Taylor and McGuire 1988). To be sure, the decision rule need not be tit-for-tat. Maynard-Smith (1978) has shown that the location of an interaction can also serve as a behavioral rule, leading to a mutually beneficial "bourgeois" strategy of deferring to the other individual when one is on the other's turf. Other formalizations include Hirshleifer's "tender trap" (1982), a game in which any rule of behavior that permits an actor to predict what others will do is preferable to the absence of rules. All these models can be used to develop Trivers's original insight that reciprocity can produce mutually beneficial social cooperation among nonkin, even in circumstances of short-term loss to the cooperator (Aristotle *Ethics* 5.5.1132b–5.6.1134b).

This approach can readily explain not only nepotism and mutual benefit, but also virtue or, to use the language of rational actor theory, the choice of collective goods. Although this choice may be rare in other species, humans occasionally act in the group interest even when reciprocity is unlikely or is deferred beyond the temporal framework of the alternatives. Game theory is a useful way to illustrate the origins of such sociality or virtue, especially because it reveals the critical role of coercive restraints imposed by an impersonal and bureaucratic state.

Although the problem of collective goods can be analyzed in terms of an n-person Prisoner's Dilemma (R. Hardin 1971; McLean 1981), for heuristic purposes it is clearer to consider a similar model that Garrett

Hardin popularized as the "Tragedy of the Commons." In these situations, one individual can be considered to be playing a game against
each of many neighbors.

> Picture a pasture open to all. It is to be expected that each herds-
> man will try to keep as many cattle as possible on the com-
> mons. . . . As a rational being, each herdsman seeks to maximize
> his gain. . . . Adding together the component partial utilities, the
> rational herdsman concludes that the only sensible course for
> him to pursue is to add another animal to his herd. And another;
> and another. . . . But this is the conclusion reached by each and
> every rational herdsman sharing a commons. Therein is the trag-
> edy. Each man is locked into a system that compels him to in-
> crease his herd without limit—in a world that is limited. (G. Har-
> din 1968)

Many ecologists have agreed with Hardin's argument that this situation approximates a wide range of phenomena, from the exhaustion
of scarce natural resources to the pollution of the environment (Cole
1980).

To show how game theory and inclusive fitness theory can be combined in the analysis of social institutions, consider the Tragedy of the
Commons as a game with many players choosing independently
whether or not to add to their herds. Since each knows that his decision cannot influence the choice of the others, it is inevitable that
some herdsmen will adopt conflicting strategies (here called strategy
A and strategy B). Assume that, ultimately, the commons will support only the xth cow of one set of strategists (either A's or B's, but not
both). Nobody knows, however, either the value of x (that is, the
number of cows at which the carrying capacity is exceeded) or the
number of players adopting each strategy.

The game has two outcomes, one in the short run (the addition of a
single cow; figure 5.6), the other over a longer term (figure 5.7). In the
short run, everyone will add a cow, for the same reason that both
prisoners talk in the simple Prisoner's Dilemma: to do otherwise
would be a gratuitous act of sociality, incurring loss for no benefit.
Unlike the Prisoner's Dilemma, however, this selfish strategy is also
mutually beneficial in the short run (figure 5.6); it is only later that
losses are encountered.

If the carrying capacity of the commons is exceeded in the long run
(figure 5.7), the mutual harm to all participants will be incommensur-
ably large. Virtue (not adding cows) entails a loss, particularly compared to the strategy of nepotism or private self-interest; but the danger that everyone will seek such a selfish outcome makes self-restraint

Figure 5.6
Tragedy of the Commons: Short Run—Add 1 Cow

Strategy A

	Don't Add Cow	Add Cow
Don't Add Cow	A= -1 B= -1 MUTUAL HARM	A= +1 B= -1 NEPOTISM*
Add Cow	A= -1 B= +1 SOCIALITY*	A= +1 B= +1 MUTUAL BENEFIT

Strategy B

Game matrix for the short-run outcomes of the Tragedy of the Commons.
Assumptions: An n-person game in which each actor knows that only two strategies
exist, and that others are free to choose either. All cows have a marginal utility =
+1. For the nongame theoretic presentation of this choice situation, see Hardin
*1968. *As in figures 5.2–5.5, nepotism (private self-interest) and sociality*
(virtue) are defined in terms of A's payoffs.

relatively beneficial as soon as there is a high enough probability that mutual harm can be prevented. The problem is that no one knows which will be the xth cow. Hence, without some form of organization, it is impossible to focus on the long-term game, the players continue to calculate only immediate benefits and costs, and the tragedy seems inevitable.

Transforming the players into two groups is a way out. If those adopting strategy B could coerce the A's into limiting their herds, while the B's themselves added cows, the latter could gain the benefits of nepotism; but for the losers, virtue still has its rewards, since the outcome of being coerced is preferable to mutual harm. By not adding cows, the A strategists avoid catastrophe even though they know that their rivals may be less than perfectly virtuous. And if the commons or collective goods can be expanded—for example, by joint work or by conquest—even the group with the relatively inferior strategy can gain the mutual benefits of extending the short-run game beyond the original limits of the resource base.

Figure 5.7
Tragedy of the Commons Long Run—Add Xth Cow

Strategy   A

	Don't Add Cow	Add Cow
Don't Add Cow	A= X−1 B= X−1 MUTUAL BENEFIT	A= X+1 B= X−1 NEPOTISM
Add Cow	A= X−1 B= X+1 SOCIALITY	A= X−1000 B= X−1000 MUTUAL HARM

Strategy B

Game matrix for long-term outcome of the Tragedy of the Commons. Same assumptions as in figure 5.6, except that the addition of cows reaches the limit at which the commons can support an xth cow if added by either A strategists or B strategists, but not by both groups; value of x is unknown. Note how the strategic situation in which both A's and B's "Add Cow" is transformed from mutual benefit (short-term outcome in figure 5.6) to mutual harm. The solution of having only one group of individuals that gains the additional benefits of "adding cows," while giving the A's a relative advantage over the B's, also gives the B's an advantage over their own outcome if both groups seek to perpetuate short-term benefits. For implications, see Hardin 1968 and Ophuls 1973, 1977.

From this perspective, citizens can benefit from the political community only by accepting the risk that those with power will gain disproportionately from their role as enforcers of the social contract (Margolis 1982, chap. 9). Governments thus can be described as providing the service of coordinating social behavior, exacting a "side-payment" for protecting the collective goods (Laver 1981, chap. 3). Once begun, such institutions can create considerable mutual benefits for all members as long as obedience to social rules prevents a Tragedy of the Commons. Under these conditions, it can be rational for self-interested individuals to form a political society, even if it will occasionally entail self-sacrifice or virtue, including paying taxes, serving in the army, and even dying in defense of the community (Alexander 1978; Hirshleifer 1982; R. Hardin 1971).

It is relatively straightforward to move from such simplified models of game theory to more precise versions of rational choice theory (Olson 1965; Laver 1981; Hirshleifer 1987). Not only does this approach suggest that the economists' distinction between selective benefits and collective goods can be founded on evolutionary biology, but it explains the origin of the state and its ultimate fragility and disintegration (Campbell 1983). Cooperation can readily arise in small groups of extended kin (figure 5.3) and can even expand to mutually beneficial exchanges between nonkin (figure 5.6). But as soon as collective goods come into question—for instance, when groups compete for nondivisible resources or the ecological carrying capacity is approached—the risk of mutual harm increases the benefits of enforceable norms; free riders can be punished by a coercive government, and well-organized groups often have the option of conquering weaker or less cohesive groups.

Anthropologists have long debated whether the state arose from intragroup cooperation or intergroup conflict (Cohen and Service 1978). The present approach suggests that both hypotheses are likely to be correct. Indeed, both processes were probably necessary to overcome the great selective disadvantage of extending sociality to a society of hundreds of thousands of nonkin (in which mutual benefit cannot be based on personal reciprocity or individual recognition of the free riders). Once established, however, social cooperation within a state can create extensive mutual benefits, as symbolized by the awesome growth in the human population that has been associated with the spread of centralized political institutions over the last ten thousand years.

Paradoxically, it is the very success of the state that creates its vulnerability. Legal rules that are enforced by a government constitute collective goods that are subject to violation in order to reap selfish benefits. Empirical evidence seems to confirm that the decline of prior civilizations is related to, if not caused by, overexploitation of environmental resources associated with a lack of individual self-restraint and virtue. With good reason, Garrett Hardin (1968) reminds us that the mere existence of the state does not guarantee immunity from the Tragedy of the Commons (Machiavelli *Discourses on Titus Livy* 1.2, 3.1; Plato *Republic* 8.546a–547c; Aristotle *Politics* 5.2.1302–1302b, 5.12.1316a–1316b).

Inclusive Fitness Theory and Political Philosophy

It should not be surprising that models of rational decision-making can be so easily related to inclusive fitness theory: both deduce social behavior from a calculus of individual costs and benefits. But recent evolutionary theory can be linked to more traditional approaches in political science as well. In Western political philosophy, for example, definitions of human nature and the origin of the state frequently parallel the concepts of evolutionary biology. This proposition can be readily illustrated by considering the thought of some of the best-known modern political theorists.

Hobbes's political theory is easily translated into the terms of inclusive fitness and rational actor models. The Hobbesian "natural condition of mankind" is marked primarily by nepotism or selfishness, since cooperation is essentially limited to the kin group based on "natural lust." As a result, social interaction readily degenerates into mutual harm ("war of all against all") unless, for reasons of mutual benefit ("natural right"), individuals are induced to agree ("social contract") to form a political community or state ("commonwealth"). Hobbes thus not only denies that sociality, or virtue, is natural; he is unable to justify any case of self-sacrifice on the basis of natural right alone. Individuals can—and, if rational, always will—reclaim their natural independence whenever they fear for their continued safety and self-interest (Hobbes *Leviathan* 1.13–14).

Hobbes's state of nature is like a Prisoner's Dilemma or Tragedy of the Commons (Ophuls 1973b; McLean 1981) and can be escaped only through a freely accepted arbiter or a sovereign capable of imposing restraints on short-term self-interest. In other words, the Hobbesian solution can be viewed as an n-person game (as in figures 5.6 and 5.7) in which each A strategist agrees with the other A's to accept the rule of a B strategist or strategists who, as "sovereign," is not party to the social contract. Even though such a sovereign may reap a selfish benefit compared to each individual subject, it is rational to form a commonwealth because the result permits the A strategists to avoid the large negative payoffs of mutual harm ("war of all against all") while preserving short-term mutual benefits.

The same cost-benefit calculus persists within society as in the state of nature. Since "no man can transfer, or lay down his right to save himself from death, wounds, and imprisonment," even convicted criminals can be expected to try to escape legitimate and just punishment: "For man by nature chooseth the lesser evil, which is danger of death in resisting; rather than the greater, which is certain and present death in not resisting" (Hobbes *Leviathan* 1.14). Pure sociality or virtue benefiting the group as a whole cannot be relied upon, since men are "not bound to hurt themselves," nor are they bound "to warfare, unless they voluntarily undertake it" (Hobbes *Leviathan* 1. 21).

Neither mutual benefit nor sociality (virtue) can exist without a centralized state to induce self-sacrifice through fear.

> Therefore before the names of just, and unjust can have place, there must be some coercive power, to compel men equally to the performance of their covenants, by the terror of some punishment, greater than the benefit they expect by the breach of their covenant; and to make good that propriety, which by mutual contract men acquire, in recompense of the universal right they abandon; and such power there is none before the erection of a commonwealth. (Hobbes *Leviathan* 1.15, 113)

Contract—and hence presumed mutual benefit—is the only reliable ground on which humans will risk their lives to defend the state and the nonkin who live in it, but even a contract is binding only if there is a sovereign capable of enforcing it.

Rousseau criticized Hobbes in two different ways, each of which becomes clearer if formulated in terms consistent with evolutionary biology. First, he attacks Hobbes for presuming that the family, and therewith a warlike state of nature between kin groups, is natural (Rousseau *Second Discourse* pt. 1). Since asocial or purely egoistic behavior is a conceivable means of survival in some species, institutions based on the perpetuation of a bond between parents cannot be taken for granted. And once the family is analyzed as the result of a prior evolution away from asociality, the original state of nature must be presumed to have been "peaceful" and "solitary," at least as a heuristic model or a hypothesis.

> Let us conclude that wandering in the forests, without industry, without speech, without domicile, without war and without liaisons, with no need for his fellow-men, likewise with no desire to harm them, perhaps never even recognizing anyone individually, savage man, subject to few passions and self-sufficient, had only the sentiments and intellect suited to that state. . . . (Rousseau *Second Discourse* pt. 1, 137)

According to Rousseau, therefore, Hobbes makes the mistake of taking as natural a condition that is the result of historical change (Masters 1968, chap. 3).

Rousseau's second major criticism of Hobbes is diametrically opposed to the first. Having argued that the original condition of the species was less social than Hobbes assumed, Rousseau also concludes that cultural institutions can be more social or virtuous than the Hobbesian commonwealth. Rousseau's *Social Contract* criticizes

Hobbesian theory for focusing on mutual benefit rather than on a patriotic community for which individuals would virtuously sacrifice their lives. Whereas Hobbes limits reciprocity or mutualism to those common institutions that are in the individual's self-interest, Rousseau seeks a logic of reciprocity ("principles of political right") that could generate binding obligations constituting the group's collective interest ("general will").

Like Hobbes, Rousseau explicitly treats the agreement to found a society as a calculation of cost and benefit: "Let us reduce the pros and cons to easily compared terms. What man loses by the social contract is his natural freedom and an unlimited right to everything that tempts him and that he can get; what he gains is civil freedom and the proprietorship of everything he possesses" (Rousseau *Social Contract* 1.8). But unlike Hobbes, Rousseau insists that consent to enter the political community generates a duty to sacrifice for it—that is, the essential condition of sociality that Rousseau explicitly calls the "virtue" of the "citizen" (Rousseau *First Discourse; Emile* 1). The willingness to die in defense of the state, dismissed by Hobbes as not binding without a specific contractual commitment, becomes a moral obligation of citizenship for Rousseau (*Social Contract* 2.4).

Rousseau thus seeks to reconstruct an evolutionary theory of the origins of the civilized community, accepting Hobbes's critique of theories that assume natural sociality, but nonetheless achieving a level of communal unity that Hobbes rejects as naturally impossible. Rousseau agrees that one must adopt a social contract model of the origin of the state, but disagrees with Hobbes's concept of human nature both as an original condition and as a limit of political possibility. The paradoxical mixture of individualism and collectivism, which has led many readers to accuse Rousseau of inconsistency (Charvet 1974), can therefore be traced to a single view of human evolution: Precisely because humans were not competitive in the original state of nature, they could develop virtue in a freely constituted political community (Masters 1978b, 1980b, 1968).

Kantian ethics, in this view, transform Rousseau's understanding of virtue by seeking to remove its limits. Whereas Rousseau's social contract cannot bind anyone who does not share the patriotic spirit symbolized by ancient Sparta and Rome (Rousseau *Geneva Manuscript* 1.2; *Political Economy*), Kant seeks a principle of social obligation that is pure and free of all empirically determined or emotional limitations (Kant, *Metaphysical Foundations of Morals*, 140–208). Although Kant is often regarded as an abstract metaphysician whose thought is unrelated to natural science (and especially to biology), this interpretation is highly questionable (Hjort 1938; Stent 1979); rather, Kantian ethics can be viewed as a scientific response to the "natural" limitations on social cooperation adduced by both Hobbes and Rousseau.

Kant's ethical teaching is based on the observation that the "disposition" or motive of "duty" is never observed unambiguously:

> If we attend to the experience of men's conduct, we meet frequent and, as we admit ourselves, just complaints that there is not to be found a single certain example of the disposition to act from pure duty. Although many things are done in conformity to what duty prescribes, it is nevertheless always doubtful whether they are done strictly out of duty. (Kant, *Metaphysical Foundations of Morals*, 154)

Kant saw that pure altruism would require a motive uncontaminated by self-interest, and the existence of such a motive is "always doubtful." As contemporary social biology indicates, there is reason enough to raise this question with regard to humans as well as to other species (Wispé 1978; Kummer 1979b). Kant answers by denying that morality could ever be deduced from "particular attributes of human nature," insisting that it is only in abstraction from empirical interests and facts that a man-made, rational "imperative" to self-sacrifice is possible: "every empirical element is not only quite incapable of aiding the principle of morality, but is even highly prejudicial to the purity of morals" (Kant, *Metaphysical Foundations of Morals*, 174). Hence, Kant's categorical imperative is "unconditional," "not grounded in any interest," and thereby sharply different from considerations of "market price" or mutual benefit that could apply to the behavior of other animals (ibid. 180, 182).

Kant maintains that there is no naturalistic ground for virtue other than an act of the free human will imposing on itself a rational obligation as an end in itself. The individual, generalizing his rule of choice ("maxim") into a law governing all rational beings, engages in a logical transformation of the situation that is not unlike Rousseau's "general will"—except that for Kant, the categorical imperative is addressed to all humans as rational beings, not to all fellow-citizens as members of the same admittedly contingent political community (Rousseau, *Political Economy*, 218–20). This means that, for Kant, moral obligation is a pure case of sociality, since the individual acts morally without any expectation of personal gain in the short or long run. Whereas Trivers's "reciprocal altruism" includes elements of mutual benefit and even of nepotism, Kant thus provides a logic of freely willed virtue without any conceivable admixture of self-interest.

Hegel's *Philosophy of Right* is an extraordinary attempt to transcend the divergences between the theoretical perspectives of Hobbes, Rous-

seau, and Kant. The first part, "Abstract Right," could be viewed as
the perspective of Hobbes (Hegel, *Philosophy of Right*, 37–74); the second, dealing with morality, focuses on the dimension that Rousseau
and especially Kant found lacking in Hobbes (ibid. 75–102), and the
third, "Ethical Life," presents Hegel's mode of transcending the contradictions in prior political thought. The third part is itself divided
into three sections: "The Family," "Civil Society" (or the market economy), and "The State." Thus the Hegelian dialectic of right, morality,
and ethical life moves from the perspective of the individual's calculus
of costs and benefits (rights or claims) to a Kantian notion of pure
duty or virtue as uniquely human (morality), and then to human
institutions as social systems integrating all constitutive levels (ethical
life).

Although detailed analysis of Hegel is impossible here, note that he
explicitly treats both marriage and economic activity—"needs and the
means of satisfying them"—as transformations of "natural" or "animal" functions (ibid. par. 161, p. 111; par. 190, p. 127). In contrast, the
state for Hegel is "a self-dependent organism"; its constitution is the
manifestation, in "the objective world," of the "self-development of
the Idea" (ibid. par. 259, p. 160; par. 267, p. 163). In more familiar
usage, the state is a cultural, or man-made, phenomenon; rather than
being a transformation of a natural or animal need, the state is thus a
purely human construction dependent on the self-conscious activity
of its citizens and the evolution of human thought (Hegel's "world
mind").

This summary of political philosophy in terms consistent with contemporary social biology could easily be expanded to include the ancients. For example, the pre-Socratics' analysis of individual costs and
benefits leads to a social contract theory parallel to that of Hobbes,
whereas Plato's *Republic* offers a model of group selection for sociality
by destroying both the family and the market economy; Aristotle, like
Hegel, develops a complex balance between institutions at the level of
family, economic system, and polity (Masters 1978a). Although the
specific vocabulary differs, the issues posed by contemporary biological theory are fundamentally similar to the traditional questions in
Western political thought.

The understanding of human nature and politics in the "great
books" of philosophers thus needs to be reconsidered in the light of
scientific research. From the perspective of biology, the logic of inclusive fitness can explain such supposedly selfish behaviors as parent-
offspring conflict, sibling rivalry, and a host of other frequently observed human traits (Trivers 1981). But, in recognizing the ubiquity of
egoistic motives and behaviors, evolutionary theory also points to the

countervailing tendencies toward cooperation, particularly in a species that experiences prolonged helplessness in infancy, predators in its environment, and scarcity of food requiring cooperative hunting and food sharing (Alexander 1979, 1987). From the earliest epochs, therefore, we can assume that human nature exhibited a complex of both cooperation and competition (Morin 1973; Masters 1977; Isaac 1978).

In theoretical terms, this means that Hobbes's definition of the state of nature as a mutually harmful "war of all" among selfish individuals, like Rousseau's assertion of human asociality or Kant's formulation of a pure and universal duty of virtue, cannot fully describe the origins of the state. This is tantamount to saying that the accounts of human nature and political institutions found in Hobbes, Rousseau, or Kant are only partially correct heuristic models. Each is true as a formal description of human behavior under some circumstances; none is a global definition of the unchanging basis of human nature.

The fact that the major political thinkers of the past have elaborated systems that are incomplete or partial should not be taken to indicate that traditional political philosophy is irrelevant or useless. Each of the major theorists discussed above analyzes a particular issue or transformation with archetypical clarity. Of the five basic modes of behavior—asociality, nepotism, mutual benefit, sociality, and mutual harm—different philosophers have tended to isolate specific situations and to explore with great depth how they relate to political experience. For example, Hobbes shows how nepotism, under circumstances producing mutual harm, can be transformed into mutual benefit only by the construction of a man-made "commonwealth." Rousseau spells out how humans could have evolved from an asocial condition (the "pure state of nature") into a Hobbesian condition of mutual harm, as well as how a political community could go beyond the mutually beneficial contracts of Hobbes to a patriotic community united by feeling and civic virtue. And Kant indicates how even such a form of virtue would fall short of the pure demands of a moral obligation, thus suggesting an inevitable tension between private self-interest and group interests.

The Return to Naturalism

From the perspective of evolutionary biology, famous Western political theorists have, contrary to the claim of historicists, addressed perennial issues of human social life (Strauss 1953; Bloom 1987). Reconsidering the "great books" of Western political philosophy is not

merely an act of intellectual piety, snobbishness, or ideological con-
formism. Rather, there are sound practical as well as theoretical reasons for linking the traditionally distinct concerns of political theory
and evolutionary biology.

Unifying the discipline of political science and relating it to the
natural sciences, which has long been a dream (Marx, *Economic and
Philosophic Manuscripts of 1844*, 143), now seems possible. Although
cost-benefit theories (whether game theory, conventional economics,
or decision-making models) need not be modified fundamentally in
order to be linked with inclusive fitness theory, by doing so one gains
a heightened awareness of the limited but important domain within
which collective decisions can be derived from the aggregation of
individual choices based on a cost-benefit calculus (Alexander and
Borgia 1978; Masters 1981b). Political philosophy, long divorced from
the "hard" sciences, can only be strengthened by the realization that
famous thinkers have described the categories and transformations of
behavior central to a scientific understanding of human political experience (Masters 1977, 1978a, 1978b, 1983b).[5] And empirical theories of
the state, based on rival models of conflict and of functional integration, can now be combined in a more comprehensive approach to
political and social history.

This integration of disciplines is not merely of abstract theoretical
interest. New and more significant empirical research should be a
goal of anyone claiming to be engaged in a scientific study of human
behavior. Hitherto unsuspected implications of political phenomena
are often discovered when studied from the perspective of the life
sciences. An example will help. In other species, it is well known that
mating patterns vary widely depending not only on the degree of
physical difference between males and females (sexual dimorphism),
but on such other factors as predation, the scarcity of resources, or the
costs and benefits of parental investment in the young. In analyzing
these relationships, Alexander and others have advanced the hypothesis that the establishment of the centralized state greatly increases the
selective advantage of monogamous mating systems (Chagnon and
Irons 1979, 402–35). Whatever the extent to which early hominids
established lasting pair-bonds—and on this question there is considerable disagreement (Lovejoy 1981; Hrdy and Bennett 1981)—the cen-
tralization of political power apparently changed the environmental
constraints on the kinship systems elaborated by various cultures
(van den Berghe 1979).

Where the bureaucratic state does not exist, human societies exhibit
a wide variety of kinship patterns; where centralized governments
have been institutionalized—whether as hereditary monarchies or ar-

istocracies, one-party dictatorships, or constitutional democracies—
the monogamous family seems to predominate. Political institutions
can have important consequences for the domains usually considered
as "private" in modern Western society. In fact, many practices that
are conventionally treated as prepolitical or beyond legitimate interfer-
ence by governments may be, at least in evolutionary form, the product of the centralized state.

Whereas most social scientists stress economic variables in the
study of politics, theories of the state also need to make explicit the
relationship between familial (or kinship) institutions, ecological constraints, and political behavior. Such a broadening of theoretical perspectives reveals a serious difficulty with conventional views of public
and private life. Individual ownership of property, for example, takes
a different form, or does not exist at all, in societies whose kinship
system is not organized in the monogamous nuclear family of the
modern state (Fortes and Evans-Pritchard 1940; Bohannan 1963; Harris 1977). What have long appeared to be "natural rights" or "human
rights" on which the state is based—such as the right to privacy
within the nuclear family or the individual ownership of property—
are social institutions whose current form was influenced by and depends upon the centralized state.

The standards usually used when judging the legitimacy of government actions are thus called into question by the study of politics as a
biological phenomenon. Issues like abortion, birth control, inheritance taxes, equality of the sexes, and homosexuality are today discussed in terms of abstract "rights" that are presumed to be more
basic or fundamental than governments and laws. If so-called natural
or human rights are institutions that evolved historically due to the
interaction between biological and cultural factors, these principles of
political legitimacy and ethical judgment are themselves in need of
foundation.

In the twentieth century, commonly accepted standards of right
and morality have been based on either theological doctrine or historical contingency. For some, political rights are derived from a divine
source; for others, all law and custom is man-made. Neither of these
alternatives can be sustained on theoretical grounds without radical
reconsideration. Given the links between evolutionary biology, social
science, and political philosophy, it is time to return to a more naturalistic foundation of our political principles.

This involves a momentous change since, in modern times, policy
proposals and ethical judgments have typically been divorced from
scientific knowledge. From an evolutionary perspective, the radical
division between scientific knowledge and practical wisdom is increas-

ingly difficult to sustain. In principle, standards of human preference can hardly be viewed as mere whim, especially insofar as models of rational choice and inclusive fitness can explain them; in practice, research in the life sciences has rendered moot the presumed autonomy of subjective choice and confronts policymakers with decisions that require biological expertise (Caldwell 1964; Kass 1971; Blank 1981). Just as medical science involves the application of biological knowledge to the care and treatment of the ill, public policy and ethics can, and doubtless will, utilize objective findings in the life sciences as their foundation.

The transformation in perspective can be called a return to the naturalism represented by thinkers like Aristotle. To be sure, there is a risk in using "nature" as a concept to justify policy choices and moral judgments. As inclusive fitness theory reminds us, the individual interpreting scientific findings as they relate to human affairs has a self-interest in the result. Evolutionary theory also makes it clear, however, that this danger is inevitable regardless of the terminology or perspective being used: the nihilist or the doctrinaire theologian is also an individual human being with the selfish tendencies recognized by theorists and prophets since antiquity.

Although it has often been said that the "naturalistic fallacy" is committed whenever scientific facts are related to decisions about values (Brecht 1959; Lewontin, Rose, and Kamin 1984; Ruse 1986), inclusive fitness theory contradicts the conventional image of biology by establishing differences of judgment as natural and inevitable. Recall how the categories in figure 5.1 relate to the various situations set forth in figures 5.2 to 5.5 and 5.6 to 5.7. In every case, the description of an outcome depends decisively on the individual who is making the judgment: what is virtue for actor A is nepotism for B, and vice versa. According to evolutionary biology, as for Aristotle, what is in accordance with nature is not given or rigidly fixed, but changes depending on circumstances; a biological perspective on human politics and ethics takes the grounds of opposed concepts of justice seriously, if only because alternative views often reflect predictable responses to very real social problems (Aristotle *Politics* 1.6.1255a; 3.9.1280a–3.11.1282b).

Far from being a logical fallacy, an evolutionary naturalism thus perpetuates a philosophical tradition with a long and noble history. It does not, however, resurrect older natural law teachings that presumably enforce absolute standards regardless of time and place. Rather, a return to naturalism on scientific grounds points toward a biological and cultural equivalent of the theory of relativity in physics (Capra 1975). Social biology promises an understanding of both "special relativity" (why individuals within any society or culture have ethical disagreements, based on their differing perspectives) and "general relativity" (why different societies and cultures have different laws and customs, based on their environment and history). Yet this new naturalism would account for such cultural variations without falling into the opposite excess of mere relativism, since evolutionary theory provides a standard against which human behavior can be measured.

Lest this view be dismissed as a return to the discredited view that "whatever is, is right," one should recall Aristotle's emphasis on nature as a criterion of ethical judgment (*Politics* 1.1.1252a–1.2.1253a; *Ethics* 2.1.1103a, 5.7.1134b–1135a). In medicine, no one would maintain that, because a ruptured appendix can occur in the "natural course of events," people ought to die of appendicitis. Those who have confused bad biology with a so-called naturalistic fallacy should—especially in an age dominated by the threat of nuclear war, genetic engineering, and pervasive terrorism—make it clear what they propose as the foundation of ethical judgment. The fact-value dichotomy may sound innocuous and reasonable in calm and tranquil times, but as Leo Strauss pointed out so effectively, in our day it amounts to "retail sanity and wholesale madness" (Strauss 1953, 4). If legal institutions and governments are not to be viewed as merely man-made conventions or arbitrary manifestations of human will (Plato *Republic* 4.428a–444e), it behooves us to follow the Socratic tradition of seeking standards of what is right or just according to nature.

PART IV

Political Philosophy and Justice

Organized government is usually taken for granted by the citizens of today's industrial societies. In the study of human behavior, as in the other natural sciences, commonly accepted phenomena often need to be analyzed without presuming that we know why they exist. Not the least of the benefits of a biological approach to politics is that it makes possible such a reexamination of contemporary institutions and patterns of behavior. The centralized state is vulnerable over the long run precisely because it can be so successful in generating mutual benefits and collective goods in the short-term horizon of an individual's conscious decision making.

From the perspective of evolutionary biology, the survival of a mature civilization depends in good part on the virtue of its members: the quest for selfish advantage, made possible by the security of the state, can easily lead to the destruction of a stable cultural order (or, to use the Hobbesian phrase, to a "war of all against all"). This risk of overexploiting the benefits of civilization can arise either from the behavior of elites, who seek to gain benefits beyond those available from social surpluses, or from the population at large, unable to justify restraints in private consumption. The logic of the Tragedy of the Commons can apply both within the centralized bureaucracy and at the level of the private consumer. In either case, the traditional philosophic teaching of the natural basis of human virtue provides a salutary alternative to the terror of punishment.

At a theoretical level, concepts developed to study the process of natural selection thus illuminate the origins and survival of the centralized state. By placing the study of political systems on a scientific foundation, moreover, evolutionary biology can contribute to the reunification of the natural and social sciences and therewith to the reinvigoration of traditional political philosophy. Such a prospect presupposes, however, that the theory developed to this point is not contradicted by the empirical evidence concerning the origins and decline of bureaucratically organized political institutions.

Not all states are, of course, the same. The types of political institutions observed in history can be described as modes of organizing the human potential for social participation. In so doing, the effects of different regimes become evident, since some kinds of states deprive most of their members of opportunities for social participation that have been typical for our species for millions of years. If so, constitutional regimes combining the rule of law and widespread political participation come closer to fulfilling the natural potentials of our social nature than do autocratic or tyrannical governments.

As the Epilogue and Notes indicate, this approach challenges the prevailing belief in the impossibility of discovering a naturalistic foundation for standards of justice. Once human social behavior is understood as a biological phenomenon, it becomes possible and necessary to transcend the value-free stance of contemporary social science and the nihilism of Western philosophy since Nietzsche. Over the past two centuries, it has often seemed necessary to choose between moral relativism and dogmatic absolutes, as if political and social institutions were either divinely ordained or arbitrary human creations. From the perspective of evolutionary biology, we are led to see that neither extreme is tenable; rather, human moral and political values can be judged by objective criteria that are relative to time and place.

CHAPTER 6

Why Bureaucracy?

The Centralized State as an Empirical Question

If the centralized state is in some sense unnatural from an evolutionary perspective, what circumstances in the last ten thousand years permitted the formation of such large political systems? This question is especially important for political philosophy because it is known that societies of this scale were previously impossible or unnecessary. Before a naturalistic perspective can be taken seriously, it must be able to account for the facts. The first test of a theory of politics must be its empirical accuracy.

There is a decisive advantage in reconsidering the origin of the state and bureaucracy from the perspective of evolutionary biology (Alexander 1979; Rosenberg 1980; Masters 1975, 1983a). For both political philosophers and game theorists, the benefits that accrue from cooperative or helping behavior directed to potential competitors are usually deduced from the consequences of actions or the motivations of the actors on the assumption that the environment is constant. In contrast, the concept of natural selection treats the traits and behaviors of animals as adaptations to changing environments. As cultural anthropologists and biologists have shown, if the environment is modified, the consequences of any particular behavior for reproductive success can be expected to change (Whiting 1969; Harris 1977; Durham 1979). Hence the empirical effects of alternative actions in specific environments, and not disembodied motivations, become of central importance.

According to the social contract theories of traditional political philosophers, cooperation arises when humans find it mutually beneficial to obey a common set of laws; from Antiphon the Sophist to Rousseau, the logic of obedience has therefore been explored in cost-benefit terms that parallel recent models of rational choice and collective goods (Downs 1957; Barry 1970; Olson 1982; Masters 1982a, 1982b). In all these theoretical approaches, the critical problem is the free rider or selfish defector, who appears to cooperate while secretly cheating and thereby gains more than the virtuous member of the group.

To counter this logical obstacle to cooperation, political philosophers generally concluded that coercive authorities enforcing common rules would be necessary. Hence the state was seen as a solution to the unbridled competition that Hobbes called the "war of all against all." Benefits from social institutions were created through the mechanism of legal punishments that increased the costs of violating agreed-upon rules and thereby secured the benefits of large-scale social communities.

While social contract theory is an elegant logical answer to the problem of the origin of the state, it begs an important empirical issue. In practice, large-scale societies need to organize the procedures of lawmaking and enforcement. A division of labor is required, with the result that those who make and enforce the rules seem to gain disproportionately from the formation of the state. As Thrasymachus pointed out sarcastically to Socrates in Plato's *Republic*, those in power make the laws in order to further their own self-interest: "justice is the interest of the stronger" (Plato *Republic* 1.338c–341d). Any government, not to mention a complex bureaucracy, creates selective benefits for those in power that exceed the advantages for the ruled. It follows that participation in a large-scale community or state is possible only under environmental circumstances in which the benefits to subjects outweigh the comparative disadvantage of obeying rulers who gain even more from their powerful positions.

In short, analysis of states and bureaucracies from an evolutionary perspective has the advantage of focusing our attention on the circumstances of ecology and social environment that might have overcome the selfish or nepotistic limits on broad-scale social cooperation. There is no evidence that fundamental characteristics of human nature were radically different before the state emerged or in the stateless societies that persisted into the twentieth century (Lévi-Strauss 1962; Leakey and Levin 1977; Ortner 1983). We know that the state has emerged only under specific historical conditions, that some states have been able to grow into massive empires based on highly articulated bureaucracies whereas others have failed despite the efforts of their leaders, and that states have periodically collapsed in virtually every cultural setting where they have been observed. Hence theoretical discussion of the origins and limits of bureaucratic institutions can and should, from the outset, focus on the environmental conditions that modify the calculus of cost and benefit in ways that make possible the state and its bureaucratic institutions, or that undermine and destroy them.

The Origins of the State

Broadly speaking, the origins of the state have been explained by anthropologists, political scientists, and evolutionary biologists in three different ways: (1) balance of power theories, in which the state is a response to intergroup conflict; (2) economic or technological theories, in which the state is a model of intragroup cooperation; and (3) feedback models, in which so-called autocatalytic, synergistic, or catastrophic processes account for the state. Not surprisingly, these alternatives echo the perspectives of traditional philosophers who considered the state to have originated in the competition for power (Thrasymachus, Hobbes), in the cooperation demanded by the productive process (Plato, Marx), or in a complex interaction of the two (Aristotle, Rousseau). When restated in terms consistent with contemporary evolutionary biology, perhaps the older theories are more amenable to empirical test.

BALANCE OF POWER THEORIES OF THE STATE

Among contemporary biologists who have studied human evolution, Richard Alexander has made perhaps the most sophisticated attempt to link inclusive fitness theory to the origin of the state (Alexander 1978, 1979). In assessing the theoretical issue outlined above, Alexander points to the nearly ubiquitous evidence of intergroup competition in human history:

> The necessary and sufficient forces to explain the maintenance of every kind and size of human group above the nuclear family, extant today and throughout all but the earliest portions of human history, were (a) war, or intergroup competition and aggression, and (b) the maintenance of balances of power between such groups. . . . I am not implying that no other forces influence group sizes and structures but that balances of power provide the basic sizes and kinds of groups upon which secondary forces like resource distribution, population densities, agricultural and technological developments, and effects of diseases exert their influences. (Alexander 1979, 222–23)

As Willhoite (1981, 1986) also argues, this process can explain how hominids were forced to expand the scale of social groups by orders of magnitude as a result of intergroup competition.

It is not hard to think of examples of military expansion at the origin of large-scale communities with centralized governments: again and again, we find evidence that conquest played a critical role in establishing the authority of states and empires. Nor is this process hard to explain from the perspective of inclusive fitness theory. If two societies are in competition, all members of each society share a common private interest in avoiding devastating conquest or invasion. Inversely, and perhaps more important, if one society can conquer the other, the result would have enormous benefits for the kin of all individuals among the victors: not only are the resources of the defeated community likely to be valuable, but members of the rival group themselves can sometimes be useful (either as low-status laborers and slaves or, as in many cases when males of the losing society were exterminated, for breeding purposes).

Once conflict between societies begins, moreover, it can readily have a snowball effect: one group's success in war or warlike conflict with another will have immediate consequences for a third society in contact with the winner. Thucydides' *History of the Peloponnesian War* describes graphically how the dynamics of rivalry can compel societies to prepare and conduct war on an expanding scale. The logical outcome of such a process has often, though not always, been the establishment of states and on occasion large-scale empires. Such political systems, particularly if they reach the size of empires, are based on functionally specific institutions devoted to the government of the society and include the rudiments of bureaucracy if not well-articulated bureaucratic institutions (Deutsch 1963; Easton 1965a, 1965b).

Empirical evidence in support of this model is not hard to locate (Carniero 1970; Cohen and Service 1978). A recent study of the emergence of the pre-Hispanic Central American state of Xochicalco (Hirth 1984) provides a less well known but particularly interesting example. Since this urban center illustrates the process of state formation in a circumstance that did not give rise to extensive literary references in the Western intellectual tradition, it can be used as independent evidence of the adequacy of a theory as old as Thrasymachus and Thucydides.

Like many other states known in history, Xochicalco was the center of a political system based on military conquest. Hirth summarizes the findings of recent archaeological research as follows:

> The appearance of regional city-states in pre-Hispanic Central Mexico corresponds with the disruption of socioeconomic relationships throughout Teotihuacan's political domain after 650 A.D. Surface reconnaissance and mapping at Xochicalco provided information on the growth and organization of one of these urban centers. The data indicate that Xochicalco was a well-planned ur-

ban center and capital of a regional city-state that extended its domain throughout western Morelos by military conquest. (Hirth 1984, 579)

Other examples, from ancient Mesopotamia and Egypt to China, Africa, and the New World, could easily be mentioned; obviously, state formation has often resulted from intergroup rivalry and warfare.

ECONOMIC AND TECHNOLOGICAL THEORIES OF THE STATE

Despite the evidence noted above, there are difficulties with the balance of power theory of the state as an explanation of the earliest departures from band or tribal societies in which cooperation is limited to a face-to-face group of extended kin or reciprocating kin groups. The principal question is one of scale. Hunter-gatherer bands typically do not exceed one hundred to two hundred members; tribal populations in segmentary lineage systems may be numbered in the thousands but typically are composed of local villages or groups that are not much larger than the largest of the hunter-gatherer bands. City-states like that based in Xochicalco in Central Mexico, not to mention the empires in Mesopotamia and Egypt, grew until they were several orders of magnitude larger. What is the missing link, so to speak? How did social groups grow large enough to fight full-scale wars, and can this process also explain why, in many areas of the world, Western explorers from the fifteenth to the nineteenth centuries encountered preliterate peoples who had not developed social systems encompassing such large populations?

In addition to this empirical question, a frequently ignored issue is embedded in the balance of power theory. One of the motivations or forces most typically cited as driving the intergroup model of state formation concerns population pressure. But how or why should populations be able to grow to the point of putting this much pressure on a society's resource base? Even assuming that population size is a critical factor in the relative power of states, how could group size have been manipulated, either as a matter of policy or as a latent consequence of intergroup competition? If mechanisms limiting population growth were effective over millions of years of hominid evolution, something presumably occurred to favor the formation of larger groups, or at least to reduce selection pressures against population growth, prior to the open conflict between states. An evolutionary model of the state cannot ignore the many leaders who actively sought to create states and empires but failed to do so: where states have occurred, they seem to have overcome the disincentives against social cooperation in groups largely composed of nonkin or even of distant kin.

In the archaeological studies of pristine states (that is, states formed at an epoch or location where no such institutions had hitherto existed), two facts stand out as confirming the relevance of this question. First, paleoarchaeology has provided demographic assessments of population sizes throughout the era of state formation; where this data has been analyzed, it appears that population growth begins before the emergence of the state (Hassan 1983), not after it as would be assumed from the balance of power theory of the state. Second, at the earliest periods of rivalry between city-states, the evidence seems to show communities that are not surrounded by walls or devoted to military conquest; on the contrary, everything seems to suggest the existence of more or less peaceful communities that grew and then came into conflict. If so, this seems to indicate that the first stages of expanded social cooperation were primarily economic or technological rather than military and expansionist (Masters 1983a).

In this view, the balance of power theory is most effective in explaining the emergence of very large state systems rather than the original extension of social cooperation beyond the band or village. A critical element of the economic and technological process prior to such intergroup rivalry clearly seems to have been the development of agriculture based on irrigation systems making it possible to control water supplies (Harris 1977). According to one widely known theory of empire formation, even at the scale of much larger communities this factor was the principal basis for the emergence of the agricultural surpluses that alone made possible the survival of central bureaucracies and the large populations they governed (Wittfogel 1957). At one well-studied site of a nascent state among the Maya, estimates of the manpower needed to construct the irrigation system seem clearly beyond the capacity of groups as small as a tribal band or village (Turner and Harrison 1981).

The case of Xochicalco, cited above, is instructive. There seems to have been a period prior to the intergroup rivalry and military conquest during which agricultural development permitted the formation of expanded social groups:

> The earliest occupations at Xochicalco date to the Middle and Late Formative periods when the population was concentrated in a few small settlements overlooking the Tembembe River. Two small Middle Formative hamlets (500 to 900 B.C.) covering 0.21 ha were located on the river's lower alluvial terrace . . . where a

high subsurface water table made year-round agriculture possible with the aid of small-scale irrigation techniques. The area and density of settlement increased during the Late Formative period (500 B.C. to A.D. 200), and communities shifted from the narrow alluvial terraces to the arid upland valley above the Tembembe River. Settlement covered a total of 5.5 ha. . . . [This] is an important demographic shift found throughout western Morelos and reflects an increased reliance on rainfall agriculture during this period. (Hirth 1984, 580)

Here we have evidence of a key shift in settlement patterns and agricultural techniques, requiring social cooperation and resulting in expanded population size—or, in evolutionary terms, increased reproductive success for all members of the society. While military conquest in the context of a balance of power system seems to explain the much larger city-state of Xochicalco, which emerged at this site after 650 A.D. and covered approximately 2.04 square kilometers (Hirth 1984, 581–85), the original transition away from very small social groups was apparently associated with economic change rather than military expansion or intergroup conflict.

The hypothesis of socioeconomic change as a primary factor in the emergence of larger-scale social cooperation, which is stressed by some cultural anthropologists (Whiting 1969; Harris 1977), can therefore not be dismissed out of hand. Other cases of social cooperation beyond the local village, seemingly akin to pristine states formed without evidence of military conflict, could be cited (Lekson et al. 1988). From an evolutionary perspective, technological changes often function as a means of altering the ecological constraints within which humans live. One can think of major changes in the mode of livelihood of a human population as the equivalent of a change in a species' ecological niche. Where all kingroups in a society can gain proportionately by cooperating in the exploitation of a new habitat or ecological strategy, such social cooperation among distant kin or unrelated families would be analogous to the expanded social groups formed by animals that rely on prey that is large and difficult to kill (Alexander 1979, 60–63).

Chief among the examples of such a technological change is the development of large-scale irrigation systems in the the Tigris, Euphrates, Nile, and other river valleys associated with early civilizations. Such systems were feasible only as the result of the coordinated labor of very large populations. Yet once they were in place, all members of the society could gain from the increased reliability and quantity of food supplies. If the emergence of empires depends on substantial and regular productive surpluses, without which it is impossible to support a central bureaucracy (Eisenstadt 1963), and if such surpluses are associated with cooperative technologies that must be studied as an autonomous source of state formation (Wittfogel 1957), it would follow that socioeconomic cooperation is an independent factor that cannot be deduced from intergroup conflict.

FEEDBACK MODELS OF STATE FORMATION

In analyzing human evolution from a biological perspective, Wilson (1975) suggests that rapid rates of morphological and social change could best be explained by a more complex process than those described above. To account for hominid social behavior, he outlines an "autocatalytic" model based on the interaction of ecological, physiological, and cultural factors. In Wilson's view, a process in which change in one variable influences other variables, which in turn have feedback consequences driving an entire system beyond previous limiting conditions or thresholds, was particularly important in the emergence of the centralized state (Wilson 1975, 565–74).

Other writers have discussed similar "multifactorial," or feedback, models. Sometimes associated with "catastrophe" theory in mathematics, this kind of process in nature generally, and especially in the origins of human social life, has been described by Corning as *The Synergism Hypothesis* (1984). In this view, phenomena at one level of organization have effects at other levels, making it impossible to consider evolutionary processes as the result of a single factor; the "combinatorial effects" of all factors—including behavioral initiatives of individuals that, in other species, would have been unlikely to shape a species' behavioral repertoire—could thus play a joint role in the evolution of complex sociocultural systems organized as states with centralized bureaucracies (Corning 1984, 224–312).

This approach has the great merit of reminding us that the emergence of a new form of social cooperation did not eradicate previously evolved elements of the human behavioral repertoire. For example, even where helping behavior between nonkin in a face-to-face society is supported by reciprocity (Trivers's "reciprocal altruism"), the advantages of favoring close kin (nepotism) persist, producing the well-known tensions between friends and relatives in human social behavior. Similarly, the formation of larger communities to which individuals contribute goods and services, occasionally at a net cost (sociality), does not obliterate the kin-based local units of simpler social systems. On the contrary, the kinship system continues to function. Indeed, from the perspective of the individual, the considerations of inclusive fitness continue to operate, *taking the broader human social organization as part of the "natural" environment.*

In a feedback model of state origins, therefore, the individual actor confronts previously evolved social, economic, or political patterns as inseparable parts of the context determining the payoff to be gained from alternative behavioral strategies. This perspective helps to explain the persisting role of individuals and kinship groups in very large societies. To cite a striking instance from the example of Xochicalco, social cooperation within the city-state was organized around what seem to have been kinship units:

> The people appear to have been organized into extended family groups that occupied residence compounds between 350 and 1000 m² in size. Individual families occupied rooms or structures within a compound, which faced onto or was connected to a central patio. Residence compounds were enclosed by walls, or structures were built adjacent to one another to form a continuous walled façade on the exterior of the compound. These compounds formed the basic economic unit in the society and available data indicate that craft production was organized at the family level. . . . Resources appear to have been shared by members of the residence compound. (Hirth 1984, 583)

In other states as well, as we know in most detail from the history of ancient Greece and Rome (Fustel de Coulanges 1956), the kinship group retained a primary importance in daily life.

This relatively obvious point has further significance for the dynamics of state formation. Just as kinship groups remain a focus of social life during and after the transition from band or tribe to centralized state, so the individual leader can be of continued importance in broadened social communities. Traditional historical scholarship treated leadership as one of the principal factors in human societies; philosophers like Machiavelli (*Discourses on Titus Livy* 1.9–11) and Rousseau (*Social Contract* 2.7) emphasized the role of the "legislator" at the founding of states. Clearly, at particular times, evidence suggests that individual leaders of the quality of Moses, Augustus Caesar, or Lenin had some effect in the formation of legal or political systems. Without ignoring the critical importance of other factors, it is hard to deny that leaders treat the existing circumstances as a resource, on occasion exploiting the situation to form new social institutions that might benefit their own kin group as well as a broader social system.

From this perspective, it is not necessary to presume that the leader acts solely or even primarily in a conscious effort to enhance inclusive fitness. There are, of course, numerous cases of individuals who sought to found dynastic systems of rule, using what could clearly be described as nepotistic strategies. But even where this attempt is transparent, as in the case of Napoléon, the means have often involved the formation of bureaucratic institutions to promulgate and enforce a uniform legal system regulating large populations that were previously independent. For instance, Napoléon wrote his brother Joseph (who had been installed as the king of Naples as part of his familial strategy for controlling Europe): "You must establish the civil code in your states; it will fortify your power, since by it all entails are cancelled, and there will no longer be any great estates apart from those you create yourself. This is the motive which has led me to recommend a civil code and to establish it everywhere" (Markham 1963, 173). Although reducing the power of autonomous feudal aristocrats or local social groups did have a short-run benefit for Napoléon and his kin, obviously the generalized adoption of the *Code Napoléon* had vast social and economic effects in the era of the formation of the European nation-state and the spread of industrialized economies.

The interaction of intergroup rivalry, intragroup cooperation, and individual behavioral strategies might thus account for the emergence of states and bureaucracies more effectively than any single-factor theory (Masters 1981b; Langton 1988). But this means that one must consider the social situation at any moment as a critical component of the environmental setting. Because behavioral strategies at the level of the individual and kinship group will continue to function within the structures associated with states and bureaucracies, inclusive fitness theory may be most effective in explaining the way in which individuals adapt to changing cultural and social systems (van den Berghe 1979). Just as individual violations of traditional norms (Chagnon 1982) or choices of cooperative partners (Essock-Vitale and McGuire 1985) treat the culture as a part of the environment to which individuals respond, so phenomena at the level of states and bureaucracies interact with individual behavioral strategies (see White and Losco 1986).

The Functions of Bureaucracy

The analysis of the origins of states from an evolutionary perspective provides helpful insight into the functions performed by bureaucratic institutions. Although functionalism in sociology (like that associated with Talcott Parsons or Marion J. Levy) has often been criticized as biased toward the status quo, biological theory permits one to undertake functional analysis without implying an evaluative preference. It is hard to imagine an evolutionary explanation of the heart that does not analyze the role or function that this organ plays in the body; one can say that the heart functions to maintain blood circulation at specified rates without concluding that the heart of a particular human individual ought to continue to function, or that a patient ought to receive a heart transplant. While the study of immediate physiological causes of development or behavior differs from functional analysis of systemic consequences, both are necessary in the evolutionary study of living beings (Simpson 1969; Handler 1970; von Cranach 1976).

In a functional study of bureaucracy, three general areas can be distinguished, each broadly associated with one of the levels of causation just described. First, insofar as there are collective goods or mutual benefits to all in the group (presumably the mechanism by which intergroup conflict leads to state formation), bureaucracies provide the element of coercion requisite for sociality in very large groups of nonkin. Second, insofar as new modes of socioeconomic cooperation create collective benefits, the coordination of behavior needed in their adoption and spread is made possible or at least facilitated by bureaucratic institutions. Finally, the central administrative organization has the consequence, for the bureaucrats and their kin, of providing selective benefits, which constitute effective strategies for enhancing their own inclusive fitness at the individual level.

COERCION AS A REQUISITE FOR SOCIALITY

Analysis of the problem of human sociality—the very large groups of nonkin comprising the societies in which states and bureaucracies emerge—has focused on the cost-benefit calculus typical of rational choice theory in discussing collective goods. For example, if the conquest of another society's territory or population represents a collective benefit (as in Alexander's balance of power model of state formation), clearly the individual male could gain even greater benefits if all others risked their lives in war while he remained in safety. And, as rational choice theorists are fond of pointing out, everyone should be presumed to make the same assessment of the situation.

It follows that rules are needed to specify the obligations of each member of the society. Once in place, however, the law recreates the same invitation to cheat; as Paul emphasizes (*Romans* 7:7–11), law can actually increase the temptation to selfish behavior by pointing out the specific actions that ought to be avoided. A coercive agency capable of detecting free riders and punishing their violations of the rules will therefore have advantages for all members of the group insofar as all gain something from the resulting collective benefits.

This argument, as has been remarked, characterizes the so-called social contract theories of philosophers as diverse as Antiphon the Sophist, Thrasymachus, Hobbes, Locke, and Rousseau; it also forms the basis of Garrett Hardin's account of the Tragedy of the Commons and the way in which coercive central authorities can resolve it (Hardin 1968). But when the origins of the state are studied from the perspective of evolutionary biology, it becomes clear that the state is not a disembodied being. Particularly in complex societies like our own, the institutions of the state require specifically designated officials who form the institutions known as a bureaucracy. Indeed, whatever the form of legitimacy, some type of bureaucratic structure seems to be associated with the emergence of large-scale social systems governed by states. Whether linked with religious ritual (in the guise of a priesthood), with military functions, or with the socioeconomic roles of monitoring taxation and rule compliance, individual leaders cannot extend the scope of their legal enactments without some human organization that facilitates the identification and punishment of free riders.

The apparent exceptions prove the utility of a neo-Darwinian approach to human sociocultural phenomena. Not all forms of the state have had as highly developed bureaucracies as did the early empires of Mesopotamia, Assyria, Egypt, China, or Rome; while the modern nation-state may resemble these ancient forms in its bureaucratic infrastructure, the leaders of some states or statelike systems did not rely on the kind of centralized institutions we take for granted. In feudal societies, the organization of political authority typically depends upon personal ties between lord and vassal as well as on obligations within extended kinship groups and local communities. What Weber called "traditional" legitimacy is thus often a complex system in which a leader with only a rudimentary central bureaucracy extends personalized control by using reciprocity and kin loyalties over broader areas than were possible in the face-to-face band or segmentary lineage system.

The fundamental differences between a fully articulated bureaucracy (in Weber's sense, a "rational-legal" system) and a feudal state are revealed by the way institutional means are used to apply coercive control from the center. In feudal systems, the mechanisms of social cooperation that characterize face-to-face society are extended over large populations, but the scope of control is in fact quite variable over time and space. Since primary loyalties are to lords or nobles, who are free to shift their allegiances as a means to further selfish ambition, the feudal state expands and contracts as a function of the ability and good fortune of its leader.

Weber's definition of the centralized bureaucratic state as an institution with a "monopoly of the legitimate use of physical force within a given territory" (Weber 1946, 78) is well known. Unlike feudal states, in which vassals repeatedly rebel when they see benefits in so doing and find allies to support them, fully bureaucratized states impose central authority as uniformly as possible throughout a fixed area. But this means that feudal states are more immediately responsive to the ability of their leaders. One could as well say that, thanks to the role of the bureaucracy, Weber's "rational-legal" state has a monopoly on the legitimate use of incompetence within a given territory. Feudal lords, without an extensive bureaucracy to depend on, must rely on their own wits, skill and courage, using personal charm, marriage, kinship, and military strategy to maintain or expand the scope of their power.

In terms of inclusive fitness theory, the primary role of kinship and personal reciprocity as the basis of both loyalty and conflict in feudal society should hardly be surprising. These systems come closest to approximating Alexander's balance of power model of the state in its pure form, since virtually the only collective good provided by the suzerain is defense against intraspecific predation. In feudal systems, there are few collective goods requiring commonly agreed-upon policies and coordinated social behavior for their realization; the economy tends to be local and to have little dependence on the center. For instance, although money is a collective good of great importance in the functioning of centralized bureaucracies (Weber 1946, 204–9), in feudal states it is less necessary to have a common medium of exchange throughout the entire territorial area.

For present purposes, it is not necessary to inquire whether, historically, such weakly articulated systems arose prior to the early centralized state or whether what we call feudal epochs are a secondary phenomenon, arising after the collapse of more highly centralized states. In either case, feudal systems have relatively undeveloped bureaucracies because their origins and maintenance are not primarily dependent on the provision of technological or economic benefits shared by all members of the society. The contrast between feudal and modern states thus confirms the difference between the functions of centralized government that arise from intergroup competition and those facilitating intragroup cooperation.

POLICY IMPLEMENTATION

The coercive functions of the state, while undeniable, clearly do not exhaust the activities of fully developed bureaucratic systems. On the contrary, the socioeconomic processes made possible within a larger population normally require the promulgation of information and the coordination of behavior even where mutual self-interest minimizes the free rider problem. For example, the original construction of an irrigation system may well be a collective good that could be accomplished only by an element of coercion (since any individual or kin group that could utilize the system without having labored to build it would obviously benefit relative to others in the society). But the same degree of coercion will typically not be needed when disseminating information on how to use the system once it has been built or, more generally, whenever all members of the society can improve their reproductive success by utilizing newly available social or ecological resources.

In this sense, policy implementation is a quite distinct function of any fully developed bureaucratic system. The determination of the particular means most likely to serve the generally shared goals in a large society becomes all the more important once a state has come into existence. As a common language, shared technological or cultural behavior patterns, and broader economic exchanges spread through a population, many decisions are mutually beneficial if and only if a subset of the society is available to make them. It probably does not matter to the reproductive success of the individual citizen of a modern society whether automobiles drive on the right or the left of highways; it obviously matters to the reproductive success of all that there be an unambiguous rule, and that some bureaucrats be able to inform drivers of temporary obstacles making it necessary to deviate from the basic pattern (Hirshleifer 1987). Coercion is not needed for citizens to support the policeman who directs traffic around a rock slide in the middle of a snowstorm.

The more complex the social system, of course, the more complex the goals and the means of implementing them. It follows that very large societies are likely to encounter situations in which there is a difference of opinion concerning the optimum means of satisfying social goals (White and Losco 1986). This is especially likely because individuals and groups in different socioeconomic situations or geographical areas will see specific policies as having quite different costs and benefits. Combined with the persistence of the free rider problem, this means that policy implementation invariably will be linked not only to disagreements concerning specific means but with coercive enforcement as well. While most motorists can understand and agree that the 55 M.P.H. speed limit on American superhighways has resulted in lower gasoline consumption and lower death rates, truck drivers who lose income because of the lower highway speeds have a different opinion.

It follows that policy implementation by the bureaucracy has feedback effects on coercive rule enforcement: each new strategy for securing the collective good defines new alternatives for violating the laws and thereby creates a new excuse for expanding the bureaucratic apparatus. When citizens or governments become aware of the feedback processes that contribute to increasing the size of bureaucracies, one common tendency is to appoint a study commission or bureaucratic agency (like the Government Accounting Office in the United States) to consider or implement policies that will control the process. In the broadest sense, it is difficult to find nonbureaucratic solutions to satisfy the functions of bureaucracy.

In this respect, terminology is often misleading. The proper allocation of social functions between the public and private sector has become a major issue in contemporary American politics. But even in the private sector, large-scale business firms are highly bureaucratic organizations; in terms of neo-Darwinian evolutionary theory, as for Max Weber, a business corporation can be analyzed in much the same way as a state, except that the benefits accrue to individuals as a function of ownership and individual remuneration rather than political or legal status as public officials (Weber 1946, 198). It may well be that private interest is the most effective way to secure social goods, but inclusive fitness theory warns us not to assume that this maxim is less applicable to the bureaucrat than to the businessman. The selective benefits that public bureaucracies provide for the individual bureaucrat need to be considered before concluding that there is a massive difference, in principle, between a bureaucratic institution in the public sector (as in virtually all states prior to the emergence of industrialized economies) and the bureaucracies that characterize businesses, labor unions, and other private organizations in the modern world.

THE BUREAUCRAT'S SELECTIVE BENEFITS

From its origins, as has been noted, the state has had the peculiar property of making possible the formation of larger social groups than had existed during the preceding millennia of hominid evolution in hunter-gatherer bands. From the perspective of natural selection, this can only mean that individuals generally increased their net reproductive success by joining and remaining in larger social communities. But the state has a cost. As one can see in the archaeological evidence of those higher civilizations associated with early empires, the bureaucrats and leaders of the state tend to be remunerated handsomely for their services to the mutual or collective benefits of the society. The evidence of early Egyptian or Assyrian tombs in our museums provides a graphic illustration that, in terms of rational choice theory, there is a selective benefit gained by the bureaucrat as an individual.

Formalized models of choice theory originally did not consider this outcome. Trivers's model of reciprocal altruism (1971) is based on the hypothetical scenario of two individuals, one of whom is drowning in a river. Axelrod and Hamilton (1981) present their findings using the heuristic of a repeated two-person Prisoner's Dilemma; such models thus do not focus on complex social hierarchies (Taylor and McGuire 1988). While it is possible to expand the logic of these situations to larger groups, such as the n-person Prisoner's Dilemma (R. Hardin 1971) or the Tragedy of the Commons (G. Hardin 1968), in doing so one finds that some individuals will require the inducement of a side-payment in order to insure the provision of collective goods (Margolis 1982). As Balch (in White and Losco 1986) shows, the need to keep subordinates from overly exploiting their positions is a key factor in explaining many traditional bureaucratic institutions (such as the use of slaves, eunuchs, or captives whose kin were not available as recipients of selective benefits). Hence there are both theoretical and practical reasons to assume that among the functions of bureaucratic institutions will be the provision of selective benefits to the bureaucrats as individuals.

If so, there may be less difference than is popularly assumed between private businesses that adopt bureaucratic structures and the public organizations we conventionally call bureaucracies. Particularly in the era of the multinational firm, it is evident that corporations have become large-scale organizations resembling nonterritorial states specialized in distinct productive and distributional tasks. In many previous states and empires (one thinks immediately of Rome), comparable organizations were part of the state bureaucracy. Whether formally public or private, the members of the bureaucracy gain selective benefits for providing a service to nonkin distributed over a wide geographic area. Indeed, if we compare nondemocratic or autocratic industrial states to business corporations, the similarities are sufficient to give one pause (Masters 1983b).

The modern industrial corporation, of course, does not usually have a territorial base, and its coercive powers are strongly limited by the legal systems of the nation-states within which it operates. For the user or even the employee, moreover, exit from relations with the firm is generally far easier than exit from the state. But here we are dealing with matters of practice that vary widely from one state to another and from one private business to another; bureaucratic organizations that Americans presume to be in the private sector, like labor unions or universities, are often public institutions in other industrialized societies. As Hirschman (1974) has shown, while exit is more characteristic of economic institutions than of political communities, the distinction is hardly a rigid one and processes in the economic and political spheres often greatly resemble each other.

These reflections suggest that the latent functions of bureaucratic organizations, as they have been discussed above, may be far more general than would be supposed from the discussion of their origins in the context of the formation of states and empires. That the owners and executives of the modern corporation benefit more than the consumers of that corporation's product may be notable merely for the high ratio of selective to collective benefits; the existence of a private interest in the provision of public goods could well be a basic cost of civilized social environments. It follows that the failures of public bureaucracies, which have so often been manifested by the disintegration of centralized states and empires, could be instructive for both public and private institutions in the modern context.

The Failures of Bureaucracy

Analysis of the origins and functions of bureaucratic systems from a neo-Darwinian perspective indicates that these institutions are exceptionally complex. The specific contribution of an evolutionary approach is not, however, the finding that similar social roles can arise in the public or private sectors, or that the coercive authority of the state can depend on bureaucratic enforcement to a greater or lesser degree (as is evident in the difference between the feudal and the modern state); Weber demonstrated these features of bureaucracy quite convincingly. Nor is biology necessary to elucidate the problems of coercion and free riders emphasized by rational choice theory.

The particular contribution of an evolutionary approach is the concept that human social or cultural institutions become a critical part of the environment within which individuals act. The refrigerator is as much, or more, a part of the ecological setting of the contemporary urban family as the rainfall, influencing human behavior in the way in which environmental conditions affect other animals. Similarly, a bureaucratic structure modifies the behavioral options open to the members of a centralized state. Considerations of the individual's inclusive fitness remain important even when economic infrastructures or intergroup conflicts create collective benefits for all members of the society. When an official of the state apprehends a counterfeiter, arrests a drunken driver, or investigates a tax evader, the functional success of the bureaucracy from the community's perspective is a failure for the individuals seeking selective benefits by cheating. In speaking of the failures of a bureaucratic system, it is therefore necessary to specify the level of analysis at which the failure is being assessed.

If it is assumed that there are collective benefits that a centralized bureaucracy is capable of providing, the self-interest of the potential free riders are a necessary condition of the system. The bureaucratic failures of relevance here are not such conflicts of interest, but rather contradictions between the different functions associated with bureaucracy. Three main areas of such bureaucratic failure are of general importance: bureaucratic rigidity, incompetence, and nepotism. In each case, apparently inappropriate responses of bureaucracies are related to behavior that emphasizes one of the three functions identified above to the exclusion of the other two.

BUREAUCRATIC RIGIDITY

We have all encountered cases of what appears to be irrational rigidity when dealing with bureaucrats. What is more frustrating than the words: "If I did it for you, I would have to do it for everyone?" In the enforcement of rules one often encounters unforeseen circumstances. Even when the request for exemption is not a classic attempt to achieve free rider status, individual interest can conflict with the general class of situations to which a rule originally applied. It is virtually impossible to foresee all contingencies when making rules for a large-scale society. As a result, contradictions are inevitable between the appropriate enforcement of a rule (as a means of securing the collective benefits that require compliance throughout the society) and the inappropriate enforcement of that same rule in cases not related to its objective (or more properly considered in the light of other rules).

While courts and legal systems can sometimes adjudicate these contradictions, their existence is a necessary feature of the bureaucratic enforcement of legal norms. This follows from the sheer complexity of the social system as a whole; it also follows from the perspective of the individual bureaucrat, who maximizes his or her self-interest by simplifying the decision-making process and ensuring that every decision is fully justified in terms of the existent set of rules (see Peterson and Losco, in White and Losco 1986). Bureaucratic rigidity, in this sense, becomes all the more inevitable insofar as the selective benefits of the bureaucrat as an individual will lead to the narrowest possible use of discretion—unless, as with the case of nepotism to be mentioned below, there are greater personal benefits from discretion than from rigidity.

It is not usually noticed that this very rigidity can be understood, from the point of view of the consumer, as an element increasing individual freedom. This seems to be a paradox because we think of instances of rigidity primarily in the context of our own efforts to do something that a bureaucracy or an individual bureaucrat will not allow. But in some of these circumstances we are seeking, even with the best of conscious intentions or rationalizations, to be free riders. To assess the phenomenon of bureaucratic rigidity from a perspective that excludes these cases of appropriate rule enforcement, it is necessary to contrast the rigid application of a rule to alternative mechanisms for coordinating behavior.

In a large and impersonal community, the individual need not rely on kinship or personal reciprocity as the basis of gaining help. The very rigidity of bureaucracies arises from their provision of more or less identical services to all members of the community, without reference to individual identity in terms of friendship or kinship. This means that the normal situation of the citizen in a complex society includes a vast array of activities in which individual choice is facilitated by the very pattern of rule enforcement that occasionally gives rise to the impression of failure. Why, then, do we hear such frequent condemnations of bureaucratic rigidity and treat bureaucracy as a pejorative term instead of a praiseworthy quality?

The phenomenon that strikes one as bureaucratic rigidity illustrates the extent to which humans take an existing social system for granted, constantly seeking to maximize additional benefits on the assumption that the existing system is robust and will continue to operate. Coercive rule enforcement gets out of hand most often when the bureaucrats seek to avoid being involved in complex circumstances at the margins of what previously appeared to be simple norms with a clearly circumscribed set of applications. But this problem is as much a consequence of the inventiveness of citizens, who use the freedom of choice that bureaucratic life expands in order to make new or more complex claims on the system, as it is a fault of the individual bureaucrat.

When confronted with bureaucratic rigidity, one frequent response is an attempt to develop new rules and new officials to administer them. The definition of these rules is of ever-increasing complexity because the new norms must consider both the novel behaviors that manipulate the existing system for private benefit and the original goals of the law. The history of the Internal Revenue Code of the

United States, and the difficulties that American citizens normally feel as a result of their interaction with the bureaucracy that enforces tax payments, are a good illustration of the continuous feedback between the public perception of rigidity and the formulation of new rules or bureaucratic structures.

INCOMPETENCE: THE PETER PRINCIPLE

Not all failures of bureaucracy arise because a rule has been applied under circumstances that seem to some (or many) members of a society as too rigid and inappropriate. In other cases, the failure is due to the fact that bureaucrats, as individuals, often make mistakes in conforming to their own procedural rules. The forms are filled out incorrectly, the wrong information is supplied, the office has lost the appropriate record. Any indication that entropy applies in human affairs as well as in closed physical systems can be the occasion for blaming bureaucratic inefficiency for behavior that the official, as an individual, ought to have avoided.

In defining incompetence, it is appropriate to exclude actions that are beyond the probable abilities of a human serving in the relevant bureaucratic role (Peterson, in White and Losco 1986). In asserting that bureaucracy has failed to function adequately, one is presumably concerned with instances when normal standards of competence are not maintained by individuals capable of doing the work correctly. In fact, many of the errors we call incompetence may be due to inevitable fatigue, overwork, or failures of support systems for which the bureaucrat in question is not personally responsible. Even these mistakes are often impetuously attributed to individual incompetence, on the presumption that the standard of judging performance is the perfect completion of the administrative task at hand.

Once again, the paradox of bureaucracy as an instrument of individual freedom should be kept in mind. The high standards we set for bureaucrats reflect the user's tendency to take the continued functioning of the system for granted and to focus all attention on the specific case at hand. I recall vividly my annoyance on discovering that the purchasing office of a bureaucratic organization had not paid a routine bill for over two months, with the result that the vendor was holding up urgently needed deliveries. I did not consider that the secretary gave an appropriate explanation when she solemnly said that her office sent out two hundred checks each day. Competent performance on a portion of bureaucratic tasks is never treated as an excuse for failure to handle the particular instance in which one is interested.

Inclusive fitness theory explains why the client has a far greater interest in his own case than does the bureaucratic official—and why the bureaucratic official has a self-interest in discovering modes of work that limit the physical and mental demands of job performance. As a result, most of the time officials fall short of utter perfection in the performance of their duties. The most successful, as Lawrence Peter eloquently demonstrated in formulating the principle that carries his name, tend to be promoted—and promoted until they reach the level at which the self-interest in further advancement for the purpose of salary and power exceeds the ability to perform at a very high degree of accuracy and reliability (Peter and Hull 1969).

In short, the self-interest of the administrator generates not only a tendency to rigidity (to minimize the risk of criticism from superiors), but a systematic likelihood of the nonperformance of some proportion of the routinely handled tasks of the bureaucracy. At the same time, the self-interest of the client generates an increased sensitivity to any failure in the individual case, if only because the expectation of perfect performance by the bureaucrat has been built into the individual's strategy of behavior. It follows, from this convergence of frustration, that bureaucracies are described in pejorative terms by users even if— or rather, especially if—they are providing extensive collective goods to the vast majority of the members of a society.

NEPOTISM: DOING WELL BY DOING GOOD

The foregoing failures of bureaucracy represent instances in which the application of general rules in individual cases produces frustration for the client. But another class of bureaucratic dysfunction arises when the bureaucrat limits the services of his office to users who provide additional side-payments beyond the official prerequisites of the position. In evolutionary terms, we can attribute all such failures to nepotism—that is, behaviors that increase the bureaucrat's individual benefits; more specifically, nepotistic behaviors channel the services of the bureaucracy to the bureaucrat's kin or to individuals chosen in terms of reciprocity (favoritism).

History records many cases in which the problem of nepotism on the part of officials was a primary concern of leaders (see Balch, in White and Losco 1986). Many high functionaries in the early empires of the Middle East and Asia were either eunuchs or slaves. Often chosen from remote parts of the empire in order to minimize contact with kin or with ethnic minorities, such officials were more likely to serve the governing authorities responsibly because their opportunities for nepotism were consciously limited. Similarly, the use of celibate orders as the core of the papal bureaucracy, a strategy that became formal policy when the church became a major source of economic and political power, was far from the only instance of forcing the bureaucrat to forgo some of the most obvious opportunities for nepotistic gain in return for a position of influence and security.

Even in more modern cases, nepotism (either in the form of political or familial favoritism) is far from unusual. In periods of security and abundance, however, the risk of disapproval for the open violation of rational-legal norms typically constrains the spread of nepotism. Changes in the ecological setting that produce economic crisis can therefore have a major effect, creating scarcity and increasing the frequency and importance of nepotistic redirection of bureaucratic services. In the Third World, for example, there seems to be greater evidence of bureaucratic failure than in the industrialized West and, in particular, a greater development of kin-based nepotism, personal favoritism, or the outright sale of services. As the overall stability of the state and effectiveness of its policies in providing collective goods comes into question, it is only to be expected that citizens will demand such favored treatment, bureaucrats will be tempted to give it, and the alternative of providing equal services to all will become increasingly impossible.

Where the stability of resource flows has frequently been interrupted, particularly in societies with a high degree of social stratification, the consequences for overall behavioral strategies can be quite extensive (Masters 1984). The feedback that drives social systems to elaborate ever more complex bureaucracies can suddenly function in the direction of giving individuals with privileged access more and more preferential treatment. The consequence is a loss in the expectation of regularized, impartial bureaucratic service and a trend toward the ever-expanding reliance on kinship, personal reciprocity, and other ties based on individualistic rather than collective criteria. The willingness to contribute to collective goods tends to decline as a consequence. Over the long run, even when states do not disintegrate entirely, they cease to provide the large measure of individual freedom of choice and mobility that citizens of Western industrialized nations take for granted.

The Cyclical Pattern of Public Institutions

The foregoing account of bureaucracy will probably not strike the reader as particularly unusual (or particularly dependent upon neo-Darwinian theory). The evolutionary perspective has, however, the merit of bringing together traditional political philosophy, rational choice theory, anthropology, and Weberian or Marxian sociology, focusing them on the dynamic properties of institutions that provide collective goods for large-scale societies. In addition, this approach makes clear that human cultural institutions arise and maintain themselves in time, so that success in one setting or period becomes a given for following generations. In biology, it is taken for granted that the evolution of greater complexity in no way ensures immortality; when studying human society, evolutionary analysis should no longer be presumed to justify the status quo as the highest or best conceivable way of life.

Given the human propensity to favor kin or personally known, reciprocating individuals as recipients of cooperative or helping behavior, the state—and particularly the centralized, bureaucratic state—can arise only if the community provides countervailing benefits to the subjects. Three explanations have been suggested for the origin of the bureaucratic state: intergroup competition (in which one of the key benefits is defense from other societies as well as conquest), intragroup cooperation (based on the benefit of new technological, economic, or cultural resources that create collective goods on a new scale), and feedback between these factors (typically manipulated for nepotistic benefit by talented leaders). While many philosophers and theorists have debated which of the first two theories is primary, the third, which stresses "autocatalytic" or "synergistic" interactions between numerous variables is probably necessary to account for the historical emergence of large-scale societies.

The interaction of intergroup competition and intragroup cooperation is particularly relevant to the explanation of those states in which a complex bureaucratic apparatus engages in policy implementation as well as coercive rule enforcement. Military defense and conquest require formal rules concerning liability for military service and taxation, and, of course, the coercive means to enforce such rules. The provision of technological or economic infrastructures is even more dependent upon detailed policy making and implementation: one cannot construct irrigation systems, introduce money, or build a road network without trained officials capable of implementing centrally determined plans with some degree of fidelity. As a result, the public functions of bureaucracies necessarily include both the articulation of public rules and their enforcement.

These functions are, however, purchased by human societies at a price, since selective benefits for the individual bureaucrat are a functional requisite for the mutual benefits and collective goods that make possible large-scale communities. Bureaucratic institutions serve the nepotistic interests of the bureaucrats as well as the collective interests of the state, and the resulting tension between the ideal and the actual functioning of the organization creates a dynamic underlying historical change. Crudely outlined, the process has a sequence of recognizable stages. Even though each is not a narrowly determined or inevitable progression from the last, historical evidence tends to confirm that bureaucratic states pass through five phases: origin, maturity, loss of control, renewal, and collapse.

At its origin, the state emerges out of a prior evolution away from the small, relatively autonomous band, village, or tribal societies associated with preliterate cultures. At some point, the dynamic of intragroup cooperation and intergroup competition gives rise to an open conflict; city-states have often emerged and passed through a phase of competition in classic balance of power systems. Sometimes, as in Mesopotamia and Egypt, one state successfully establishes hegemony and a lasting regional empire; on other occasions, as in ancient Greece and medieval Italy, active attempts to gain hegemonic authority either fail completely or give rise to relatively fragile and superficial personal conquests. In the former instance, a threshold seems to have been crossed, permitting (but also produced by) the formation of a centralized bureaucracy; in these early empires, the resulting bureaucratic system not only extracts resources, but also provides some forms of collective benefit, making possible an effective cultural community on a broader social scale.

The mature empires of antiquity left behind massive monuments as evidence of the ability of their bureaucrats to coordinate large-scale labor forces. Although ceremonial and public wonders like the Pyramids are striking symbols of a collective identity, which often seem to lack any other productive function, other centrally administered activities include irrigation systems, roads, granaries, money, and defense. Indeed, it is mature bureaucratic empires that provide the clearest evidence of the functions needed to explain the origins of the state in its various forms.

The very success of the mature bureaucratic system generates increasing loss of control. Some of the causes of this transition have been outlined above in discussing bureaucratic dysfunctions or failures. In many cases, the original impetus to decline has been external: for example, climatic changes can reduce agricultural output, cut surpluses, and hence reduce the effective net gain to the individual member of the society. In other instances, internal social dynamics may reduce the effectiveness of the state: as more people become dependent on the goods and services of the bureaucracy, individuals and groups consider past benefits to be a part of the natural environment and defend their specific advantages against reductions justified in the name of the collective good (Olson 1982). In cultural areas as different as ancient Egypt and China, the centralized state fell into a "time of troubles" or conflict in which the bureaucracy lost effective control over large geographic and functional areas it formerly serviced.

Conventional historical accounts typically understate the importance of these periods of loss of control. On the one hand, by definition we have better records from the epochs of maturity and stability, during which great public monuments were constructed; on the other, historians themselves living in a centralized state are perhaps more likely to understand and value those previous eras with similar principles of stability and public organization. The conventional terminology for the period of loss of control in Western history is revealing: the *Middle* Ages (between the states of classical antiquity and the modern nation-state) or the *Dark* Ages (lacking the enlightenment of modern public life). Nonetheless, there is no reason to exclude these epochs from our understanding of the evolution of human communities, nor to presume that such institutional forms are inferior to centralized states at all costs (Masters 1983b).

Periodically, a bureaucratic system that has encountered loss of control and decline has been able to reverse this trend. In ancient Egypt and China, periods of internal conflict and upheaval were followed by a renewed assertion of central power. These epochs could be described as a return to the favorable configuration marking the transitions to maturity at an earlier point in the historical process. Indeed, conventional histories generally imply as much, treating the leaders of renewal with the same deference as those associated with the origins and growth of centralized bureaucratic institutions. In each case, it is to be presumed that very precise empirical conditions made possible the renewal of bureaucratic control. But, as was argued in discussing alternative theories of the origin of the state, it is probable that the individual leader's skill and foresight were equally important contributing causes to the period of renewal.

If the seeds of the decline of bureaucratic institutions lie in their very success, the phase of renewal must be as impermanent as that of maturity. Eventually, ecological conditions change, rival powers armed with new technologies emerge, established social groups claim greater benefits from the system than resources allow. Nepotism, personal favoritism, and sheer stupidity can be counted upon as continuing factors in the human condition. Sooner or later, political systems decline and collapse as it becomes impossible for them to provide the collective goods needed to convey a sense of legitimacy and to extract resources from the populace. Under the pressure of predatory invasions and ecological catastrophe, centralized bureaucracies and large-scale communities have disappeared, even though they must have appeared exceptionally vigorous in their prime. But the human populations associated with these cultures have not always vanished totally.[1] The surviving populations, often organized in feudal systems, typically persist; what has become extinct is the bureaucratic state and not the entire culture or society.

This account reflects our general knowledge of the early empires of Mesopotamia, Egypt, Rome, and China. The less well known example of Xochicalco, cited above, is no different.

> Xochicalco decreased in importance at the end of the Epiclassic, and the site was largely abandoned by 900 A.D. The subsequent Early Postclassic period (900 to 1250 A.D.) marks the end of both Xochicalco's regional political hegemony and its broader ceremonial influence. . . . It is possible that Xochicalco's decline was stimulated by the migration of hostile groups into the region from the Valley of Toluca and northern Guerrero.
>
> The site was partially reoccupied during the Late Postclassic period (1250 to 1519 A.D.) shortly after the arrival of Nahuatl-speaking Tlahuica groups in Morelos. Xochicalco grew to 92.4 ha during the late 13th and 14th centuries when a new civic-ceremonial precinct was constructed on the lower slopes of Cerro Temascal. Xochicalco was abandoned during the century preceding Spanish contact and is not mentioned in the early 16th-century sources either as one of the 60-odd Tlahuica city-states in Morelos or a subsidiary shrine, and the Pyramid of the Plumed Serpent was an important ancient monument. (Hirth 1984, 584–85)

Clearly the period of renewal, even when it occurs, has not precluded the ultimate collapse of bureaucratic states.

We tend, of course, to think that such events could only happen in history books. It remains to be seen, however, whether similar dynamics characterize modern bureaucratic institutions in exactly the same way (Masters 1983b). If neo-Darwinian evolutionary theory is correct, the process of evolution is not a guaranteed progress to ever higher and better forms; death and extinction are as much a part of life as birth and growth. This truth should apply as much to bureaucracy and the centralized state as to any other form of life.

CHAPTER 7

The Biology of
Social Participation

Evolutionary Concepts and Social Science

Critics of the extension of evolutionary reasoning to human behavior have failed to understand the extensive congruence between models based on natural selection and approaches conventionally accepted within the social sciences: the methods of the natural sciences can be extended to the study of political life. Paradoxically, however, reconceptualizing theories of politics in terms consistent with the life sciences challenges the assumed gulf between science (fact) and evaluative judgment (value). A naturalistic perspective both provides a scientific foundation for the study of social behavior and makes it possible to restore natural justice to its traditional place at the center of political philosophy.

The relationship between these two points can best be introduced by considering a representative and widely respected work in contemporary social science: Albert O. Hirschman's attempt to integrate economics and political science in *Exit, Voice, and Loyalty*. Although Hirschman's conceptual framework was elaborated without reference to evolutionary biology, the natural repertoire of social behavior provides a scientific foundation for his work. At the same time, a theoretical reassessment of economics and politics in naturalistic terms suggests limited but important conclusions about natural justice and injustice.

Hirschman first published *Exit, Voice, and Loyalty* in 1970. An economist by training, Hirschman bridged the gap between economics and political science by noting that the former traditionally deals with markets as institutions that permit, and indeed invite, individuals to leave as soon as the costs of participation exceed the benefits. In political institutions and behavior, on the other hand, participants try to modify outcomes by intervening directly in the decision process.

Because the buyer's way of influencing the seller is to cease to purchase goods at the current price, quality, or design, Hirschman describes the decision to leave a market as a form of exit. In this view, politics typifies the institutions in which individuals use voice to protest, support, or implement decisions binding on the group, whereas markets are usually regulated by voluntary exit.

As Hirschman points out ([1970] 1974), exit is sometimes possible in politics, just as voice is possible in economics. Political dissidents can emigrate rather than protest, just as purchasers in a market can complain about service rather than shift to another seller. In either case, the exercise of exit and voice is often inhibited by loyalty. In the market, brand preference or habit may prevent the buyer from seeking alternatives or from complaining, and thereby shelter the producer from the consequences of inadequacy in quality or design. In politics, similar patterns of attachment lead individuals to accept decisions without either trying to modify them or leaving the society. Because the effects of exit and voice cannot be analyzed without estimating the strength and character of individual loyalties, Hirschman was able to develop many surprising insights on the basis of this threefold conceptualization (see also Hirschman 1971, chaps. 9–12).

Although the concepts of exit, voice, and loyalty map well onto the basic dimensions of animal social behavior, Hirschman himself was not fully aware of the relevance of ethology. Hirschman did introduce one example from baboon social behavior early in his book, but only to contrast the "marvel of gradualness and continuity" of changes among primates with "the violent ups and downs to which human societies have always been subject" (Hirschman [1970] 1974,5–6). Observing that productive "surplus" in human society gives rise to "slack" and the possibility of "occasional decline as well as prolonged mediocrity," Hirschman then left the baboons to one side and focused on the way exit and voice serve as responses to deterioration in economic firms, social organizations, and political systems.

In fact, biological research both helps to explain the importance of the dimensions emphasized in *Exit, Voice, and Loyalty* and reveals important shortcomings in Hirschman's presentation. The premise that change is always more gradual and peaceful in primate social groups than in human societies has been contradicted by observations of chimpanzees (de Waal 1982, 1986; Goodall 1986a) as well as langurs (Hrdy 1981). More important, while Hirschman treats exit and voice as social mechanisms that are more primary than loyalty, ethological data reminds us that loyalty is far more than the "residual" category he describes.

Loyalty is a lasting disposition that is critical when the individual faces an alternative between social participation (voice) or exit. Among many animals, individuals are bonded to others of their species but leave that particular group or activity (exit) or engage in social interaction (voice) depending on the costs and benefits of alternatives. The three factors identified by Hirschman are thus equally fundamental elements of social behavior (Masters 1976a).

These categories are not merely artificial constructs, since they correspond to the natural repertoire of social behavior discussed in chapter 2. The human facial displays and emotional cues described as "happiness/reassurance," "anger/threat," and "fear/evasion," which are closely parallel to gestures of nonhuman primates, are congruent with Hirschman's exit (flight), voice (threat or attack), and loyalty (bonding). For both theoretical and empirical reasons, Hirschman's conceptualization in *Exit, Voice, and Loyalty* reflects the natural foundations of human social behavior, a fact that probably helped him to integrate economics and political science.

It may at first seem paradoxical to treat flight or departure as an intrinsic part of social interaction. Although irreversible exit marks the limit beyond which active cooperation with other group members ceases, this response is often adaptive in evolutionary terms. Departure from the group has the functional consequence of producing exogamy, limiting the extent of genetic inbreeding. Exit and group fission are thus important factors among other primates (Wrangham 1979; Lancaster 1986) and are generally assumed to have played an important role in early hominid hunter-gatherer bands (Fox 1975; Lovejoy 1981).

Even more important as a component of normal social behavior may be the role of intention movements and displays associated with exit. Short of exit, the displays of flight intention are well marked and decoded reliably from facial displays and other body movements, from paravocal cues, and from verbal messages. Although such cues indicate the absence of aggressive intent in subordinate individuals, they can also be signs of impending loss of status when exhibited by a dominant animal (de Waal 1982). When fear and evasiveness are shown by human leaders, such displays produce negative emotional responses and judgments regardless of the viewer's prior attitudes (Masters et al. 1986; Sullivan and Masters 1988).

Discovering the naturalistic basis of social science is more than an intellectual curiosity. Often, an evolutionary perspective illuminates unsuspected gaps in an otherwise sound theoretical model. Despite its insights, Hirschman's *Exit, Voice, and Loyalty* assumed that human societies normally produce a surplus ("slack"), failed to analyze bureaucratic or political command as an institutionalized form of voice, and understated the role of forced exit (expulsion or ostracism). Of these, the latter is perhaps the most interesting if one is to understand the foundations of human social participation (Gruter and Masters 1986).

Ostracism as Coerced Exit

From time to time, among animals as well as in human societies, some individuals are excluded from normal social interaction with all or virtually all of a group's members. This phenomenon, often called ostracism, can be defined as a pattern of social behavior in which one or more individuals are singled out and isolated from ongoing relationships of which they would otherwise be a part. Human examples range from the informal process of giving someone the "cold shoulder" within adolescent peer groups to ritualized customs like shunning. Precisely because ostracism seems to mark a rupture in normal social life, such practices can provide valuable insight into the processes underlying human societies.

Assuming that flight or exit is a fundamental dimension of social behavior, along with threat and reassurance, ostracism could be called involuntary or coerced exit. From this perspective, what makes ostracism particularly interesting is its paradoxical combination of exit, which is otherwise a voluntary departure from a group or activity, with the coercion associated with threats directed at those whose loyalty prevents flight. Such a distinction makes it possible to classify the different forms of human society in terms of their evolutionary origins and consequences.

In most preliterate human tribes and among other primates, groups frequently split and reform. Deviance and disagreement therefore lead to either individual departure or group fission, voluntary forms of exit (Chagnon and Irons 1979, chap. 4). This process has several evolutionary functions of importance. First, as mentioned above, it produces outbreeding, particularly in species where young males tend to move to the periphery of the group as they mature and then to leave it after agonistic interactions with the dominant males (DeVore 1965). Second, individual exit or group fission tends to balance the size of social groups, permitting populations of human hunter-gatherers to exploit marginal ecological settings with considerable efficiency. Finally, but most important, institutionalized exit (whether by individuals or subgroups) serves as a fundamental mechanism maintaining group consensus in preliterate tribes without political institutions. This third function requires an additional comment.

In many hunter-gatherer populations that survived into the twentieth century, as well as in other preliterate tribes often called segmentary lineage systems, there is no formal government (Fortes and Evans-Pritchard 1940; Barkun 1963; Masters 1964). Decisions are made by consensus after a more or less informal process of debate. This consensus is reinforced by traditions of reciprocity among group members ("reciprocal altruism") and by "moralistic aggression" or informal punishment directed toward those who deviate from group norms (Trivers and Willhoite, in White 1981). In such face-to-face groups, exit is a vital resource, providing disaffected members of a group with a credible sanction on overly ambitious or ineffective leaders. Independently chosen exit (whether by individuals or subgroups) is typical of many primates as well as of technologically primitive humans, and bands with this structure are a conceivable model of early hominid social life (Fox 1975).

The emergence of agriculture radically altered the potential implications of voluntary exit. Once agricultural techniques had been perfected, it was often necessary that fields be cleared and harvests collected by cooperative labor. Surpluses became possible but had to be stored. Therefore the group as a whole was more vulnerable to attack or predation by rival groups. Under these circumstances, as the story of Moses and the Pharaoh reminds us (*Exodus* 5–15), exit tends to be actively discouraged or subjected to regulation.

As wealth was accumulated, sedentary populations became more stratified. When political institutions were formed, resources were usually available to provide selective benefits for those in power; in return, political authorities provided services that maintained collective goods in the form of agricultural irrigation, law and order, and defense against outsiders. In place of informal procedures of consensus, formalized institutions established both legal norms governing behavior and authoritative roles for enforcing them (Margolis 1982, chap. 9; Masters 1983a).

Prior to the emergence of the state, exit was always an option, albeit sometimes a dangerous one, for those disaffected by the group in which they found themselves. Ostracism could also occur when virtually all members of a band abandoned a disliked individual (for an example, see Lévi-Strauss [1955] 1974, chap. 28). Although technologically simpler human groups could punish a disliked individual by collective exit, leaving the offending person isolated, agriculture and the state inverted this picture by making it possible to coerce a group member for whom exit was impracticable. In place of voluntary exit (by followers who choose to abandon a leader or by a leader who chooses not to contest a challenge), governments punish by organizing and enforcing involuntary or coerced exit (in which a majority of the group prevents one of its members from engaging in normal social interaction).

As Rousseau pointed out in Part 1 of the *Second Discourse*, coercive ostracism is impossible without institutions that block voluntary exit. If individuals can survive as well by leaving the group as by remaining within it, extreme conflict will lead to group fission or individual flight (as is the case among most primates). Ostracism is therefore particularly revealing because it shows both the strength of social bonds (Hirschman's loyalty) and the mechanisms by which coercion can be used to reinforce social norms. It would therefore be an error to limit the analysis of ostracism to its most informal mode (mere avoidance by others in the group), since legal punishments for the violation of social rules are a closely related phenomenon.

From this perspective, imprisonment, enslavement, and death are particularly important forms of ostracism. With the origin of the centralized state, governments could legislate more explicitly and in greater detail. Insofar as the state provides both security and relative control over the supply of food and other resources, those in power gain considerable leverage as social groups of a size previously impossible among primates emerge. Such societies can only be held together by legal norms including punishments for deviant behavior and limitations on voluntary exit (emigration). While this involves a cost for the subject, the benefits in terms of reproductive success have apparently been so massive that they usually outweigh the risks of punishment.

The foregoing analysis suggests that ostracism is far more important than might appear from the role usually attributed to it by social science. The most obvious examples of ostracism are informal and highly coercive patterns of social rejection in tribal societies based on segmentary lineage systems, groups of preschool children, or cohesive religious groups (Gruter and Masters 1986). In a complex industrial society like our own, such events seem somehow primitive and unpleasant. On reflection, however, it has to be admitted that the formal legal system of the modern state has institutionalized ostracism in the form of incarceration, the death penalty, or, in some societies, exile. Whether they take place in preliterate societies without a formal state or in our own society, phenomena akin to ostracism seem to reflect the limits of the fundamental process of social participation.

If this interpretation is correct, ostracism grew in importance and in formal institutionalization along with the emergence of the centralized state governed by a bureaucracy and functioning to amass a material surplus. Human social and political systems can therefore be classified in terms of the processes used to exclude people from social participation. Whereas political theory has usually emphasized institutions of decision making, shifting the focus to modes of ostracism makes it easier to assess the consequences of different regimes. The comparative study of legal forms of ostracism can, for example, suggest the relative costs and benefits of constitutional and totalitarian political regimes in our own day.

The Functions of Ostracism

In order to classify human social systems in terms of their institutionalized patterns of excluding or cutting off members, it is important to reemphasize the theoretical linkages between social bonding (Hirschman's loyalty), active participation in group decisions (voice), and various modes of voluntary and involuntary exit. Ostracism, defined as coercive or involuntary exit, presupposes social bonds that inhibit individual flight or group fission; as such, the greater the cost of voluntary exit, the more likely the occurrence of coercive or involuntary forms of excluding an individual from social participation. Conversely, where an active social role in decision making takes the form of participating in a face-to-face process of consensual agreement, it is most likely that ostracism will occur in the informal manner called "moralistic aggression" (Trivers 1981). As social processes are bureaucratized and institutionalized by formal governments, both voluntary exit and informal social ostracism tend to be replaced by legally defined punishments.

Over the last 3.5 million years of hominid evolution, most evidence suggests that our ancestors lived in relatively small bands of fifty to two hundred members (Leakey and Lewin 1977; Lovejoy 1981). While there is little direct evidence of the prehistory of behavior, such face-to-face groups, like similar bands in surviving hunter-gatherers, were probably open to fission and voluntary exit. Lacking rigid dominance hierarchies, face-to-face societies are characterized by an extensive participation (voice), either in the form of discussion leading to social consensus or as challenges to the leader's dominant status. Indeed, even in chimpanzee groups, ongoing social participation by all members of the group is reinforced by the possibility of temporary or lasting exit (Goodall 1982, 1986a, 1986b; de Waal 1982, 1986).

The function of ostracism, first in the informal patterns observed in many preliterate tribes and later in the legal punishments familiar to our own society, is thus inseparable from social bonds and the consequential cost of exit. In face-to-face societies where social participation remains open to most adults (or at least most adult males), ostracism is most likely to occur in its informal or consensual mode, as in the shunning among the Amish (Gruter 1986). Where social dominance is not organized on the basis of a complex, bureaucratized state, ostracism cannot be delegated to specific officials and institutions such as prisons; in face-to-face groups, most if not all members have to be recruited in order to exclude the ostracized from social participation. This informal mode of denying a voice to those who are deemed morally reprehensible (literally silencing them) is thus the counterpart of social relations in small groups that combine intense personal interaction and carefully regulated reciprocity.

The bureaucratic state has, therefore, a paradoxical effect on the process of managing social relationships. The institution of formalized legal procedures in a large-scale, often impersonal society makes it possible to replace informal or consensual ostracism with graded formal punishments. As a result, civilized societies often appear as a liberation from the constraints of the small-scale, agricultural community. No longer is the individual, and particularly the deviant individual, bound to the rigors of subtly calculated reciprocities with every other member of the local community. Diffuse moralistic aggression is therefore not as easily used to isolate and control individuals who refuse to be bound by social consensus.

Not all regimes have the same structure, of course. The interplay between participation and coercion is widely variable depending on the specific kind of political system in question. Constitutional democracies like those of Western Europe provide considerable opportunities for social participation (voice), even for citizens with little status or power. In contrast, more rigidly organized states—be they hereditary monarchies like the ancient regime in France or modern autocratic regimes ranging from the Soviet Union under Stalin to Chile under Pinochet—reduce the scope of active participation to a small segment of the entire population.

In civilized societies, reduction in the legitimacy and importance of relatively spontaneous social and political participation (voice) should therefore be correlated with increasing recourse to legalized or bureaucratic punishments amounting to institutionalized ostracism. In all nation-states, voluntary exit has become more difficult than it was centuries ago. To cross most frontiers, one needs a passport; to reside in most societies, one needs a visa or other form of bureaucratic permission. But in democratic regimes, exit remains a formal right of most citizens (unless convicted of serious crimes), and formally institutionalized ostracism is generally limited to incarceration or (for the most serious crimes, especially by individuals from marginal social strata) the death penalty. In contrast, autocratic and totalitarian regimes have elaborated both more rigid barriers to voluntary exit and a wide variety of devices for silencing or ostracizing those whose participation in decision making is deemed illegitimate.

Consider Nazi Germany. Exit was inhibited by all sorts of bureaucratic and political obstacles, while institutionalized ostracism took a number of forms that are relatively rare in constitutional democracies. These included arbitrary arrest, forced labor, denial of work, restriction of free movement from place to place or of access to the press, massive campaigns of vilification, petty bureaucratic harassment, and above all the systematic extermination of Jews and others deemed undesirable by Hitler's regime. Similar kinds of bureaucratic, governmentally organized ostracism have, of course, been observed in the Soviet Union and elsewhere. Often, as in the career of Alexander Solzhenitsyn, a single individual will be subjected to many of these varied forms of ostracism, including coerced exile. In other settings, as in several Latin American and African states under military rule, it appears that paralegal groups more or less inspired by some members of the elite have been responsible for the disappearance and assassination of presumed critics of the government. Wherever modern societies seek to repress dissent and silence the critics of the ruling elite, one finds the recurrence of formally institutionalized ostracism in its governmentally organized or bureaucratic form.

It would be naïve to assert that Western democracies never resort to analogous methods of reducing the impact of dissent, but both the legitimacy and extent of bureaucratic devices for denying participatory voice are markedly reduced in constitutional regimes. Under a government of law, such forms of formally institutionalized ostracism as massive disappearances, concentration camps, or press censorship usually seem either unavailable or too costly. In the United States, efforts to ostracize critics of the war in Vietnam usually took the form of politically motivated uses of the criminal justice system: voluntary exit, such as the flight of draft resistors to Canada, was never effectively blocked, and even attempts to stop leaks of information within the administration were, by totalitarian standards, relatively ineffective.

From this perspective, five general forms of social organization can be distinguished. Each kind of regime can be characterized in terms of the social bonds (loyalty), openness (exit), and political participation (voice) available to individuals. Of the five types, two arise in social situations in which centralized political institutions are lacking:

1. *Migratory or loosely organized face-to-face bands.* Characterized by

threat, exit, and group fission, simple hunter-gatherer bands with little or no obstacle to exit resemble some primate troops. Social participation is typically open to members of the group without rigid, institutionalized forms of ostracism. Individuals who do not cooperate or reciprocate are likely to be threatened and, if need be, abandoned (either by individual exit or group fission).

2. *Sedentary or closed face-to-face societies.* Such groups are governed primarily by consensus, with moralistic aggression being directed at nonconformists. While most members participate in ongoing social interaction, ostracism develops as a concerted form of punishment decided upon and determined by the collective judgment of the elders or other subgroups responsible for the community's social organization, defense, and ritual.

With the emergence of formal political institutions and legal systems, informal moralistic aggression is replaced by specific procedures and punishments for deviant behavior. Symbolized by the substitution of the "cities of refuge" for the passion of feud and ostracism (*Numbers* 35:9–34), the apparent freedom from local particularism is combined with new forms of social control on a broader scale. For theoretical purposes, three additional forms of social interaction can be distinguished within the broad class of state or statelike systems.

3. *Socially stratified states.* In early states and empires as well as in feudal systems, social stratification is typically marked; only some groups or classes have access to wealth and political power. Usually losers in warfare, whether held in slavery or in socially impotent lower-class status, are in effect ostracized as a collective category. At the local or village level, processes characteristic of closed face-to-face groups often persist.

4. *Constitutional government.* Formal legal procedures provide greater participation in the political process and easier exit as well as broader realms of freedom. The result is a decline in coercive ostracism because all citizens are considered to have legal rights, which can sometimes even be claimed against the state itself.

5. *Totalitarian or authoritarian government.* In contrast to constitutional regimes, repressive systems introduce rigid controls that radically lower political participation and individual freedom while increasing coercive ostracism. All individuals become vulnerable as competing bureaucracies (secret police, army, party) are used by a seemingly omnipotent leader to silence dissent through generalized fear and terror. As governments silence critics and demand unlimited loyalty, coercive ostracism becomes a central mechanism of political control.

From an evolutionary perspective, the balance of voice and voluntary exit characteristic of hominid bands prior to the development of large-scale agriculture is more closely approximated in the constitutional democracies of the West than in autocratic or totalitarian regimes. By maintaining avenues for widespread social and political participation and by restricting coercive exit to specified legal procedures of a public nature, societies ruled by law provide the benefits of a highly industrial civilization without the costs of more repressive societies. In contrast, highly authoritarian or totalitarian regimes seem to prevent large sectors of the population from engaging in behaviors typical of the human social repertoire. To exclude all but a small proportion of society from effective political participation, not only must voluntary exit be minimized, but coercion must be used to silence potential critics and ostracize those bold enough to voice dissent.

Social Participation and Natural Justice

The political implications of ostracism and social exclusion have long been studied as a problem in political theory. The first extensive discussion of the practice of ostracism as it relates to the law may well be Aristotle's treatment of the issue in the *Politics*.

> From this it is clear that legislation must necessarily have to do with those who are equal both in stock and capacity, and that for the other sort of person there is no law—they themselves are law. It would be ridiculous, then, if one attempted to legislate for them. They would perhaps say what Antisthenes says the lions say when the hares are making their harangue and claiming that everyone merits equality.[1] Hence democratically run cities enact ostracism for this sort of reason. For these are surely held to pursue equality above all others, and so they used to ostracize and banish for fixed periods from the city those who were held to be preeminent in power on account of wealth or abundance of friends or some other kind of political strength. The tale is told that the Argonauts left Heracles behind for this sort of reason: the Argo was unwilling to have him on board because he so exceeded the other sailors. Hence also those who criticize tyranny and the advice Periander gave to Thrasyboulus must not be supposed to be simply correct in their censure. It is reported that Periander said nothing by way of advice to the messenger who had been sent to him, but merely lopped off the preeminent ears of corn and so leveled the field. When the messenger, who was in igno-

rance of the reason behind what had happened, reported the incident, Thrasyboulus understood that he was to eliminate the preeminent men. This is something that is advantageous not only to tyrants, nor are tyrants the only ones who do it, but the matter stands similarly with respect both to oligarchies and to democracies; for ostracism has the same power in a certain way as pulling down and exiling the preeminent. And the same thing is done in the case of cities and nations alike by those with [military] power under their authority—for example, the Athenians in the case of Samians, Chians, and Lesbians, for no sooner was their [imperial] rule firm than they humbled these [cities,] contrary to the compacts [they had with them]. And the king of the Persians frequently pruned back the Medes and Babylonians and others who had harbored high thoughts on account of once exercising [imperial] rule themselves. (Aristotle *Politics* 3.13.1284a–1284b)

Reflecting the Athenian practice (Rehbinder, in Gruter and Masters 1986), Aristotle viewed ostracism as a widely practiced political institution both within and between societies. Individuals or entire societies that presented a threat to those in power were subjected to exile or coercive repression by "all regimes generally, including correct [that is, just] ones" (*Politics* 3.13.1284b).

Like a modern biologist studying the behavior of another species, Aristotle therefore assesses the functional consequences of ostracism without regard to the type of regime or the ethical quality of its implementation. He notes that ostracism occurs "when a certain person or persons are greater in power than accords with the city and the power of the governing body; from such persons there customarily arises a monarchy or a dynasty. Hence in some places they have the custom of ostracism—at Argos and Athens, for example" (*Politics* 5.3.1302b).

Despite Aristotle's objective description of ostracism, he counsels against its use: "It is better to see to it from the beginning that no one is preeminent to such an extent, however, than to let them arise and to heal [the malady] afterwards" (ibid.). Political participation (voice in the sense used by Hirschman) is characteristic of the human behavioral repertoire: although some individuals may not be well suited to playing an active role in community life, Aristotle calls our species the "political animal" (*zoon politikon*) precisely because participation in social activity is a central characteristic of human nature.

Social problems can arise, of course, if one individual is vastly superior to all others. While granting that "it is surely not proper to execute or exile or ostracize a person of this sort" (*Politics* 3.17.1288a),

Aristotle suggests that, at least in the Greek communities he knows best, such radical differences between the abilities of men do not exist:

> But since this is not easy to assume, there being none so different from the ruled as Scylax says the kings in India are, it is evident that for many reasons it is necessary for all in similar fashion to participate in ruling and being ruled in turn. For equality is the same thing [as justice] for persons who are similar, and it is difficult for a regime to last if its constitution is contrary to justice. (*Politics* 7.14.1332b)

Although Aristotle was not a modern egalitarian, he takes a perspective that combines a clinical if not scientific objectivity with the capacity to make discriminations based on the natural capacities of our species.

In our own time, there is no reason why contemporary evolutionary biology cannot provide the foundation for a similar approach to social and political life. Descriptions of different regimes and an understanding of their historical, economic, and social causes need not entail the inability to express preferences based on a knowledge of the human behavioral repertoire. When Aristotle speaks of "natural justice" (for example, *Politics* 1.5.1254a–1255a; *Ethics* 5.7.1134b–1135a), he points to precisely such a judgment and not to a presumed "natural law" that cannot be violated without immediate disaster or divine punishment. From a contemporary perspective, one can identify social systems that are closer to the central tendency of human behavior produced by our evolutionary past while understanding the specific circumstances leading to more extreme and less desirable social systems.

Explaining a social phenomenon does not require that it be considered either consistent with human nature or desirable. The emergence of different forms of political regimes depends on environmental or historical factors, whereas criteria of judgment depend on the behavioral repertoire of the species as it has evolved over millennia. A naturalist stance in the social sciences can thus resemble Aristotle's political theory both in its capacity to explain variation and in its emphasis on natural justice as an evaluative criterion.

If the foregoing reasoning is correct, modern totalitarian and autocratic regimes subject large portions of the community to behavioral constraints that are not typical of our primate heritage or of the patterns of hominid behavior that evolved over the last five million years. Insofar as the repertoire of human behavior has not changed in the last twenty thousand years, arbitrary and bureaucratically imposed coercive ostracism is more distant from the center of our species-typical range of behavior than the kinds of ostracism observed in stateless societies and constitutional legal systems. Even though diseases may be produced by natural processes, medical science can distinguish between sickness and health.

It is not possible here to present a comprehensive analysis of the historical causes of repressive or totalitarian regimes. In general, one or more of the following is likely to be involved: (1) the need to control large-scale populations in order to produce forced savings, and particularly to capitalize rapid industrialization; (2) fears that the reliable flow of resources can be maintained only by rigid control over the decision-making process; (3) rigidified social stratification, reinforced by attempts to prevent downward social mobility by members of social classes whose socioeconomic status is insecure; (4) resentment or fear of the loss of national identity or power; and (5) the breakdown of cultural or religious patterns under the impact of rapid technological and economic change. Any combination of these pressures may engender so much insecurity that major segments of a society are willing to exchange immediate security for the loss of voice. As Tocqueville warned a century and a half ago, modern populations often surrender their political freedoms to tyrannical regimes legitimized by egalitarian principles.

The incidence of repressive regimes seems to be correlated with two variables that influence the social behavior of other species and the norms of human cultures more generally: the extent of social stratification and the unpredictability of resource flow (Masters 1983b, 1984). In this hypothesis, derived from inclusive fitness models of natural selection, societies confronting ecological or economic crises and characterized by rigid dominance hierarchies are most likely to resort to devices like bureaucratic or totalitarian ostracism. Conversely, abundance and easy social mobility not only reinforce individual freedom and social participation, but reduce the pressure to ostracize social or political outsiders.

It would be inaccurate to describe the bureaucratic ostracism in a totalitarian regime like Nazi Germany as impossible: history has demonstrated all too well that such behavior is within the range of human possibilities. But it would be equally incorrect to claim, in the name of presumed scientific objectivity, that evolutionary biology is totally irrelevant to the preference for political freedom on which Western constitutional government is based. Modern biology provides grounds for understanding the widely shared hostility to institutionalized forms of coercive ostracism.

Many contemporary scholars have strong reservations about the argument that some cultural or political patterns are more natural than others. In biological research, the observation that a response is characteristic of the behavioral repertoire of a species in many or all of its typical habitats or evolutionary settings does not imply that other responses will not be inevitable in different environments (cf. Aristotle *Ethics* 1.3.1094b; 5.6.1134a-5.7.1135a). When a naturalistic approach is used in political science, it does not follow that we can say nothing about the relative desirability of different regimes. Such a conclusion would make as little sense as the assertion that the science of medicine makes it impossible to define health and prefer it to illness.

Because cancer occurs naturally and its probability is increased by heavy smoking, can science say nothing about the desirability of smoking or cancer on the grounds that all such statements would be purely arbitrary values? While extreme versions of the fact-value dichotomy pose interesting epistemological problems (to which I will return), such a stance entails a degree of skepticism that is not found in the day-to-day judgment of virtually all reasonable citizens. When one encounters other domains of modern scientific research, it is customary and reasonable to distinguish between necessity and desirability.

The Return to Natural Justice

That neo-Darwinian evolutionary principles can be the foundation of human political and ethical standards will strike many (including some biologists and philosophers) as paradoxical. That the shape of the human rights and duties arising on the basis of the life sciences will resemble the classical natural right teaching of political philosophers like Plato and Aristotle—thinkers who seemingly deny the existence and importance of evolution—will at first be even more surprising (Masters 1978a). It must be remembered, however, that similarity is not identity: while the classics used nature as a basis for judging human affairs, their concept of nature was not exactly the same as ours. The new naturalism will inevitably differ in many ways from the specific doctrines of the past.

Let it not be said that my thesis is merely a return to the ethical and political ideas of Aristotle. I am far from believing that industrial civilization should be abandoned in order to create the *polis* of antiquity or that the existence of natural slavery is demonstrated by the study of hominid evolution. To say that Aristotle and other classical political philosophers remain relevant to an understanding of the human condition is not an invitation to pretend we are ancient Greeks and Romans, living in the very different world of the pagan city-state. Evolutionary biology teaches the importance of change as well as of continuity.

What, then, are the standards of the good life? If the biological sciences provide a route to the rediscovery of human goals and purposes "in accordance with nature" (to use the phrase so frequently employed by the Platonic Socrates), how do these ends resemble those taught by the ancients, how do they differ, and what explains the changes in perspective? It should be obvious from the mere statement of the question that it is very different from the focus of this book. One cannot do everything at once, and while contemporary culture leads us to impatience, it is often a mistake in philosophy, as in life, to be in too much of a hurry.

Even so, the outlines of the ethical and political values grounded on twentieth-century evolutionary biology are not hard to see. Based on the understanding of human nature and society described above, we can identify three broad features that are likely to characterize the new naturalism: respect for human individuality and cultural difference; the duties of virtue entailed by social obligation; and the concern for human justice.

While a preliminary statement of these principles cannot claim to be definitive, it is proper to conclude this inquiry into the nature of politics with an outline, admittedly tentative, of these principles of natural justice. As is implied by what has gone before, there is relatively little that is radical or new, but much that is profoundly reassuring, in this rediscovery of the soundness of the Western tradition.

RESPECT FOR INDIVIDUAL AND CULTURAL DIFFERENCES

The first principle of natural justice that should attract our attention is the respect for other human beings entailed by our common humanity. If the phenotype is merely the vehicle by which genes replicate themselves, every human being is equal in a more profound sense than has been realized in most secular political teachings. Difference is not inferiority: who can know which of us carries a mutant gene that is a valuable adaptation to a future environment and will someday spread throughout the human gene pool? At one level, the human species can be defined only by the statistical frequencies of different gene alleles at each genetic locus: each genotype is merely a sampling of this realm of possibilities, and none can ever be said, a priori, to be better than another, if only because the natural selection that will test differential survival lies in the future.

Nothing is more threatening to the survival of a species than the disappearance of naturally occurring genetic variation. This is why many agronomists have insisted that hybrid species of corn and wheat, while extraordinarily well adapted to produce high yields under contemporary conditions, should not be allowed to eliminate all representatives of older strains of seed. Evolutionary principles teach us to expect humans to overvalue their own interests, perspectives, and importance; nepotism or selfishness is, to an extent, natural. Evolutionary principles also teach us, however, that this selfishness of the human phenotype is a behavioral strategy of the gene pool and that, in the case of our species at least, such behavior is naturally balanced by social cooperation, without which we could not have evolved and cannot now survive.

Because human societies, and most particularly modern civilizations, depend on reciprocity, respect for others is enjoined on us by the very nature of the social system in which we live. Discovery of the difference between one human culture and another, which leads the superficial to believe in relativism, has to be understood in this context. It is true that the specific cultural norms of each human society are different: relations between males and females were relatively equal among the !Kung bushmen, highly unequal in traditional India, and are between these extremes in the contemporary United States (Masters 1984). The fact of cultural differences and social change has always been at the foundation of political philosophy (*Republic* 1.327a): the question is how to interpret this fact from the perspective of modern biology.

A comprehensive theory of cultural evolution, based on biological principles and suggesting hypotheses that account for such different social norms, would obviously have important philosophic implications. On scientific grounds, the same theory should account for the social practices and laws of the !Kung bushmen and the ancient Indian caste system. Even if our self-interest leads us to understand and prefer one of these systems to the other, we cannot deprecate that which is strange or displeasing and pretend that such customs are due to ignorance and folly from which we ourselves are exempt. More important, we cannot pretend that our way of life represents progress over older, less sophisticated societies: evolution is not progress, and change is not always improvement. The new naturalism based on the synthetic theory of evolution therefore leads to respect for different human cultures; humility—not the pride associated with Marxism or the Social Darwinism of the Victorians—is one of the first obligations of natural justice.

THE DUTIES OF VIRTUE

A second principle arising from evolutionary principles flows from the first. Those who live in a civilized society governed by the centralized state find themselves in a particularly complex, often comfortable, but ultimately precarious situation. This form of social system is extraordinarily rare in nature: a very unusual combination of circumstances is required for a mammalian species to engage in the cooperative behaviors needed to support bureaucratic governments and very large-scale societies. For those living in a civilized world, many comforts and benefits depend upon collective goods generated by the state. As analysis from an evolutionary perspective shows, however, these systems are vulnerable and fragile both in theory and in practice.

The principle of reciprocity can suffice as the basis of a face-to-face group, like the kin groups comprising a stateless society; mere reciprocity will not maintain the centralized state. Evolutionary principles lead us to expect selfishness, but also to recognize its dangers. To seek more for oneself may be natural but, under some circumstances, to live in a state has become natural too; once the centralized state evolved, the virtues associated with this new social and cultural environment emerged. Natural justice requires, then, a willingness to balance one's own immediate selfish needs not only by cooperation with others in the hopes of reciprocity, but even by acts of self-sacrifice that contribute to the collective good without reciprocity (Plato *Crito* 50a–54d).

The same theoretical principles that provide a foundation for the classical notion of virtue teach us to beware of the use of this concept by the political leadership. The centralized state, as an institution, stands or falls according to the extent to which its citizens are capable of pursuing their own interests in a virtuous manner. But the leaders, as individuals, are only too readily tempted to use this argument to their own selfish advantage. The tension between leaders and the led is inherent in human politics. Precisely for this reason, the natural foundation of justice cannot enjoin obedience in all circumstances without contradicting the common humanity of rulers and ruled that is its first principle.

Unlike contemporary political opinions, the new naturalism can therefore best be interpreted in terms of self-imposed moral obligation. Unlike some absolute moral teachings, these obligations depend on circumstances, cannot legitimately be invoked by governments as a reason for unquestioning obedience, and can produce genuine humanity in relations with others. Perhaps it would be more comforting to have simpler standards of right and wrong that never vary in any respect, but in practice, no code of ethical or religious teaching has long survived unless it could adapt to changed circumstances, provide grounds to challenge corrupt rulers, and serve as the basis for decent social relationships.

The extension of evolutionary principles to human life, unlike the seventeenth-century teachings of natural right, is thus not restricted to equal "rights to life, liberty, and estate" —abstract claims that produce social conflict without providing natural grounds for self-restraint in the exploitation of either the physical environment or other peoples. The natural right doctrines of Hobbes and Locke gave rise to colonialism and the destruction of natural resources. In the name of these principles, the vast majority of the indigenous population of North America was subjected to virtual genocide. Like older views of ethics, natural justice can and should recognize the claims of others. In terms of the traditional virtues, moderation and temperance in seeking one's own interest as well as courage in defense of the community are perfectly reasonable and just obligations of the civilized human being.

NATURAL JUSTICE

The claim that justice is a natural virtue would be all well and good, it might be objected, if one could only discover what it means. That individuals and even governments disagree about the definition of justice in concrete circumstances has been obvious, however, to the generations of serious philosophers who asserted that there is a natural distinction between just and unjust actions. Precisely because politics is a biological phenomenon, disagreement on practical matters is virtually inevitable. Indeed, this is probably the true lesson to be derived from the often-noted human dependence on learning and culture as means of adapting to the environment.

In one sense, disagreement is a sign that a society is responding to changing or complex circumstances; if so, disagreement should invite tolerance and dialogue rather than impatience and anger. In another sense, however, social conflict reflects the inevitable tension between the collective goods required for the survival of civilization and the continued selfishness of those who seek the added benefits of the free rider. Those who contribute virtuously to maintain a civilization are likely to direct "moralistic aggression" toward the deviant, the criminal, or the political dissident (Trivers 1981; Willhoite 1981, 1986).

It follows, from evolutionary principles, that there is no single political system that can claim to be perfectly natural in all social and ecological conditions. Although this might seem an invitation to relativism, naturalism leads in a different direction. The question of what is or is not just cannot be entirely divorced from circumstances any more than the question of what is or is not healthy food or exercise can be defined abstractly for all humans in all environments. Standards of good food and exercise differ for the child, the adult, or the aged; what is proper is relative to the individual's situation, without it thereby being concluded that health is entirely a question of subjective value or personal preference (cf. Aristotle *Politics* 4.1.1288b).

Health is a useful analogy to justice for more than one reason. Standards of a healthy way of life differ depending on the individual and the circumstances, but for practical purposes the most evident measure of health is its absence. We may disagree on the definition of perfect physical condition, exercise, or food, and still readily recognize illness. In much the same way, standards of natural justice are probably most useful in identifying injustice. Humans have adopted many different cultural and individual ways of life, none of which can claim to be ordained by natural selection in the sense that religion ordains a mode of life as divinely given. Since all of these patterns are built on a natural repertoire of behaviors, the study of human nature may be most useful in teaching us the limits beyond which the presumption of respect for another might properly be replaced with indignation in the face of injustice.

Three fundamental elements of the social repertoire have been identified as particularly important in human societies: bonding to the group (loyalty), threat (voice), and flight (exit). Humans naturally compete as well as cooperate; opportunities to leave the group are as important as opportunities to influence it. As a first approximation, one could presume that an unjust violation of natural standards of behavior is likely when individuals or groups are coercively and unfairly denied access to these fundamental elements of the human repertoire of social behavior. When power or violence is used to exclude some from a group, to silence them by precluding their participation in decision making, and yet to prevent their exit, the basic element of reciprocity on which societies usually rest appears to be destroyed (Gruter and Masters 1986). Genocide and attempted genocide, using the power of the state as a means to destroy masses of humans, is naturally unjust.

Within the industrialized world, constitutional democracies, however imperfect they may be, come closer than other regimes to providing institutionalized arenas within which individuals can express loyalty, challenge those in authority, or freely submit (as evidenced by a choice to remain rather than to flee). What we describe as "natural" or "civil rights" is, most often, a legal expression of much this same judgment. Respect for the different opinions of others requires that we permit them to speak and participate in political life, even when our ideas diverge. Virtue and a willingness to contribute to the common good requires that we exhibit loyalty to a community that provides collective benefits to us. Neither political debate nor loyalty can be fully effective if silent obedience cannot be interpreted as a choice because there is no option to live elsewhere.

Although this formulation might not satisfy every reader, it is not my intention to seek universal agreement. Indeed, it will be enough to have made it legitimate to discuss, with the seriousness it deserves, the question of natural justice and injustice. No understanding of the human condition, however elegant on other grounds, is complete if it cannot help us to judge such events as Hitler's attempted Final Solution, Stalin's use of purges and terror, and other abuses of bureaucratized power in the twentieth century. Survival of the fit cannot conceivably mean survival of individuals or ways of life that can persist only by the violent destruction of helpless masses of humans: even though it is true that extinction is a natural event, humans who take the fate of populations—or of the entire species—into their own hands know not what they do. Nuclear war and other uses of industrial technology that create hitherto inconceivable horror may be possible; such means of securing political advantage cannot be just.

Contemporary biology supports the view that human life has a meaning beyond the immediate pleasures or pains of the individual. As a species with an evolutionary history, we are not merely the unconditioned, self-creating beings imagined by nihilists. That humans learn much of their behavior does not prove the absence of a natural foundation for cultural variation and change; as Aristotle puts it, "all art and education" tend to "supply the element that is lacking in nature" but, in so doing, should follow "the distinction of nature" in such matters as age, ability, and excellence (*Politics* 7.17.1337a). If either science or philosophy have any role in the future, surely it is to perpetuate the tradition of rational discourse about ends as well as means. Humans cannot understand their own humanity without asking to what extent the way they live is consistent with human nature.

EPILOGUE

The study of the life sciences makes it necessary to change our understanding of human nature and history. Research in hominid evolution, ethology, neurophysiology, sociobiology, and linguistics can no longer be ignored by anyone seriously interested in human political and social behavior. The task is difficult because it is necessary to integrate biology, political philosophy, and the social sciences in an age of academic specialization. And the results will be controversial because they challenge prevailing opinions concerning science, ethics, and human nature.

The naturalistic approach described in the preceding chapters has three principal consequences. First, it provides a new foundation for the social sciences. Second, it offers an objective basis for moral judgment. Finally, it gives us a deeper understanding of our species' place in the world. Because such a profound change in attitude is involved, a detailed summary of the argument as it applies to each of these three issues is appropriate.

Science and the Study of Human Behavior

Behaviorism is dead. Behaviorist theorists sought universal "laws of behavior" that could predict the response of any organism to specific stimuli (Skinner 1965); contemporary biology shows that different species—and often individuals of different development or age within a single species—respond to a given stimulus in very different ways. The behaviorist view that the organism is a passive "black box," with few innate responses beyond reflexes (Kuo 1967), has been contradicted by research in ethology, neurology, and social psychology. The cues stimulating an organism are often preprogrammed in the central nervous system; a particular stimulus can elicit different responses depending on the individual or the social context. The effects of conditioning and experience stressed by behavioral psychologists cannot alone provide a comprehensive explanation of human behavior.

The behaviorist movement in social science was nonetheless useful. It has often been asserted that human life is impossible to study in the light of natural science: for phenomenologists, historical determinists, nihilists, deconstructionists, and traditionalists alike, purpose and subjective experience render our species unique. Although this belief has now been disproven by advances in the life sciences, behaviorism was long the primary school that challenged the comforting but erroneous myth of the autonomy of human will.

The difficulty with behaviorism was not, as its critics charged, that it sought to link the natural and the social sciences, but rather that the behaviorist approach used an inappropriate scientific discipline as its model. In discovering patterns of conditioning and response that do occur—albeit not with the universality supposed by the movement's founders—behaviorists sought to build upon the science of physics (Taijfel and Peters 1968); in economics and political science, attempts to discover a scientific basis for understanding human society were likewise based on Newtonian physics (Goldberg 1963). As a movement in the social sciences, behaviorism generally failed to appreciate the impact of Darwinian biology (Schubert 1981), not to mention the extent to which the physical sciences themselves had been transformed by quantum mechanics and the theory of relativity.

Many of the reasons against a scientific study of human social life disappear when the biological sciences are taken as its theoretical foundation. Newtonian physics appeared to establish relationships between cause and effect that were independent of time and place; transposed into human affairs, such a perspective could only appear reductionist and determinist, to cite two frequent criticisms. Evolutionary biology leads in a different direction. Because of the multiplicity of causal levels in living systems, as one leading neo-Darwinian put it, reductionism is "absurd" in biology (Simpson 1969). Determinism implies causal links that always move in one direction, on the model of the transmission of force by billiard balls, which became the implicit metaphor for political theory (Hobbes *Leviathan,* chaps. 2–3; Bentley 1908). Living systems are infinitely more complicated, since causal processes operate simultaneously at the levels of the ecosystem (webs of interaction among species as well as between living beings and the physical environment), the species (natural selection of gene frequencies), the group (the stimulation of organisms by events in the physical and social environment), and the individual (irreversible developmental and idiosyncratic events).

Discoveries in the life sciences challenge a number of principles that have been generally shared by social scientists. First, instead of seeking deterministic relationships (whether defined as the influence of the environment or the action of genes), the life sciences focus on probabilities. The laws of behaviorism assumed that all organisms respond in the same way, so that experiments with mice and rats could illuminate human behavior; most economic theories likewise presume that different individuals respond to market forces in the same way. Beneath this approach has been the assumption that all organisms, like all atoms of hydrogen, are essentially similar. The life sciences, on the other hand, prove that each individual (with the exception of identical twins) is genetically different.

Philosophers have long spoken of the nature of man. Evolutionary biology teaches us that "man" does not exist. Rather, populations of human beings encounter varied environments that elicit distinct attributes from the range of human responses produced by natural selection. To speak of man confuses the individual, the group, and the species, and blurs the difference between males and females. Individuals have different natures, and without such naturally occurring variation, evolution could not occur. Biological processes can, in general, be described as the production of a multitude of variants among which some are selected depending on context and prior history.

Second, innate ideas and biological processes seem necessary to explain many otherwise puzzling aspects of human behavior. The natural propensities of the human organism—generally dismissed since the triumph of Locke and empiricist philosophy—are as important as the environment in forming individual behavior. Evidence is mounting that such divergent traits as mathematical or musical genius, dyslexias, schizophrenia, depression, criminality, and other personality traits have an organic substrate (Masland 1983; Wilson and Herrnstein 1985; Rushton et al. 1986; Izard, Hembree, and Huebner 1987; Eaves 1988; Kagan, Reznick, and Snidman 1987, 1988). As more is learned about genetic and hormonal influences on behavior, there is no reason to assume that the inheritance and development of personal characteristics will be impossible to explain in a nonreductionist, probabilistic model of the interaction of nature and nurture throughout the life cycle.

The argument against naturalistic explanations of human behavior was, at its inception, in part political (though not thereby unreasonable). Natural differences between individuals, such as the father's power over the family, were once viewed as divinely ordained grounds for political authority; as Locke argued in the *First Treatise of Government*, such arguments do not withstand scrutiny. Because environmental determinism had served as a foundation for the Western constitutional principle that all citizens are equal before the law, it is hardly surprising that a biological perspective on human affairs was long opposed on the grounds that it would be inherently conservative or reactionary.

Modern genetics removes this difficulty. Insofar as the phenotype is simply a "vehicle" for genetic replication (Dawkins 1976), no individual can claim to be naturally superior in all respects. None of us can know which genes will turn out, in future environments, to be essential for continued human life. All one can know for certain is that variation is essential to every living species; homogeneous gene pools are peculiarly vulnerable to unanticipated disaster. Far from being a sign of inferiority, differences are often advantageous (as in the case of those dyslexics whose reading disability is the counterpart of genius in tasks requiring nonverbal, spatial integration). Respect for each individual can be based on genetics and the theory of natural selection.

Finally, the change and complexity that are at the center of the life sciences require more sophistication and caution than have hitherto characterized research in the social sciences. Psychologists and pedagogues have pretended that one could understand the way humans think without a knowledge of the structure of the central nervous system; now we know not only that different cognitive processes tend to be localized precisely, but that individuals have quite different aptitudes, reflecting different neurological structures and functioning.

Such knowledge increases our ability to change outcomes, just as modern medicine enhances our ability to overcome diseases. Knowing the localized source of diverse types of dyslexia makes it easier to teach those afflicted how to read (Ellis 1984; Denckla 1986a, 1986b). Many sociologists and anthropologists have analyzed cultural norms as if they could be chosen at will by human groups, whereas ethology and sociobiology reveal predictable relationships between behavior and ecology or social environment that apply to humans as well as to other species. Knowing these relationships might make it easier to understand the contradictions between what humans desire and what they can attain—and thereby help avoid social conflict, war, and tyranny.

Given the complexity of the new naturalism, it is understandable that most people have questioned the possibility or relevance of scientific studies of human affairs. Hostility to the very concept of a science of human behavior carries with it, however, the implication that we are totally unfettered by natural constraint. As more is learned in ecology, neurobiology, and molecular genetics, the presumption that human behavior is uncaused or controlled by free will becomes less and less tenable. In place of the hubris of either the behaviorists (who sought to "engineer" human behavior on the model of mechanical engineering) or the humanists (for whom all social life is a question of choice), a biological perspective calls for humility and dignity.

Knowledge of the causes of human behavior does not limit human freedom. Contrary to popular belief, the more we know about physiological and genetic causation, the more independent from accident and blind determinism our choice can become. Discovery of the genetic and cellular processes involved in cancer has not made those with the disease any less free. If anything, the problem is quite the opposite, since a science of human behavior creates choices that most people are ill prepared to make.

In this as in many other respects, modern medicine provides a revealing indication of the potential and the dangers of a more comprehensive science of politics and social behavior. Expanding knowledge of human biochemistry, genetics, and ethology is not likely to be prevented by philosophic arguments about science and free will. Instead, as genetic engineering and chemical modification of behavior become practical realities, discoveries in the life sciences will force us to make decisions with awesome ethical implications. As in medicine, the question is no longer whether humans can influence events and processes that were hitherto neither understood nor controlled by human choice. Now, we must decide if we ought to do things that are made possible by scientific knowledge.

Toward a Natural Basis for Ethics

At first, it appears that natural science cannot be a foundation for any moral teaching beyond the justification of the status quo: Whatever is, is right. Were humans not endowed with such complex central nervous systems, permitting the most diverse responses to identical situations, this objection might have force. As it is, humans are all too liable to mistake their own self-interest, committing folly and wickedness on a scale unknown among other species. Traditional moralists from Plutarch ("That Beasts Use Reason," *Moralia*) to Rousseau (*Second Discourse*) had no difficulty showing that so-called lower animals are often more in tune with nature than humans. Evil arises because of the very traits that many contemporary thinkers describe as signs of human excellence: rationality, cultural diversity, scientific knowledge, rapid social change—in short, what Morin (1963) called our "hypercomplexity."

Because humans appear to have emancipated themselves from the instinctive or mechanical causes found in other species, modern social and ethical theorists have typically concluded that nature can no longer be a standard of ethical evaluation. As a result, Western civilization since the eighteenth century has been confronted with a pervasive opposition between nihilists or historicists (for whom all values are subjective or relative) and doctrinaires (for whom theological or ideological principles can be imposed on others by force if need be). A way out of this profound dilemma can now be found by using evolutionary biology as the basis of ethical judgment.

Both relativism and dogmatism can be transcended by a naturalist approach to human life. Logical positivism, which proclaimed that a "gulf" between "fact" and "value" precludes any scientific basis for judgments of right and wrong (Brecht 1959), is insufficient as an account of the relationship between science and human behavior. Although skeptics and historicists had good reason to challenge absolute dogmas parading as natural law, neo-Darwinian biology provides the foundation for ethical standards consistent with the Western tradition yet open to change and reasoned debate. These assertions are, however, so contrary to contemporary opinions that they need to be explained in some detail.

BEYOND NIHILISM

In one form or another, relativism and nihilism have dominated Western secular thought since Nietzsche. Advances in physics destroyed the image of a divinely ordained cosmic order, confronting us with the picture of a universe based on chaotic and random processes. If the human meaning of a physical observation depends on one's location in time and space, it seems obvious that all moral judgment will likewise be relative. For over a century, Darwin's theories had the same effect when they were used to challenge the literal interpretation of the Bible: a species descended from the apes and adapted to varied environments does not appear to be governed by a divinely ordained and universally valid natural law.

Arguments for the existence of God based on the presumed harmony of nature, while predominant in the eighteenth century, were indeed an inappropriate foundation for ethical or political principles. The tendency to claim that one's own beliefs are naturally superior to those of others was compounded by Social Darwinism, which misinterpreted evolutionary principles and transformed them into an apology for Victorian differences in social class and status. Given such palpably false and self-serving uses of the concept of nature, it is little wonder that most intellectuals and scientists preferred skepticism or even nihilism to dogmatism and ideological deception.

In the philosophy of science, this mood took the form of the fact-value dichotomy. Reason and logic seemed to show that it was a naturalistic fallacy to claim one outcome is preferable to another on scientific grounds. Like the pre-Socratics in ancient Greece, logical positivists open the way to a scientific perspective on social behavior, but their relativism cannot provide an adequate philosophic account of human life. For the relativist or nihilist, each individual's values are as good as another person's: "Do your own thing." Ultimately, such a perspective is in contradiction with its own premises.

Thoroughgoing relativism presumes that one cannot make moral judgments of others because no one can fully share another's perspective. Language is taken as a totally arbitrary set of conventions. Were this entirely true, there would be no reliable means of communication and no science. The Greek Heraclitus had said that one "cannot step into the same river twice"; his follower Cratylus, taking this argument to its logical conclusion, argued that one can't step into the same river even once, therewith stopped speaking, and merely waved his finger.

If all language and human culture were totally arbitrary conventions, science would also be arbitrary and all communication merely a form of compulsion. Were this an adequate account, natural scientists could neither describe nor predict the world around us. To be consistent, thoroughgoing relativists and nihilists would have to refuse to benefit from modern medicine and technological devices based on science, for by doing otherwise they tacitly admit that some humans can discover and communicate truths about the world, and implicitly give the scientists who do so uncontested power.

In practice, relativism and nihilism usually become a rationalization for hedonism. Once traditional morality and religion have been rejected in the name of scientific objectivity, the only basis of ethical judgment comes to be subjective value. Given this choice, that most people prefer their self-interest and pleasure is predictable from the theory of natural selection. The individual's desire for self-preservation and comfort, taken as a value by some philosophers of science, is surely one of the central facts of an application of evolutionary biology to human affairs (Alexander 1979).

The logical positivist's argument that values cannot be deduced from facts is thus doubly contradictory. On the one hand, the most widely chosen value—individual hedonism or at least self-preservation—is quite obviously a biological fact; when the physician says a patient ought to have an operation because the facts show appendicitis, the patient is unlikely to complain about a fallacious logical deduction. On the other hand, the logical positivists themselves have unwittingly derived a value (it is bad to defer to ethical doctrines based on authority) from a presumed fact (traditional dogma seems to be inconsistent with natural science).

Just as Plato and Aristotle transformed the hedonism of the Greek

Sophists into a scientific and philosophic tradition capable of lasting to our own day, contemporary naturalism can go beyond relativism and nihilism. Arguments rejecting traditional orthodoxy in the name of new scientific perspectives overstate the human relevance of chance, accident, and chaos. In neo-Darwinian theory, natural selection is driven by events that have neither meaning nor purpose, but it results in living beings whose behavior has meaning and purpose within the constraints of time and place. For Aristotle, human ethics were derived from biology, not from physics (Masters 1978a, 1987). The discovery that the cosmos lacks the harmony of the Newtonian worldview may contradict eighteenth century theological doctrines; it does not lead ineluctably to Nietzschean principles.

BEYOND DOGMATISM AND A PRIORI MORALITY

The insufficiency of relativism and hedonism should not blind us to the truth contained in the challenge to traditional dogma. Inclusive fitness theory teaches that humans, like other animals, typically behave in ways that benefit their physical health and welfare. Those in power, benefiting from the perquisites of status and wealth, can be expected to justify the existing state of affairs as natural and appropriate; the greater the social or political inequality, the more likely it is that such justification will take the form of dogmatic orthodoxies. Ethical absolutes, whether rooted in theology or in a presumed natural law, can readily be used by elites to justify customs or policies in their own self-interest.

Moral relativism is profoundly egalitarian. If values are *sui generis*, each individual's choices (as long as they are sincere) would seem to be beyond ethical criticism. It is no accident that relativism and hedonism were developed as a challenge to doctrines of divine or natural law rooted in medieval thought: with the rise of the market economy and constitutional democracies, each citizen needed to take responsibility for his own life. As historicists and Marxists like to point out, doctrines like those of the logical positivists have political implications.

In a world of change, no human action can be judged without reference to time and place. The imposition of abstract norms without regard to circumstances is naturally unjust, for such a priori standards inevitably favor some people over others. Precisely because each human genotype is of equal importance from an evolutionary perspective, a naturalistic ethics cannot be dogmatic, intolerant, and absolutist. While most secular philosophers would accept this argument as a reason for rejecting doctrinaire religious fundamentalism, it extends to Kantian rationalism and other a priori ethical theories.

An example will illustrate the defect of ethical absolutes. Debates concerning the equality of the sexes in contemporary Western industrial society often reflect the quest for a universal solution. For some, men and women should be equal in all respects; for others, the traditional family, and therewith the distinct roles of men and women, are the foundation of civilization. From both perspectives, it is usually assumed that those with the contrary view are shortsighted and selfish. The difficulty lies in the assumption that there is a single answer to the question of the appropriate role of each sex.

In socially stratified cultures as diverse as medieval Europe and traditional India, it was customary for men and women to have different political rights and privileges; in many hunter-gatherer societies, the two sexes have roughly equal status. While some might use these differences as evidence of cultural relativism, they can readily be explained as responses to the social and physical environment (Harris 1977). Since similar differences in gender roles are found in other species, a naturalistic approach explains why some cultures invest equally in males and females, whereas others treat the two sexes quite differently (Weinrich 1977; Dickemann 1979; Masters 1984).

To assume that there is a single logic of male and female social and political roles, without reference to time and place, is contrary to evolutionary biology. While it would be absurd to claim that the practices of the caste society of traditional India should be a guide in Western industrial democracies, it is equally unwarranted to dismiss all social norms unlike our own as based on ignorance and vice. It is understandable enough that people describe their own customs as natural, but this label does not justify the imposition of universal ethical criteria on others living in very different circumstances. Such ethnocentrism is all the more suspect today because contemporary doctrines of equality are suited to a market economy and have been used to extend the power and wealth of capitalist societies at the expense of the Third World.

Moral or political doctrines that are in one's own self-interest cannot be forced on others contrary to their interests without thereby using an ostensibly true theory as an instrument of power (Kass 1971). This caveat applies not only to theological intolerance and dogmatism, but to the a priori ethical reasoning that has become philosophically stylish since Kant. The categorical imperative seems to provide an appealing foundation for a rational ethics. Insofar as it is impossible to define a norm of behavior without reference to circumstance, however, ethical abstractions can ultimately enshrine parochial customs and interests in a rationalist garb.

One example should suffice. Rawls's celebrated *Theory of Justice*

(1971) proclaims that a rational norm must be one that could be adopted behind a "veil of ignorance." Like the Kantian categorical imperative, Rawls's principle of justice requires that the individual be unaware of his circumstances in life. At one level, this could be described as an approximation of the principle of natural selection on future generations: since none of us can predict the exact social situation of our grandchildren, each has an interest in establishing cultural norms that would not favor some classes or groups against others. The restatement of Rawls's principle in this form indicates, however, that it applies to social situations in which rapid social mobility is considered normal—and even there, only over the long run. In day-to-day behavior, context matters; to treat everyone in exactly the same way would make all forms of reciprocity immoral. No primate behaves toward others as if it is behind "a veil of ignorance"; inclusive fitness theory shows that reciprocal altruism—and hence what Axelrod (1983) calls the "tit-for-tat" strategy—is more reasonable on naturalistic grounds than an a priori ethics ignoring the past behavior of others.

It is worth noting, in fact, that a priori ethical doctrines tend to be enunciated by males. As Carol Gilligan (1983) has shown, women are more likely than men to insist that concrete circumstances should qualify abstract moral rules. While formal definitions of rights and duties are appropriate in some areas, such as legislation that will be binding on an entire society across generations, they cannot be taken as the only mode of ethical reasoning without imposing a style of judgment contrary to evolutionary principles and inconsistent with the practice of many humans. A naturalistic ethics must consider differences of time and place, and therefore provides an alternative to both religious and philosophic dogmatism.

RELATIVE OBJECTIVITY AND MORAL REASONING

That both moral relativism and doctrinaire universalism are unsound is an easily resolved paradox. The human brain tends to code concepts in binary pairs (up-down; in-out; right-left); many cultural norms reflect linguistic or symbolic systems in which such mental structures are embedded (Lévi-Strauss 1949). Although ethical theorists often engage in similar antinomies, there are other logical and mental structures besides simple dualism (as Plato teaches in the *Sophist*). To comprehend the world in a way that transcends the limits of one's own time and place, it is necessary to use conceptual tools like the Socratic dialectic.

In contemporary physics, no measurement is true without reference to the point in space and time from which it is made (Hawking 1988). Water boils at a different temperature at sea level and on a mountain top. When it is 3:00 P.M. in New York, it is noon in San Francisco. Such obvious propositions seem to be forgotten as soon as moral principles are at issue. On the one hand, people pretend that their own cultural standards are universally true; on the other, the discovery of historical or cultural differences is used to demonstrate that ethical principle is merely a question of subjective preference.

Relativity and relativism do not mean the same thing merely because the words are similar. In the sciences, objectivity can be attained only by abandoning the pretense that a human can be in the position of a divine observer whose judgments were true without qualifications of time and place. One might wish to have the power of the invisible but omniscient narrator of a nineteenth-century novel, but such is not the situation of any living being. The closest approximation to truth accessible to us, whether in science or in ethics, presupposes the qualification of principles in terms of the domains to which they apply and the perspective from which they are uttered.

Historicists and Marxists are fond of emphasizing this principle, using the relativity of things to show that alternate theories or customs are time-bound. Evolutionary biology teaches that all living species are organized in ways that depend on the past as well as on the present. Unlike historical determinists, biologists do not imply that the process of change is one of improvement or that we can necessarily predict the future. A new naturalism, like contemporary physics, leads to moral reasoning that is based on "relative objectivity": truths that depend on time and context are nonetheless truths.

Ethical judgment depends on the point of view of the observer as well as on the action being observed.[1] Traditional religious and ethical doctrines often recognized this elementary fact. Indeed, only since Kant, whose ethics imply a degree of rationality once attributed to God alone, have philosophers pretended that truly universal standards of right and wrong could be discovered by unaided human reason. It is time to adopt a humbler way of judging affairs.

Human Nature

The new naturalism described here requires profound changes in our attitude toward both science and morality. Although the point of view set forth in this book may be highly controversial, advances in the life sciences give us no choice. Now that biology is capable of explaining the mysteries of thought as events in the central nervous system and the differences of human culture as adaptations to the environment, traditional doctrines of human nature are at odds with contemporary science. We will have to abandon one or the other.

Humans have a nature, but it is complex and changing. Societies are responses to the social and physical environment, but they are virtually never in stable equilibrium. Because the contradictory intentions and behaviors in any social group need to be reconciled, politics is natural to an animal using speech and language to supplement the genes as a means of encoding and transmitting information. Social conflict can therefore never be solved, nor can perfect human institutions be invented.

Differences in judgment are inevitable, for individuals have distinct innate temperaments as well as unique experiences; increasingly, neurological and psychological evidence demonstrates that people have different ways of processing identical information. Such variability in perception and judgment is clearly an adaptive trait, particularly for a species living in varied and changing environments. While few contest this conclusion of an evolutionary approach to human cognition, it has political and ethical consequences.

Differences in the way events are perceived is not always evidence that one person is right and others wrong. In the scientific community, propositions are formed in a way that permits disconfirmation of hypotheses and hence a slow but significant process of distinguishing plausible and accurate statements about the universe. In politics and ethics, however, one is forced to judge individual events and to choose specific courses of action before knowing their outcomes. In social life, therefore, the plurality of modes of cognition is a desirable and necessary way of gaining information in an uncertain world.

Unless one human being truly attains supernatural wisdom, it will probably be the case that no single person could provide perfect political or ethical guidance for an entire society. Any understanding of the world, even if based on extensive scientific knowledge, is necessarily limited when applied to a wide variety of individual cases and specific social problems. From this perspective, as from the evolutionary considerations raised in chapter 7, political systems based on the rule of law seem more in accord with nature than totalitarian or autocratic regimes. The democratic political processes associated with republican or constitutional forms of government, like the informal decisions in hunter-gatherer bands and other face-to-face groups, are "naturally right" or healthy for human societies.

A naturalistic approach to human life leads to a philosophical perspective remarkably like that of Aristotle, for whom an objective analysis of all forms of government showed that "ruling and being ruled in turn" was basis of the best regime described in Book 7 of the *Politics*. On the one hand, observation and explanation of the different political regimes are possible; on the other, ethical judgment of better and worse can be derived from theoretical reflection on the human condition. The divorce between the human and natural sciences can be overcome, though at the cost of abandoning beliefs and attitudes that have been accepted in the West for several centuries. By rediscovering human nature, we must change our understanding of what it is to be human as well as what nature means.

THE HUMAN IN HUMAN NATURE

Our concept of the species *Homo sapiens* has been marked by unnecessary and indefensible hubris since the Renaissance and, more particularly, since the industrial revolution. With the decline of medieval Christianity and the acceptance of Bacon's projected conquest of nature through science, Western civilization set forth to dominate the known world; the very success of these goals led ineluctably to the presumption that human rationality and freedom were the highest form of life. As secular interests replaced belief in God as the central force in human affairs, many have come to think of themselves as if humans were either individually or collectively endowed with divine power.

Evolutionary biology does not permit such an exaggerated view of human nature. We are living beings, no more precious than any other living form except in our own eyes. Because we can eat or kill virtually all other animals in the environment, we are technically called "top carnivores." But this does not mean that we are independent of natural necessity or in control of our evolutionary destiny. Political doctrines that seek to abstract human beings from the natural world cannot be true representations of our situation.

Philosophers pretend that our reason can be the foundation of an ethical life superior to that of other animals (the "beasts," as it is said). On the contrary, observation of other species and analysis of the human brain leads to the surprising conclusion that morality is more a phenomenon of emotion than of reason. All too often, logic and rationality are used to justify self-interest; moral feeling is precisely that— the feeling of outrage at injustice, unfairness, or selfishness. Similar responses occur among other animals, forming the basis of the kind of social repertoire discussed in ethological terms in chapter 2. Among humans, the linguistic and symbolic capacities analyzed in chapter 3 make it possible to repress or disguise the feelings we share with other primates. Cultural tradition and individual learning produce error and evil as well as wisdom and truth. From a naturalistic perspective, it is therefore appropriate to lower our assessment of the human condition. Wounded pride may well be a price worth paying for the preservation of life on earth.

THE NATURE IN HUMAN NATURE

If Western culture since the Renaissance has overestimated the faculties and dignity of human beings, it has also depreciated nature. In our culture, natural things are all too often merely to be used, controlled, and manipulated to the benefit of transient human desires. In political theory, this attitude is well illustrated by the labor theory of value, shared by such otherwise different thinkers as Locke and Marx. For most moderns, nature provides resources or raw materials, but without human activity, these materials are nothing more than worthless potentialities.

The counterpart of this outlook in philosophy is the belief that meaning is solely derived from human thought and language. From seventeenth-century nominalists to contemporary deconstructionists, it is taken for granted that humans are the only source of intention and substantive meaning in the universe. Nature is treated as impermeable and dead matter, without purpose, intention, or intrinsic value comparable to the ideas and goals of men.

Naturalism directly challenges this view of the world. If selfishness and altruism have a meaning for humans, it is because the social consequences of individual behavior are similar for animals generally. Neither consciousness nor cultural variation are unique to our species (Crook 1981; Bonner 1980). Beauty, play, and humor may be highly developed among humans, but their roots are in nature, not in arbitrary convention (Lorenz 1966; Alexander, in Gruter and Masters 1986).

Those tempted to resist these assertions would do well to reflect on Jane Goodall's prolonged study of chimpanzees (Goodall 1983, 1986a, 1986b), particularly because on so many points it has been confirmed by other observers (DeVore 1965; Reynolds 1967; de Waal 1982, 1986). Individual self-consciousness, intentionality, laughter, deceit, pity, murder, and warfare have now all been observed among chimpanzees. If these phenomena are at the root of meaning, then surely humans cannot pretend that meaning itself is absent from the animate world.

Our difficulty in this regard may be more theological than philosophic. Because many seventeenth- and eighteenth-century thinkers used the observation of natural harmonies to buttress religious belief against secularism, the attribution of meaning to nature has been associated in the modern mind with divine intention. In this view, nature would or could represent purpose if and only if a caring God created the whole with the intention of thereby demonstrating his omnipotence and love to mankind. Such arguments went out of fashion, particularly under the impact of twentieth-century physics.

The philosophy of ancient Greece (not to mention many Eastern schools of thought) should testify to the existence of alternative ways of relating to nature. Aristotle, for example, explicitly denied the view that meaning and purpose in nature depended on the existence of an intentional supernatural agency or divine principle. As Aristotle put it in the *Physics* (199b), nature is like "a doctor doctoring himself": natural purpose is immanent in living things, not extrinsic to them. Animate nature, not physical processes, can be the natural point of reference for humans; what the Greeks called *logos* is more readily seen in the organization of information in all living systems than in physical systems governed by the second law of thermodynamics.

A new naturalism suggests not only that biology replace physics or mathematics as the "queen of the sciences" (Simpson 1969), but that nature thereby should be revalued as the source of meaning and purpose in the world. While the recent concern for preserving ecological balance and protecting endangered species reflect the beginnings of such a shift, it is not enough to pretend to manage natural processes. Confronted by technologies that permit us to produce new species at will, our culture faces—as none before us—the challenge of coming to terms with nature. The potential of realizing the Baconian project, complete with the invention of "new natures," may be far more horrifying than has yet been realized.

THE PLACE OF HUMAN NATURE IN THE COSMOS

These issues lead to metaphysics and theology, which are far from the focus of this work. Since my approach has been intentionally based on secular reasoning, it would be both impudent and unwise to pretend to assess the implications of modern biology for belief in God. No one individual can pretend to know everything; it is surely quite enough to have suggested the renewed importance of questions that were central during past epochs of Western philosophical or religious inquiry.

There is no doubt, of course, that Darwinian biology has been perceived as a direct challenge to revealed religion. The history of the reception of evolutionary principles and the opposition to teaching them in public schools should remind secular or scientifically oriented readers of the pervasive theological issues posed by modern biology. Creation science, although clearly not a science as that concept has been used in the West, is obviously a persistent challenge to the biological theories and findings discussed in this book.

In suggesting that a new naturalism can provide the grounds for ethical principles as well as for a more objective science of human behavior, it has not been my intention to attack religion; one can question intolerant dogmatism without implying that all theological beliefs are false. On the contrary, there is little of substance in this naturalist perspective that could not be said to be consistent with many, though not all, religious doctrines.[2] Humility, virtue, the rule of law, respect for others and for the natural world—none of these consequences of a naturalist perspective on the human condition need be viewed as a threat by the religious believer.

It is true enough that a literal interpretation of the biblical account of creation is at odds with evolutionary biology, and, indeed, with the scientific and philosophic spirit more generally. But some of the most serious and profound religious thinkers of the Judaeo-Christian tradition have not had difficulty on this score. If Saint Thomas Aquinas could reconcile Aristotelian philosophy and Christian belief, surely it is not out of the question that a return to principles like those of Aristotle could be viewed as complementary to religious faith rather than as antagonistic to it. Three principles of meaning have characterized our civilization: science, ethics, and religious belief. It would surely be tragic for Western culture if harmonizing two of these three could be achieved only at the cost of the third.

These broad reflections on the place of human beings in the cosmos may be out of place in a work intended to raise much narrower issues. Since the time of Socrates, political theory has been devoted to an inquiry into human nature and its consequences for social life. Among the Greeks, it was presumed that the knowledge of nature had fundamental implications for a philosophical understanding of the human condition. A return to this element of our tradition is needed, for scientific research can no longer be ignored in the practice of philosophy. The biological sciences must come to the center of our attention if the Socratic injunction, "Know thyself," is to remain alive.

NOTES

1. Animal Behavior and Human Altruism

1. The term hedonism is traditionally used by philosophers to describe the view that human behavior is determined solely by the individual's pleasures and pains. Since pleasure-seeking and pain-avoidance are presumed to be natural, "altruism" is defined as an act of helping others that entails pain. In this context, "hedonism" is often used to mean natural selfishness (Campbell 1972), and will be given this meaning in this chapter wherever the discussion focuses on theories equating selfishness and pleasure. The reader should be warned, however, that some ethologists have used the related word "hedonic" to refer to pleasurable behaviors that include displays of social greeting and interaction. In the study of animal behavior, "hedonic" or pleasurable displays include cooperative social behaviors and are contrasted with "agonic" or competitive behavior (Chance 1976). Research in social psychology and political science has found that humans also distinguish between "negative" or competitive feelings and "positive" emotions, akin to the ethologists' "hedonic" behavior, that include pleasures arising from social cooperation (Plutchik 1980; Abelson et al. 1982; Masters et al. 1986; Marcus, in press). Although the ethological approach will be introduced in chapter 2, here the term "hedonism" refers solely to theories of individualistic human selfishness. As is often the case, terminological precision is needed at the outset of a technical argument: for ethologists, both competition and cooperation are forms of social behavior, not properties of individuals acting in isolation.

2. In general, all quotations from philosophic texts are taken from the editions listed in the references, using short-form classical citations.

3. Because of the importance of this passage, it might be interesting for the reader to compare this literal version by Carnes Lord to an earlier translation in McKeon's edition of *The Basic Works of Aristotle* (1941):

> The family is the association established by nature for the supply of men's everyday wants. . . . But when several families are united, . . . the first society to be formed is the village. And the most natural form of the village appears to be that of a colony from the family. . . . When several villages are united in a single complete community, large enough to be nearly or quite self-sufficing, the state [*polis*] comes into existence, originating in the bare needs of life, and continuing in existence for the sake of a good life. And therefore, if the earlier forms of society are natural, so is the state [*polis*], for it is the end of them, and the nature of a thing is its end. For what

each thing is when fully developed, we call its nature, whether we are speaking of a man, a horse, or a family. . . . Hence it is evident that the state [*polis*] is a creation of nature, and that man is by nature a political animal. And he who by nature and not by mere accident is without a state [*polis*] is either a bad man or above humanity.

It is clear from either version that Aristotle provides, in compressed form, an evolutionary account of the origin of civilized human communities.

4. Direct evidence of behavior in hominid evolution is tantalizingly difficult to secure. To be sure, tools reflect the behavior of toolmaking, and fossilized bones can be used to infer mode of life when dental structures and wear are correlated with food consumption (Coppens et al. 1976; Leakey and Lewin 1977; Isaac 1978; Lovejoy 1981). Social behavior, however, can only be associated with such evidence on the basis of multiple assumptions. Even undeniably cultural and symbolic activities like prehistoric cave painting and sculpture leave us with the greatest uncertainty. We can agree that the images on cave walls or a sculpture like the "Dame de Brassempouy" are art, that they represent different animals or humans, and that they reflect intention and planning on the part of the artist; we do not know what the paintings or sculptures mean or whether social behavior was associated with them (Bataille 1980). Were cave paintings part of a social ritual to improve success at the hunt, an initiation into shamanism for a few select individuals, or a purely artistic creation? The only unambiguous behavior demonstrated by these works of art is the artist's experience of observing the species depicted—and the hand movements needed to create the representation. Very rarely, other behaviors leave more direct traces than mere artifacts. For example, in the prehistoric cave of Pech-Merle in France, there are a number of footprints fossilized in what was, thousands of years ago, a muddy point in the cave floor. Even here, experts disagree: Several years ago, visitors to the cave were told that the footprints were of a mother and an infant (implying that social rituals of the entire group took place in the cave); more recent analysis suggests that all the imprints may have been made by the feet of a single adolescent male. In at least one case, however, footprints seem to establish social behavior at a very early stage of human evolution. Two sets of hominid footprints found at Laetoli in Tanzania include "a dual trail in which the footsteps of the leading individual are almost exactly overprinted by a second set of tracks" (Leakey 1981). In addition to providing unambiguous evidence of bipedal locomotion, the circumstances of preservation make the tracks difficult to interpret without admitting that one individual was following another. As this exception confirms, the precise nature of prehistoric social behavior is extraordinarily difficult to determine because the observable evidence we see is a mute material object.

2. Bonding, Aggression, and Flight

1. In prior epochs, nonverbal cues were mainly seen by the audience that was physically present; when the general public learned of political discourse

only through printed reports or by word of mouth, displays of emotion primarily had their effect by focusing the attention of influential opinion leaders, who then disseminated some statements rather than others to the masses. As long as printing was the main source of political communication, therefore, leaders' messages often appeared as verbal statements when they reached the average citizen. Televised press conferences, campaign debates, and other aspects of routine media coverage heighten the impact of the nonverbal displays of leaders, who can now be seen regularly in close-up images by the general public. This process may help explain the general presumption that television has transformed the political life of Western democracies (Blumler et al. 1978; Ranney 1983; Atkinson 1984). The resulting changes are often associated with increased attention to personality and a decline in partisanship as a determinant of election outcomes: "with the decline of political parties, performance assessments are now much more clearly candidate centered than in the past" (Ostrom and Simon 1985; Conover 1981).

2. It does not follow, as is sometimes argued, that females are more accurate than males in decoding nonverbal cues in all contexts. For example, in an experiment using television news stories of political issues, males were more accurate than females in describing the silent facial displays of President Reagan that were seen in the background (Sullivan et al. 1984). Differences between the genders with regard to facial display behavior are complex (Plate 1984), reflecting the many factors involved in male and female roles in human social behavior (Schubert 1983a, 1985).

3. While one sector of the brain can often compensate for damage or dysfunction in another and the brain as a whole interacts, contemporary neuroscientists are thus effectively exploring what behaviorists long considered inaccessible cognitive phenomena. This research shows that while cognitive tasks are "not performed by any single area of the brain," they are composed of operations that are "strictly localized" (Posner et al. 1988, 1627). Care is needed, however, in assessing popular discussions of the localization of emotional and cognitive responses in the human brain, especially with reference to lateralization between the two hemispheres of the cerebral cortex (see figure 2.2a). Much has been said of the general tendency for linguistic responses and other linear analytic tasks to be lateralized in the left hemisphere of normal right-handed subjects, with tasks associated with music, emotion, or spatial and visual pattern processing being more likely to be performed in the right hemisphere (Geschwind and Galaburda 1987). Even in a task like mental imaging, however, some component processes are more effectively performed in each hemisphere (Kosslyn 1988). Individual experience may also influence some of these processes: for instance, trained musicians sometimes process melodic recognition in the left hemisphere, perhaps because they have converted musical experience into symbolic categories that can be processed analytically like speech. While the relevance of cerebral localization to social and political behavior requires further study, preliminary observation of brain-damaged patients with Dr. Mitchell Ross has suggested its relevance to the processing of political information. Patients with specific brain

lesions were shown photographs of a number of political figures, some of whom have been president of the United States. One brain-damaged subject with left-hemispheric deficits showed an inability to name any political leader or his political party, but could point with perfect accuracy to those who had been president and could use the phrases "number 1," "number 2," or "neither" to distinguish between presidents, vice-presidents, and others. This patient accurately named the emotions in facial expressions, and could identify a politician's party by the verbal images "elephant" and "donkey" even though the verbal labels "Republican" and "Democrat" were inaccessible. Clearly much political information is coded by images and nonverbal cues that are processed differently than left-hemispheric verbal information. In another case, postoperative examination after corpus callostomy (cutting the fibers connecting the left and right hemispheres) revealed not only a loss of emotional response, but a decline in cognitive accuracy. Such findings might be interpreted as evidence that some humans code and process political information in terms of emotional and visual cues associated with right-hemispheric processing, rather than relying entirely on linguistic or "rational" information of the sort typically described as left-hemispheric. At the moment, such observations are little more than intuitively interesting hypotheses; since controls with normal adults show a wide variation in the way individuals process the same stimuli, careful observation and research will be needed to determine the precise relevance of lateralization and other localization of brain function for political and social behavior.

4. The verbal report of an emotion—by definition a nonverbal experience—poses a more fundamental theoretical difficulty than might at first appear. Because individuals attach slightly different meanings to words, it does not go without saying that an emotional response has been accurately described by a single term without that word itself generating or modifying the response. Differences in personal experience that are linked to single words can be minimized by using clusters of terms associated with related emotional experiences; experimental subjects respond more reliably to triads of emotionally descriptive words ("angry," "threatening," "aggressive"; or "comforting," "helpful," "reassuring") than to single words like "angry" or "comforting" alone (Izard 1972, 1977; McHugo, Smith, and Lanzetta 1982). Whatever the explanation, because responses to the triads of words in table 1 seem to have greater reliability than other verbal self-reports of emotion, this type of question has been used in the experimental studies described later in this chapter.

5. In one excerpt, viewers perceived the difference between an angry/threatening facial display and a reassuring verbal message. As will be shown below, the channel of communication plays a distinct role in subjects' emotional responses and judgments of leaders. (See also Lanzetta et al. 1985; McHugo et al. 1985.)

6. If the mathematical constraints on the factor analysis are relaxed somewhat (technically by accepting additional factors explaining approximately 10 percent or more of the variance but having eigenvalues less than 1.0), the

result is a three-factor solution. In most experimental conditions, the three factors correspond to happiness/reassurance, anger/threat, and fear/evasion, although in some cases both agonic responses are on one factor, with distinct factors for hedonic emotions of happiness/reassurance and of interest or activation.

7. Since some citizens in contemporary society leave television sets on without attending to the sound, the finding that the image of a leader can have strong effects when seen without an accompanying verbal message also has political significance. Voters who are exposed to the sight of leaders without attending to what is being said may be especially influenced by differences in the nonverbal cues to which they have been exposed.

8. The statistical procedures used in multiple regression analysis assume that a series of factors are weighted in producing the observed result. Recent models of the central nervous system suggest that this approach provides a reasonable picture of the way the brain actually functions (Georgopoulos et al. 1986). Because the central nervous system integrates inputs from so many neurons, some such analysis is necessary.

9. The more such a ratio departs from 1, the more homogeneous the perception of happiness and reassurance; for example, the average of this ratio for the entire sample varies from 4.5:1 to 9:1 in viewers' descriptions of Reagan's displays of happiness/reassurance (depending on the excerpt). In our French experiment, the excerpt of Fabius's happiness/reassurance was perceived as more nearly blended (average hedonic/agonic ratio = 3.85:1) than that of Chirac (average hedonic/agonic ratio = 5.4:1).

3. Society, Language, and Cultural Change

1. The classic example of feedback between cultural and biological factors is sickle-cell anemia, a disease due to natural selection in favor of a hemoglobin mutant that is lethal when homozygous; in heterozygotes, sickle-cell hemoglobin produces relative immunity to malaria, which had been inadvertently induced by the adoption of slash-and-burn agricultural techniques in tropical climates. Incidence of the mutant gene is correlated with the number of years that a tribe has practiced slash-and-burn agriculture (Dobzhansky 1962, 150–54; Brace and Montagu 1965, 316–20; Wiesenfeld 1969). For the genetic mechanisms involved, see McKusick (1964, 61–67). Once in existence, moreover, material environments and human populations with sickle-cell mutants can have consequences for cultural norms. Many tribes in West Africa had a taboo on the consumption of newly ripened yams prior to a festival celebrating the harvest of this food staple. Since the new yam festivals usually did not occur until after stocks from the preceding year had been exhausted, these customs prohibited hungry people from eating an available food supply; hence they provide a striking example of a cultural taboo that seems to repress natural desires. In an unpublished conference paper, Durham (1981) showed that new yam festivals occurred in malarial environments with a "little dry" sea-

son and were timed to coincide with this climatic phenomenon (which marks the end of the most serious malaria pandemic). Even more interesting, he suggested the hypothesis that yam consumption might have had the effect of counteracting sickling in hemoglobin, so that the taboo would have preserved sickle-cell resistance to malaria during the rainy season, while the consumption of yams at the festival coincided with the decline of malaria and would have contributed to maintaining sickle-cell heterozygotes (and even homozygotes) in the population. Although recent evidence has called into question the precise biochemical mechanism originally presumed to be responsible (Durham, personal communication), these institutions remain likely examples of the natural selection of a human cultural norm.

2. The use of affixes in Mayan writing is not evidence of what is here called triadic patterning, because the symbols attached to or inserted in a Mayan glyph were themselves carriers of meaning (Thompson 1950). By contrast, the letters of an alphabet, like phonemes, do not convey symbolic meaning apart from their place in well-formed structures or "strings." As this example indicates, the triadic pattern described above represents a special type of hierarchical organization.

3. For present purposes, the evolutionary trend toward the invention of phonograms (symbols representing sounds) in hieroglyphic writing systems will be ignored, though consideration of this phenomenon and the limited form it took prior to the emergence of alphabetic writing would only strengthen the argument. Note, however, that the first stage in this evolution from pictogram or hieroglyph to phonetic alphabet seems to have been the rebus— that is, the extension of a symbol from an easily recognized referent to a more abstract homonym (Brown 1958, 62–64).

4. In human speech, as has been pointed out, morphemes are usually arbitrary representations except for onomatopoeia; phonemes are equally arbitrary insofar as they carry no meaning in themselves. But in alphabetic writing, the lowest level of coding units—namely, letters—is iconic or imitative, since "the properties of the denotata" [the spoken phonemes] "can be mapped onto properties of the corresponding message" that has been written. Conversely, as a means of representing speech itself, pictographic or hieroglyphic writing generally tends to be arbitrary, since the sign has no iconic (imitative) relationship to the verbal sound or morpheme; exceptions, such as the rebus glyphs of Mayan writing, represent an evolutionary trend toward phonetic writing. The situation, at least for most pictograms and some ideograms, is reversed if one considers the relationship between the written sign and the thing denoted rather than the relationship between written sign and spoken word. With reference to denotation, it is alphabetic writing that is arbitrary and nonalphabetic writing that is or can be iconic. Since the role of imitation or iconic representation therefore depends in part on the perspective of the analyst, it cannot be the foundation of meaning (cf. Plato *Republic* 6.504c–7.518b).

5. For alternative hypotheses of the RNA codes involved, see Beadle and Beadle (1966, 202–3) and Bonner and Mills (1964, 57) as well as Steitz (1988).

As is often the case in science, the choice between alternative hypotheses need not be essential in determining the truth of ideas at a higher level (Plato *Republic* 6.509d–511e). The highest questions concern the forms that alone give coherence to the visible things humans can see (Gleick 1987). While public opinion focuses on the empirical evidence for varied hypotheses, knowledge ultimately concerns the apprehension of formal relationships or shapes. Doubtless this explains the reasoning of those mathematicians and physicists who suggest "that the reason why mathematics has the uncanny ability to provide just the right patterns for scientific investigation may be because the patterns investigated by mathematicians are *all* the patterns there are" (Steen 1988).

6. By "twofold redundancy," Hershey means the dual strands of DNA that make up the famed "double helix" of the chromosome. It is not quite certain that Hershey's point has all the force he attributes to it. The phonemic system of a spoken language contains a degree of redundancy similar to that of DNA: "The actual number of distinctive features (i.e., the binary oppositions creating phonemic contrasts) thus is predicted to be close to double the minimum number, permitting a redundancy of 50%. In languages which have been analyzed, this estimate has been borne out" (Gerard, Kluckhohn, and Rapoport 1956, 20). Moreover it can be questioned whether, in Hershey's hypothetical spoken message composed of sentences A–Z, the transformation of the sequence to A–YA or A–Y would leave the message substantially unchanged; since the redundancies of speech that "minimize errors of transmission" occur at the level of phonemic contrasts and syntax, redundant sentences often do alter meaning. Gertrude Stein's "A rose is a rose is a rose" surely has a different meaning from the statement "A rose is." Finally, the function of the redundant sentence Z in Hershey's example reminds one of genetic "buffering," which serves to minimize errors in hereditary transmission (Waddington 1953).

7. This distinction should not be overstated, since both DNA strings and human utterances often communicate messages that reflect environmental conditions; rather, it is a question of the degree to which the coding system exhibits the design feature called "productivity" or "openness" (Altmann 1967, 346–47). Since part of the class of context-free languages can be shown to be a subset of the class of context-sensitive languages (Spanier 1969, 338), it is in any event impossible to think of the two as polar opposites.

8. Although the more extreme versions of Whorf's hypothesis that language constitutes thought (Whorf 1956) are questionable, modern psycholinguistics shows that naive epistemological realism is also untenable (Brown 1958; Lenneberg 1957; Landar 1966). The primordial importance of language and symbolic structures in human cultures and behavior has been especially stressed by the so-called structuralist movement in France led by Lévi-Strauss in anthropology, Lacan in psychoanalysis, and Derrida in philosophy. When limited to the recognition of the role of language in human history, this school tends to the nihilist conclusion that meaning is the product of accident or freely created will (as in the deconstructionist movement in literary criticism).

Although the symbolic systems of human culture are by no means always verbal languages (Hall 1959), chapter 2 has provided evidence of the way even nonverbal cues take on symbolic or ritualized meaning.

4. Politics as a Biological Phenomenon

1. For many reasons, it is best to leave to one side the acrimonious debate on the inheritance of IQ (Jensen 1969; *Harvard Education Review* 34 [Spring 1969]: 273–356; [Summer 1969]: 449–631; Richardson and Spears 1972). Although human intelligence is quite obviously complex and heterogeneous (Gardner 1983), the concept of an intelligence quotient assumes that it is possible to discover a single measure of mental abilities; this procedure is largely based on statistical assumptions and manipulations rather than on experimental or observational evidence of specific abilities and their actual variation in human populations. Because IQ testing was developed for practical and in part political reasons (Kamin 1974), the charge that this procedure has been used as an ideological justification of social status (Bowles and Gintis 1972) seems difficult to refute; the theoretical assumptions behind the notion of a single measure of intelligence, like IQ, are easily traced to the psychological tradition of Hobbes. Recent studies of learning confirm the heterogeneity of cognitive processes: that the specific abilities needed for excellence in music, mathematics, verbal manipulation, problem solving, and spatial representation would all depend on a single genetic factor (or even a set of related genes) is highly implausible. On the other hand, there is increasing evidence that some mental abilities may be traits with variable reaction ranges that are inherited (Rose et al. 1974; Eaves 1988). As more is learned about the localization of brain function and its dependence on hormonal as well as environmental stimulation, it is not unlikely that knowledge of the biological bases and interpersonal differences in learning abilities will increase (rather than decrease) the capacity of providing remedial help for those with learning deficits (Bayliss and Livesey 1985).

2. This "epigenetic" position (Lehrman 1956; Schneirla 1956; Kuo 1967), strikingly in contrast to the work of many European ethologists (Lorenz 1956, 1967; Hass 1970; Eibl-Eibesfeldt 1971), cannot be pushed too far. For many behavioral traits, reaction ranges will be broader than for physiological structures whose development is to some extent "buffered" against the influence of minor environmental variation. Nonetheless, it is possible to classify species by similarities in behavior as well as by structural likeness (Lorenz [1931–63] 1970–71); genetic inheritance can be as much a factor in the development of behavior patterns as in the determination of bodily structures (Mayr 1958; Caspari 1958; Emerson 1958, 313–15). Compare Aristotle *Nicomachean Ethics* 5.7.1134b18–1135a4.

3. This formulation leaves open the issue of whether some aspects of behavior first learned or acquired by organisms are subsequently passed on genetically. Biologists have customarily rejected such a Lamarckian view of evolu-

tion, which was emphasized by the Soviet biologist Lysenko for political reasons, because it seems inconsistent with neo-Darwinian theory and has been contradicted by most experimental tests. While it now seems highly unlikely that Lamarckian processes operate independently of genetic change, attention has been paid to the so-called Baldwin effect, by which acquired modifications that improve chances of survival and reproduction increase the probability of genetic mutations or recombinations fixing the adaptive trait. This process is now viewed as consistent with evolutionary theory by some (Waddington 1953, 1956; White and Smith 1956; Haldane 1956; Emerson 1958), especially because it seems necessary in order to account for much animal behavior. Hence Mayr, who criticized the concept of the Baldwin effect with primary reference to morphology (1963, 610–12) took a more open view when discussing the evolution of animal behavior (1958, 354–55). In particular, the instinctive behaviors that ethologists call ritualizations (Lorenz 1966; Morris 1956; Tinbergen 1967; Masters et al. 1986) seem difficult to explain without reference to something like the Baldwin effect.

4. This error has important consequences, since Deutsch, like many contemporary social scientists, seems to overstate the extent to which a human society can be "self-steering" (Deutsch 1963, chap. 5; Etzioni 1968). Response to environmental pollution and other threats to collective goods suggests that most people have difficulty coping with the contradiction between short term benefits and long run catastrophe (Hardin 1968; Meadows et al. 1972; Ophuls 1977). Such effects, however, are only evident when biological phenomena are studied at the level of populations and ecosystems.

5. Easton uses the term "political system" (1953, 1965a, 1965b) to refer to something more inclusive than the "regime," since he defines a political system as "those interactions through which values are authoritatively allocated for a society" (1965b, 21). My usage here is perhaps closer to that of Deutsch, who speaks of political systems as "networks of decision and control" (1963, 145). The central issue is whether politics is reduced to competition for power and authority, or is understood to encompass a broader range of functions defined in terms of social communication.

5. The Nature of the State

1. To represent the difference between psychological assessments and social institutions, in this chapter the former will be printed in quotation marks and the latter in italics. Hopefully this trivial device will make it easier to see an intelligible distinction that has not been kept in mind with sufficient clarity by many social scientists. Compare Plato *Republic* 9.368d–368e.

2. In a functional sense, such terms as nepotism and nonkin are relative even though sociobiologists sometimes speak of the coefficient of relatedness as a fixed quantum (for example, Wilson 1975, 118). Relatedness is fixed if one considers the relative closeness of brother and sister ($r = 1/2$) when compared to mother's brother and son, or father's sister and son ($r = 1/4$). But nepotism

or kin selection, defined as a preference for close kin, will depend on the extent to which individuals with a high coefficient of relatedness are present in the actor's environment. For other animals, with less geographical mobility than modern humans, it can often be assumed that mutualism and nepotism are relatively unambiguous; in human societies, these terms are far more relative and indeed may help explain such variable phenomena as ethnic cooperation among immigrants (Wilson 1975, 75; Hamilton 1964, in Caplan 1978, 195).

3. For the classic exposition of the dialectical relationships between sociality, mutual benefit, and cheating, see the story of the "ring of Gyges" in Plato's *Republic* (2.359b–360d). The extent to which both mutually beneficial reciprocity and sociality are vulnerable to cheating, providing the violator can remain unknown, had in fact been clearly spelled out by the pre-Socratics, as is illustrated by Antiphon the Sophist's *On Truth* (in Barker 1968, 95–98). Compare Masters (1977, 74–77; 1978a).

4. I am greatly indebted to Evelyn Fink for pointing out the effect of lowered punishment for joint defection, which I had failed to notice in earlier publications (Masters 1982b, 1983a). She suggests that the problem can be formalized as follows. Let the transitivity of the payoffs in the four outcomes (the definitional requirement of a Prisoner's Dilemma) be represented as T ("defector" who talks while other is silent) > R (both cooperating by remaining silent) > P (both talk and are punished) > S (the "sucker" or virtuous individual who was silent when the other talked). In figure 5.2, this condition is met: $+10 > +9 > -9 > -10$. For a Prisoner's Dilemma between close kin, such as full siblings, to become a cooperative game, cooperation must yield a higher payoff either if the other player cooperates, a condition that can be formally represented as: $(R + 1/2R) > (T + 1/2S)$, or, if the other player defects, as: $(S + 1/2T) > (P + 1/2P)$. The first version of the Prisoner's Dilemma with close kin, in figure 5.3, met both of these requisites for cooperation, first because $(R + 1/2R) = 13.5 > (T + 1/2S) = 5$, and second because $(S + 1/2T) = -5 > (P + 1/2P) = -13.5$. The interested reader can see, by inserting the payoff values of figure 5.4, that these requisites for cooperation are not always met. In general terms, for the payoffs $T = +10$; $R = +9$; and $S = -10$, a joint punishment payoff between $+9$ and -3.33, while still consistent with transitivity, will not produce cooperation among kin with a coefficient of relatedness of 1/2; in this case, it is necessary to increase the joint punishment to a value greater than -3.33 to induce cooperation. To go further in formalizing these outcomes, one must use indifference curves like those of economic theory (Chase 1980a; Hirshleifer 1978, 1985; Margolis 1982) rather than a game theory matrix, whose heuristic simplicity requires the limitation to specific numerical outcomes.

5. The extension of political philosophy to empirical and even experimental research, illustrated by this book, is developed further in my forthcoming *The Nature of Obligation*, which brings together representative studies challenging the conventional isolation of the natural and social sciences from each other and from moral judgment (Masters 1983b, 1984, 1986, 1987). For the prehis-

tory of experimental reasoning in political philosophy, see Plato *Republic* 4.436c–436e, 439e–440a; Aristotle *Politics* 1.11.1259a, 2.4.1262a; Hobbes *Leviathan* 1.13.

6. Why Bureaucracy?

1. See Plato *Republic* 8.545d–547c; Aristotle *Politics* 4.11.1295a–1296b; 5.1.1301d–5.7.1307b; 7.15.1334a; Rousseau *Social Contract* 3.10–11. One of the most striking defects of contemporary political theory has been the failure to understand the importance of this fact. Although political philosophers like Plato, Aristotle, or Rousseau are often taxed with idealism when contrasted to a materialist like Marx, they have been more realistic about the decline of political institutions than the apparently scientific thinkers for whom human social and political history is inherently a pattern of progress.

7. The Biology of Social Participation

1. "Where are your claws and your teeth?" (Aristotle *Politics* 3.13, ed. C. Lord, note 37). Compare the famous Melian dialogue in Thucydides' *History of the Peloponnesian War*.

Epilogue

1. To fail to recognize this elementary fact of life is to engage in the deceptive (and self-deceptive) tactic of hiding one's own potential self-interest in the norm or principle used. Let it not be claimed that the present argument is subject to this logical flaw (technically described as "reflexivity"): a naturalistic ethics is obviously in the interest of the philosophic or scientific observer when compared to the average citizen or the believer. To think otherwise would be to deny the legitimacy of science and philosophy as a way of life. Since the time of Socrates, our civilization has depended on the ability to question accepted opinions in the name of knowledge. What makes the self-interest of the philosopher or scientist unusual is the collective benefit made possible by philosophic activity. Those who would deny this fact use abstract logic in a shortsighted if not unjust manner. Open discussion and scientific inquiry have redounded to the benefit of those who contest the legitimacy of science and philosophy in the most literal way. The explosion of population since these practices were institutionalized in the West represents an increase in the reproductive success of most individuals in the recent history of our civilization.

2. While the ultimate consistency of naturalism and religion is most easily defended in realms associated with standards of human behavior, theology may also be founded more securely on contemporary physics and cosmology

than on the metaphysical concepts traditionally used in the West. Theories of relativity, quantum mechanics, and cosmology show that Newtonian physics is valid only for a limited domain of phenomena and hence does not constitute a universal or absolute system of nature as a whole (Bohr 1958; Heisenberg 1958). The visible world is only part of a cosmos that humans cannot, in principle, perceive completely; because there are regions of the universe from which light can neither reach our point in space-time nor be reached by any signal or event from us—domains of space-time called "elsewhere" by Hawking (1988)—the human capacity to understand the whole is necessarily incomplete. The principles of deterministic processes and linear mathematical equations do not apply to the phenomena of form and transformation that are central to the explanation of change, uncertainty, and chaos (Gleick 1987). Models of the origin of the visible world, such as the "big bang," are perfectly consistent with an incorporeal, eternal, and omnipotent being. If, to use a phrase I once heard, God is a human name for "the total system of simultaneous nonlinear equations capable of governing this or any conceivable universe," it is not evident that the resulting theological understanding would depart in any meaningful way from the teachings of *Genesis*. That the universe is closed is no longer inconsistent with the postulate of its infinity; that the principles of nature are eternal is no longer inconsistent with the certainty that the visible world came into being—and in a profound sense was created by these eternal principles. Modern physics of course challenges the naive view that God is an anthropomorphic being attending individually and separately to each human being as a human father cares for his children within a monogamous family in a stable human civilization; as Hawking (1988) notes, such a God would have nothing to "do" in a cosmos governed by the principles discovered in contemporary physics. Since this anthropomorphic view of God is not entailed by the biblical account of creation, it remains to be seen whether the principal difficulty arises from the gap between popular opinion and science rather than from science itself. Perhaps there is more truth in the Platonic distinction between knowledge and belief (see chap. 3, n. 5) than in its modern equivalent, the divorce between science and religion. Although further consideration of the theological implications of physics or cosmology is beyond my technical competence, reflection on these matters suggests that the nihilist and relativist reaction to modern science may be as unwarranted in the physical sciences as in evolutionary biology and human history. In practice, however, such speculations are probably less useful than the demonstration that the principal foundations of human ethics concern the life sciences rather than physics—and that, on such a basis, there is no longer good reason to dismiss the view that standards of justice and virtue can be derived from nature.

REFERENCES

Given the range of disciplines covered and the sheer quantity of scientific publications, it would be absurd to claim completeness for this bibliography. Specialists will note, for example, that the works cited are not always the classics in each field. Rather than pretending to a perfection that would in any event soon be obsolete, these references illustrate the range of scientific materials that need to be considered in a philosophic treatment of human nature and indicate the particular sources upon which I have relied.

Abelson, Robert P.; Kinder, Donald R.; Peters, M. D.; and Fiske, Susan T. 1982. Affective and Semantic Components in Political Person Perception. *Journal of Personality and Social Psychology* 42:619–30.

Alexander, Richard D. 1974. Evolution of Social Behavior. *Annual Review of Ecology and Systematics* 5:25–83.

———. 1977. Natural Selection and the Analysis of Human Sociality. In C. Goulden, ed., *Changing Scenes in Natural Sciences, 1776–1976*, 283–337. Special Publication 12. Philadelphia: Philadelphia Academy of Natural Sciences.

———. 1978. Natural Selection and Societal Laws. In T. Englehardt and D. Callahan, eds., *Morals, Science, and Society*. Vol. 3. Hastings-on-Hudson, N.Y.: Hastings Center.

———. 1979. *Darwinism and Human Affairs*. Seattle: University of Washington Press.

———. 1981. Evolution, Culture, and Human Behavior: Some General Considerations. In R. D. Alexander and D. W. Tinkle, eds., *Natural Selection and Social Behavior: Recent Research and Theory*, 504–20. New York: Chiron Press.

———. 1986. Biology and Law. In M. Gruter and R. Masters, eds., *Ostracism: A Social and Biological Phenomenon*, 19–25. New York: Elsevier.

———. 1987. *The Biology of Moral Systems*. Hawthorne, N.Y.: Aldine de Gruyter.

Alexander, Richard D., and Borgia, Gerald. 1978. Group Selection, Altruism, and the Levels of the Organization of Life. *Annual Review of Ecology and Systematics* 9:449–74.

Alexander, Richard D., and Sherman, Paul D. 1977. Local Mate Competition and Parental Investment in Social Insects. *Science* 196:494–500.

Alland, Alexander, Jr. 1967. *Evolution and Human Behavior*. Garden City, N.Y.: Natural History Press.

Altmann, Stuart A. 1967. The Structure of Social Communication. In
S. Altmann, ed., *Social Communication among Primates*, 325–62. Chicago:
University of Chicago Press.

Altmann, Stuart A., ed. 1967. *Social Communication among Primates*. Chicago:
University of Chicago Press.

Anderson, P. W. 1972. More Is Different. *Science* 177: 393–96.

Aquinas, St. Thomas. 1957. *The Political Ideas of St. Thomas Aquinas*. Ed.
D. Bigongiari. New York: Hafner.

Ardrey, Robert. 1963. *African Genesis*. New York: Atheneum.

Aristotle. 1941. *The Basic Works of Aristotle*. Ed. R. McKeon. New York:
Random House.

———. 1952. *Politics*. Ed. E. Barker. New York: Oxford University Press.

———. 1984. *The Politics*. Ed. C. Lord. Chicago: University of Chicago
Press.

Arnhart, Larry. 1981. *Aristotle on Political Reasoning*. DeKalb, Ill.: Northern
Illinois University Press.

Atkinson, Max. 1984. *Our Masters' Voices: The Language and Body Language of
Politics*. London: Methuen.

Attah, E. B. 1973. Racial Aspects of Zero Population Growth. *Science*
180:1143.

Axelrod, Robert. 1980a. Effective Choice in the Prisoner's Dilemma. *Journal
of Conflict Resolution* 24:3–25.

———. 1980b. More Effective Choice in the Prisoner's Dilemma. *Journal of
Conflict Resolution* 24:379–403.

———. 1981. The Emergence of Cooperation among Egoists. *American
Political Science Review* 75:306–18.

———. 1983. *The Evolution of Cooperation*. Cambridge, Mass.: Harvard
University Press.

Axelrod, Robert, and Hamilton, William D. 1981. The Evolution of
Cooperation. *Science* 211:1390–96.

Ayala, Francisco J. 1978. The Mechanisms of Evolution. *Scientific American*
239:56–69.

Babchuck, Wayne A.; Hames, Raymond B.; and Thomason, Ross A. 1985.
Sex Differences in the Recognition of Infant Facial Expressions of
Emotion: The Primary Caretaker Hypothesis. *Ethology and Sociobiology*
6:89–102.

Bach, E. 1964. *An Introduction to Transformational Grammars*. New York:
Holt, Rinehart & Winston.

Barash, David. 1974. The Evolution of Marmot Societies: A General Theory.
Science 185:415–20.

———. 1977. *Sociobiology and Behavior*. New York: Elsevier.

Barker, Ernest. 1960. *Greek Political Theory*. New York: Barnes & Noble.

———. 1968. *Greek Political Thought*. New York: Barnes & Noble.

Barkow, Jerome. 1978. Culture and Sociobiology. *American Anthropologist*
80:5–20.

Barkun, Michael. 1963. *Law Without Sanctions*. New Haven: Yale University
Press.

Barner-Barry, Carol. 1981. Longitudinal Observational Research and the Study of Basic Forms of Political Socialization. In M. Watts, ed., *Biopolitics: Ethological and Physiological Approaches*, 51–60. New Directions for Methodology of Social and Behavioral Science, no. 7. San Francisco: Jossey-Bass.

Barry, Brian. 1970. *Sociologists, Economists, and Democracy*. London: Macmillan.

Bastian, J. 1965. Primate Signalling Systems and Human Languages. In I. DeVore, ed., *Primate Behavior*, 585–606. New York: Holt, Rinehart & Winston.

Bataille, Georges. 1980. *La peinture préhistorique: Lascaux ou la naissance de l'art*. Paris: Skira.

Bayliss, Janet, and Livesey, P. J. 1985. Cognitive Strategies of Children with Reading Disability and Normal Readers in Visual Sequential Memory. *Journal of Learning Disabilities* 18:326–32.

Beadle, George W. 1963. The Language of the Gene. In P. LeCorbeillier, ed., *The Languages of Science*, 57–84. New York: Basic Books.

Beadle, George W., and Beadle, Muriel. 1966. *The Language of Life*. Garden City, N.Y.: Doubleday.

Beals, Allan R., and Siegel, Bernard J. 1966. *Divisiveness and Social Conflict*. Stanford: Stanford University Press.

Beckoff, Marc, and Wells, Michael C. 1980. The Social Ecology of Coyotes. *Scientific American* 242:130–48.

Bentley, Arthur F. 1908. *The Process of Government*. Chicago: University of Chicago Press.

Bert, J.; Ayats, H.; Martin, A.; and Collumb, H. 1967. Note sur l'organisation de la vigilance sociale chez le babouin *Papio papio* dans l'est sénégalais. *Folia Primatologica* 6:44–47.

Birdwhistell, R. L. 1970. *Kinesics and Context: Essays on Body Motion Communication*. Philadelphia: University of Pennsylvania Press.

Bischoff, Norbert. 1972. Biological Foundations of the Incest Taboo. *Social Science Information* 9:7–36.

Blank, Robert H. 1981. *The Political Implications of Human Genetic Technology*. Boulder, Colo.: Westview Press.

Bloom, Allan. 1987. *The Closing of the American Mind*. N.Y.: Simon & Schuster.

Bloom, Benjamin S. 1964. *Stability and Change in Human Characteristics*. N.Y.: John Wiley.

Blumler, Jay G.; Cayrol, Roland; and Thoveron, Gabriel. 1978. *La télévision, fait-elle l'élection*. Paris: Presses de la Fondation des Sciences Politiques.

Blurton-Jones, Nicholas G. 1987. Tolerated Theft, Suggestions about the Ecology and Evolution of Sharing, Hunting, and Scrounging. *Social Science Information* 26:31–54.

Bohannan, Paul. 1963. *Social Anthropology*. N.Y.: Holt, Rinehart & Winston.

Bohr, Niels. 1958. *Atomic Physics and Human Knowledge*. N.Y.: Science Editions.

Bonner, D. M., and Mills, S. E. 1964. *Heredity*. 2d ed. Englewood Cliffs, N.J.: Prentice-Hall.

Bonner, John Tyler. 1980. *The Evolution of Culture in Animals*. Princeton, N.J.: Princeton University Press.

Bordes, F. H. 1960. Evolution in Paleolithic Cultures. In S. Tax, ed., *The Evolution of Man*, 99–110. Chicago: University of Chicago Press.

Bounak, V. V. 1958. L'origine du langage. In *Les processus de l'hominisation*, 99–110. Paris: CNRS.

Bouthoul, Gaston. 1970. *L'infanticide différé*. Paris: Hachette.

Bowles, Samuel, and Gintis, Herbert. 1972. IQ in the U.S. Class Structure. *Social Policy* (Nov./Dec. 1972–Jan./Feb. 1973): 65–96.

Boyd, Robert. 1988. Is the Repeated Prisoner's Dilemma a Good Model of Reciprocal Altruism? *Ethology and Sociobiology* 9:211–22.

Brace, C. L., and Montagu, M. F. A. 1965. *Man's Evolution*. N.Y.: Macmillan.

Braidwood, R. J. 1960. Levels in Prehistory: A Model for the Consideration of the Evidence. In S. Tax, ed., *The Evolution of Man*, 143–51. Chicago: University of Chicago Press.

Brecht, Arnold. 1959. *Political Theory*. Princeton, N.J.: Princeton University Press.

Britten, R. J., and Davidson, E. H. 1969. Gene Regulation for Higher Cells: A Theory. *Science* 165:349–57.

Brown, Roger. 1958. *Words and Things*. N.Y.: Free Press.

Brown, Roger, and Bellugi, U. 1964. Three Processes in the Child's Acquisition of Syntax. In E. Lenneberg, ed., *New Directions in the Study of Language*, 121–61. Cambridge, Mass.: MIT Press.

Cacioppo, J. T., and Petty, R. E. 1979. Attitudes and Cognitive Response: An Electrophysiological Approach. *Journal of Personality and Social Psychology* 37:2181–99.

Caldwell, Lynton Keith. 1964. Biopolitics: Science, Ethics, and Public Policy. *The Yale Review* 54:1–16.

Campbell, Donald T. 1960. Blind Variation and Selective Retention in Creative Thought as in Other Knowledge Processes. *Psychological Review* 67:380–400.

———. 1965a. Variation and Selective Retention in Socio-cultural Evolution. In H. R. Barringer, G. I. Blanksten, and R. W. Mack, eds., *Social Change in Developing Areas*, 19–48. Cambridge, Mass.: Schenkman.

———. 1965b. Ethnocentric and Other Altruistic Motives. In D. Levine, ed., *Nebraska Symposium on Motivation, 1965*, 283–311. Lincoln, Neb.: University of Nebraska Press.

———. 1972. On the Genetics of Altruism and the Counter-Hedonic Components in Human Culture. *Journal of Social Issues* 28:21–37.

———. 1975. On the Conflicts Between Biological and Social Evolution, and Between Psychology and Moral Tradition. *American Psychologist* 30:1103–26.

———. 1978. On the Genetics of Altruism. In L. Wispé, ed., *Altruism, Sympathy, and Helping*. N.Y.: Academic Press.

———. 1983. Legal and Primary-Group Social Controls. In M. Gruter and P. Bohannan, eds., *Law, Biology, and Culture*, 159–71. Santa Barbara: Ross-Erikson.

Caplan, Arthur, ed. 1978. *The Sociobiology Debate*. N.Y.: Harper & Row.

Capra, Fritjof. 1975. *The Tao of Physics*. Berkeley: Shambala.

Carlotti, Stephen J. 1988. *The Faces of the President*. Unpublished Senior Fellow's thesis, Dartmouth College.

Carniero, Robert L. 1970. A Theory of the Origins of the State. *Science* 169:733–38.

Caspari, Ernst. 1958. Genetic Basis of Behavior. In A. Roe and G. G. Simpson, eds., *Behavior and Evolution*, 103–27. New Haven: Yale University Press.

———. 1968. Selective Forces in the Evolution of Man. In M. F. A. Montagu, ed., *Culture: Man's Adaptive Dimension*, 259–69. N.Y.: Oxford University Press.

Cavalli-Sforza, Luigi, and Feldman, M.W. 1981. *Cultural Transmission: A Quantitative Approach*. Princeton, N.J.: Princeton University Press.

Chagnon, Napoleon. 1982. Some Limits of *r* in the Sociobiology of Kinship and Mating. In King's College Sociobiology Group, eds., *Current Problems in Sociobiology*, 281–318. Cambridge: Cambridge University Press.

Chagnon, Napoleon, and Irons, William, eds. 1979. *Evolutionary Biology and Human Social Behavior: An Anthropological Perspective*. North Scituate, Mass.: Duxbury Press.

Chance, M. R. A. 1967. Attention Structure as the Basis of Primate Rank Orders. *Man* 2:503–18.

———. 1976. The Organization of Attention in Groups. In M. von Cranach, ed., *Methods of Inference from Animal to Human Behavior*. The Hague: Mouton.

Changeux, Jean-Pierre. 1983. *L'homme neuronal*. Paris: Fayard.

Charvet, John. 1974. *The Social Problem in Jean-Jacques Rousseau*. Cambridge: Cambridge University Press.

Chase, Ivan D. 1980a. Cooperative and Noncooperative Behavior in Animals. *American Naturalist* 115:827–57.

———. 1980b. Social Process and Hierarchy Formation in Small Groups: A Comparative Perspective. *American Sociological Review* 45:905–24.

———. 1982. Behavioral Sequences during Dominance Hierarchy Formation in Chickens. *Science* 216:439–40.

Chevalier-Skolnikoff, S. 1973. Facial Expressions of Emotion in Nonhuman Primates. In P. Ekman, ed., *Darwin and Facial Expression*, 11–89. N.Y.: Academic Press.

Chomsky, Noam. 1965. *Aspects of the Theory of Syntax*. Cambridge, Mass.: MIT Press.

Clark, Kenneth B. 1971. The Pathos of Power. Presidential address to the American Psychological Association Convention, Washington, D.C.

Cloninger, C. Robert. 1986. A Unified Biosocial Theory of Personality and Its Role in the Development of Anxiety States. *Psychiatric Developments* 3:167–226.

———. 1987. A Systematic Method of Clinical Description and Classification of Personality Variants. *Archives General of Psychiatry* 44:573–88.

Cohen, Ronald, and Service, Elman R., eds. 1978. *Origins of the State.* Philadelphia: Institute for the Study of Human Issues.

Cole, John N. 1980. Learning a Hard Lesson in Aroostook County. *Country Journal* (November): 42–46.

Conover, P. J. 1981. Political Cues and Perception of Candidates. *American Political Quarterly* 9:423–48.

Coppens, Yves; Howell, F. Clark; Isaac, Glynn L.; and Leakey, Richard E. F. 1976. *Earliest Man and Environments in the Lake Rudolf Basin.* Chicago: University of Chicago Press.

Corning, Peter A. 1971a. The Biological Bases of Behavior and Some Implications for Political Science. *World Politics* 23:321–70.

———. 1971b. Evolutionary Indicators. Boulder, Colo.: University of Colorado, Institute of Behavior Genetics.

———. 1984. *The Synergism Hypothesis: A Theory of Progressive Evolution.* N.Y.: McGraw-Hill.

Corning, Peter A., and Corning, Constance Hellyer. 1972. Toward a General Theory of Violent Aggression. *Social Science Information* 11:7–35.

Corover, Stephen. 1973. Big Brother and Psychotechnology. *Psychology Today* (October).

Coulomb-Gully, Marlene. 1986. Le feuilleton politique des informations télévisées. DEA de Lettres Modernes, Faculté de Amiens (France).

Critchley, Macdonald. 1960. The Evolution of Man's Capacity for Language. In S. Tax, ed., *The Evolution of Man*, 289–308. Chicago: University of Chicago Press.

Crook, John H. 1967. Evolutionary Change in Primate Societies. *Science Journal* (June): 2–7.

———. 1981. *The Evolution of Human Consciousness.* Oxford: Oxford University Press.

Darwin, Charles. n.d. [1859]. *Origin of Species.* N.Y.: Modern Library.

———. [1872] 1965. *The Expression of the Emotions in Man and Animals.* Chicago: University of Chicago Press.

Dawkins, Richard. 1976. *The Selfish Gene.* N.Y.: Oxford University Press.

———. 1982. Replicators and Vehicles. In Cambridge Sociobiology Study Group, eds., *Current Problems in Sociobiology*, 45–64. Cambridge: Cambridge University Press.

———. 1987. *The Blind Watchmaker.* N.Y.: Norton.

Dayhoff, M. O. 1969. Computer Analysis of Protein Evolution. *Scientific American* 221:86–95.

Dearden, John. 1974. Sex Linked Differences of Political Behavior. *Social Science Information* 13:19–45.

Deleurance, Ed. Ph. 1956. Analyse du comportement batisseur chez 'Polistes' (*Hymenopteres vespides*). In M. Autuori et al., *L'instinct dans le comportement des animaux et de l'homme*, 105–41. Paris: Masson.

Denckla, Martha. 1986a. The Neurology of Social Competence. *ACLD Newsbriefs* (June/July 1986): 1.

————. 1986b. Application of Disconnexion Concepts to Developmental Dyslexia. Geschwind Memorial Lecture presented to the 37th annual meeting of the Orton Dyslexia Society, Philadelphia, Pa., November 1986. Inglewood, Calif.: Audio-Stats Educational Services, tape #916R–34.

Derrida, Jacques. 1967. *De la grammatologie.* Paris: Editions de Minuit.

Deutsch, Karl W. 1963. *The Nerves of Government.* N.Y.: Free Press.

Deutsch, Kenneth, and Soffer, Walter. 1987. *The Crisis of Liberal Democracy: A Straussian Perspective.* Corrected Edition. Albany, N.Y.: State University of New York Press.

DeVore, Irven, ed. 1965. *Primate Behavior.* N.Y.: Holt, Rinehart & Winston.

DeVore, Irven, and Hall, K. R. L. 1965. Baboon Ecology. In I. DeVore, ed., *Primate Behavior,* 20–52. N.Y.: Holt, Rinehart & Winston.

DeVore, Irven, and Washburn, Sherwood L. 1967. Baboon Ecology and Human Evolution. In N. Korn and F. Thompson, eds., *Human Evolution,* 137–60. N.Y.: Holt, Rinehart & Winston.

de Waal, Frans. 1982. *Chimpanzee Politics.* London: Jonathan Cape.

————. 1984. Sex Differences in the Formation of Coalitions among Chimpanzees. *Ethology and Sociobiology* 5:239–68.

————. 1986. The Brutal Elimination of a Rival among Captive Male Chimpanzees. In M. Gruter and R. Masters, eds., *Ostracism: A Social and Biological Phenomenon,* 89–103. N.Y.: Elsevier.

Dickemann, Mildred. 1979a. The Ecology of Mating Systems in Hypergynous Dowry Societies. *Social Science Information* 18:163–95.

————. 1979b. Female Infanticide, Reproductive Strategies, and Social Stratification: A Preliminary Model. In N. Chagnon and W. Irons, eds., *Evolutionary Biology and Human Social Behavior,* 321–67. North Scituate, Mass.: Duxbury Press.

Dobzhansky, Theodosius. 1955. *Evolution, Genetics, and Man.* N.Y.: John Wiley.

————. 1962. *Mankind Evolving.* New Haven: Yale University Press.

Dorfmann, D. D. 1978. The Cyril Burt Question: New Findings. *Science* 201:1177–86.

Downs, Anthony. 1957. *An Economic Theory of Democracy.* N.Y.: Harpers.

Dubos, René. 1968. *So Human an Animal.* N.Y.: Charles Scribner's.

Dunbar, Robin I. M. 1988. *Primate Social Systems.* Ithaca, N.Y.: Cornell University Press.

Duncan, Hugh Dalziel. 1968. *Symbols in Society.* N.Y.: Oxford University Press.

Dunn, Judy. 1979. Understanding Human Development: Limitations and Possibilities in an Ethological Approach. In M. von Cranach et al., eds., *Human Ethology,* 623–41. Cambridge: Cambridge University Press.

Durham, William. 1979. Toward a Coevolutionary Theory of Human Biology and Culture. In N. Chagnon and W. Irons, eds., *Evolutionary*

Biology and Human Social Behavior, 39–59. North Scituate, Mass.: Duxbury Press.

———. 1981. Coevolution and Law: The New Yam Festivals of West Africa. Paper presented to Hutchins Center–Goethe Institute Conference on Law and Behavioral Research, Monterey Dunes, Calif., September 1981.

Easton, David. 1953. *The Political System.* N.Y.: Alfred A. Knopf.

———. 1965a. *A Framework for Political Analysis.* Englewood Cliffs, N.J.: Prentice-Hall.

———. 1965b. *A Systems Analysis of Political Life.* N.Y.: John Wiley.

Eaves, Lindon J. 1988. Genetic and Social Causes of Personality Differences. Paper presented to meeting of American Association for the Advancement of Science, Boston, Mass., February 1988.

Edelman, Murray. 1964. *Symbolic Uses of Politics.* Urbana: University of Illinois Press.

Ehrlich, Paul; White, Raymond; Singer, Michael; McKechnie, Stephen; and Gilbert, Lawrence. 1975. Checkerspot Butterflies: A Historical Perspective. *Science* 188:221–28.

Eibl-Eibesfeldt, Iraneus. 1971. *Love and Hate.* N.Y.: Holt, Rinehart & Winston.

———. 1979. Ritual and Ritualization from a Biological Perspective. In M. von Cranach et al., eds., *Human Ethology*, 3–55. N.Y.: Cambridge University Press.

Eisenstadt, S. N. 1963. *The Political Systems of Empires.* London: Free Press of Glencoe.

Ekman, Paul. 1978. Biological and Cultural Contributions to Body and Facial Movement. In J. Blacking, ed., *Anthropology of the Body*, 39–84. N.Y.: Academic Press.

———. 1979. About Brows: Emotional and Conversational Signals. In M. von Cranach et al., eds., *Human Ethology*, 169–249. N.Y.: Cambridge University Press.

Ekman, Paul, and Friesen, Wallace V. 1982. Felt, False, and Miserable Smiles. *Journal of Nonverbal Behavior* 6:238–52.

Ekman, Paul; Friesen, Wallace V.; and Ellsworth, Phoebe. 1972. *Emotion in the Human Face.* N.Y.: Pergamon.

Ekman, Paul; Levenson, R. W.; and Friesen, Wallace V. 1983. Autonomic Nervous System Activity Distinguishes among Emotions. *Science* 221:1208–10.

Ekman, Paul, and Oster, Harriet. 1979. Facial Expressions of Emotion. *Annual Review of Psychology* 30:527–54.

Ellis, Andrew. 1984. *Reading, Writing and Dyslexia.* Hillsdale, N.J.: Lawrence Erlbaum.

Emerson, A. E. 1958. The Evolution of Behavior among Social Insects. In A. Roe and G. G. Simpson, eds., *Behavior and Evolution*, 311–35. New Haven: Yale University Press.

Englis, Basil G.; Vaughan, K. B.; and Lanzetta, J. T. 1982. Conditioning of

Counter-Empathetic Emotional Responses. *Journal of Experimental Social Psychology* 18:375–91.

Ervin, S. M. 1964. Imitation and Structural Change in Children's Language. In E. Lenneberg, ed., *New Directions in the Study of Language*, 163–89. Cambridge, Mass.: MIT Press.

Essok-Vitale, Susan M., and McGuire, Michael. 1985. Women's Lives Viewed from an Evolutionary Perspective, I–II. *Ethology and Sociobiology* 6:137–73.

Etzioni, Amitai. 1968. *The Active Society*. N.Y.: Free Press.

Feierman, Jay R., ed. 1987. The Ethology of Psychiatric Populations. Supplementary number of *Ethology and Sociobiology* 8:1s–164s.

Ferris, N. P., Jr. 1969. The Biochemistry of Anxiety. *Scientific American* 220:69–75.

Fetzer, James H., ed. 1985. *Sociobiology and Epistemology*. Dortrecht and Boston: D. Reidel.

Fisher, Helen C. 1987. The Four-Year Itch. *Natural History* October: 22–33.

Fishman, J.; Ferguson, C. A.; and Das Gupta, J., eds. 1968. *Language Problems of Developing Nations*. N.Y.: John Wiley.

Fodor, Jerry A., and Katz, Jerrold, eds. 1964. *The Structure of Language: Readings in the Philosophy of Language*. Englewood Cliffs, N.J.: Prentice-Hall.

Fortes, Meyer, and Evans-Pritchard, E. E. 1940. *African Political Systems*. London: Oxford University Press.

Fox, Robin. 1967. In the Beginning: Aspects of Hominid Behavioral Evolution. *Man* 2:415–33.

———, ed. 1975. *Biosocial Anthropology*. London: Malaby.

Fraser, C.; Bellugi, U.; and Brown, R. 1968. Control of Grammar in Imitation, Comprehension, and Production. In R. C. Oldfield and J. C. Marshall, eds., *Language* 48–49. Baltimore: Penguin.

Frey, Siegfried; Hirshrunner, H-P; Florin, A.; Daw, A.; and Crawford, R. 1983. A Unified Approach to the Investigation of Nonverbal and Verbal Behavior in Communication Research. In W. Doise and S. Moscovici, eds., *Current Issues in European Social Psychology*, 143–97. Cambridge: Cambridge University Press.

Fridlund, A. J., and Izard, C. E. 1983. Electromyographic Studies of Facial Expressions of Emotions and Patterns of Emotion. In J. T. Cacioppo and R. E. Petty, eds., *Social Psychophysiology: A Sourcebook*, 243–86. N.Y.: Guilford Press.

Fridlund, A. J.; Schwartz, G. E.; and Fowler, S. C. 1984. Pattern Recognition of Self-Reported Emotional State from Multiple-Site Facial EMG Activity during Affective Imagery. *Psychophysiology* 21:622–37.

Frost, Robert. 1949. *The Complete Poems of Robert Frost, 1949*. N.Y.: Henry Holt.

Fuller, Watson, ed. 1974. *The Biological Revolution*. Garden City, N.Y.: Doubleday Anchor.

Fustel de Coulanges, Numa. 1956. *The Ancient City*. N.Y.: Doubleday Anchor.

Galaburda, Albert M. 1986. Human Studies on the Anatomy of Dyslexia. Paper presented to the 37th annual meeting of the Orton Dyslexia Society, Philadelphia, Pa., November 1986. Inglewood, Calif.: Audio-Stats Educational Services, tape #916R–18.

Galdikas-Brindamour, Biruté. 1975. Orangutans, Indonesia's "People of the Forests." *National Geographic* 148:444–73.

Galle, Omer R.; Gove, Walter R.; and McPherson, J. Miller. 1972. Population Density and Pathology: What Are the Relations for Man? *Science* 176:23–30.

Gal-Or, Benjamin. 1972. The Crisis about the Origin of Irreversibility and Time Anistropy. *Science* 176:11–17.

Gardner, Howard. 1983. *Frames of Mind*. N.Y.: Basic Books.

Garn, S. M. 1967. Culture and the Direction of Human Evolution. In N. Korn and F. Thompson, eds., *Human Evolution*, 100–112. N.Y.: Holt, Rinehart & Winston.

Gaylin, Willard. 1972. We Have the Awful Knowledge to Make Exact Copies of Human Beings. *N.Y. Times Magazine* (March 5): 12–13, 41–43.

Geertz, Clifford. 1965. The Impact of the Concept of Culture on the Concept of Man. In John R. Platt, ed., *New Views of the Nature of Man*, 93–118. Chicago: University of Chicago Press.

Georgopoulos, A. P.; Schwartz, A. B.; and Kettner, R. E. 1986. Neuronal Population Coding of Movement Direction. *Science* 233:1416–19.

Gerard, Ralph W. 1960. Becoming: The Residue of Change. In S. Tax, ed., *The Evolution of Man*, 255–67. Chicago: University of Chicago Press.

Gerard, Ralph W.; Kluckhohn, Clyde; and Rapoport, Anatol. 1956. Biological and Cultural Evolution: Some Analogies and Exploration. *Behavioral Science* 1:6–34.

Gernet, Louis, ed. 1923. *Antiphon: Discours suivi des fragments d'Antiphon le Sophiste*. Paris: Editions les Belles Lettres.

Geschwind, Norman, and Galaburda, Albert. 1987. *Cerebral Lateralization*. Cambridge, Mass.: MIT Press.

Gilbert, Martin. 1981. *Winston Churchill*. Boston: Houghton Mifflin.

Gilinsky, Alberta Steinman. 1984. *Mind and Brain*. N.Y.: Praeger.

Gilligan, Carol. 1983. *In a Different Voice*. Cambridge, Mass.: Harvard University Press.

Gleick, James. 1987. *Chaos*. N.Y.: Viking.

Goodall, Jane. [1982] 1983. Order Without Law. Reprinted in M. Gruter and P. Bohannan, eds., *Law, Biology, and Culture*. Santa Barbara: Ross-Erikson.

———. 1986a. *The Chimpanzees of Gombe: Patterns of Behavior*. Cambridge, Mass.: Harvard University Press.

———. 1986b. Social Rejection, Exclusion, and Shunning among the Gombe Chimpanzees. In M. Gruter and R. Masters, eds., *Ostracism: A Social and Biological Phenomenon*, 79–88. N.Y.: Elsevier.

Gould, P. R. 1963. Man Against His Environment: A Game Theoretic
Framework. In A. P. Vayda, ed., *Environment and Cultural Behavior*, 234–
51. Garden City, N.Y.: Natural History Press.

Gould, Stephen J. 1977. *Ontogeny and Phylogeny*. Cambridge, Mass.:
Harvard University Press.

———. 1981. *The Mismeasure of Man*. Cambridge, Mass: Harvard University
Press.

Gould, Stephen J., and Eldredge, Niles. 1977. Punctuated Equilibria: The
Tempo and Mode of Evolution Reconsidered. *Paleobiology* 3:115–51.

Gray, J. 1963. The Language of Animals. In P. LeCorbeiller et al., eds., *The
Languages of Science*, 85–99. N.Y.: Basic Books.

Green, Philip, and Walzer, Michael, eds., 1969. *The Political Imagination in
Literature*. N.Y.: Free Press.

Greenstein, Fred. I. 1982. *The Hidden Hand Presidency: Eisenhower as Leader*.
N.Y.: Basic Books.

Griffin, Donald R. 1976. *The Question of Animal Awareness*. N.Y.: Rockefeller
University Press.

Gross, Charles G. 1983. Visual Functions of Inferotemporal Cortex. In
R. Jung, ed., *Handbook of Sensory Physiology*, 8:3 N.Y.: Springer Verlag.

Gruter, Margaret, and Bohannan, Paul, eds. 1983. *Law, Biology, and Culture*.
Santa Barbara: Ross-Erikson.

Gruter, Margaret, and Masters, Roger D., eds. 1986. *Ostracism: A Social and
Biological Phenomenon*. N.Y.: Elsevier.

Haldane, J. B. S. 1956. Les aspects physico-chimiques des instincts. In
M. Autuori et al., *L'instinct dans le comportement des animaux et de l'homme*,
545–57. Paris: Masson.

Hall, Edward T. 1959. *The Silent Language*. Greenwich, Conn.: Fawcett.

———. 1969. *The Hidden Dimension*. Garden City, N.Y.: Doubleday Anchor.

Hall, K. R. L. 1967. Tool Using Performances as Indicators of Behavioral
Adaptability. In N. Korn and F. Thompson, eds., *Human Evolution*, 173–
91. N.Y.: Holt, Rinehart & Winston.

Hall, K. R. L., and DeVore, Irven. 1965. Baboon Social Behavior. In
I. DeVore, ed., *Primate Behavior*, 52–110. N.Y.: Holt, Rinehart & Winston.

Halle, Louis J. 1965. *The Society of Man*. N.Y.: Harper & Row.

Hamilton, William D. 1964. The Genetical Evolution of Social Behavior.
Journal of Theoretical Biology 7:1–52. Partly reprinted in A. Caplan, ed.,
The Sociobiology Debate, 191–209.

Handler, Philip. 1970. *Biology and the Future of Man*. N.Y.: Oxford
University Press.

Hardin, Garrett. 1968. The Tragedy of the Commons. *Science* 162:1243–48.
Reprinted in H. E. Daly, ed., *Economics, Ecology, Ethics*, 100–114. San
Francisco: W.H. Freeman, 1980.

Hardin, Russell. 1971. Collective Action as an Agreeable *n*-Prisoners'
Dilemma. *Behavioral Science* 16:472–81.

Harlow, Harry F. 1971. *Learning to Love*. N.Y.: Ballantine.

Harlow, Harry F., and Harlow, Margaret K. 1963. A Study of Animal

Affection. In C. Southwick, ed., *Primate Social Behavior*, 174–84. Princeton, N.J.: Van Nostrand Reinhold.

Harris, Marvin. 1977. *Cannibals and Kings*. N.Y.: Random House.

Hass, Hans. 1970. *The Human Animal*. London: Hodder and Stoughton.

Hassan, Fekri A. 1983. Earth Resources, and Population: An Archeological Perspective. In D. J. Ortner, ed., *How Humans Adapt*, 191–226. Washington, D.C.: Smithsonian Institution.

Hawking, Stephen W. 1988. *A Brief History of Time*. N.Y.: Bantam Books.

Hearne, Vicki. 1987. *Adam's Task*. N.Y.: Viking.

Hegel, G. W. F. 1945. *Philosophy of Right*. Trans. T. M. Knox. Oxford: Clarendon Press.

———. 1956. *Philosophy of History*. Trans. J. Sibree. N.Y.: Dover.

Heisenberg, Werner. 1958. *Physics and Philosophy*. N.Y.: Harper & Row.

Hemphill, Michael. 1973. Pretesting for Huntington's Disease. *Hastings Center Report* 3:12–13.

Herbst, P. 1975. Foundations for Behaviour Logic. *Social Science Information* 14:81–100.

Hershey, Alfred. 1968. The T4-lambda Universe. *Carnegie Institution of Washington Year Book 1967*, 562–68. Washington, D.C.: Carnegie Institution.

Hinde, Robert A. 1982. *Ethology*. Glasgow, Scotland: William Collins.

Hinde, Robert A., and Stevenson, J. G. 1971. Les motivations animales et humaines. *La Recherche* 2:443–56.

Hirschman, Albert O. 1971. *A Bias for Hope*. New Haven: Yale University Press.

———. [1970] 1974. *Exit, Voice, and Loyalty*. 2d ed. Cambridge, Mass.: Harvard University Press.

Hirshleifer, Jack. 1977. Economics from a Biological Viewpoint. *Journal of Law and Economics* 20:1–52.

———. 1978. Natural Economy vs. Political Economy. *Journal of Social and Biological Structures* 1:319–37.

———. 1982. Evolutionary Models in Economics and Law: Cooperation versus Conflict Strategies. *Research in Law and Economics* 4:1–60. Greenwich, Conn.: JAI Press.

———. 1985. The Expanding Domain of Economics. *American Economic Review* 75:53–68.

———. 1987. *Economic Behavior in Adversity*. Chicago: University of Chicago Press.

Hirth, Kenneth. 1984. Xochicalco: Urban Growth and State Formation in Central Mexico. *Science* 255:579–86.

Hjort, Johann. 1938. *The Human Value of Biology.* Cambridge, Mass.: Harvard University Press.

Hobbes, Thomas. [1651] 1962. *Leviathan*. Ed. M. Oakeshott. London: Colliers Macmillan.

Hockett, Charles F. 1958. *A Course in Modern Linguistics*. N.Y.: Macmillan.

———. 1959. Animal "Languages" and Human Language. In J. N. Spuhler, ed., *The Evolution of Man's Capacity for Culture*, 32–39. Detroit: Wayne State University Press.

Hoffman, Martin L. 1981. Is Altruism Part of Human Nature? *Journal of Personality and Social Psychology* 40:121–37.

Holden, Constance. 1987. The Genetics of Personality. *Science* 237:598–601.

Holland, Henry M., Jr., ed. 1968. *Politics through Literature*. Englewood Cliffs, N.J.: Prentice-Hall.

Holloway, Ralph. 1968. Cranial Capacity and the Evolution of the Human Brain. In M. F. A. Montagu, ed., *Culture: Man's Adaptive Dimension*, 170–98. N.Y.: Oxford University Press.

Hrdy, Sarah Blaffer. 1981. *The Woman Who Never Evolved*. Cambridge, Mass.: Harvard University Press.

Hrdy, Sarah Blaffer, and Bennett, William. 1981. Lucy's Husband: What Did He Stand For? *Harvard Magazine* 83:7–9, 46.

Hummel, Ralph P. 1973. A Psychology of Charisma. Paper presented to the 9th Congress of the International Political Science Association, Montreal, Canada, August 1973.

Humphrey, N. K. 1976. The Function of the Intellect. In P. P. G. Bateson and R. H. Hinde, eds., *Growing Points in Ethology*, 303–17. Cambridge: Cambridge University Press.

Hundert, E. J. 1987–88. The Thread of Language and the Web of Dominion: Mandeville to Rousseau and Back. *Eighteenth-Century Studies* 21:169–91.

Isaac, Glynn. 1978. The Food-Sharing Behavior of Protohuman Hominids. *Scientific American* 238:90–108.

Izard, Carroll E. 1972. *Patterns of Emotions: A New Analysis of Anxiety and Depression*. N.Y.: Academic Press.

———. 1977. *Human Emotions*. N.Y.: Plenum.

———. 1988. Emotion Expressions in Early Development: Continuity and Change. Paper presented to meeting of American Association for the Advancement of Science, Boston, Mass. February, 1988.

Izard, Carroll E.; Hembree, Elizabeth A.; and Huebner, Robin R. 1987. Infants' Emotion Expressions to Acute Pain: Developmental Change and Stability of Individual Differences. *Developmental Psychology* 23:105–13.

Jacob, François. 1977. Evolution and Tinkering. *Science* 196:1161–66.

Jacob, François; Jakobson, Roman; Lévi-Strauss, Claude; and L'heritier, Philippe. 1968. Vivre et parler. *Les Lettres Françaises*, nos. 1221–22.

Jakobson, Roman. 1970. Relations entre la science du langage et les autres sciences. In *Tendances principales de la recherche dans les sciences sociales et humaines*. The Hague: Mouton-UNESCO.

Jay, Phillis. 1963. The Indian Langur Monkey (*Presytus entellus*). In C. Southwick, ed., *Primate Social Behavior*, 114–23. Princeton, N.J.: Van Nostrand Reinhold.

———. 1965. The Common Langur of North India. In I. DeVore, ed., *Primate Behavior*, 197–249. N.Y.: Holt, Rinehart & Winston.

Jensen, Arthur R. 1969. How Much Can We Boost IQ and Scholastic Achievement? *Harvard Educational Review* 39:1–123.

Johnston, Francis E.; Malina, Robert M.; and Galbraith, Martha A. 1971. Height, Weight, and Age at Menarche and the 'Critical Weight' Hypothesis. *Science* 174:1148–49.

Kagan, Jerome; Reznick, J. Steven; and Snidman, Nancy. 1987. The Physiology and Psychology of Behavioral Inhibition in Children. *Child Development* 58:1459–73.

———. 1988. Biological Bases of Childhood Shyness. *Science* 240:167–71.

Kamin, Leon. 1974. *The Science and Politics of IQ*. Potomac, Md.: Lawrence Erlbaum.

Kant, Immanuel. 1964. *Metaphysical Foundations of Morals*. In C. J. Friedrich, ed., *The Philosophy of Kant*, 140–208. N.Y.: Modern Library.

Kaplan, Morton A. 1957. *System and Process in International Politics*. N.Y.: John Wiley.

Kass, Leon R. 1971. The New Biology: What Price Relieving Man's Estate? *Science* 174:779–88.

Katz, S. H.; Hediger, M. L.; and Valleroy, L. A. 1974. Traditional Maize Processing Techniques in the New World. *Science* 184:765–73.

Kaufman, I. Charles. 1974. Mother/Infant Relationships in Monkeys and Humans: A Reply to Professor Hinde. In N. White, ed., *Ethology and Psychiatry*, 47–68. Toronto: University of Toronto Press.

Kawamura, Syunzo. 1963. The Process of Sub-Culture Propagation among Japanese Macaques. In C. Southwick, ed., *Primate Social Behavior*, 82–90. Princeton, N.J.: Van Nostrand Reinhold.

Kendon, Adam, ed. 1981. *Nonverbal Communication, Interaction, and Gesture*. The Hague: Mouton.

Keohane, Nanerl. 1982. "But for her sex . . .": The Domestication of Sophie. In Jim MacAdam et al., *Trent Rousseau Papers*, 135–45. Ottawa: University of Ottawa Press.

Kitcher, Philip. 1985. *Vaulting Ambition: Sociobiology and the Quest for Human Nature*. Cambridge, Mass.: MIT Press.

Kling, Arthur. 1986. Neurological Correlates of Social Behavior. In M. Gruter and R. Masters, eds., *Ostracism: A Social and Biological Phenomenon*, 27–38. N.Y.: Elsevier.

———. 1987. Brain Mechanisms and Social/Affective Behavior. *Social Science Information* 26:375–84.

Köhler, Wolfgang. 1959. *The Mentality of Apes*. N.Y.: Vintage.

Kolata, Gina Bari. 1977. Overlapping Genes: More Than Anomalies? *Science* 196:1187–88.

Korn, Noel, and Thompson, Fred, eds. 1967. *Human Evolution*. N.Y.: Holt, Rinehart & Winston.

Kosslyn, Stephen M. 1988. Aspects of Cognitive Neuroscience of Mental Imagery. *Science* 240:1621–26.

Kraut, R. E., and Johnston, R. E. 1979. Social and Emotional Messages: An Ethological Approach. *Journal of Personality and Social Psychology* 37:1539–53.

Kroeber, A. L. 1952. *The Nature of Culture.* Chicago: University of Chicago Press.

Kummer, Hans. 1971. *Primate Societies.* Chicago: Aldine Atherton.

———. 1979a. On the Value of Social Relationships to Nonhuman Primates: A Heuristic Scheme. In M. von Cranach et al., eds., *Human Ethology,* 381–95. Cambridge: Cambridge University Press.

———. 1979b. Analogs of Morality among Nonhuman Primates. In G. Stent, ed., *Morality as a Biological Phenomenon,* 31–47. Berkeley: University of California Press.

Kuo, Zing-Yang. 1967. *The Dynamics of Behavior Development.* N.Y.: Random House.

Lacan, Jacques. 1966. *Ecrits.* Paris: Le Seuil.

Laird, J. D. 1974. Self-Attribution of Emotion: The Effects of Expressive Behavior on the Quality of Emotional Experience. *Journal of Personality and Social Psychology* 29:475–86.

Lancaster, Jane. 1986. Primate Social Behavior and Ostracism. In M. Gruter and R. Masters, eds., *Ostracism: A Social and Biological Phenomenon,* 67–77. N.Y.: Elsevier.

Landar, H. 1966. *Language and Culture.* N.Y.: Oxford University Press.

Langacker, R. W. 1968. *Language and Its Structure.* N.Y.: Harcourt, Brace, and World.

Langton, John. 1988. Publius and Political Anthropology. *American Behavioral Scientist* 31:484–96.

Lanzetta, John T., and Orr, Scott P. 1980. Influence of Facial Expressions on the Classical Conditioning of Fear. *Journal of Personality and Social Psychology* 39:1081–87.

———. 1981. Stimulus Properties of Facial Expressions and Their Influence in the Classical Conditioning of Fear. *Motivation and Emotion* 5:225–34.

Lanzetta, John T.; Sullivan, Denis G.; Masters, Roger D.; and McHugo, Gregory J. 1985. Viewers' Emotional and Cognitive Responses to Televised Images of Political Leaders. In S. Kraus and R. Perloff, eds., *Mass Media and Political Thought.* Beverly Hills, Calif.: Sage.

Larsen, R. R. 1973. Leaders and Non-Leaders: Speculation on Charisma. Paper presented to the 45th Meeting of the Southern Political Science Association, Atlanta, Ga., November 1973.

Lau, Richard R., and Erber, Ralph. 1985. Political Sophistication: An Information Processing Approach. In S. Kraus and R. Perloff, eds., *Mass Media and Political Thought,* 37–63. Beverly Hills, Calif.: Sage.

Laver, Michael. 1981. *The Politics of Private Desire.* Harmondsworth, England: Penguin.

Layzer, David. 1978. Altruism and Natural Selection. *Journal of Social and Biological Structures* 1:297–305.

Leakey, Mary D. 1981. Tracks and Tools. *Philosophical Transactions of the Royal Society of London* 292:95–102.

Leakey, Richard E., and Lewin, Roger. 1977. *Origins.* N.Y.: E. P. Dutton.

Lehrman, Daniel S. 1956. On the Organization of Maternal Behavior and the Problem of Instinct. In M. Autuori et al., *L'instinct dans le comportement des animaux et de l'homme*, 475–514. Paris: Masson.

Lekson, Stephen H.; Windes, Thomas C.; Stein, John R.; and Judge, W. James. 1988. The Chaco Canyon Community. *Scientific American* 259:100–109.

Lenneberg, Eric H. 1957. A Probabilistic Approach to Language Learning. *Behavioral Science* 2:1–12.

——. 1964. A Biological Perspective of Language. In E. H. Lenneberg, ed., *New Directions in the Study of Language*, 65–88. Cambridge, Mass.: MIT Press.

Leventhal, Howard. 1984. A Perceptual Motor Theory of Emotion. In K. R. Scherer and P. Ekman, eds., *Approaches to Emotion*, 271–91. Hillsdale, N.J.: Lawrence Erlbaum.

Lévi-Strauss, Claude. [1944] 1967. The Social and Psychological Aspects of Chieftainship in a Primitive Tribe. In R. Cohen and J. Middleton, eds., *Comparative Political Systems*, 5–62. Garden City, N.Y.: Natural History Press.

——. [1955] 1974. *Tristes tropiques*. N.Y.: Atheneum.

——. 1958. *Anthropologie structurale*. Paris: Plon.

——. 1962. *La pensée sauvage*. Paris: Plon.

——. 1968. *Mythologiques III: L'origine des manières de table*. Paris: Plon.

Levy, Marion J., Jr. 1952. *The Structure of Society*. Princeton, N.J.: Princeton University Press.

Lewontin, Richard; Rose, Richard; and Kamin, Leon. 1984. *Not in Our Genes*. N.Y.: Pantheon.

Lockard, Joan S., ed. 1980. *The Evolution of Human Social Behavior*. N.Y.: Elsevier.

Lopreato, Joseph. 1984. *Human Nature and Biocultural Evolution*. Boston, Mass.: Allen and Unwin.

Lorenz, Konrad Z. [1931–63] 1970–71. *Studies in Animal and Human Behavior*. Vols. 1–2. Cambridge, Mass.: Harvard University Press.

——. 1956. The Objectivistic Theory of Instinct. In M. Autuori et al., *L'instinct dans le comportement des animaux et de l'homme*, 51–64. Paris: Masson.

——. [1961] 1966. *On Aggression*. N.Y.: Harcourt, Brace, and World.

——. 1967. *Evolution et modification du comportement*. Paris: Payot.

——. 1974. Analogy as a Source of Knowledge. *Science* 185:229–34.

Lorenz, Konrad Z., and Leyhausen, Paul. 1973. *Motivation of Human and Animal Behavior*. N.Y.: Van Nostrand Reinhold.

Lovejoy, C. Owen. 1981. The Origin of Man. *Science* 221:341–50.

Lumsden, Charles J., and Wilson, Edward O. 1980a. Translation of Epigenetic Rules of Individual Behavior into Ethnographic Patterns. *Proceedings of the National Academy of Sciences, USA*, 77:4382–86.

——. 1980b. Gene-Culture Translation in the Avoidance of Sibling Incest. *Proceedings of the National Academy of Sciences, USA*, 77:6248–50.

————. 1981. *Genes, Mind, and Culture*. Cambridge, Mass.: Harvard University Press.

McClintock, Barbara. 1967. The States of a Gene Locus in Maize. *Carnegie Institution of Washington Year Book 1966*, 664–72. Washington, D.C.: Carnegie Institution.

McEachron, Donald L., and Baer, Darius. 1982. A Review of Selected Sociobiological Principles: Application to Hominid Evolution. II. The Effects of Intergroup Conflict. *Journal of Social and Biological Structures* 5:121–39.

McGuire, Michael T., and Raleigh, Michael J. 1986. Behavioral and Physiological Correlates of Ostracism. In M. Gruter and R. Masters, eds., *Ostracism: A Social and Biological Phenomenon*, 39–52. N.Y.: Elsevier.

Machiavelli, Niccolò. 1970. *Discourses on Titus Livy*. Ed. B. Crick. Harmondsworth, England: Penguin.

McHugo, Gregory J., and Lanzetta, John T. 1986. Emotional and Mental Reactions to Televised Images of Political Leaders. Paper presented to the annual meeting of the American Psychological Association, Washington, D.C.

McHugo, Gregory J.; Lanzetta, John T.; Sullivan, Denis G.; Masters, Roger D.; and Englis, Basil. 1985. Emotional Reactions to Expressive Displays of a Political Leader. *Journal of Personality and Social Psychology* 49:1513–29.

McHugo, Gregory J.; Smith, C. A.; and Lanzetta, John T. 1982. The Structure of Self-Reports of Emotional Responses to Film Segments. *Motivation and Emotion* 6:365–85.

McKusick, V. A. 1964. *Human Genetics*. Englewood Cliffs, N.J.: Prentice-Hall.

Maclay, George, and Knipe, Humphry. 1972. *The Dominant Man*. N.Y.: Delacorte.

McLean, Ian. 1981. The Social Contract in *Leviathan* and the Prisoner's Dilemma Supergame. *Political Studies* 29:339–51.

MacLean, Paul. 1983. A Triangular Brief on the Evolution of the Brain and Law. In M. Gruter and Paul Bohannan, eds., *Law, Biology, and Culture*, 74–90. Santa Barbara, Calif.: Ross-Erikson.

McNeill, D. 1968. The Creation of Language. In R. C. Oldfield and J. C. Marshall, eds., *Language*, 21–31. Baltimore: Penguin.

Macpherson, C. B. 1962. *The Political Theory of Possessive Individualism*. Oxford: Clarendon Press.

Madson, Douglas. 1985a. A Biochemical Property Related to Power-Seeking in Humans. *American Political Science Review* 79:448–57.

————. 1985b. Power Seekers Are (Biochemically) Different: Further Evidence. Paper presented to the meeting of the International Political Science Association, Paris, France, July 1985.

Marais, Eugene. 1969. *The Soul of the Ape*. N.Y.: Atheneum.

Marcus, George. 1988. The Structure of Emotional Appraisal: 1984 Candidates. *American Political Science Review* 82:737–62.

Margolis, Howard. 1981. A New Model of Rational Choice. *Ethics* 91:265–79.

———. 1982. *Selfishness, Altruism, and Rationality.* Cambridge: Cambridge University Press.

Markam, Felix. 1963. *Napoleon.* N.Y.: Mentor.

Marler, Peter. 1965. Communication in Monkeys and Apes. In I. DeVore, ed., *Primate Behavior*, 544–84. N.Y.: Holt, Rinehart & Winston.

Martin, R. D. 1972. Concepts of Human Territoriality. In P. Ucko, R. Tringham, and G. W. Dimbley, eds., *Man, Settlement, and Urbanism*, 427–45. Cambridge, Mass.: Schenckman.

Marx, Karl. 1964. *Economic and Philosophic Manuscripts of 1844.* Ed. D. Struik. N.Y.: International Publishers.

———. 1974. *German Ideology.* Pt. 1. N.Y.: International Publishers.

Masland, Richard L. 1983. Neurological Aspects of Dyslexia. In G. T. Pavlidis and T. R. Miles, eds., *Dyslexia Research and Its Applications to Education*, 35–66. N.Y.: John Wiley.

Masters, Roger D. 1964. World Politics as a Primitive Political System. *World Politics* 16:595–619.

———. 1968. *The Political Philosophy of Rousseau.* Princeton, N.J.: Princeton University Press.

———. 1970. Genes, Language, and Evolution. *Semiotica* 2:295–320.

———. 1971. Gènes, langage, et évolution. *La Recherche* 2:825–33.

———. [1973a] 1976. Functional Approaches to Analogical Comparisons between Species. In M. von Cranach, ed., *Methods of Comparing Animal and Human Behavior*, 73–102. The Hague: Mouton.

———. 1973b. On Comparing Humans—and Human Politics—with Animal Behavior. Paper presented to the 9th Congress of the International Political Science Association, Montreal, Canada, August 1973.

———. 1975a. Politics as a Biological Phenomenon. *Social Science Information* 14:7–63.

———. 1975b. Vers une science? *Contrepoint* 16:109–22.

———. 1976a. The Impact of Ethology on Political Science. In A. Somit, ed., *Biology and Politics*, 197–233. The Hague: Mouton.

———. 1976b. Exit, Voice, and Loyalty in Animal and Human Behavior. *Social Science Information* 15:78–85.

———. 1977. Nature, Human Nature, and Political Thought. In R. Pennock and J. Chapman, eds., *Human Nature in Politics*, 69–110. N.Y.: New York University Press.

———. 1978a. Classical Political Philosophy and Contemporary Biology. Paper presented at the Conference for the Study of Political Thought, Chicago, Ill., April 1978. To appear in Kent Moors, ed., *Politikos.* Pittsburgh, Pa.: Duquesne University Press.

———. 1978b. Jean-Jacques Is Alive and Well: Rousseau and Contemporary Sociobiology. *Daedalus* (Summer): 93–105.

———. 1978c. Of Marmots and Men: Human Altruism and Animal

Behavior. In L. Wispé, ed., *Altruism, Sympathy, and Helping*, 59–77. N.Y.: Academic Press.

———. 1979a. Beyond Reductionism. In M. von Cranach et al., eds., *Human Ethology*, 265–84. Cambridge: Cambridge University Press.

———. 1979b. On the Ubiquity of Ideology in Modern Societies. *Revue européenne des sciences sociales et cahiers Vilfredo Pareto* 17:159–72.

———. 1980a. Sociobiology. *American Medical News* 23:7.

———. 1980b. Nothing Fails Like Success: Development and History in Rousseau's Political Teaching. In J. MacAdam et al., *Trent Rousseau Papers*, 99–118. Ottawa: University of Ottawa Press.

———. 1981a. Linking Ethology and Political Science: Photographs, Political Attention, and Presidential Elections. In M. Watts, ed., *Biopolitics: Ethological and Physiological Approaches*, 61–80. New Directions for Methodology of Social and Behavioral Science, no. 7. San Francisco: Jossey-Bass.

———. 1981b. The Value—and Limits—of Sociobiology. In E. White, ed., *Sociobiology and Human Politics*, 135–65. Lexington, Mass.: Lexington Books.

———. 1982a. Is Sociobiology Reactionary? The Political Implications of Inclusive Fitness Theory. *Quarterly Review of Biology* 57:275–92.

———. [1982b] 1983. Evolutionary Biology, Political Theory, and the Origin of the State. In M. Gruter and P. Bohannan, eds., *Law Biology and Culture*, 171–89. Santa Barbara: Ross-Erikson.

———. 1983a. The Biological Nature of the State. *World Politics* 25:161–93.

———. 1983b. Evolutionary Biology and the Welfare State. In R. F. Thomasson, ed., *Comparative Social Research*, 6:203–41. Greenwich, Conn.: JAI Press.

———. 1983c. The Duties of Humanity: Legal and Moral Obligation in Rousseau's Thought. In F. Eidlin, ed., *Constitutional Democracy: Essays in Comparative Politics*, 83–105. Boulder, Colo.: Westview Press.

———. 1984. Explaining "Male Chauvinism" and "Feminism": Cultural Differences in Male and Female Reproductive Strategies. In M. Watts, ed., *Biopolitics and Gender*, 165–210. N.Y.: Haworth Press.

———. 1986. Ostracism, Voice, and Exit: The Biology of Social Participation. In M. Gruter and R. Masters, eds., *Ostracism: A Social and Biological Phenomenon*, 231–47. N.Y.: Elsevier.

———. 1987. Evolutionary Biology and Natural Right. In W. Soffer and K. Deutsch, eds., *The Crisis of Liberal Democracy*. Albany, N.Y.: SUNY Press.

Masters, Roger D., and Mouchon, Jean. 1986. Les gestes et la vie politique. *Le Français et le Monde* 203:85–87.

Masters, Roger D., and Muzet, Denis. In preparation. La rhétorique et l'image des hommes politiques à la télévision: Analyse experimentale.

Masters, Roger D., and Sullivan, Denis G. 1986. Nonverbal Displays and Political Leadership in France and the United States. Paper presented to the meeting of the American Political Science Association, Washington, D.C., August 1986.

Masters, Roger D.; Sullivan, Denis G.; Lanzetta, John T.; and McHugo, Gregory J. 1985. Facial Displays as a Political Variable. Paper presented to the meeting of the International Political Science Association, Paris, France, July 1985.

Masters, Roger D.; Sullivan, Denis G.; Lanzetta, John T.; McHugo, Gregory J.; and Englis, Basil G. 1986. The Facial Displays of Leaders: Toward an Ethology of Human Politics. *Journal of Social and Biological Structures* 9:319–43.

Maynard-Smith, John. 1978. The Evolution of Behavior. *Scientific American* 239:176–92.

Mayr, Ernst. 1958. Behavior and Systematics. In A. Roe and G. G. Simpson, eds., *Behavior and Evolution*, 341–62. New Haven: Yale University Press.

———. 1963. *Animal Species and Evolution*. Cambridge, Mass.: Harvard University Press.

———. 1974. Teleological and Teleonomic, a New Analysis. *Boston Studies in the Philosophy of Science* 14:91–117.

Meadows, Denis, et al. 1972. *The Limits to Growth*. N.Y.: Signet.

Mehler, Jacques. 1986. Language Comprehension: The Influence of Age, Modality, and Culture. Paper presented to the 37th annual meeting of the Orton Dyslexia Society, Philadelphia, Pa., November 1986. Inglewood, Calif.: Audio-Stats Educational Services, tape #916R–21.

Meltzoff, A., and Moore, M. 1977. Imitation of Facial and Manual Gestures by Human Neonates. *Science* 198:75–78.

Merton, Robert K. 1949. *Social Theory and Social Structure*. Glencoe, Ill.: Free Press.

Mettler, Fred A. 1962. Culture and the Structural Evolution of the Central Nervous System. In M. F. A. Montagu, ed., *Culture and the Evolution of Man*, 102–13. N.Y.: Oxford University Press.

Mills, C. Wright. 1959. *The Sociological Imagination*. N.Y.: Oxford University Press.

Monod, Jacques. 1970. *Le hasard et la nécessité*. Paris: Le Seuil.

Montagner, Hubert. 1977. Silent Speech. *Horizon—BBC2*, July 28, 1977. Videotape.

———. 1978. *L'enfant et la communication*. Paris: Stock.

Montagu, M. F. Ashley, ed. 1968. *Man and Aggression*. N.Y.: Oxford University Press.

Moorhead, Paul, and Kaplan, Martin M., eds. 1967. *Mathematical Challenges to the Neo-Darwinian Interpretation of Evolution*. Philadelphia: Wistar Institute.

Morin, Edgar. 1973. *Le paradigme perdu*. Paris: Le Seuil.

Morison, Samuel Eliot. 1965. *Oxford History of the American People*. N.Y.: Oxford University Press.

Morris, Desmond. 1956. The Function and Causation of Courtship Ceremonies. In M. Autuori et al., *L'instinct dans le comportement des animaux et de l'homme*, 261–84. Paris: Masson.

————. 1967. *The Naked Ape*. N.Y.: McGraw-Hill.

————, ed. 1969. *Primate Ethology*. Garden City, N.Y.: Doubleday Anchor.

Moyer, K. E. 1969. Kinds of Aggression and Their Physiological Basis. *Behavioral Biology* 2:65–87.

Muller, Herman J. 1960. The Guidance of Human Evolution. In S. Tax, ed., *The Evolution of Man*, 432–62. Chicago: University of Chicago Press.

Newton, James; Masters, Roger D.; McHugo, Gregory J.; and Sullivan, Denis G. 1988. Making up Our Minds: Effects of Network Coverage on Viewers' Impressions of Leaders. *Polity* 20:226–46.

Nur, Uzi; Werren, John H.; Eickbush, Danna G.; Burke, William D.; Eickbush, Thomas H. 1988. A "Selfish" B Chromosome That Enhances Its Transmission by Eliminating the Paternal Genome. *Science* 240:512–14.

Oakley, Kenneth P. 1959. *Man the Tool-Maker*. Chicago: University of Chicago Press.

Ohloff, Gunther. 1971. L'odorat et la forme des molécules. *La Recherche* 2:1068–70.

Ohman, A., and Dimberg, U. 1978. Facial Expressions as Conditioned Stimuli for Electrodermal Responses: A Case of "Preparedness"? *Journal of Personality and Social Psychology* 38:1251–58.

Olson, Mancur, Jr. 1965. *The Logic of Collective Action*. Cambridge, Mass.: Harvard University Press.

————. 1982. *The Rise and Decline of Nations*. New Haven: Yale University Press.

Ophuls, William. 1973. Leviathan or Oblivion? In H. E. Daly, ed., *Toward a Steady-State Economy*, 215–30. San Francisco: W. H. Freeman.

————. 1977. *Ecology and the Politics of Scarcity*. San Francisco: W. H. Freeman.

Orr, Scott P., and Lanzetta, John T. 1980. Facial Expressions of Emotion as Conditioned Stimuli for Human Autonomic Responses. *Journal of Personality and Social Psychology* 38:278–82.

Ortner, Donald E., ed., 1983. *How Humans Adapt*. Washington, D.C.: Smithsonian Institution.

Osgood, Charles E. 1966. Dimensionality of the Semantic Space for Communication via Facial Expression. *Scandinavian Journal of Psychology* 7:1–30.

Ostrom, Charles W., and Simon, Dennis M. 1985. Promise and Performance: A Dynamic Model of Presidential Popularity. *American Political Science Review* 79:334–58.

Papousek, Hanus, and Papousek, Mechthild. 1979. Early Ontogeny of Human Social Interaction: Its Biological Roots and Social Dimensions. In M. von Cranach et al., eds., *Human Ethology*, 456–78. Cambridge: Cambridge University Press.

Pattee, Howard H., ed. 1973. *Hierarchy Theory*. N.Y.: George Braziller.

Peter, Lawrence J., and Hull, Raymond. 1969. *The Peter Principle*. N.Y.: W. Morrow.

Peters, Richard, and Taijfel, Henri. 1972. Hobbes and Hull: Metaphysicians of Behavior. In M. Cranston and R. S. Peters, eds., *Hobbes and Rousseau,* 165–83. N.Y.: Doubleday Anchor.

Petty, Richard E., and Cacioppo, John T. 1981. *Attitudes and Persuasion: Classic and Contemporary Approaches.* Dubuque, Iowa: William Brown.

Piaget, Jean. 1970. *Le structuralisme.* 4th ed. Paris: Presses Universitaires de France.

Pieron, Henri. 1956. L'évolution du comportement dans ses rapports avec l'instinct. In M. Autuori et al., *L'instinct dans le comportement des animaux et de l'homme,* 677–95. Paris: Masson.

Pierotti, Raymond. 1980. Spite and Altruism in Gulls. *American Naturalist* 115:290–300.

Pittendrigh, Colin S. 1958. Adaptation, Natural Selection, and Behavior. In A. Roe and G. G. Simpson, eds., *Behavior and Evolution,* 390–416. New Haven: Yale University Press.

Plate, Elise. 1984. The Double-Bind Phenomenon in Politics: The Influence of Nonverbal Expressive Behavior of Male and Female Political Candidates on Impression Formation. Senior honors thesis, Dartmouth College.

Plato. 1968. *Republic.* Ed. A. Bloom. N.Y.: Basic Books.

Plomin, Robert, and Daniels, Denise. 1987. Why Are Children in the Same Family So Different from One Another? *Behavior and Brain Science* 10:1–30.

Plutchik, Robert. 1980. *Emotion: A Psychoevolutionary Synthesis.* N.Y.: Harper & Row.

Portmann, Adolf. 1961. *Animals as Social Beings.* London: Hutchinson.

Posner, Michael I.; Petersen, Steven E.; Fox, Peter T.; and Raichle, Marcus E. 1988. Localization of Cognitive Operations in the Human Brain. *Science* 240:1627–31.

Price, Trevor; Kirkpatrick, Mark; and Arnold, Steven J. 1988. Directional Selection and the Evolution of Breeding in Birds. *Science* 240:798–99.

Pritchard, James B., ed. 1958. *The Ancient Near East.* Princeton: Princeton University Press.

Raleigh, Michael J., and McGuire, Michael T. 1986. Animal Analogues of Ostracism: Biological Mechanisms and Social Consequences. In M. Gruter and R. Masters, eds., *Ostracism: A Social and Biological Phenomenon,* 53–66. N.Y.: Elsevier.

Ranney, Austin. 1983. *Channels of Power: The Impact of Television on American Politics.* N.Y.: Basic Books.

Rawls, John. 1971. *A Theory of Justice.* Cambridge, Mass.: Harvard University Press.

Real, Leslie A. 1980. Fitness, Uncertainty, and the Role of Diversification in Evolution and Behavior. *American Naturalist* 115:623–38.

Rensch, Bernhard. 1966. *Evolution above the Species Level.* N.Y.: John Wiley.

Reynolds, Vernon. 1966. Open Groups in Hominid Evolution. *Man* 1:441–52.

———. 1967. *The Apes.* N.Y.: Harper Colophon.

————. 1968. Kinship and the Family in Monkeys, Apes, and Man. *Man* 3:209–23.

Reynolds, Vernon; Falger, Vincent S. E.; and Vine, Ian, eds. 1987. *The Sociobiology of Ethnocentrism*. London: Croom Helm.

Richardson, Ken, and Spears, David, eds. 1972. *Race and Intelligence*. Baltimore: Penguin.

Rifkin, Jeremy. 1983. *Algeny*. N.Y.: Viking Press.

Ripley, Suzanne. 1967. Intertroop Encounters among Ceylon Grey Langurs (*Presbytis entellus*). In S. Altmann, ed., *Social Communication among Primates*, 237–53. Chicago: University of Chicago Press.

Rodman, Hillary, and Gross, Charles. 1987. Temporal Cortex. In George Adelman, ed., *Encyclopedia of Neuroscience* 2:1194–96. Boston: Birkhaüser.

Roe, Anne, and Simpson, George Gaylord. 1958. *Behavior and Evolution*. New Haven: Yale University Press.

Roelofs, Wendell; Comeau, Andre; Hill, Ada; and Milicevic, G. 1971. Sex Attractant of the Codling Moth: Characterization with Electroantennogram Technique. *Science* 174:297–99.

Rose, Richard J.; Harris, E. L.; Christian, J. C.; and Nance, W. E. 1979. Genetic Variance in Nonverbal Intelligence: Data from the Kinships of Identical Twins. *Science* 205:1153–54.

Rosenberg, Alexander. 1980. *Sociobiology and the Preemption of Social Science*. Baltimore: Johns Hopkins Press.

Rosenblatt, Joseph D.; Cann, Alan J.; Slamon, Dennis J.; Smallberg, Ira S.; Shah, Neil P.; Fujii, Joyce; Wachsman, William; and Chen, Irvin S.Y. 1988. HTLV-II Transactivation Is Regulated by the Overlapping *tax/rex* Nonstructural Gene. *Science* 240:916–19.

Rousseau, Jean-Jacques. [1750–55] 1964. *First and Second Discourses*. Ed. R. Masters. N.Y.: St. Martin's Press.

————. [1755–62] 1978. *Social Contract, with Geneva Manuscript and Political Economy*. Ed. R. Masters. N.Y.: St. Martin's Press.

Ruse, Michael. 1986. *Taking Darwin Seriously*. Oxford: Basil Blackwell.

Rushton, J. Phillipe; Littlefield, Christine H.; and Lumsden, Charles J. 1986. Gene-Culture Coevolution of Complex Social Behavior: Human Altruism and Mate Choice. *Proceedings of the National Academy of Science, USA*, 83:7340–43.

Sagan, Carl. 1977. *The Dragons of Eden*. N.Y.: Random House.

Sahlins, Marshall, and Service, Elman R., eds. 1960. *Evolution and Culture*. Ann Arbor: University of Michigan Press.

Sapir, E. 1970. *Le langage*. Paris: Payot.

Sapir, Selma. 1985. *The Clinical Teaching Model*. N.Y.: Bruner/Maazel.

Schaller, George B. 1965. *The Year of the Gorilla*. N.Y.: Ballantine.

Schneirla, T. C. 1956. Interrelationships of the "Innate" and the "Acquired" in Instinctive Behavior. In M. Autuori et al., *L'instinct dans le comportement des animaux et de l'homme*, 387–439. Paris: Masson.

Schreider, Eugène. 1972. Les limites de l'adaptabilité humaine. *La Recherche* 3:47–62.

Schubert, Glendon. 1981. The Sociobiology of Political Behavior. In
E. White, ed., *Human Sociobiology and Politics*, 193–238. Lexington, Mass.:
Lexington Books.

———. 1982. Nonverbal Communication as Political Behavior. In M. K.
Ritchie, ed., *Nonverbal Communication Today: Current Research*. Berlin:
Mouton.

———. 1983a. The Biopolitics of Sex: Gender, Genetics, and Epigenetics. In
M. Watts, ed., *Biopolitics and Gender*, 97–128. N.Y.: Haworth Press.

———. 1983b. Psychobiological Politics. *Political Science Review* 16:535–76.

———. 1985. Sexual Differences in Political Behavior. *Political Science Review*
15:1–68.

———. 1986. Primate Politics. *Social Science Information* 25:647–80.

Schubert, James. 1986. Human Vocalizations in Agonistic Political
Encounters. *Social Science Information* 25:475–92.

Schwartz, G. E.; Fair, P. L.; Salt, P.; Mandel, M. R.; and Klerman, G. L.
1976. Facial Muscle Patterning to Affective Imagery in Depressed and
Nondepressed Subjects. *Science* 192:489–91.

Scott, William. 1820. *Lessons in Elocution; or, a Selection of Pieces in Prose and
Verse for the Improvement of Youth in Reading and Speaking*. Leicester: Hori
Brown.

Sebeok, Thomas A. 1962. Coding in the Evolution of Signalling Behavior.
Behavioral Science 7:430–42.

———. 1965. Animal Communication. *Science* 147:1006–1114.

———. 1967a. Aspects of Animal Communication: The Bees and Porpoises.
ETC: A Review of General Semantics 24:59–83.

———. 1967b. Discussion of Communication Processes. In S. Altmann,
ed., *Social Communication among Primates*, 363–69. Chicago: University of
Chicago Press.

———, ed. 1968. *Animal Communication*. Bloomington: Indiana University
Press.

Shepherd, Gordon M. 1983. *Neurobiology*. N.Y.: Oxford University Press.

Shirer, William L. 1941. *Berlin Diary*. N.Y.: Alfred Knopf.

Simpson, George Gaylord. 1958. The Study of Evolution: Methods and
Present Status of Theory. In A. Roe and G. G. Simpson, *Behavior and
Evolution*, 7–25. New Haven: Yale University Press.

———. 1967. *The Meaning of Evolution*. Rev. ed. New Haven: Yale
University Press.

———. 1969. *Biology and Man*. N.Y.: Harcourt, Brace, and World.

Skinner, B. F. 1965. *Science and Human Behavior*. N.Y.: Free Press.

Slobodkin, Lawrence B. 1964. The Strategy of Evolution. *American Scientist*
52:342–57.

Smith, W. J. 1969. Messages of Vertebrate Communication. *Science* 165:145–
50.

Somit, Albert. 1968. Toward a More Biologically Oriented Political Science.
Midwest Journal of Political Science 12:550–67.

———, ed. 1976. *Biology and Politics*. The Hague: Mouton.

Sorenson, James R. 1971. Social Aspects of Applied Human Genetics. *Social Science Frontiers, #3*. N.Y.: Russell Sage Foundation.

Southwick, Charles; Beg, Mirza Azhar; and Siddiqui, M. Rafiq. 1965. Rhesus Monkeys in North India. In I. DeVore, ed., *Primate Behavior*, 111–59. N.Y.: Holt, Rinehart & Winston.

Spanier, E. 1969. Grammars and Languages. *The American Mathematical Monthly* 76:335–42.

Sparks, John. 1969. Allogrooming in Primates: A Review. In D. Morris, ed., *Primate Ethology*, 190–225. N.Y.: Doubleday Anchor.

Spielman, Richard S.; Migliazza, E. C.; and Neel, J. V. 1974. Regional Linguistic and Genetic Differences among Yanomama Indians. *Science* 184:637–44.

Sprout, Margaret, and Sprout, Harold. 1971. Ecology and Politics in America. *Module 3018*. N.Y.: General Learning Press.

Spuhler, John N. 1959. Somatic Paths to Culture. In J. Spuhler, ed., *The Evolution of Man's Capacity for Culture*, 1–13. Detroit: Wayne State University Press.

———, ed. 1959. *The Evolution of Man's Capacity for Culture*. Detroit: Wayne State University Press.

Stauffer, Robert B. 1971. The Role of Drugs in Political Change. *Module 3016*. N.Y.: General Learning Press.

Stebbins, G. Ledyard. 1966. *Processes of Organic Evolution*. N.Y.: Prentice-Hall.

———. 1967. The Dynamics of Evolutionary Change. In N. Korn and F. Thompson, eds., *Human Evolution*, 34–51. N.Y.: Holt, Rinehart & Winston.

Stebbins, G. Ledyard, and Ayala, F. 1985. The Evolution of Darwinism. *Scientific American* 253 (July):72–82.

Steen, Lynn Arthur. 1988. The Science of Patterns. *Science* 240:611–16.

Steitz, Joan Argetsinger. 1988. "Snurps." *Scientific American* 258:56–63.

Stent, Gunther. 1969. *The Coming of the Golden Age*. N.Y.: Natural History Press.

———. 1972. Cellular Communication. *Scientific American* 227:49–51.

———. 1977. You can take the ethics out of altruism, but you can't take the altruism out of ethics. *Hastings Center Report* 7:33–36.

———, ed. 1979. *Morality as a Biological Phenomenon*. Berkeley: University of California Press.

Steward, Julian. 1955. *The Theory of Culture Change*. Urbana: University of Illinois Press.

Stoffaes, Christian. 1973. De l'impot negatif sur le revenu. *Contrepoint* 11:31–50.

Strauss, Leo. 1953. *Natural Right and History*. Chicago: University of Chicago Press.

———. 1964. *The City and Man*. Chicago: Rand McNally.

Strayer, Fred F. 1981. The Organization and Coordination of Asymmetrical Relations among Young Children: A Biological View of Social Power. In

M. Watts, ed., *Biopolitics: Ethological and Physiological Approaches*, 33–50. New Directions for Methodology of Social and Behavioral Science, no. 7. San Francisco: Jossey-Bass.

Strayer, Fred F., and Trudel, M. 1984. Developmental Changes in the Nature and Function of Social Dominance among Young Children. *Ethology and Sociobiology* 5:279–95.

Sugiyama, Yokimaru. 1967. Social Organization of Hanuman Langurs. In S. Altmann, ed., *Social Communication among Primates*, 221–36. Chicago: University of Chicago Press.

Sullivan, Denis G., and Masters, Roger D. 1988. Happy Warriors: Leaders' Facial Displays and Viewers' Emotions, and Political Support. *American Journal of Political Science* 32:345–68.

Sullivan, Denis G.; Masters, Roger D.; Lanzetta, John T.; Englis, Basil G.; and McHugo, Gregory J. 1984. The Effect of President Reagan's Facial Displays on Observers' Attitudes, Impressions, and Feelings about Him. Paper presented to the meeting of the American Political Science Association, Washington, D.C., September 1984.

Sullivan, Denis G.; Masters, Roger D.; Lanzetta, John T.; McHugo, Gregory J.; Plate, Elise; and Englis, Basil G. In preparation. Facial Displays and Political Leadership. In G. Schubert and R. Masters, eds., *Primate Politics*.

Sullivan, Denis G.; Nakamura, Robert T.; and Winters, Richard F. 1980. *How America Is Ruled.* N.Y.: John Wiley.

Tax, Sol, ed. 1960. *The Evolution of Man.* Chicago: University of Chicago Press.

Taylor, Charles E., and McGuire, Michael T., eds. 1988. Reciprocal Altruism: 15 Years Later. *Ethology and Sociobiology* 9:67–258.

Taylor, Gordon Rattray. 1968. *The Biological Time-Bomb.* N.Y.: Mentor.

Terrill, Ross. 1980. *Mao: A Biography.* N.Y.: Harper & Row.

Thass-Thienemann, T. 1968. *Symbolic Behavior.* N.Y.: Washington Square Press.

Thompson, J. E. S. 1950. *Mayan Hieroglyphic Writing.* Washington, D.C.: Carnegie Institution.

Thompson, Philip R. 1976. A Behavior Model for *Australopithecus africanus. Journal of Human Evolution* 5:547–58.

Thorson, Thomas Langdon. 1970. *Biopolitics.* N.Y.: Holt, Rinehart & Winston.

Thucydides. 1839–1845. *The History of the Grecian War.* Trans. by T. Hobbes. In Thomas Hobbes, *The English Works of Thomas Hobbes.* London: J. Bohn. Vols. 8–9.

Tiger, Lionel. 1969. *Men in Groups.* N.Y.: Random House.

———. 1979a. *Optimism: The Biology of Hope.* N.Y.: Simon & Schuster.

———. 1979b. Biology, Psychology, and Incorrect Assumptions of Cultural Relativism. In N. Chagnon and W. Irons, eds., *Evolutionary Biology and Human Social Behavior*, 511–19. North Scituate, Mass.: Duxbury Press.

———. 1987. *The Manufacture of Evil.* N.Y.: Harper & Row.

Tiger, Lionel, and Fox, Robin. 1971. *The Imperial Animal*. N.Y.: Holt, Rinehart & Winston.

Tinbergen, Niko. 1967. *La vie sociale des animaux*. Paris: Payot.

Tranel, Daniel, and Damasio, Antonio R. 1985. Learning Without Awareness: An Autonomic Index of Facial Recognition by Prosopagnosics. *Science* 228:1453–54.

Trivers, Robert. 1971. The Evolution of Reciprocal Altruism. *Quarterly Review of Biology* 46:35–57.

———. 1981. Sociobiology and Politics. In E. White, ed., *Sociobiology and Human Politics*, 1–43. Lexington, Mass.: Lexington Books.

Tsumori, Atsuo. 1967. Newly Acquired Behavior and Social Interactions of Japanese Monkeys. In S. Altmann, ed., *Social Communication among Primates*, 207–19. Chicago: University of Chicago Press.

Turner, B. L. II, and Harrison, P. D. 1981. Prehistoric Raised-Field Agriculture in the Maya Lowlands. *Science* 213:399–405.

van den Berghe, Pierre L. 1979. *Human Family Systems*. N.Y.: Elsevier.

van Hooff, J. A. R. A. M. 1969. The Facial Displays of Catyrrhine Monkeys and Apes. In D. Morris, ed., *Primate Ethology*, 9–81. N.Y.: Doubleday Anchor.

van Lawick-Goodall, Jane. 1969. Mother-Offspring Relationships in Free-Ranging Chimpanzees. In D. Morris, ed., *Primate Ethology*, 365–436. N.Y.: Doubleday Anchor.

Vaughan, K. B., and Lanzetta, John T. 1980. Vicarious Instigation and Conditioning of Facial Displays and Autonomic Responses to a Model's Expressive Display of Pain. *Journal of Personality and Social Psychology* 38:909–23.

von Cranach, Mario, ed. 1976. *Methods of Inference from Animal to Human Behavior*. The Hague: Mouton.

von Cranach, Mario, et al., eds. 1979. *Human Ethology*. Cambridge: Cambridge University Press.

Waddington, C. H. 1953. The Evolution of Adaptations. *Endeavor* 12:124–39.

———. 1956. Genetic Assimilation of the Bithorax Phenotype. *Evolution* 10:1–13.

Wade, Michael J. 1980. Kin Selection: Its Components. *Science* 210:665–67.

Wahlke, John. 1979. Prebehavioralism in Political Science. *American Political Science Review* 73:9–32.

Washburn, Sherwood L., and Avis, V. 1958. Evolution of Human Behavior. In A. Roe and G. G. Simpson, *Evolution and Behavior*, 421–36. New Haven: Yale University Press.

Washburn, Sherwood L., and Hamburg, David A. 1965. The Study of Primate Behavior. In I. DeVore, ed., *Primate Behavior*, 1–13. N.Y.: Holt, Rinehart & Winston.

Washburn, Sherwood L., and Howell, F. C. 1960. Human Evolution and Culture. In S. Tax, ed., *Evolution of Man*, 33–56. Chicago: University of Chicago Press.

Watts, Meredith, ed. 1984. *Biopolitics and Gender*. N.Y.: Haworth Press.

Weber, Max. 1956. *From Max Weber: Essays in Sociology*. Ed. H. H. Gerth and C. W. Mills. N.Y.: Oxford University Press.

Weinrich, James D. 1977. Human Sociobiology: Pair-Bonding and Resource Predictability (Effects of Social Class and Race). *Behavioral Ecology and Sociobiology* 91–118.

Wheelwright, Philip. 1966. *The Presocratics*. N.Y.: Odyssey.

White, Elliott, ed. 1981. *Sociobiology and Human Politics*. Lexington, Mass.: Lexington Books.

White, Elliott, and Losco, Joseph, eds. 1986. *The Biology of Bureaucracy*. Lanham, Md.: University Press of America.

White, Fred N., and Smith, Hobart M. 1956. Some Basic Concepts Pertaining to the Baldwin Effect. *Turtox News* 34:51–53, 66–68.

Whiting, J. W. M. 1969. Effects of Climate on Certain Cultural Practices. In A. P. Vayda, ed., *Environment and Cultural Behavior*, 416–55. Garden City, N.Y.: Natural History Press.

Whorf, Benjamin. 1956. *Language, Thought, and Reality*. Cambridge, Mass.: MIT Press.

Wickler, Wolfgang. 1972a. *The Biology of the Ten Commandments*. N.Y.: McGraw-Hill.

————. 1972b. *The Sexual Code*. Garden City, N.Y.: Doubleday Anchor.

Wiegele, Thomas C. 1979. *Biopolitics*. Boulder, Colo.: Westview Press.

————, ed. 1982. *Biology and the Social Sciences*. Boulder, Colo.: Westview Press.

Wiesenfeld, S. L. 1969. Sickle-cell Trait in Human Biological and Cultural Evolution. In A. Vayda, ed., *Environment and Cultural Behavior*, 308–31. Garden City, N.Y.: Natural History Press.

Willey, Gordon R. 1960. Historical Patterns and Evolution in Native New World Cultures. In S. Tax, ed., *Evolution of Man*, 11–41. Chicago: University of Chicago Press.

Willhoite, Fred H., Jr. 1981. Rank and Reciprocity: Speculations on Human Emotions and Political Life. In E. White, ed., *Human Sociobiology and Politics*, 239–58. Lexington, Mass.: Lexington Books.

————. 1986. Political Evolution and Legitimacy. In E. White and J. Losco, eds., *Biology and Bureaucracy*, 193–232. Lanham, Md.: University Press of America.

Williams, George C. 1966. *Adaptation and Natural Selection*. Princeton, N.J.: Princeton University Press.

Wilson, David Sloan. 1979. *The Natural Selection of Populations and Communities*. Menlo Park, Calif.: Benjamin Cummings.

Wilson, Edward O. 1975. *Sociobiology*. Cambridge, Mass.: Harvard University Press.

————. 1978. *On Human Nature*. Cambridge, Mass.: Harvard University Press.

Wilson, James Q., and Herrnstein, Richard D. 1985. *Crime and Human Nature*. N.Y.: Simon & Schuster.

Wispé, Lauren. 1978. *Altruism, Sympathy, and Helping.* N.Y.: Academic Press.

Wittfogel, Karl. 1957. *Oriental Despotism.* New Haven: Yale University Press.

Wrangham, Richard. 1979. On the Evolution of Ape Social Systems. *Biology and Social Life* 18:335–68.

———. 1980. Review Essay: Sociobiology. *Biological Journal of the Linnean Society* 13:171.

Wynne-Edwards, A. C. 1962. *Animal Dispersion in Relation to Social Behavior.* Edinburgh: Oliver and Boyd.

———. 1963. Intergroup Selection in the Evolution of Social Systems. *Nature* 200:623–26.

Zivin, Gail. 1977. Facial Gestures Predict Preschoolers' Encounter Outcomes. *Social Science Information* 16:715–29.

INDEX

Adaptation: to environmental change, 72, 111; human social systems as, 73; of political institutions, 112

Alexander, Richard D., 158, 180, 189, 199

Altman, Stuart E., 86–87

Altruism: as a result of convention, 4; in terms of natural selection, 7; fighting between groups, 7; in non-human primates, 8–9; sociocultural in origin, 10, 21; transmitted genetically in vertebrates, 16; influenced by heredity, 17; in terms of evolution, 19; in preliterate society, 20 (diagram), 193–94; as opposed to sociality, 153–54, 157; kin vs. nonkin, 194–95; definition, 251

Ancients vs. moderns. *See* Philosophical debates

Anthropocentrism, 126

Anthropology (cultural): causes for cooperation and competition, 18. *See also* Lévi-Strauss, Claude

Antiphon the Sophist: hedonism, 3–4, 151; selfishness in human nature, 6; pleasure-pain calculus, 33, 36, 68, 152

Aquinas, Saint Thomas, 151, 249

Aristotle: writing on science, xi, 251; *Zoon Politikon*, xiii, 139, 224; natural justice, xv, 225; altruism, 3, 151; contradicting sophist hedonism, 4–5, 22; emotion in human thought, 61; reciprocal agreements, 102; ambivalence of human nature, 117; causal processes, 117, 144, 146; natural change, 148;

Politics, 151; and Hegel, 178; naturalism, 182, 225, 227, 233, 245–46; origin of the state, 189; ostracism, 223–25; denial of divine principle, 248

Australopithecus africanus, 18, 26

Baboons, 8, 19, 24, 109, 126, 214

Bacon, Francis, 147, 149

Balance of power theory. *See* Political behavior

Barash, David, 11–15

Barry, Brian, 163

Behaviorism, 234–36

Bentham, Jeremy, 146

Bible, 70

Bonding (social): consummatory behavior, 36; reason for classification, 36; in mating, 77; as result of symbolic acts, 101, 103; as result of human speech, 102; as result of loyalty, 213–14; as tied to ostracism, 219–20

Brain (human): size for childbirth, 22; cranial capacity, 22, 25 (diagram), 26; in natural selection, 24; evolution of in terms of altruism, 26; in perceiving nonverbal behavior, 42, 44–45 (diagrams), 46, 254; triune, 67; capacity for language, 87, 88–89 (diagrams); response to sensory stimulation, 136–37; information processing, 138, 243, 253

Bureaucracy: description of, 153–54; in terms of neo-Darwinism, 159, 203, 208–09, 212; functions of, 197, 199–200, 202–03, 209; origin, 198, 209–10; policy implementation,